THE ZODIAC

Willem Koppejan was born in Amsterdam in 1915. He began his study of astrology at an early age and pursued this interest throughout his life. At the same time he developed his knowledge of medicine and it was his unique combination of these two disciplines which led him to be considered as one of the best Dutch medical-astrologers. He moved to Glastonbury, England in 1977 and there devoted the last years of his life entirely to astrological research. Willem Koppejan died in 1979.

Born in 1927, Helene Koppejan is of Dutch Huguenot origin. She studied social psychology in Amsterdam and then went on to meet Willem Koppejan in 1953 who taught her astrology. She had an astro-psychology practice in The Hague until 1970 where she worked with her husband and spent several years as a freelance astrology writer. The Koppejans moved to England and founded *The Glastonbury Experience* – a centre for holistic living. Helene continues as managing director of this centre today and also works as a freelance astro-psychological counsellor and writer.

By the same author

The Zodiac Image Handbook
The Fixed Signs

The Zodiac Image Handbook
The Mutable Signs

THE ZODIAC IMAGE HANDBOOK

THE CARDINAL SIGNS
Aries · Cancer · Libra · Capricorn

Helene and Willem Koppejan

Series Editor
Steve Eddy

ELEMENT BOOKS

First published in Great Britain in 1990 by
Element Books Limited
Longmead, Shaftesbury, Dorset

Designed by David Porteous
Cover design by Max Fairbrother
Typeset by Selectmove Ltd, London
Printed and bound in Great Britain by
Billings Ltd, Hylton Road, Worcester

British Library Cataloguing in Publication Data
Koppejan, Helene 1927–
The zodiac image handbook : the cardinal signs,
Aries, Cancer, Libra, Capricorn.
1. Signs of the zodiac
I. Title   II. Koppejan, Willem 1913–1979
133.52

ISBN 1–85230–192–9

CONTENTS

ABOUT THE AUTHORS

Helene Van Woelderen Koppejan

Born 20 August 1927 at 17.10 hrs. (see 27th Sag.) in Flushing, of Dutch Huguenot origin. Her father, being a burgomaster and in the Resistance movement, was captured during World War II by the Nazi occupiers. She went to the Latin school on the island of Walcheren and studied social and colour psychology in Amsterdam, where she graduated in 1956.

She met Willem Koppejan in 1953. He taught her astrology and opened her eyes to esoteric knowledge. In 1957 she travelled to the USA where she stayed for over a year, meeting Marc Edmund Jones several times in his home. He wrote about her in one of his Sabian Symbol newsletters. When staying in Beverly Hills she had frequent contact with Dane Rudhyar, for whom the Koppejans later organised some courses in the Netherlands, also introducing him to his Servire publishers. Both Jones and Rudhyar were very interested in the research Willem Koppejan had done on the degree symbols and urged him to publish in English. No one could have thought this wish would take thirty years to be fulfilled.

Helene had her own astro-psychology practice in The Hague, which she gave up after her marriage to Willem Koppejan in 1970. She was a staff-writer on astrology for a woman's magazine, *De Vrouw en haar Huis* for several years and also carried on freelance work. She published several books in Dutch, German and English. *Wie anders dan Andersen* is a biography of the Danish fairy-tale writer with a chapter on his astrological chart. *Strange Parallel* (in Dutch *Wondere Parallel*) draws an analogy between the Hebrew tribe of Zebulon and the character of the Dutch people.

She moved in 1977 with her husband to the little English town of Glastonbury, with its ancient legends and tradition. There they started a centre, 'The Glastonbury Experience', a complex of bookshop, healing, crafts and courses on holistic living. Since the passing of Willem in 1979, Helene continues to be leader of this activity.

Willem A. Koppejan

Willem Ary Koppejan was born in Amsterdam on 19 August, 1913 at 04.00 hrs. (conception corrected ASC. 15°56 Le; see 16th and 17th Le).

He went to school in The Hague. His grandfather left him a book on astrology, which he began to read as a child. At the age of 16 he came across the degree symbols of La Volasfera. He also began to read theosophical literature.

Against the will of his father, a modernistic thinker, he schooled himself in astrology. His parents also being against his medical studies, Willem had to earn his own college fees at Leyden University, which he did by giving lectures and astrological counselling as well as selling cheeses and setting up a little eating-house for students. At the age of 22 he refused military service on religious grounds and as a result he was banned from the university for several years. During this period he developed his astrological practice.

In 1938 he met the philosopher Ouspensky, who gave a summer school at Wassenaar. Willem became his secretary during that six-week period. After the war he was asked to set up Ouspensky groups in Holland. Lack of time prevented him from pursuing this. During World War II Willem hid Jews in his home. From 1945 to 1960 he developed a vast medical-astrological practice in The Hague and founded his own Medical Paedagogical Institute. Having a lifelong interest in the Great Pyramid of Giza, he published a book in 1953 *The 20th August 1953 Horary* (in Dutch). In 1956 his loose-leaf book *The 360 Degrees of the Zodiac* came out in Dutch.

He was considered to be one of the best Dutch medical-astrologers. During his lifetime he kept up a vast correspondence with astrological researchers over the entire Western world, such as Luc de Marré (Belgium), Barbault and Gauquelin (France), Charles Jayne, Rudhyar and Sucher (USA) and personal contact with Charles Harvey and members of the Astrological Association in England, for which he lectured.

He married Helene van Woelderen in 1970. They moved to Glastonbury in England where he devoted his last years entirely to astrological research. His vast archives with charts of prominent people is still kept by Helene. Willem's friend and co-worker Niek Scheps carries on the astrological research next door to her at The Landmark. They hope to publish more of Willem's original concepts in due course.

This *Zodiac Image Handbook* is Willem's major lifetime work.

Helene and Willem Koppejan at their Glastonbury home, 12th May 1979

CONCEPTION CORRECTION

One of the main reasons for working with the degree symbols and the interpretation as we have done in this book, is that they prove the conception method to be invaluable.

The conception method used in this book is based on the original work of E.H. Bailey. It was used by several Dutch astrologers, such as Gorter in Indonesia. Willem Koppejan refined this method basing it on the medical principles of the possible length of pregnancies. He tested this method in thousands of cases. Through this calculation one can find the exact moment of conception and consequently the precise minute of birth. Niek Scheps contributed much to this book in the form of re-calculating and checking all the conception corrected charts cast by Willem Koppejan.

The charts of prominent people published in this book have all been calculated by conception correction method by hand, as Willem and Niek's principle was that one enters into contact with the soul or Higher Self of the person right from the moment that one starts to calculate. Therefore there have been thousands of hours of thought and calculation in order to get the right conception corrected degree symbol for the rising sign.

Nowadays there are very few astrologers in the world working with the conception correction method because the method has not yet been tested enough.

In this book we want to put forward the conception correction method as a valuable tool for serious astrologers.

ACKNOWLEDGEMENTS

This book has been based on Willem A. Koppejan's *De 360 gradenbeelden van de Dierenriem*, published in Holland in 1956. After our move to Glastonbury, England, we planned to rewrite the book in English and add the new material, such as the Biblical parallels, the Grail in the zodiac signs and a selection of about one thousand charts of prominent people from all walks of life. Willem had spent forty years assembling his vast collection of data and charts, which he had calculated by hand and corrected with a refined conception method. His aim was to prove the validity of the degree symbols as shown in the life and work of well-known people. His sudden passing in May 1979 was a blow to the work and the group of helpers around him. It took me seven years to write the English version.

Ayliffe Hervey was invaluable as a typist. Elizabeth Gaythorpe was a great help in correcting double-dutch expressions and grammar, as English is my second language. My thanks also go to Steve Eddy for his editing.

Two of our best friends and lifelong workers with Willem's astrological principles, lawyer Jhr. Willem van Panhuys and musician Niek Scheps, have given years of their time and knowledge to advise, correct and calculate. Niek Scheps, our neighbour in Glastonbury, first checked and recalculated all the charts by hand and when the computer became available double-checked the ones pre-dating 1850 with the Electric Ephemeris. At the same time he wrote two books of his own, using the same astrological system, one on the connections between music and astrology, and the other an exposition of the conception correction method which has been used throughout this book. That subject cannot be covered here, but his book *The Trutine of Hermes* (Element Books, 1990) is an invaluable companion to the present work. It teaches the reader step by step how to calculate the conception time according to the ancient rule of Hermes in order to correct the moment of birth. Basing his work on the many years of research by Willem Koppejan on this subject, Niek has refined this conception-correction (CC) method and made it available in clear language to English and American readers. If one is not interested in calculations, the book is still a must for readers of the present handbook, as it takes as examples ten of the conception-corrected charts, presented in our work, such as Salvador Dali (see page 176) and Rodin (see page 377). Niek Scheps shows in these ten monographs how the corrected degree symbol on the Ascendant of these historical people can be that one zodiac image and no other. His work is new and original, and I can warmly recommend it. In the present volume the terms in the sample charts 'CC WAK and NS' mean: conception-correction calculated by Willem A. Koppejan and Niek Scheps.

The interpretations in this book are based on the series of degree symbols by Janduz, pen-name for Mrs J. Duzéa, who was professor at the Centre d'Astrologiques de France in Paris. One may read more about the origins of her symbols in the next chapter.

The other series of images or degree symbols on which this book has been based come from Dr Marc E. Jones and Dane Rudhyar. I met both these astrological researchers during my first visit to California as a student in 1957. Dr Jones reported my visit in his 'Fortnightly Field Notes' of 21 Dec. 1957 and wrote:

The hours of discussion with Dr van Woelderen were exceptionally fruitful because of the chance to examine the difficulties in dealing with ideas of this sort across the lines of language. Dr W. A. Koppejan, a medical psychologist who has established an astrologically centered research group in the Hague, is orientated rather basically to the symbolized degrees of the zodiac with special recognition for the series of J. Duzea Janduz. Dr Koppejan's judgment of these two series is that Janduz works 'from the outside to the inside' and myself 'from the inside to the outside'. He speaks of a projected reconciliation of the insights from the two points of view, together with an expanded interpretation to be given illustration in the lives of world-prominent individuals for each degree, as a life work of illimitable possibility. The whole time was a species of signature for me. While this was contact with a group of keen and rigorously trained minds abroad rather than any activity directly within the Sabian framework, it yet

revealed the extent to which there are quickening minds for fulfilling
the destiny of the occult tradition brought to its present crest in the
great transitions. Here was certification of my judgment that there is
genuinely high potentiality in the creative activities now coming to
focus in the Sabian group.

We had a deep personal connection with Dane Rudhyar
as well as a longstanding correspondence, in which he often
showed his eagerness for the English publication of Willem's
book, and I thank him for his encouragement to finish the work
after Willem's passing. I am sorry that this great man Rudhyar,
who did so much for humanistic astrology, left this earth in 1985
before seeing the publication of our degree book.

This book is also based on the psychology of Dr C. G.
Jung (see under 28th Cap.). We often use his terms relating
to the unconscious, archetypes, projection and the need for
individuation.

Although we have never been Anthroposophists, the insights
of Rudolf Steiner (see under 14th Sc.) are invaluable. We have
used his terms for the etheric, which Willem equates with
the Moon-plane in the chart and the denser planets; and the
astral, which reflects the working of the further planets Uranus,
Neptune and Pluto.

Though we have never been affiliated to any denomination,
the philosophy behind this book is humanistic psychology and
individuation, Western Christianity and Hebrew Kabbalah. As
such we acknowledge the influence on our thinking of the
profound teachings of our personal friend the Jewish Friedrich
Weinreb, whose introductory work *Roots of the Bible* is now
available in English (Merlin Books, Braunton, UK 1986).

The Biblical parallels, which we have collected over the years
and which are only a beginning for further research, have been
taken from the King James version, unless otherwise stated.

The excerpt quoted from Dane Rudhyar's *An Astrological
Mandala: The Cycle of Transformations and its 360 Symbolic Phases*
is copyright material, used with the kind permission of Random
House, Inc.

The photograph of Queen Beatrix appears with the kind
permission of John Thuring.

A Note on the Text

We have used the word 'image' in the title of this book and there is mention of Divine Imagery throughout. It is based on the belief that mankind was brought forth as a living entity, imaged in the Mind of God and patterned to that image. Nothing can exist if the image or pattern is not held in the Divine Mind. Image-making is a divine business, which can be utilised by us humans to gain spiritual insight. There is a perfect set of 360 Divine Images as pores around the zodiac, but mankind as a whole has lost them. This book is an attempt to gain back some of this lost Divine Imagery or patterns. However, the series of Janduz-Jones images do not claim to be perfect. They are not more than fragments of the Divine degree symbols. They are bound by the vision of our time and space. Coming generations may see different things in them. However, it is a first step towards regaining the imagery lost for centuries.

The most important thing to remember is that these images or degree symbols contain cosmic energy, which means essential spiritual food for our inner growth and for the future of this planet earth, which is patterned in the Divine Image as 'The Kingdom of Heaven on earth' of which the Biblical prophets repeatedly speak.

In our esoteric astrological interpretation we also use three more planets, based on a longstanding research since the 1940s in Holland by the Astrologische Werkgemeenschap. These are the higher ruler of Taurus, called Persephone, the higher ruler of Gemini called Hermes and the higher ruler of Cancer called Demeter. In this introduction we can do no more than mention them.

We should also point out that in our esoteric system of interpretation Pluto is the higher ruler of Aries and not of Scorpio. I know that this is presently not a popular view since the school of Witte in Germany in the 1950s started to equate Pluto with Scorpio. It is, however, as a result of years of painstaking research by Willem Koppejan and those working with his system, that we stick to this rulership.

Abbreviations

CC conception correction
N northern latitude
NS Niek Scheps
NS New Style
Opp opposition
OS Old Style
RB Registrar of births
W/E western/eastern latitude
WAK Willem Ary Koppejan
Ar. Aries
Tau. Taurus

Ge. Gemini
Cn. Cancer
Le. Leo
Vi. Virgo
Li. Libra
Sc. Scorpio
Sag. Sagittarius
Cap. Capricorn
Aq. Aquarius
Pi. Pisces

Sources of Birthtimes

The Koppejan archives are based upon fifty years of research between 1930 and 1980 by Willem Koppejan. Additions between 1980 and 1990 are by Helene Koppejan and Niek Scheps.

For the Netherlands, Germany, France and other countries which have used the Napoleonic Code since 1815, the Registers of Births have been used. There was intensive exchange of data and birthtimes with Luc de Marre in Antwerp, whose archives are vast and exact. There was also correspondence with Francesca Snethlage and the Gauquelins in France. For Germany the researchwork of the Ebertins in Aalen with their EPA-bulletin was helpful and so were the magazines *Astrologische Auskunftbogen* and *Sein und Werden* by Edith Wangemann, Wuppertal.

For England and the USA there are no registered birth-times, so that one has to rely on family books, Bibles and personal information. That is why there are relatively few of these charts in this book. The databank of the Astrological Association also was helpful.

Notable Nativities by Alan Leo and consequently Marc E. Jones in *Sabian Symbols* (1953 edn) often gave wrong data and hours. These have been corrected in correspondence with Dr Jones and in this book, but one might still find the wrong data occurs in other astrological literature. An unknown source was Gavin Arthur's archive in San Francisco, which HK researched in 1951. After his death it seems to have been lost.

TWO STREAMS OF
DEGREE SYMBOLS AND
THEIR ORIGINS

It is the privilege of the end of the twentieth century and the beginning of the twenty-first to rediscover the ring of symbolic images around the zodiac, which have existed as a pictorial script from times immemorial. Glimpses of its forms have been dug up through the ages. Some fascinating new research has been done recently by a Dutch astronomer, who prefers to remain anonymous. He has traced the series of the French Janduz back through sixteenth-century Italy and Spain to ancient Greece. More about this astrological archaeology in a moment. See also his introduction in the volume on the Cardinal Cross.

The special importance of the degree images for our time lies in the fact that modern psychologists and therapists are rediscovering the healing values of inner visualisation. Guided meditation is 'in'. 'Imagine yourself in a meadow with the birds whistling in the trees; you hear the rushing water of a stream' and so forth. This sort of thing takes people away from the outer horrors of images on television and gives them inner strength and centers them. However, the inner images are often fragmented and not personalised. If only one could tune into one's own archetypal images.

It is the great advantage of our time that the research on the 360 zodiacal degree symbols based on clairvoyant vision, can now be combined with the modern technique of easy access to the birthchart by computer-calculation. In a matter of minutes one can find the exact degree symbols on which to meditate.

In the twentieth century two seemingly separate streams of zodiac degree symbols have been rediscovered. One series of 360 images leads us from Wales to California, where the great names of research fellows are Dr Marc Edmund Jones and Dane Rudhyar, whose publications on the degree symbols are the only ones available. They are termed the 'Sabian Symbols'. Marc Jones made use of the medium Elsie Wheeler, who tuned into the ancient Welsh seers, a lost source, from which the astrologer Charubel also drew his series, the same source as used by Alan Leo. However, Willem Koppejan found Jones-Wheeler much more exact than Charubel-Leo and so we have used this series in the present book. See for Jones under 11th Sc. rising, for Rudhyar under 14th Sag., for Wheeler under 28th Tau., for Charubel under 13th Sc. and for Alan Leo under 28th Le. in this twelvefold book.

The other stream leads us towards the Netherlands and into France, where the series of '360 degrees cf the Zodiac' was published by Janduz in Paris in 1939, just before World War II broke out, making all international contact impossible. That is probably why the Americans Jones and Rudhyar (though of French origin) had not heard of the Janduz symbols when I first visited them in 1957. As Janduz' images, based on the traditions of the degree symbols in Italy and ancient Rome, have never been translated from the French into English, it is for the first time here in this book, that the two streams of the American Sabian symbols and the French Janduz symbols are reunited. I say *re*-united advisedly, since they must have come originally from one source, older than the Sabians, probably from Atlantis if we take the word of clairvoyants for the truth.

In the Netherlands over the past fifty years quite a group of individual therapists and astrologers have, not always openly, worked with the degree symbols of the zodiac. My husband's book on the subject was published in 1956, sold out and was never translated. Dutch astrologers like Mellie Uyldert propagated and worked with Koppejan's degrees in her classes. Willem's great strength in dealing with the degrees was his clear and precise vision of how the two streams, the American and the French, although so different in their images, really belong together. Dane Rudhyar's book *The Astrology of Personality* was translated into Dutch as early as 1936, and the descriptions of the Sabian symbols in the present work are still more often based on this first edition than on Rudhyar's revised and shortened version of 1973.

World War II broke out and the German occupation of Holland in 1940 closed all international contact with astrologers, whose profession was made illegal. Willem, then still in his twenties and in semi-hiding as a medical student, concentrated his visionary capacity on combining the two streams of degree symbols, which had been published shortly before this time, Jones–Rudhyar in 1936 and Janduz in 1939. Divine fate gave him five terrible war years of physical danger, curfew and hunger to test the working of the degrees in the lives of his patients and pupils, and in the charts of celebrities. He found that it worked: his theory is that the Sabian symbols as used by the Americans reflect on an inner, astral level the same energy expressed by the European Janduz images in the external environment and lives of those he tested. Thus his Dutch publication of 1956 and the content of this present English book have been based on the testimony of thousands of clients, mostly Dutch, in a vast astro-psychological practice with his staff over a period of more than twenty years, mainly between 1940 and 1960. Holland seemed a good testing ground. It is a country full of water, and astrologically it comes under Cancer. The Dutch psyche responds easily to visualisation and seems to mirror these Moon symbols stored in the etheric and astral realms quite easily. Thus Holland became the breeding ground for this present book. It gives new tools in the English language for the imagery-work of the new consciousness.

This present book is definitely Dutch-based. I myself and Niek Scheps (who carried out or checked all the conception correction calculation of Willem's material, since his passing in 1979) were youngsters in the 1940s. As pupils of Willem we began to work with the degree symbols in our twenties and have never ceased to do so. Another example is the lawyer Willem van Panhuys, whose help and correction of this book are greatly appreciated. He became a good friend of Willem as early as 1943 and has worked and absorbed the degree symbols, as interpreted by WAK, ever since.

Back to the question of how old the degree symbols might be. Another of Willem's pupils and co-workers 'played' with the zodiac images from his childhood, while his mother studied the degree symbols under Willem's staff. As a university-based astronomer he is still playing with these degree symbols, which he knows by heart. His historical research led him to the following sources on which Janduz must have based her series.

Madame J. Duzéa, who wrote under her pen-name Janduz, is original in her Kabbalistic interpretation of her degree symbols, which means that she takes four different levels of spiritual awareness into account, for which she bases herself on Papus (see the description of his rising degree under 18th Le.). However, she remains vague in her foreword of 1939 as to the exact source of her images. She mentions the seventeenth-century English physician and astrologer Robert Fludd, who published a series of degree images, each of which he described merely as 'good' or 'bad'. This may have to do with the source of our Welsh stream. However, she hints at a more important link for our present research by mentioning that she based herself on Anton Borelli though she knows that both Ptolemeus and Manilius occupied themselves with these degree symbols.

Borelli was a seventeenth-century Italian astronomer. However, the Dutch research brought a much older source to light. I have now a photocopy of the *Astrolabium Planum* by the thirteenth-century Pietro d'Abano (Abanus) in the first printed edition of 1502 by Johannes Angelus in Latin. An original is in the Koninklijke Bibliotheek (Royal Library) in The Hague, and another one in the Warburg Library, Woburn Square, London. Each square chart contains a primitive picture of the degree on the Ascendant at the left. See the illustrations in Volume II and compare the sixteenth-century version of these 27th–30th degree drawings with the ones by Claude Lhuer in the Janduz edition of 1939 and our description in Volume II. Moreover, the Palazzo Chifanoia in Ferrara and the Palaza della Regione in Padua in Italy have friezes with series of these images. Their meaning has been totally lost, but our Dutch researcher immediately recognised them a few years ago. Another line is Alfonso el Sabia (Alphon the sage) in Spain, who knew d'Abano in the thirteenth-century. He had Arabian books translated into Latin containing degree symbols used in ancient Greece. We are getting nearer to the source of our two streams, the American Sabian Symbols and the French Janduz ones.

A definite proof that the ancient Greeks equated symbolic and mythological images with certain degrees can be seen in

Sphaera by Franz Boll, printed by George Holms, Hildesheim in 1903, reprinted at Schors, Amsterdam in 1967. Boll describes a manuscript written by Teuchros the Babylonian in AD 50, which includes Greek texts indicating that each degree of the zodiac had a picture of its own, on which the first-century Manilius must have based his work.

This piece of astrological archaeology is only a tiny grain in the rediscovering work to be done, but it is fascinating to know that Janduz' symbols have been kept relatively pure and are of great antiquity. Janduz' artist, Miss Lhuer, often tuned into a Greek kind of imagery, which goes with the French text, to which we have stuck in our translation, which sometimes differs from the not always correctly translated 1956 Dutch edition.

All this historical research aside, the main thing is to let the degree images work for yourself. Forget how others have pictured them and create your own inner version from deep within your own magnetic field and aura and create your own attunement with these ever-renewing pores of energies around the zodiac.

THE USE OF THE DEGREES

The fact that every degree of the zodiac, totalling 360 degrees, has two symbolic images, one on the outer Moon-level and one on the inner Sun-grail-level, adds a totally new dimension to astrological interpretation.

The entire chart can be interpreted in images. This is a blessing for the thousands who think in images and to whom the mathematical and the more abstract horoscope interpretations are stumbling-blocks. The modern mind is thinking more and more through visualisation, helped by the widespread use of television for instance. Therefore the use of the degree images will become popular for future astrologers, and the general public wanting to improve their self-knowledge.

The use of degree images goes back to the fourth century BC in Greece and is probably much older, but the rediscovery of them is new in our time. Hardly any psychologists or astrologers use them as yet. Using them involves the technique of visualisation and in order to interpret the images one needs to have some cosmic schooling. Every symbol comes under a certain astrological sign. It is for instance obvious that a lion in an image refers to the sign of Leo. However, the matter can be more complicated: a white dove comes under Libra as the sign of peace, but birds as a whole come under Gemini.

All this is the background knowledge for the interpretation of these degree images. We do not claim to have all the answers. It is only a beginning and readers and researchers will find much more in these degree symbols in the coming centuries. Symbols also change with the times. When we read about a glider in an image, this may be coloured by the American Marc E. Jones who picked up this image. In former and future days one may see a silently moving UFO in it. However, the symbolism and the response of the inner psyche on the visualisation of a majestically silent object in the sky remains the same regardless of one's place in time. The degree images are therefore timeless, as they can be interpreted on many levels, as will become apparent in this book.

The interpretation often starts with the low level of awareness, as is natural on a dense plane. There is no good or bad in the images. There are levels of consciousness of light and darkness. Some very advanced souls may have to work in very dark areas of imagery. Therefore one should never 'feel bad' about having a degree image in one's horoscope which shows lots of difficulties. It is always a challenge and the message of this book is that there is always an inner energy-level and light with which the consciousness or the Higher Self can overcome the lower images and help to improve the outer level of the Moon-situation or one's psychic surroundings. Divine imagery is bringing the Spirit, the Christ-light, or the energy of the heart into the psyche's chart. Imaging one's own or someone else's chart is a tool for understanding and ultimately for healing, because it gives a new flow of energy.

It does not require a lot of astrological knowledge to visualise the degree symbols of one's chart. Start with the Sun, Moon and Ascendant. If Sun is in 26°38 Leo, then the image is the 27th of Leo, not the 26th! In the beginning it is more important to visualise the image within oneself than to read the interpretation, because it is a good exercise to try to interpret the symbol for oneself first. Having absorbed this, one can visualise the degrees of all one's planets in the chart.

For professional astrologers and counsellors this is a study in itself and a handbook to help with horoscope interpretation. Many degrees have one or more example horoscopes of well-known people, with conception correction calculation computer-checked by Niek Scheps (see page ix). Counsellors should find it helpful to use these images with their clients.

The book can also be read as a daily meditation. I suggest that one reads the image degree where the Sun is that day. One needs an ephemeris to be exact. On 20 August for instance the Sun is sometimes in 27th Leo, but can often be in 28th Leo if it is a leap year. There are 360 degrees divided over 365 days. The idea of this kind of meditation is to be in tune with the Sun's energies through the pore of the degree symbol.

At the same time one learns the degree symbols literally by heart.

Last but not least one may use this book to learn esoteric astrology in general. It has a wealth of material on the meaning of each sign. Reading all thirty degrees of a sign through, one can see a development of the sign of Leo for instance from the first to the 30th of Leo.

When one has got the full 360 degrees, one can then make circles of, for instance, all the twelve first degrees of the zodiac and see what message they contain collectively. Willem Koppejan wrote an example of all 27th degrees in his book on the Pyramid of 1953. If one had the Sun for instance in the 26th of Leo, it would be very useful to know the 26th of Cancer and the 26th of Virgo, as part of one's own Leo grail and the message they contain for one's spiritual being.

The possibilities are endless, once you are tuned in to symbolic thinking and cosmic imagery. It will undoubtedly become a major working tool in the Aquarian Age, as it must have been in the Age of Leo, at the dawn of creation.

GRAIL ASTROLOGY

In the first volume of *The Zodiac Image Handbook* under the heading of Leo, I described the principles of grail astrology in general and for the fixed cross in particular. The same general principles apply of course to the cardinal cross. One can imagine a goblet or cup with the drinking part the same size as the root, or one may see it as two identical triangles. The beaker-part is the Sun-side of the grail, open for the pouring in of energy from the universe. The bottom triangle or foot without which the cup is unbalanced, is the Moon-side of the grail in the chart. This part contains the reflected light and represents the day-to-day experiences of being incarnated on the earth.

Many individuals nowadays have little or no awareness of the interconnections between the Sun-side and Moon-side in their grail. They have blocked themselves off in the middle of their goblet with the result that the energy cannot stream through. Thus they are either too spiritual and not grounded, or too earthbound and not open enough to receive the energy impulses from the universe.

The task of the Higher Self is to unblock these energies locked in the middle of their overflowing cup. Insight into their specific grail, for instance Sun in Aries or Cancer, will stimulate a better flow of energies. The refinement of the individual grail astrology is its application to one's own horoscope and the interplay of planets within their grail-signs. For example, for a Sun in Aries, one would look to see what planets were in Pisces and Taurus, around Aries-Sun-side, and whether there were planets in the signs on the Moon-side of the Aries Grail, which are Virgo, Libra and Scorpio.

The Sun sign is flanked by the sign behind it and the one before it. One only needs to be centred within oneself to find and benefit from one's personal grail. One then will become balanced between one's opposite signs, so that one can drink

in the cosmic energy through one's Sun sign and give it out
and into the earth via the Moon-side of one's grail-cup, and vice
versa.

THE ARIES GRAIL

The Aries grail consists on the Sun-side of Aries in the middle
surrounded by Pisces on one side and Taurus on the other,
making together the grail-cup and its brim. The foot of the
cup or Moon-side has Libra in the middle flanked by Virgo and
Scorpio.

The energy which is radiating through to the Aries Sun can
be imagined as coming from high and far in the universe. It
has the quality of fire. The energy is raw and new and it is of
a forceful and primordial kind. It is the concept of the universe
starting with a big bang. Nuclear energy and hypnotic power
come under this sign.

The Aries person directs his or her energy into independent
acts and impulsive activities. They are the ones who get things
done. They tend to be the pioneers who have the courage to
start projects on their own, often quite alone, because nobody .
believes in them (Pi.) or their plans (Ar.) or shares their vision
for the future (Tau.). However, once Arians decide to go ahead
regardless (the head comes under Ar.), they break through
existing ethics and hammer down crumbling old walls (square
Cap.) and with their spearheading actions they energise the
tired environment and worn-out milieu (square Cn.) – so much
so, that those who criticised (Vi.) and opposed (Sc.) them now
accept the new balance of power (Li.) which Aries has created
as a miracle coming from 'nowhere'. Or else the general public
experience this new impulse as something commonplace, as if
it had always been there, when in fact Aries created it out of
hard work. In any case, Arians seldom receive thanks for their
pushing power, their humble and sacrificing deeds (Vi.-Pi.) or
for their painstaking and transforming labour towards a better
future on earth (Sc.-Tau.).

The difficulty for Aries is the hind-axis Pisces–Virgo. At the
same time, one gains conscious awareness that as an Aries one
grows towards the fore-axis Taurus–Scorpio. Thus Arians reach

the inner balance and peaceful equilibrium of their opposite sign Libra. In other words: before one can open up a new field of action (Ar.), the place has to be cleansed and purified (Vi.-Pi.). One needs to get rid of useless chaos and stagnant situations (Pi.) which prevent the new from penetrating through.

Another thing which Aries seldom likes doing is sitting down and working out the practical details of what the new project is going to cost. Do the individual's humble earnings cover all these magical plans for the future? When they honour Virgo's concern for detail, Arians will often be given abundant and supernatural strength to get on with the job and to leave narrow-minded critics gasping. That happens only when Arians have done their homework well.

As soon as a plan of action has started, Aries needs to be aware that working it out and letting impulses materialise on earth will often take a long period of ripening (Tau.). The pioneer needs to work in the ground for years until he sees results. Maybe he has to wait till his resurrection, to be shown that his vision was prophetic. Or else the Aries person dies without having seen the seeds coming up and then must return in another lifetime to finish what he was doing before. In other words, Aries must take death and transformation – Scorpio – into account in order to be renewed as a more conscious being.

This reminds one of the phoenix rising out of its own ashes, reborn every 460 years. Hans Christian Andersen wrote an immortal fairy-tale about this ancient symbol of the sign Aries.

The higher energy of the Aries grail renews itself in a cyclical rhythm. When they are in touch with their inner being, calm and centered, Arians are constantly replenished with new fire burning in their hearts. Their grail-cup is truly overflowing and soaks the earth around them with new energy in pulsing waves.

The opposite sign of Aries, Libra, which so often unbalances Arians when their fire is burning them up through overactivity, can be held under control. Through the bottom of the grail-cup the Aries flow of energy will thus bring harmony into the air (Li.) in rhythmic Venusian waves. No explosive bangs of nuclear fission anymore, but 'green' energy, working out in environment-friendly 'implosion'. That is how the earth will be transformed when Aries, now or in its next phoenix-round, undoes the dangerous death-causing power in the present atmosphere.

In this last paragraph lies not only the solution for Aries, but also the problem of the entire cardinal cross. Therefore it is advisable to study and meditate upon all the four grails of the cardinal cross together as one cosmic subject.

The planets involved in the Aries grail are: Mars–Pluto in Aries and Mars in Scorpio; Venus and Persephone in Taurus and Venus in Libra (which in itself gives an interesting male–female balance); Jupiter and Neptune in Pisces; and Mercury in Virgo. This combination is quite different from the other three cardinal cross signs. This is another indication that Aries functions as a cosmic spearhead.

THE CANCER GRAIL

The Sun-side of the Cancer grail consists of Aries in the middle flanked by Gemini and Leo. Its Moon-side or the foot of the cup is formed by Capricorn in the middle, opposite Cancer, surrounded by Sagittarius and Aquarius, thus making together the solid foot of the Cancer grail.

Cancer is the most sensitive sign of the zodiac. The reactions to the spiritual energy pouring into the Sun are like images reflecting and mirroring from every possible angle and in innumerable phases. Cancerians are like hugh cosmic light-reflectors, gathering in all that which there is to experience out there and converting it here within themselves into the tiniest images repeating themselves for ever.

We begin to become familiar with the principles and working of the hologram. This represents the idea of Cancer. The hologram takes up only a tiny amount of space, but it creates an image which seems to repeat itself and thus it gives the viewer a feeling of deep wisdom and being engulfed in a cosmic wave. One experiences emotional reactions as if one is being given a deep inner insight into universal wisdom and one feels like space-travelling within the infinite universe.

The real value of what I have described here and have been given to see inside myself concerning the essence of the hologram has to be tested by the reader, because the connection between Cancer and holograms has not yet been experienced by the majority of humanity (1990).

To me the invention of the hologram is the latest example of how the Cancer grail works. Through the cosmic energy, cocooned within Cancer, (melo-) dramatic impressions (Cn.) are being formed and formatted (Cap.) in time and space (Aq.) showing as light-creations from the centre (Le.), which are optical illusions, but which appear to be indefinite by the repetitive nature of their images (Cn.). If not properly understood (Aq.) the hologram creates a split-personality problem through identification of the viewer with that illusionary image out there as a scientific miracle (Ge.) on the one hand and the astral inner self as a private inner reality on the other, to be guarded from within one and in the reality of me here (Cn.). If well handled, however, the New Age vision (Aq.) of the hologram science can create a quantum leap in consciousness. It will become an inexhaustible source of information and knowledge (Ge.). Holograms will bring about an enormous expansion of thinking and a broadening of the range of tools available for mass education (Sag.). As the Moon has it changing phases and causes the tides, so will this new model have many phases and faces before holography is firmly established in society (Cap.), free and open for everyone to enjoy it (Aq.), and bringing humanity further in their inner and outer space travel and cosmic belief-systems (Sag.).

With the idea of the hologram model as an example of the Cancer grail we have moved through the Sun-side and the Moon-side of its cup. Here are a few more indications of what the Sun in Cancer arouses on the personal level of self-knowledge.

As Cancer is so sensitive to the minutest wave and change of mood in the world around as well as within, Cancerians get easily hurt and need to armour themselves against the floods of adverse psychic attacks and unwanted channels. Too much new energy (see the Aries grail) may throw them out of balance (square Li.).

Cancer is a female sign. She is the mother and protector of the home and inner life behind closed doors and walls (opposite

Cap.). The growth towards higher spiritual consciousness (Le.) needs to be fed and nourished (Cn.) with the written and spoken word by the wisdom-teachers (Ge.) of all centuries and religions (Cap.).

The need for Cancer is to move on from filling oneself and one's image in the world with emotional illusions, too much intellectualism and superficial information without ideals and goals that have been well thought out and aim towards the future. Cancer is so hooked into the past and the traditional way of life, that it often puts an old-fashioned education, with an intellectual and competitive approach, before the attainment of greater consciousness through impersonal love (Le.) and the experience of open-ended groups and friendships with fresh alternatives for transcendental co-existence (Aq.).

Cancerians have to overcome their personal fears of being hurt and to grow into creating their own individuality and Christ-centredness within the larger group (Le–Aq.).

As with the hologram, they are at their best when creating themselves as an image of the light, which creation may then repeat itself a thousandfold, so that all those around them of the human, animal and plant kingdoms can feel, through their guiding light, that we are all homing in on our eternal being, as created in the image of the universe.

The Cancer cup is flowing over again and again, now as of old, to repeat this ageless message of wisdom, that we are created in the Image of God. Cancerians can give this message its holographic form of neverending, lifegiving sunlight and moonlight, day by day, night by night, here and now.

From all this one may gather that the Cancer grail, with the Moon and Demeter in the centre is equal in importance to the Leo grail, which symbolises the King/Creator and Sun. Here we sense the Mother and Queen, protecting the etheric and astral regions of Gaia, the earth, and co-creatrix of the universe.

In the Sun-side of the Cancer grail-cup we see the Moon, surrounded by the Sun and Mercury. The Moonside of this Cancer grail has Saturn in the middle with Jupiter on one side and Saturn with Uranus on the other side. What a cosmic hologram!

THE LIBRA GRAIL

The Sun-side of the Libra grail is composed of Libra in the middle, balanced by Virgo on one side and Scorpio on the other. Virgo is the sign that has just been passed and Scorpio is the sign which the Sun is approaching.

The Moon-side of this grail is formed by Pisces, Aries and Taurus. Thus this grail is the exact opposite of the Aries grail. The energy of the cosmos moves through the Sun into the will of the Libran in order to weigh that which is coming their way in the form of opposing energy fields. They put the pro's against the con's before they make any decision. This may unbalance them, but their basic intention is always to make, and keep, peace and harmony. Because those around them and society as a whole are often not yet ready for this, they may easily loose their equilibrium. Thus they dance from decision to doubt, to regret, to beginning again, or to crisis, to exhaustion, and at last to doing nothing at all – returning back where they started. Or as the perfect ballet-dancer they have all their movements under control, up and down and right and left, in front and behind. They dance rhythmically and totally centred in the now, amidst the disturbances caused by time and space.

Because of this centredness and therefore consequently being unattached, Libras are born judges. Seeing both sides as equal they tend to be impartial and non-judgmental, so that they can make right and just decisions from the heart.

Their weak side is Virgo, the sign which the sun in Libra has passed. Their peace of mind can be shaken by criticism and small-mindedness. To counteract this they need to be sure of their facts and pure in their motives, and not overlook any details before coming to their decisions.

The sign towards which they grow and from which they can draw a harvest in this life is Scorpio. When they have learned to be balanced and at peace, they can penetrate deep into the essence of life and death, acquiring a transforming strength and an unshakeable force when it comes to what is right. Thus they become active fighters for justice and peace in the world. They can even become generals who fight for peace, which seems a contradiction in itself. President Eisenhower was an example of this.

The Moon-side of the grail will be filled by their Sun energy and thus they show on earth how to co-operate in harmony with a new project and what a team spirit there can be amongst pioneers (Ar.). Undisturbed and unattached, they can transform destructive energy into a positive force for good. They often have to work amidst chaos and liquidation (Pi. of their Vi–Pi, hind-axis), but their peaceful attitude can bring healing and restore equilibrium. Through those who live their Libra grail fully, peace and beauty can return to earth (Tau.). Through their initiatives (Ar.) and their vision for the future (Tau.) the need for the arts, for music, for dance and for beauty in nature will be given priority again. Crafts and working with one's hands and the care for soil (Tau.) all come under the blessings of the Libra cup. One of the beatitudes in the sayings of Jesus is 'Blessed are the peacemakers for they will be called the children of God' (Matt. 5: 9).

The combination of planets in the Libra grail is an interesting one. The Sun-side has Venus in the middle surrounded by Mercury and Mars. The opposite Moon-side is filled by Mars and Pluto in the middle with Jupiter and Neptune on one brim of the cup and Venus and Persephone on the other – exactly the reverse of the Aries grail. Note how the foot of the Libra grail is filled with far more planets than the overflowing top itself. Also, both Mars and Venus appear twice. It shows that the Aries and Libra grails are there to bring an equal balance between male and female, activity and passivity, doing and undoing, about which Eastern philosophy has much to say.

THE CAPRICORN GRAIL

The Sun-side of the Capricorn grail consists of Capricorn, with its ruler Saturn, in the middle, flanked by Sagittarius and Aquarius. The Moon-side has Cancer in the middle, surrounded by Gemini and Leo.

One could imagine the Capricorn cup chiselled out of a pure white rock-crystal, which is the purest form of Capricorn itself. This earthly form is also esoterically known as the true symbol of the grail. A ball of rock-crystal mirrors the complete earth. Hence the use of crystal balls for scrying. If one had eyes to see, one could encompass all earthly experiences and impressions.

As the mirror comes under Cancer, there is a cosmic logic in the fact that Cancer is the opposite sign of Capricorn. In Cancer, all etheric and astral levels are mirrored. The two signs cannot function without each other.

For those Capricorns living in the northern hemisphere there is the spiritual need to be fully awake and not to be bedevilled by the cold and lack of sunshine coming through their grail-cup in the darkest days of the year. They need to let their light shine in the darkness and within the homes of which Cancer is the symbol. It is the time for meditation on the passing of time, with yet another old year going and a new one coming. One renews one's faith (Sag.) in angels and the higher worlds (Aq.). Through these reflections on the laws of the universe the Capricorn needs to go with his light within himself into the inner chamber (Cn.) and realise that this inner chamber of the heart is being kept alive and filled by the rhythm of the constant in- and out-breath and the pumping of blood through the heart, which are the two functions of the signs around Cancer, Gemini and Leo.

Capricorn becomes aware of cosmic consciousness through its fore-axis, Aquarius–Leo. Leo is ruled by the Sun and thus by sunlight itself. That is precisely what Capricorn is lacking. To see the Sun right in the face and being led by it is the great difficulty. Capricorn has an enormous will of its own, which often appears to be modesty but it is not. It is the will of one's own ambition, of egotism and of stone-hard social drives. The ideal (Sag.) is often to achieve status (Cap.) by having faster information, outdoing rivals by being more hard-line, just a bit more clever in the commercial sector (Ge.), or a more gifted communicator (Ge.). When on this level, their Gemini–Sagittarius side tends to be misused and faith becomes fanaticism and motivated rat-racing. Thus the overruling factor for Capricorn becomes fear and worry: associated with loss of status in the eyes of the authorities and the family (Cap.–Cn.). The next typical characteristic of Capricorn is causing guilt feelings (Cap.–Cn.) in others and themselves. Before long shadows of sombre thoughts are being drawn like curtains before the sunlight. The energy of the Sun is thus prevented from shining into the grail-cup of the Capricorn and it becomes cold and empty within the heart of their crystal goblet. One builds an ivory tower around oneself to protect one from the free flow of light and love (Aq.–Le.).

To break out of this hardening process, the way out for Capricorns is to ask help from others and from transcendental forces. This is of course the essence of Aquarius, the sign towards which they need to grow. To do this one needs to overcome one's fear of humiliation. One has to break through the wall of isolation and depression and to admit that one cannot do it alone and that his own ego (lower self) is the greatest barrier to the light of cosmic consciousness. True faith and surrender to helping friends and angelic guidance is very difficult. None the less Capricorns need to be ushered over the threshold into freedom from status and towards an ethic of life where the only law is the one of loving service to one's neighbour and the community as a whole.

The ideal progression is that Capricorn does not listen to his own voice any longer, but begins to hear the intuitive flashes from the realms beyond him. The life-giving energy will overflow their cup, as if it were the waters of Aquarius already when they purify themselves through meditation and prayer.

The Moon-side of this grail will then be lit up and reflects, as it were, an inner glowing fire that burns up all the ice-cold past in their heart. Freed from fear they can become examples on earth of how to rule in wisdom from within (Le. and Ge. round Cn.). Thus they can be trusted with world leadership, free from party politics and nationalism, which they have just overcome within themselves.

The planets in the Capricorn grail form an interesting pattern. In the Sun-side of their cup, or in this case their hourglass (Sat.) we see Saturn in the middle with Jupiter in Sagittarius, and once more Saturn, now with Uranus in Aquarius.

At the Moon-side the Moon itself is central, together with Demeter, the astral mirror, and around her are Mercury and Hermes in Gemini and the Sun in Leo. Thus we see the same configuration as in the Cancer grail, only in reversed form.

Physically we can see the foot of this grail as a phenomenon in the sky in the early morning in midwinter, a few days before new moon. The moon is setting, with the morning star Mercury at her right side. On her left is the sun, about to rise. It is symbolic for the simplicity and clearness of Capricorn when it mirrors

the cosmos seen from our planet in time and space. Thus the
Capricorn grail is the symbol of the purest matter on earth, the
rock-crystal cosmic insight, sought after by every knight of the
Holy Grail in the mysteries of old.

ARIES

Index of Aries Ascendant Degrees

1st Degree Aries

First Image, Outer Symbol

A robust man with well-developed muscles is advancing resolutely from the left of the picture. In his right hand he balances a club; his left hand is resting on his hip. He is wearing an animal skin over his otherwise naked body. He gives the impression of quiet, decisive power. On the right, a woman in a long, revealing dress is standing in a seductive pose smiling at him.

Interpretation

This 1st degree of Aries, and of the entire zodiac, is the archetype of creation – of Adam and Eve. There are different levels of interpretation of each degree. It always depends on the strength and spiritual development of the Higher Self within the chart whether one lives this degree on an outer or physical plane, an emotional plane, or a highly evolved spiritual one. The three can intermingle within the life-span of one personality.

Here we are dealing with the 1st degree of a sign, in this case Aries. In principle, the 1st and 30th degrees symbolise the entire sign. Here we have primal energy bursting forth. It is the first impulse (Ar.) of simple, uncomplicated action and practical force. The Sun enters this degree on the first day of spring, and in our Western countries this is the bursting forth of new life in nature.

On the lower level, the man in this image is a brute, representing the more passionate and instinctive functions of creation. A man, in symbolic interpretation, stands for consciousness and is equated with the Sun in the horoscope – the spiritual aspect of both male and female. Man is supposed to be master over nature, and over his own lower nature, but here in this 1st degree this masculine side is still primitive. The man has enormous potential and undeveloped capacities. He acts without concern for anyone or anything in the world.

He is armed for 'the struggle of life' in a primitive way (the club). This means that those with this degree prominent are often ignorant about their own motives. They are propelled by a primeval power, an energy which is life itself – potent but hidden, and anything can happen.

On a low level they may be aggressive and quarrelsome, without inner control, and passionate – not in a sexual manner (more characteristic of Sc.) but in their reactions. On a higher level they have tremendous strength of character and are absolutely invincible. They believe themselves to be capable of, and indeed destined to achieve, everything. They have the power to perform the supernormal with an awe-inspiring superiority.

This is the pure symbol of the strong man, typified in Greek mythology as Hercules, who has to perform twelve miraculous labours. Those with this degree prominent do well to study these phases of development in man. In the Hercules symbolism, as well as in this 1st degree of Aries, temptation by women is always close at hand. These are phases in this person, and in the cosmos, which the Higher Self has to conquer. The masculine side is the 'positive', invincible, radiant force of upright man, corresponding to the Sun in the chart, as opposed to the 'negative', vulnerable, feminine side – symbolic of the lower emotions and uncontrolled moods in human beings, equated in cosmology with the Moon and Venus. Here, as with Eve, the woman seems to represent the temptation to unguided action without effect. It is the feminine side, as opposed to the masculine side, that is the undeveloped consciousness in this image.

However, there is a far higher message contained in this degree. There is the first Aries impulse of pushing action in opposition to Libra, the sign of peace and balance. Moreover, in addition to balancing its own opposition sign (here Li.), every sign also has to overcome its own difficult hind-axis (Pi.–Vi.), and to grow towards perfection into its own fore-axis (Tau.–Sc.). In other words this image (as is the case with all the 360 images) is a creative lesson on Divine imagery, showing us in symbols what to leave behind and what to aim at.

Here we leave behind us the lower side of Pisces, which is the chaos and nebulous existence of a former cycle of that sign, and also the divisive criticism which crumbles any action into particles of sand (Vi.). This man and woman have to overcome this axis (Vi.–Pi.), find their complement in each other and become one as equal partners. Then they blend into the fore-axis of a harmonious sexuality (Sc.) and passion, not murderous but procreative and harmonious, working towards peace on earth (Tau.). Male and female together, created as God-chosen partners, will then conquer the difficult square-axis for Aries, which is Cancer–Capricorn.

The ray of energy (Ar., the man) must see the eternal globe (Cap.) as its counterpart. The receiving sea or astral mirror (Cn.) has to become aware that she owes her existence to all that is, was and will be. This, in a nutshell, is the esoteric meaning of the cardinal cross (Ar.–Cn.–Li.–Cap.): the ultimate reconciliation of all the paradoxes or contrasts which Creation embodies, such as man-wife, male-female, light-darkness, positive and negative.

Second Image, Inner Symbol

A woman just risen from the ocean; a seal is embracing her (Rudhyar 1973).

Interpretation

We endeavour in these interpretations of the 360 pairs of images, to show the link between the first symbol, on the outer physical level of existence, and the second symbol, on the higher inner level. The second image can often only be appreciated by a more esoterically developed inner eye. Here, for instance, this fairly-tale image seems more Piscean than Arien. Do not forget that humanity's collective consciousness is only just emerging from the Piscean phase in this 1st degree of Aries. Thus we have a striking elevation of the first image. Here new birth has come out of the great reservoir of the waters of life. It is the archetype and symbol of Venus rising from the foam of the sea – created out of nothingness.

There is food for deep thought upon the great secret hidden in this 1st degree of the first sign. What striking Divine imagery is this word 'seal', with its double and inner meaning! The female, God's beloved creation – whether seen in its totality or as the human soul – is *sealed*, or loved and protected, from its emergence and throughout its evolution to perfection, and cherished to that unsuspected end by undeveloped Man.

There is a very ancient belief in Ireland and Scotland about the 'seal-people'. It is said that they have a mysterious affinity with human beings, and that they carry the souls of the drowned. As the highest level of Aries is the power of the resurrection, the life and death of the seals, and their purpose on earth, may hold a lesson for us humans. The way in which seals are murdered with clubs is symbolically significant, for it exemplifies the primitive human nature of the collective 'old' Adam in his domination of Mother earth.

Biblical Parallel

Adam and Eve. See *Gen. 1: 26–28* and *2: 21–28.*

Notes

Mythology   Hercules, or Heracles. See Homer's *Iliad* and *Encycl Britt.* The 'Hercules-club' is the devil's walking stick or angelica tree.

Seals   There is serious literature about seals and their habits, as observed in the north of Scotland where they have been known to share human habitation. The outcry against the cruel killing of seals elsewhere for their skins has received world-wide publicity.

2ND DEGREE ARIES

First Image, Outer Symbol

A rider, in the noble spirit of chivalry, is approaching from the right on a richly harnessed thoroughbred, brandishing a sabre in his right hand. With his left hand he is lightly holding the reins and is easily in control of the horse, although it is rearing because some snakes, or serpents, are wriggling before its feet.

Interpretation

This 2nd degree of Aries is the image of an archetype. We might have expected the serpent in the 1st degree of Aries, but in the Divine imagery it is in the 2nd. In all religions we find man attacked by the serpent. Apollo meets Python; Krishna meets Anatha; Belmerduk meets Tiamat. In the Bible the tribe of Dan is symbolised, and even blessed, as a serpent at the roadside biting the horse's heel.

In this image the Higher Self is depicted as a man of courage. On a physical level the person with this degree on the Ascendant may be an excellent jockey, or a horse-breaker, or may be good at organising horse-shows. On a more spiritual level there is the possibility of spectacular deeds as the outcome of his high moral standing and his white-magical awareness. As rider and horse are both so well-equipped, there is a strong indication that we have a superior Higher Self here, who might like 'show' but is also extremely capable. People with hypnotic power (Pl., ruler of Ar.) come under this degree, and may express this talent in surgery or psychoanalytical studies and practice, in which their freely guided thoughts and intuition may cleanse the patients from deep-seated sexual drives and death-wishes (the snakes). These people are of high moral standing and lofty conviction. They can train their thought-life towards great heights (the rearing horse, Sag.), but they may suffer from a staggering perplexity when they realise where their thoughts and beliefs lead them. Those with an unawakened consciousness gallop through life too busy to halt and see the dangers. Those with spiritual awareness of their own powers may look into themselves and check their headlong career in time, before death (serpent, Sc.) strikes, or slander (Sc.) brings their high-powered personalities to a downfall. Pluto, the higher ruler of Aries (not of Sc.!) has everything to do with the powers released in the atom and with Mars, the lower ruler of Aries. One can use this power in an explosive, or implosive and peaceful, way.

If these people are proud, boastful and reliant on outward

glamour, there is the chance that their lack of humility will bring them many personal enemies (Sc.). If their manner is one of contempt for the masses, they may become too powerful for their own good and too dismissive of others.

It is a cosmological principle that every image in a certain zodiacal sign comprises the other two of the same element. In this case Aries is a fire sign, so we look for the two other fire signs, Leo and Sagittarius, and find them strongly portrayed. The man is very individual and courageous (Le.). The horse is richly (Le.) harnessed. The man may be very aware of his own spiritual (Le.) conviction (Sag.). The horse (Sag.) and the elevated sabre indicate a strong conviction, maybe even fanaticism (Sag.). All this is found in the pioneering fire sign of Aries. This person may well be the 'cock (Ar.) of the walk (Sag.)'.

Second Image, Inner Symbol

A·comedian is entertaining a group of his friends.

Interpretation

The rider, who has either been thrown from his horse or has quietly dismounted, has come down to the level of the group, and in both love and friendship (Li.–Aq.) he is even doing them the service (Vi.) of entertaining them with humour (Pi.). He is thus overcoming the difficult hind-axis for Aries and converting the struggle with the serpent (Sc.) into a beautiful poetic tale, or even uttering prophetic words (higher meaning of Tau.), thus perfecting himself towards the fore-axis of Taurus–Scorpio. On a lower level he could simply use humour to perpetuate the attitude of contempt shown by the horseman, by making fun of the audience, or even his friends. On whatever level, he (or she) has to make contact with the other side – in other words incorporate the opposition sign of Libra. Those with this degree prominent must turn explosive actions into inner peace, and then bring out that inner peace and direct it towards their friends.

Biblical Parallels

Jacob's blessing for his son Dan. 'Dan shall be a serpent by the way, an adder in the path, that biteth the horse heels, so that his rider shall fall backward.' *Gen. 49: 17.*

'For behold I will send serpent, cockatrices, among you, which will not be charmed, and they shall bite you, saith the Lord.' *Jer. 8: 17.*

He that sits on the white horse to make war 'and out of his mouth goes a sharp sword . . . and on his thigh a name written King of Kings and Lord of Lords.' *Rev. 19: 11–16.*

Conception Corrected Asc. 2nd Aries

Arthur Honegger   Born 10 Mar. 1892 at 07.00 hrs. in Le Havre, 49°30 N, 00°06 E. Died 27 Nov. 1955. (A second birthtime of 08.00 hrs. has been rejected, 07.00 is personal information.) CC NS for 283 days at 06.59 hrs. gives 1°43 Aries, or for 269 days at 07.01 hrs. gives 2°55 Aries (see 3rd Ar.).

Swiss composer, part of the French School, one of 'Les Six', known for his 'clashing of scale passages and rhythmic figures in contrary motion' (Encycl. Britt). His best-known works are the biblical drama *King David* (1921) and his opera *Antigone*. He wrote music to plays and well-known motion pictures of his days, such as Joan of Arc (1938). He owed much to Debussy (see 23rd Le.).

Nostradamus   If born at 11.56 hrs. gives 1°33 Aries (see 29th Pi.).

George Orwell   (E. A. Blair) Born 25 June 1903 at midnight, 00.00 hrs. in Motihari (India), 26°40 N, 84°57 E. Died 23 Jan. 1950. CC NS for 266 days at 23.56 hrs. (18.16 hrs. GMT) gives 1°33 Aries. English writer, who won a world reputation for his futuristic novels depicting totalitarian states, such as *Animal Farm* (1945) and *1984* (1949). Orwell was a stubborn defender of the underdog, the 'common man', and the Jews in Britain; he volunteered to fight against the Fascists in the Spanish Civil War. He lived in self-chosen poverty and ended his life far from civilization in the Hebrides. Much of what he predicted in *1984* has become a reality only a few decades after his death. See *George Orwell, Fugitive from the Camp of Victory* by Richard Rees (London, 1961).

3RD DEGREE ARIES

First Image, Outer Symbol

At the left, an elegantly dressed *hetaera* (Greek for female companion) is seated on a low stool in her boudoir. She has a pleasant smile on her face, her costume is elegant and her right hand is stretched out in an explanatory, or teaching, gesture towards an invisible figure. On the right, a half-naked woman is lying on a carpet in a voluptuous and provocative attitude.

Interpretation

At first sight, this symbol seems a strange combination of two possibilities in the positive fire sign Aries. Aries is the symbol of the ram. Perhaps the ladies are awaiting him? We certainly have here a Greek archetype, and that takes us much deeper than the superficial French interpretation of Janduz, who sticks to words like 'luxury', 'love-making', 'coquetry' and 'sleeping Madonnas'.

Undoubtedly on a low physical level this is true for all people, male and female, with this degree on the Ascendant, or with a prominent planet in it. It is the archetype of Eve tempting the opposite sex. A *hetaera* in ancient Greece was a public woman, either a priestess or a flute and cithern player. So both sides of this image may point to two aspects of one public woman's symbol. Venus in this degree in the horoscope tends to bring out the sensual side, and Mars the sexual desires symbolised by the half-naked woman on the right. Those with the Moon here may mirror both sides simultaneously. Saturn here brings out the hardness and egoism of the female feelings. Jupiter brings out thinking and teaching, and Uranus the hospitality and intuition of the upright companion. Neptune here inspires eroticism and music, while the Sun and/or Pluto may make this person (him or her) into a priestly soul endowed with magical powers, capable of seeing beyond the visible(Pi.). So there is much more to this degree than sexual indulgence, although in the current decline of our culture this factor is prevalent collectively and thus more tempting for people with this 3rd degree prominent.

Aries as the first sign of the zodiac is notorious for its tendency to go ahead regardless, and for its lack of discrimination. Here, however, we seem to have a dualistic image; two opposites to be very clearly distinguished within one person. Aries has two rulers: the higher, immaterial planet Pluto with its connotations of magic and resurrection, is represented in this image by the *hetaera* on the stool, whilst the female on the carpet represents the self-indulging symbol of the lower Mars forces. The two go together and blend, and that is the subtle message of this complicated Aries degree.

On the outer level, the upright woman on the left is sensitive and willing to do anything to come into a fruitful contact with her surroundings. These people are charming and good for everybody. They are joyful, loyal and frank; inviting and not timid; strong lovers of the truth, and ideal hosts and hostesses. They spread an atmosphere of harmony and though their words can sometimes be powerful and sharp, they are also quick to extend the forgiving hand and to give a soothing smile. Good companionship is their watchword. On a high level *hetaeras* are priestesses, and thus links between the visible and the invisible. However, the giving, female attitude in this degree can always revert to the possessive, greedy, sexual charms of the naked lady. It is the archetype of the character (male or female) who acts as a Madonna, but whose meetings always end in bed.

On a still higher level, blending the two together, these people strive to convert not only physical prostitutes, but also those prostituting the spirit. Their weakness is that they may lack discrimination in their offering of themselves. They may become 'too good' and thus be overpowered.

Second Image, Inner Symbol

A man's profile suggests the outlines of his country.

Interpretation

For the Higher Self schooled in conscious awareness, this second image is a striking elevation of the first one. The first image lacks boundaries – it is too open and inviting. Here we see the two opposing female sides blended into one male profile, which is the highly individual spirit of the Higher Self. The oversoul in the invisible is what the *hetaera* tried to contact. Here, this oversoul has expressed itself in the form of the individual Ego, or face, against the background of the borders within which it is incarnated.

Here the three fire signs come into a magnificent inner synthesis (Sag.) of conscious and unconscious atoms (Ar.), through which the spark of the masculine creativity (Le.) enlightens and sets its borders. As the Germans say 'In knowing one's limitations, one shows oneself to be a Master.' In the highest symbolism this country is 'Thy Kingdom come'.

Biblical Parallels

The prophet Hosea's vision of Israel as the two women in whoredom. See *Hos. 1: & 2:*

Martha and Mary as higher prototypes. See *Lk. 10: 38–42.*

The resurrection of their brother Lazarus. See *Jn. 11: 1–39.*

Note

Cleopatra is said to have been smuggled naked within a carpet into the camp of Julius Caesar, with the well-known romantic results.

Conception Corrected Asc. 3RD ARIES

Arthur Honegger   If born at 07.01 hrs. gives 2°55 Aries (see 2nd Ar.).

4TH DEGREE ARIES

First Image, Outer Symbol

A countryman approaches from the left on a path going through a wood with an undergrowth of bushes, plants and herbs of various colours. He is dressed like a peasant in the traditional costume of that area, with a hat and wooden shoes. He is walking along peacefully with his hands behind his back. On the right a hirsute man is hiding behind a bush.

Interpretation

This is a typical Aries degree with a problem. The two men, symbols of consciousness, are obviously operating on different levels. On the lower level one is apparently about to attack the other. Will the figure in the shadow kill the upright one, or will the higher powers win, so that the two men may come to terms with each other, and perhaps even co-operate? The person with this degree on the Ascendant must become aware of this duality hidden within themselves. In the French interpretation of Janduz, the emphasis is laid on 'rude independence'.

In the character of these people (men or women) there is one side that hides its instincts. They have a timidity which prevents them from coming out into the open. The impulse (Ar.) to come forward and to be themselves is counteracted by the desire to hide, which takes the form of masking (Ar.) and underhand behaviour.

If the upright man prevails in this character, we have a simple person who goes through life in a quiet and well-considered way, fulfilling his task even though he may be faced with workers or partners who are dishonest, or who try to undo his work by strikes or sabotage.

The image is a bit primitive (Ar.) on the lower physical level, where these people might have to cope with a pioneering situation, or with colonising an undeveloped country and living among the natives. They may be quiet peasants, who know they have to be in modest positions as their faculties have not yet fully developed. They might even be slightly abnormal in the eyes of others.

There is a side to this character that has not yet been cultivated. Such a person may suddenly become unreasonable and hot-tempered because they forget that other side of their character, which then takes its revenge.

The fruits of their life can be good, but the impression remains that they lack the strength and will-power to do what is good and pure. There is an energy in them which they do not dare to face yet, even though they may behave extremely independently. There is some sort of underdevelopment in this image, which does not fit in with the sign of Aries, that should give potential in all spheres of life. They are often earthbound so that they do not make the effort to ascend (Ar.) into the higher realms of the spirit.

On a higher level we see the Aries grail here. The spirit of Aries is to co-operate in peace (Li. opp.) giving impulses for new development. These people have got negative criticisms and chaos (Vi.–Pi. hind-axis) under control, and are overcoming hate and greed by working harmoniously for the new earth, to make it a paradise (Tau.–Sc. fore-axis).

On the highest level this degree is an archetype of Jahveh (the Lord God) walking in Paradise, while Adam is hiding himself and covering his body with leaves, because his light has darkened while he ate the fruit from the tree of the knowledge of good and evil, and he fears the confrontation with the Most High.

Second Image, Inner Symbol

Two lovers are strolling through a secluded park lane.

Interpretation

Here is the fullness of conscious participation in life. Here is Paradise in action. Adam and Eve, male and female, accept each other and the cycle is closed once more after the two male figures have not only seen each other but got together. The walking peasant and the hiding man are not very active (neg. Ar.) – they just let things happen. In the second image there is the positive return to the greatness of life. The shadow of expulsion

from the park (Paradise) still lies heavily over this image. There
is goodwill, but they are not yet able to be strong and definite
enough to do what is right, although there is a hidden drive in
these people to return to Paradise.

Biblical Parallels

'And the Lord God called unto Adam, and said unto him, "Where art
thou?"' *Gen. 3: 9.*

Adam and Eve expelled from the garden of Eden. See *Gen. 2: 17* and
Gen. 3: especially *verses 22–24.*

5TH DEGREE ARIES

First Image, Outer Symbol

A wide night-sky, thrown into turmoil by a violent gale.
Lightning striking through the clouds reveals a massive rock
along which a strong, muscular man is climbing. He is joyful,
determined and undisturbed by the storm.

Interpretation

Janduz calls this a degree of 'justified pretension'. One may
agree with the word 'pretension' in its literal sense of 'pre-
tendere', or 'to seize in advance'. Janduz also speaks of the
inborn privilege of good fortune, which may be put to the
service of great causes.

This person is industrious and will do anything to better their
personal standards and life in general. They like targets to aim
at, and they are at their best when striving to attain them.

However, it is too simple to identify with the man alone.
As an Aries degree this is indeed a young and energetic
consciousness, but we have to interpret the complete picture. We
then see the elements of the cardinal cross (Ar.–Cn.–Li.–Cap.)
strongly represented. The man is trying to tackle this in a
typically impulsive Aries way. Rock comes under Capricorn and

symbolises career-making, harsh society and shrewd ambition. This man is climbing the social ladder to the top, but so what? Is he unaware of the turbulent weather, which one might see as the environment of the other square sign Cancer? When he reaches the top of the rock, could this weather dethrone him at the last moment? His aim should be peace and harmony (Li. opp.) with heaven and earth, in and around himself.

We can also see the fire trine (Ar.–Le.–Sag.) represented. The man is very confident (Sag.) in himself (Le.). He is striving towards a single, very definite goal (Sag.), and his creative leadership (Le.) might become a fanatical striving to reach the top. Through this process he may become hard on himself, although not dictatorial towards others, because it is a degree which is bubbling over with energy and, as Aries, he will start a new plan of action just as soon as he reaches the next peak.

The individual with this degree prominent may be of very modest birth, but will quickly climb towards the highest, almost unattainable position (the bare rock), but it is not certain that he will grow as fast inwardly, and the lack of inner contentment (Cn.) may make his character too rigid.

However, he is a good sport and has a burning drive. He is full of fire and does not shun hardship when reaching for his goal. He may do wonders in building up a project, working it out with incredible persistence.

His weak side is that he may become an egoistic and fanatical fighter, who could not care less about the sensitivity of others or the milder elements of nature in general. He grasps what he can with his hands (Ge.) and may even challenge Fate or the Creator Himself. This is the archetypal symbol of Moses climbing Mount Sinai to claim the tablets of the Law, unaware of the emotional state of the people down below. Those with this degree prominent may well become both famous and feared. They may be guides towards the light, but the 'light' appears to them in the thundering Jahweh, not calmly and in silence.

In ordinary physical life such an individual may enjoy mountaineering, and could do well as a guide or rescue worker (Vi.–Pi. hind-axis). They have to learn to perfect themselves (Tau.–Sc. fore-axis) and thus become at peace with themselves and the earth, through awareness of the dangers of death (Sc.), by transmutation or conversion to God.

Second Image, Inner Symbol

A white triangle, made weightless by two golden wings at each side.

Interpretation

This image has that unearthly ethereal fulfilment that the first image lacks. One may fall off the top of the mountain, or one may get wings in order to disappear into other dimensions. Aries is the sign of the power of ascension, rising into invisible realms. This triangle is the symbol of the law of trinity or triads, on which all philosophies are based. Here is the comprehension of the balance within the trine of spirit, soul and body, which is finding its way back to the Source and thereby acquiring wings. Gold (Le.) is a symbol of the spirit, into which the flashes of lightning (Aq.) have turned. The uncontrolled ambitions of the first image and its turbulent background are here encapsulated within a white pyramid, which stands as an archetypal symbol of pure and very high initiation.

Biblical Parallels

Moses climbing Mount Sinai. See *Ex. 19; 24* and *34*.

The pyramid as a sign and witness in Egypt. *Is. 19: 20*

Note To understand this degree, one should study the literature on the Pyramid of Giza.

6TH DEGREE ARIES

First Image, Outer Symbol

Having taken a winding and steep route at the edge of a ravine in a mountain landscape, a man on horseback is proudly looking around him. In a deep valley below him to the right, labourers are working with pick-axes.

Interpretation

According to Janduz this is a degree of 'innate superiority', which indeed is a typical characteristic of Aries. Illustrious people may be born under this degree, says Janduz. Indeed, this person has extraordinary potential (Ar.) and a formidable talent for resisting coercion.

When Janduz speaks of an aristocratic person or even a highborn prince with a long and prosperous reign, she is fixing solely on the man on horseback. Certainly that part of this symbol indicates the talent to be a born 'chief'. He (or she) does not avoid difficult circumstances (the high road). He will not be put off by a high position and great responsibility (Cap. sq.), but will bear it with pride and fervour. He rules his own affairs, and things would go wrong if he did not do so. He is a central force: the consciousness is that of Aries, which is pioneering and exploratory; it is not the centrality of Leo (2nd fire sign). He acts on sudden impulse and by doing so he may gain honour and climb in the eyes of the world. He is himself, in that Arien sense of 'new every morning'.

He may have to face many unforeseen eventualities (the winding path), but his spirit can mirror them in advance (Cn. sq. Ar.). His position amongst others may be rather detached, and his work may leave his heart cold (distance between rider and workers).

The labourers on the right side of the image show another part of this character: the group-consciousness of work. They may be free labourers, singing joyfully, or a political pressure-group, or slaves, or prisoners from a concentration camp (different levels of the cardinal cross). The awareness of the rider overlooking the work may be that of a respected king or of a dreaded foreman.

On a high level he is protected by those above him in rank. His task is to emerge from the lower collective slave mentality and from docility by hard and independent work. He knows the meaning of slow, determined toil.

The Aries grail can be seen in this image as the slave-labour and conquering nature (Vi.–Pi. hind-axis) from which the Higher Self has become detached. What this person wants is to use white-magical power (Ar.) to work his way through the earth by transmuting matter (Tau.–Sc. fore-axis), in order to link up (Li. opp. Ar.) on whatever level the symbol may be operating.

It is a dangerous degree in terms of the spiritual dangers of the pride that may develop when service is forgotten; the man could fall from his high-riding position down into the canyon. This individual must not try to get higher than the point to which he or she is led absolutely through faith (Le.–Sag. trine Ar.).

Second Image, Inner Symbol

A black square with one of its sides illumined in red.

Interpretation

Rudhyar speaks in his commentary of 'great inner restlessness', but that seems more appropriate for the first image. However, one can see the black square as the imperturbable pre-matter which is suddenly disturbed by a flash of red energy. Red comes under Aries and it stands for a new impulse. This is the same in the first image; the man on high can give a sudden new impulse to the workers down below.

It is the task of Aries to give impulses, which bring the black inertia into unrest, so that old colourless forms get the chance to be set on fire. It is another symbol of the red phoenix burnt and rising out of its black ashes, which is an archetype of Aries.

7TH DEGREE ARIES

First Image, Outer Symbol

A solitary path in the countryside. On the left is a stone wall projecting its shadow onto the path, along which a fox is running in the direction of a copse.

Interpretation

Janduz describes this degree as 'circumspect falseness'. She sees it as a peculiar image in the sign of Aries, which normally stands for openness and fair battle.

Indeed, the fox is a biological and esoteric symbol of Virgo on its low level of negative criticism. Virgo is the sign of the zodiac (hind-axis of Ar.) which the bearer of the Aries grail has to outgrow. Note that the fox is in the shadow – indeed, in the shadow-side of the Aries grail.

As the first of the twelve 7th degrees, which all tell stories both of very dark and of powerfully light forces, this symbol opens with dualism. On the left is the symbol of the shadow and the stone wall: these are the dangerous forces of the uncontrolled square axis (Cn.–Cap.). Stone stands for Capricorn and the shadow is the unconscious part of the soul (Cn.), which can become emotionally upsetting. On the right, however, we see the peaceful countryside in full sunshine, and the copse which is a sheltered area for small animals, both peaceful symbols of Cancer–Libra.

One can see that this Aries degree has many different levels of meaning, and it depends on the rest of the horoscope how one interprets the personality of someone with this degree rising. One may find an afflicted Mercury (ruler of Vi., fox), or a difficult Mars (ruler of Ar.), or a difficult position of Saturn (ruler of Cap., the wall).

On a lower level one has to be aware that there may be hypocrisy, giving the impression of innocence and good faith, while in fact traps are being set for others. On the lower side such people may perform perfidious, mischievous acts (the fox in the shadow), but they are always about to be unmasked (the fox will soon reach the sunshine). Their foxside is quick-witted, cultivating an image of charming naivety (see the many folk-tales about foxes). The wall in shadow shows their blunt egoism. They may be without morals and very shrewd in so-called diplomacy, when covering up nasty and 'foxy' crimes (the wall protects the fox). The lower side of this character has all the negative elements of the hind-axis Virgo–Pisces: They are loners who choose their victims on the borderline of society, and may have a ruinous influence.

However, black as the left side is, the right side is to be interpreted as entirely light. The character of these people is as the sunny rural countryside in springtime (Ar.), full of the promise of young life (Ar.), while the area of the bushy copse had a deep magical meaning, as ancient rites may have been performed here, turning this spot into an open-air temple, where one is safe from approaching dangers (the fox). There are many levels of interpretation. This brings us to the second image.

Second Image, Inner Symbol

A man succeeds in expressing himself simultaneously in two realms.

Interpretation

The first image was one on the borderline of two worlds, which might make the person dishonest. Here that phase has been passed and the duality consciously accepted. One is indeed working on the edge between heaven and earth, or between God and the devil. William Blake, and the more modern 'magic-realistic' (Ar.) painters and writers, tried to express these two realms as one whole. The word 'simultaneously' is the keynote here. Above and below, good and bad, mirror each other in this archetypal and New Age degree.

Biblical Parallels

The Hebrew name for fox in the Bible is *shual*. A similar word is used for underworld or hell (sheol). See *Ps. 63:10*; *Lam. 5: 18*; *Ex. 13:4*; *Neh. 4:3* and *Luk. 13:32*.

Jesus said 'The foxes have holes . . . but the Son of man hath not where to lay his head.' *Mt. 8:20* (Head comes under Ar.)

8TH DEGREE ARIES

First Image, Outer Symbol

On the left a man in a furious temper is provoking others, who are peacefully playing ball (*jeu aux boules*) on a village green.

With a dagger in his hand he is slashing at a poster and stamping with rage, having found out that his actions have little or no effect on the players.

Interpretation

Janduz calls this a degree of 'dangerous violence'. Is this man (the consciousness) mad, or drunk, or a religious fanatic? One automatically looks at the raging man first, but people with this degree rising show an interplay of violence and calmness alternating in their character.

They get more and more furious when others do not pay them enough attention. On a low level they lack all self-control and crush everything that gets in their way. They seem to be able to start (Ar.) and lead (Le.) a project (Sag.), but soon it is evident that they are merely boasting (neg. Ar.). They cannot bear it when others see through them, so they make more noise and become more and more stubborn (neg. Ar.), and even mean in their passions. Discussions always end in quarrels, as they can never give in. They think they can win with insolent and offensive threats.

Here we have an example of Aries not controlling the square of the cardinal cross. By rude actions (Ar.), stemming from egoism (Cap.) and emotionalism (Cn.), they destroy peace and beauty (Li.). They do not see any danger for themselves, but it all bounces back on their own head (Ar.) when they find their master, who lays a whip across their shoulders, this being the only language they understand. Otherwise they go on ruining the existing peace (the players) and causing disharmony. This side of their character tends towards terrorism and revolution. They are born rebels.

On a higher level they fight the good fight with all their might, like Luther, who hung his famous statements against the existing church on the public noticeboards, thus inaugurating the Reformation. They dedicate themselves to the fight with blood, sweat and tears, full of enthusiasm.

One can see the Aries grail here. They see the liquidation of the old order as a service (Vi.–Pi. hind-axis) and they fight for peace (Sc.–Tau. fore-axis). At their best they are great adventurers, enlisting others for their army in the cause of 'Onward Christian Soldiers'. The other side of them is just the reverse. They play games and appear to be at peace while in reality they should be doing something about the turmoil of their lives. They mask themselves (neg. Ar.) against the approaching warning (man on the left). They identify with the mass of people (the group) who see life as a game – which in the end may win wars. They would do well to develop this attitude within themselves (Li. opp. Ar.), in order to attain their Aries grail-cup. They certainly have hypnotic (Ar.) personalities with suggestive power (Tau.) to transform energies (Sc.). They would be very useful if they gave themselves to a Christ-like cause. Much depends on the strength and development of their Higher Self.

Second Image, Inner Symbol

A woman's hat with streamers blown by the east wind.

Interpretation

The first image is bursting with male energy. Here we see the female side. What can be more innocent and frivolous than a lady's hat that has freed itself from its owner and just gone with the wind? That wind comes from the East!

The man and the players have to become one and to be moved by the wind (the Holy Spirit). Then the ascent to a higher realm is possible. Here there are forces capable of elevating them even higher. They may become an aerial force together, in order to overcome the negative powers in the air, symbolised by the mere lightness of a circular hat (head comes under Ar.) with streamers. Not through strife, but through soft coloured ribbons dancing in the wind, will the resistance of the Prince of the air vanish. In other words, the game has to be perfected into the art of ju-jitsu (Chinese, Li.) by which inward action or implosion conquers explosion (Ar.).

Biblical Parallels

'Proclaim ye this among the Gentiles; Prepare war, wake up the mighty men, let all the men of war draw near; let them come up.'
Joel 3:9.
The powers of the air. See *Eph. 2: 2* and *6: 12.*

9TH DEGREE ARIES

First Image, Outer Symbol

A man is standing on an elevated terrace with his arms crossed over his breast in a haughty attitude. He is regarding the city at his feet with the air of a conqueror.

Interpretation

According to Janduz this is a degree of 'infatuation'. If the devil whispers in this person's ear that the empires of the world will be at his feet if only he will worship the devil, this person would not answer, like Jesus, 'Get thee hence Satan'. The danger of this degree is indeed the wish to be admired by the world. These people expect admiration, and their self-love can be great.

They may have a justified self-esteem. The consciousness (the man) has been elevated high above the average, and he (or she) may well deserve this position. The three fire signs are strongly represented here (Ar.–Le.–Sag.). These people may be spiritual or worldly leaders of great value. The danger is that they know this only too well and become high-handed and get entangled in the cult of their own personality.

If this position is not deserved from on high, then the squares of Aries (Cn.–Cap.) may upset their entire character. They become ambitious and cold of heart (Cap., the city). They play on the emotions of the common people (Cn.) and are very keen to be talked about in town.

As Aries they may have a hypnotic and even black-magical power over others. If they do not control themselves, they may use all their energy in dominating the lower instincts of their people and their environment.

On a higher level these people see through these temptations and stand above them like Jesus. This will depend on the strength of the entire horoscope, whether the Sun is afflicted, Saturn well-placed, Neptune strongly aspected, and so forth.

These individuals may evolve from the merely physical, through the astral, towards the mental, and even the high spiritual planes. They may become noble and, with a well-deserved pride, accept the highest honours, but they have to be aware that there is always a more highly developed leader above them to whom they must give way. Thus they will attain the Aries grail cup in religious service and the sacrifice of the lower self (Vi.–Pi. hind-axis). They may become prophetic and protect their city (their own moral values) against wars and invasions (Tau.–Sc. fore-axis) and bring peace to their land. Thus they may become like a Chinese emperor whose mere presence on the high mountain ensures that the city prospers. Their capacities may be those of the highest leaders. They may be seers (Tau.) for their friends (Aq.). They may rule their own household, or the state, according to the highest vision, knowing that the Kingdom is within.

Second Image, Inner Symbol

A seer gazes with concentration into a crystal sphere.

Interpretation

The direction here is completely inward-looking. The consciousness of the man on the terrace is centred outside himself, fixed on the world, while here all energies are gathered together and fixed on the centre of the crystal, which is the highest esoteric symbol of the grail. The man becomes a seer, a 'fore-seer' of all factors in any situation.

The self-centredness of the ego now evolves into the prophetic visionary ability (high Tau.), to see through matter (Tau.). The fact that the next sign is shown in the symbol means that Aries itself may also be manifested in its highest ascension. However, even in crystal-gazing there is the danger of hypnotic power and too much concentration on a single goal. One has to ascend higher to penetrate with great caution into the centre.

Biblical Parallel

'Get thee hence, Satan.' See *Mt. 4: 8–10.*

10TH DEGREE ARIES

First Image, Outer Symbol

On the left we see a battlefield with the dead and wounded lying across each other. On the right is a hunter's spoil in the form of a heap of shot pheasants, partridges and hares. In the centre a man is standing upright, armed with a gun.

Interpretation

Janduz calls this a degree of 'triumph', and according to her this is the sort of triumph that may be overshadowed by destruction and bloodshed.

At first sight it seems to be a morbid kind of triumph. We have to be careful in our interpretation, because this is not a Scorpio degree, but an Aries one, in which the ruler of the sign, Mars, undertakes activity, often for the purposes of protection or for clearing the way (Vi.–Pi.) for a new era. This man in the centre is the Aries-consciousness.

Certainly the Higher Self of the person with this degree rising may be highly developed, standing above murder and destruction, although he may not yet see so far as to encompass the animal world in his compassion.

In ordinary life these people always have to face difficult circumstances. On the physical plane they may be adventurous leaders of expeditions. According to Janduz they may even become rich as gunsmiths or smugglers, trappers or just simple hunters. This can manifest on the psychological plane as hunters for sympathy (Ar. opp. Li.). However, on the lower plane they do not hesitate to importune others for their own collections of 'dead material', such as stamps or war trophies. Often it is easy to see through their little tricks.

On a high level one can see the Aries grail here. The man

himself is calm and balanced (Li. opp. Ar.) like a judge between two parties, without hate for either (Tau.–Sc.). In a higher sense these people may even be fighters for God and conscious of having to cleanse the earth of its dead, and its dead matter, as a service (Vi.–Pi. hind-axis) before the kingdom of peace can descend, as they realise that in practice some souls have to be sacrificed and go through the fire (Ar. fire sign).

Inwardly they are often driven by a sense of moral duty (Cn.–Cap. sq. axis) to wade through the morass of human misery. Their deeds gradually bring them into a position where it is almost impossible to remain upright without using force or even causing their own self-destruction.

On a high esoteric level they may then use either white or black magic. They know of the power of angels to destroy armies, of which there are examples in the Bible and in modern times, or of the power of Nimrod. Nimrod is the archetype of the 'mighty hunter' and according to some an incarnation of the devil himself.

One may find amongst them the courage of Aries (different from the courage of Leo), which single-handedly can put tens of thousands to flight. They can only do that because they have inwardly conquered themselves. Their task in the end is to stand up and be counted for the highest ideals, to be reached without explosion but with the power of implosion.

Second Image, Inner Symbol

A scholar creates new forms for ancient symbols.

Interpretation

The direction is now completely inward-looking. Implosion (Ar.) is a technologically advanced technique of freeing energy without explosion. This person, when overcoming the explosive side of his character, may become a scholar by using these higher potentialities and building valuable new forms by studying the ancient wisdom of the past. He can become a wise man, even a seer, foreseeing how the destruction of the earth can be avoided (Tau.–Sc. fore-axis) through the reintegration of what is already here.

Few Aries people realise that a higher force lives through them, and that they are merely the instrument and not themselves that force. If they do not see this, they can be the creators of blood-baths.

Biblical Parallels

'Even as Nimrod the mighty hunter before the Lord.' *Gen. 10: 9.*

'Now gather thyself in troops, O daughter of troops.' *Mic. 5: 1.*

'And they shall waste the land of Assyria with the sword, and the land of Nimrod in the entrances thereof.' *Mic. 5: 6.*

'A thousand shall fall at thy side, ten thousand at the right hand; . . . only with thine eyes shalt thou behold and see the reward of the wicked.' *Ps. 91: 7–8.*

Note

1. The London poet Isaac Rosenberg died at the Western Front on 1 April 1918 (Sun 10° Ar.). An insight into this degree can be gained by reading his great poems of the war: 'Break of Day in the Trenches', 'Dead Man's Dump' and 'Returning We Hear the Lark'.

2. The vision of the angels of Mons (*Belgium*) in World War I is an example of a celestial army seen by thousands.

Conception Corrected Asc. 10TH ARIES

Peter the Great (Tsar), born 30 May 1672 (OS) or 8 June (NS) or sometimes seen as 9th, at 1.00 hours (this is the 9th June, GMT 22.29 on the 8th) in Moscow 55°45 N, 37.34 E, died 8 February 1725 (NS) in (now) Leningrad. Source of his birth hour in the biography of Graham Stephen (see below). CC NS for 263 days at 1.01 hours gives 9°47 Aries.

Emperor of Russia, known as a reformer and as creator of the first Russian fleet. In order to learn Western ship-building he lived and worked one year in the Netherlands amongst the shipbuilders on the River Zaan, where his home is now a museum. He witnessed horrors as a child when his tutor and best friend were hacked to pieces, which can be seen as an expression of this 10th Aries. He was involved in wars with

Turkey. He crowned his wife as successor, which was unheard of. She became Catherine I. He suffered from convulsions, had violent passions and was deeply religious. This rising degree seems to fit him.

See *Encycl. Britt.* and *The Life of Peter the Great of Russia*, by Graham Stephen (1929, 1987).

11TH DEGREE ARIES

First Image, Outer Symbol

A young and beautiful woman 'awfully nice' and 'terribly pretty' half sits, half lies on a couch or sofa in a sensual and provocative attitude. Her gown is sliding down from her shoulders.

Interpretation

Janduz calls this a degree of 'softness and moral weakness'. According to her, people with this degree on the Ascendant, or with a prominent planet there, are physically beautiful and in love with themselves. She observes that men with this Ascendant are chased by women, while their female counterparts are imprudent and sexually desirable, and that both sexes are in favour of 'free union'.

All this applies very much to the outer physical level. When in a spiritually unawakened state, these people are indeed weak in so far as they have very little resistance to the senses, and they may live primarily for personal, sensual and sexual satisfaction. Men and women on this level have the whore, the flirt and the fancy-man within them.

However, it is an Aries degree, which means that the erotic senses (Pi. behind Ar.) need to be controlled and guided, even refined. On a higher level therefore these people are likely to organise artistic centres and literary get-togethers with a sensual undertone.

Aries is the sign of masks and magic. Here we come to cosmic and deeper meaning of this symbol. The properties of Aries are strength, energy, initiative and initiation. It represents an atom, or a first point of being. It is the passionate impulse about to break loose.

The opposition sign or the 'finishing touch' for Aries is Libra. This image here seems to show nothing but Libra symbols – the beauty and balancing out, and weighing the right relationship, the longing for partnership and the laws of emotional attraction and repulsion (Ar.–Li. sq. Cn.–Cap.) all appear. However, there are two more points noticeable to the esoterically trained eye.

In the Aries grail the difficult hind-axis is Virgo–Pisces. The woman in this symbol may give herself over completely to sexual, magical impulses (Ar.) by defiling her virginity (Pi.–Vi.). When living this hind-axis on a low level of spiritual awareness, the fore-axis of Aries (Tau.–Sc.) also comes out in a negative way. The senses can become so dominant that a throat-cutting stage is reached (Tau.–Sc.), which may grow in painful intensity. However, in the symbol of this image the feminine side (the soul) does not make victims. The only 'victim' who can bear the pain of (self) defilement, with deepening growth for the soul as the result, is this woman herself.

This lady is by no means a weakling. She is in a static pose and not at all voluptuous. That interpretation is only the all-too-easy projection of the onlooker's dynamic imagination. The irony in this degree is that of its ambivalence. Obscenity is simply not there. The female beauty is merely sitting in a feminine way on a couch. Woe to the villain who thinks of profaning her (neg. Vi.)!

This symbol of the female in the masculine sign of Aries denotes the incorruptible beauty dressed with spiritual strength. It is the archetype of the spirit dressed in matter. True it is very difficult for people with an undeveloped Higher Self or a very materialised spiritual being to live this image on a high level. The squares of Aries (Cn.–Cap.) may prove to be too strong. The appearance and illusion of the bodily form may frustrate them.

On a high level the body is the dress of the spirit, the temple of God, and it needs to be this. All the innate strength (Ar.) to make this temple outwardly shine (Cn.–Moon) with reflected light is concentrated in inward, astral reflections, so that the end-product, the form, is a kind of cloth which is spirit concentrated in form. (N.B. in the Technique of Light one visualises a shroud of white linen light around one's body. This exercise, meant for the resurrection body (Ar.) can help us to visualise the underlying degree-symbol.)

Thus we see that this lady has latent powers (Ar.) which are exemplary for a new humankind. But again, only spiritually developed individuals can demonstrate this degree in its maturity.

Second Image, Inner Symbol

The ruler of a country is being officially introduced.

Interpretation

In this second image the essence and all the highest qualities of Aries are symbolised. Again, as in the first image, what did you automatically visualise? A ruler as a man? Why? Were you again tricked by your senses and the traditions of your upbringing (Cn.–Cap.), assuming what seems obvious, but is not so, as in the first image? Why should 'a ruler' be male rather than female?

The word 'ruler' stands for a typical English concept. England as a country, and the characteristics of its people, come under Aries. Therefore we have an even deeper archetypal image here. A ruler in the English sense of the word is a leader, another English concept, which only the English people collectively can bring forth. The English are traditionally very nationalistic. Thus, by conformity to the nation, they are, paradoxically, able to fight for freedom in a one-pointed way. Thus British kingship is the pure prototype of the king (or queen) who is priest (or priestess) and leader in one. This is connected with ancient, collective wisdom, which is more appropriate now than ever before, and will be even more so in the new age to come.

Christ will only return when there are enough rulers on this planet whose souls are dressed with light. All 'rulership' that has been defiled by murder and bribery (Sc.–Tau.) has to return to the pure concept of the Aries initiation. No one will be elected anymore because of personal preference or political ambition (Cn.–Cap. sqs.), but leaders will be set apart for something radically new (Ar.), not led by past examples. There will be a new impulse, one which transcends time, which may seem repetitious and old (Cap.), but which in truth is embedded in our deepest inner condition (Cn.).

People with this degree prominent – and indeed every one of us, as the symbol is archetypal – will do well to contemplate the idea of rulership, as expressive of what is mystically needed (Pi.–Vi.), and prophetic of transformation (Sc.–Tau.).

In a world which has forgotten the potentiality of Harmony and Divine Equilibrium (Ar.–Li.), because it is blinded by egotistical ambition (Cap.), so that our true identity has been lost, genuine rulers are desperately needed. In a double sense they are the measuring-sticks, the 'rulers', of the highest standards. For this we need to return to our origins and the invisible rules by which our own astral and personality forms are being measured. For whoever takes up the burden of this symbol, there is a tremendous assignment, whereby even the strongest may be found weak, unless ruled by Divine appointment.

The soul (the woman of the first image) will be judged by her ability to live up to her high vocation. The Higher Self or the spirit who will not take on the task of 'ruler' or leader, will be weighed in the balance and found wanting.

Biblical Parallels

'. . . I will shew unto thee the judgment of the great whore that sitteth upon many waters.' *Rev. 17: 1.*

The woman clothed with the sun. See *Rev. 12: 1–6.*

Note

1. See literature on biblical origins of British kingship.
2. See Olive C B Pixley, *The Armour of Light* Part II (Glastonbury).

Conception Corrected Asc. 11TH ARIES

Annie Besant,   née Wood. Born 1 Oct. 1847 at 17.39 hrs. (her own corrected time) in London 51°30 N, 0°05 E. Died in Bombay 20 Sept. 1933. CC NS for 294 days at 17.39 hrs. gives 10°30 Aries

(10°29 Ar. given in her autobiography). Three other corrections for 5th, 6th and 14th Aries all differ from the given time.

British social reformer and Fabian Socialist, became a theosophist and champion of home rule for India. She was married to Frank Besant, an Anglican clergyman from whom she separated after seven years when she became an atheist and intimate friend of Bernard Shaw. Converted to theosophy, she became the Society's president in 1907. She became a Hindu and was elected president of the Indian National Congress. She is known for having introduced Krishnamurti (see 5th Pisces) as the new Messiah, a title he renounced in 1929 (*Encycl. Britt.* 1961). In her circle she was undoubtedly 'a ruler' (11th Ar.). See her biography *The Strange Lives of Annie Besant* (1885) by A.H. Nethercot and *Candles in the Sun* by Lady Emily Luytjens.

Barbra Streisand   Born 24 Apr. 1942 at 05.16 hrs. in Brooklyn, New York, 40°45 N, 73°58 W. CC NS for 268 days at 05.14 hrs. gives 10°14 Aries.

American actress, singer and film-star, known for her role as Nefertiti and musicals on Broadway, and her own TV show in the 1970s.

12TH DEGREE ARIES

First Image, Outer Symbol

A man holding hands with his two young children, a boy and a girl, walks with them in his garden. One sees the humble house through some branches. The father is amiable, but at the same time he seems to be obsessed by an idea (a fixed idea), which one can see mirrored in the water of a pond showing him his own reflection, but now decorated and with a sash over his breast.

Interpretation

This is a degree of 'corrosive ambition', according to Janduz. These people are deeply rooted in their concern for the needs of their family (Cn. sq. Ar.). No sacrifice or service (Pi.–Vi. hind-axis) is too much for them if it will enhance the welfare of their tribe or clique. They constantly seek security for their own group. They use all their resources to increase their family's prestige. They experience a kind of intimate joy through this. The education of their children and the beautifying of their home are in their hands. They like to talk to the clan about honour, maintaining a proud attitude with excellent behaviour, and promoting spiritual ennoblement and the idea of decorum in general.

There is nothing wrong with this. On all levels of awareness they have an innate goodness, and one cannot imagine them performing base or vulgar deeds. They may be excellent parents, good spouses and, honoured citizens – even on a planetary level. They spread a tender happiness and are not egotistical. They think only of the well-being of all who are near to their heart.

However, in this image there is a problem. This is an Aries degree, but this image has too much of the sign of Cancer, square to Aries. Therefore the entire cardinal cross is a bit distorted in it. There is the archetypal problem of Narcissus, the man in the legend who fell in love with his own image. What these people see in the water, which is the unconscious, or their past, is an illusion, and may become an obsession. Their thoughts circulate around their own, and their family's, social importance. If this is fixed in a faraway future or in a bygone time (Cap. sq. Ar.), they may even become the victims of megalomania. Often it does not get this far, as these people are usually too small-minded to take the distant view. Spiritually they are like children (the boy and girl). What is lacking is the dynamic force of Aries, the independence and the fighting spirit. Their family might well prefer to look after themselves! These characters might be woken up by a few well-placed bombs or a revolution. However, as it has already been said, they are too decent for such violence to be deserved.

On a high level of awareness they can get the cardinal cross under control. They can bring their own actions into harmony with the reality of their existing milieu and its laws. They have an inner home, and the pond indicates experiences on the inner planes through dreams and visualisation. It is a spiritual image.

They know what they want, and their sensitive emotional side should not be overlooked. There is transformation and growth (Tau.–Sc. fore-axis), symbolised by the new development of logical left brain consciousness (the boy) and the more sensitive and intuitive experiences of the right brain (the girl).

Second Image, Inner Symbol

A flock of white geese flies overhead across clear skies.

Interpretation

The goose, as a member of the Bird Kingdom, comes under Gemini, and is in itself a symbol of the purity (Vi.) of a phoenix (Sc.–Ar.), which ascends with Plutonic force above the worldly plane. Here the consciousness (man) is no longer looking down into his reflection but up towards the heavens. The illusion of the man's 'clique' has been transmuted into a close formation of flying geese, chattering like a family, but mightily impressive to look at from below. The element of water (Pi. behind Ar.) has become the element of air (Li. complementing Ar.). The lesson of this 12th degree of Aries is to discover oneself and to learn to ascend and then in full certitude to descend again in concrete and realistic self-expression.

Conception Corrected Asc. 12TH ARIES

Hans Christian Andersen Famous Danish fairy-tale writer. He had the Sun (spirit) in this degree. His writing includes stories about swans and wild geese, and he was known for his megalomania. See his Ascendant in 18th Sagittarius.

13th Degree Aries

First Image, Outer Symbol

A hill is lit up by the setting sun. On its summit the profile of an aged man, slightly bending forward, stands out against the sky holding a sceptre in his right hand and a royal crown in his left. A wide mantle hides his costume.

Interpretation

This is a degree of 'deserved reward'. Once the mountain of troubles and obstacles is conquered, these people can get what they want. In their youth their path will not be one of roses. They may be of humble descent, lacking help and protection, or, if better placed, they may be unlucky.

However, the difficulties of their existence will not discourage them. On the contrary, their daily struggle for life will turn their physical and 'moral' muscles into steel (Ar.). Their continuous zeal for work (Tau.) and their logical mind (Ge.), giving them insight into the laws of cause and effect, will make them wiser than the average person.

From the beginning of their life they are convinced that they have an almost Divine mission, which fills them with determination. In many circumstances they prove to be very audacious and they will not allow others to take advantage of them, although there is a calmness in their efforts. They are the pioneers (Ar.) every community needs.

At the dawn of their life on earth they see, more clearly than anybody else, that in the distant future they will become well-known or even famous. They foresee that they will be endowed with human and divine honours if only they can remain true to what they know is good and do not attempt to exceed their mental capacity.

The symbol is not just a hillock, but a high hill, even a small mountain, which means that their destiny is to climb high.

This can be outwardly in governmental work or in a position of command, but they probably take it further in leadership on the inner levels of magic and initiation (Ar.) as the man in the image is aged, indicating an old or highly developed Higher Self consciousness.

The rays of the setting sun indicate a strong, not hidden, radiation and shining glory. Sun is Leo, leadership and in the centre, although here declining (setting sun). The hill is a symbol of Saturn–Capricorn (sq. Ar.). There is strong social ambition (Cap.). Saturn and Sun together give the combination of a person with a character of strong will and determination, capable of reaching what they want through perseverance, without having to crush their inner and social conscience for this goal. Their honour and glory will come late, maybe even after they have passed on to another level (resurrection comes under Ar.), or may shine on those with whom they are closedly associated. The impulses (Ar.) they give out never fail. They do not know the word 'impossible'. Their intimate friends, and those on the same wavelength, are mainly those who help to spur them on to greater heights.

The setting sun from an esoteric viewpoint is an even better symbol than the rising sun. This celestial globe laden with warmth turns its rays towards the dark night. These people are meant to bring light to those who are in deepest darkness and obscurity. Of course their right choice, as with Aries in general, is to give out the impulses of white magic and not to go dabbling in its dark counterpart.

The setting sun also indicates the end of the age, or historical cycle, in which they are involved and the preparation of a new one. In some cultures (such as the Jewish) the new day starts at sunset.

With an eye to the second image, these people may have a spiritual destiny to focus energies and to discover power points and ley lines on the earth, and to open these inner points ('earth chakras') through prayer and magical rituals (crown and sceptre), for the transformation of hatred (Sc.–Tau. fore-axis). It may also be their task to send vibrations in other ways to radiate healing peace and harmony into the earth.

The sceptre and crown symbolise, in the highest instance, the Ascension of Christ and the promise of His return to rule as King over the entire planet. The mystery of ascension and levitation can be interpreted as the action of inner atomic power of 'implosion' over matter, which in the zodiac comes under Aries–Pluto. Because the place of Pluto is important in their horoscope, these forces should be studied and actually practised by those with this degree prominent.

Second Image, Inner Symbol

A bomb which failed to explode is now safely concealed.

Interpretation

This unusually modern-looking archetypal image symbolises compressed power and focused strength that stops at nothing. This is what 'magic' means. The man of the first image can use this for destruction or for good. All the potential for inner and outer existence is like a ball of atoms (Ar.) which if split can explode at any moment, bringing destruction or becoming a 'rainbow' of impulses for a new atomic age.

'Safely concealed' means there is absolute control over the magic. The Rainbow-impulse is now kept safe. Fear (Cap. sq. Ar.) has been overcome. The astral, inner planes (Cn. sq. Ar.) are being led to security.

This degree confers sudden revelation not previously seen on earth. The potential danger and contrast of the alternatives – implosion or explosion – could not be more 'archetypal'. The choice is one of life or death, of going under, as in the case of Atlantis, or being reborn in the New Kingdom of Christ.

Biblical Parallel

'. . . this same Jesus, which is taken up from you into heaven, shall so come in like manner as ye have seen him go into heaven.' See *Acts 1: 9–11*.

Conception Corrected Asc. 13th Aries

King Leopold III of Belgium   Born 3 Nov. 1901 at 15.05 hrs, or

15.15 GMT, in Brussels, 50°50 N, 04°40 E. CC NS for 283 days at 15.15 hrs. gives 12°45 Aries.

Became King of Belgium in 1934 after the death of his father in an accident. He caused the death of his wife Astrid (see 9th Ge.) in a car crash in 1935. In World War II he tried to co-operate with the Germans and was forced to abdicate in 1944. He was succeeded by his son Baudouin (see 10th Cap.) in 1951.

14TH DEGREE ARIES

First Image, Outer Symbol

A cheerful well-formed man, a kind of wine-taster, comes out of his well-stocked cellar and presents, with outstretched arm, a goblet of wine filled to the brim. In front of him sit a dog and a lion looking amiably at each other.

Interpretation

This is a friendly image. In people with this degree prominent there burns a joyful flame. Their character tends to be generous and magnanimous. They are full of confidence, gladness and loyalty. They tend to be honest and never mean. They deserve the pleasure that life gives them. They may build up quite a productive business (the well-stocked cellar) and on the physical plane they may do well in wine production and distilling, but also in public relations in areas such as the hotel industry or the diplomatic service.

On a more spiritual level they may succeed as leaders of a religious or cultural centre, where the barrels of wine then symbolise their spiritual knowledge, and the wine the potential healing they can give by their happy attitude (Vi.–Pi. hind-axis). They are not exuberant in their giving and hospitality. What they give out has inner value. They stick to the better traditions of their country and make many friends. They are held in high esteem because of what they have made of their life, in which everything falls into place. The older they become, the more they are treated as equals by people high on the social ladder and spiritually evolved men and women. They deserve, and get, special protection from within. This is not because they are hard workers, but simply through the demonstration that life can be happy and rich and noble. Their life-style is morally sound, as they have overcome the squares of Capricorn–Aries and they know how to say the right sensitive word, at the right time and place to uplift others.

They are hardly conscious of the tremendous potential (Ar.) of primordial riches they carry within them.

This image is one-pointed. It is a strong Aries degree, clearly indicated not only by the man, but also the friendly dog (symbol of Ar.). Moreover the lion, who is a symbol of Leo, has been tamed and domesticated. The giving gesture of the upright man is of Leo, the second fire sign after Aries, and so as a consequence the third fire sign Sagittarius is strongly indicated as the giving of confidence and happiness to travellers and seekers of culture. On the highest level the goblet may be seen as the grail, brought forth in a magical (Ar.) way, mystically seen by the initiates as a materialisation of atomic energies full of white light (the Pi.–Ar.–Tau. grail).

Second Image, Inner Symbol

A serpent encircles a man and woman in close embrace.

Interpretation

The first image was very positive, and manly, but lacked the close unity of the male and female, which is of the complementary sign Libra. Here are the two polarities joined by the all-embracing symbol of the serpent (the Kundalini fire). The joining together of the two poles gives a magical one-pointed strength, such as we sense in any close-knit marriage bond. Nobody can come between such partners.

The first image indicates that these people can radiate to all sides, giving outwardly. They can even burn up in this. There is the need to become receptive as well. The contact between the man and the animals, the dog and lion, is the beginning of an eye-to-eye contact of spirit and soul.

Here in this second image there is the symbol of the Michelangelo-like expression of two bodies joined together. Only out of this kind of togetherness, which cannot yet be understood, can something totally new, a new atomic being, emerge and spring up. The will of the Higher Self alone (the radiating man) cannot do it. It needs the receptive feminine earth to be impregnated by the transmuting power (Sc., the serpent), to bring it forth.

Biblical Parallels

Adam and Eve. See *Gen. 2: 22 to end of chap. 3.*

'And Moses made a serpent of brass, and put it upon a pole, and it came to pass, that if a serpent had bitten any man, when he beheld the serpent of brass, he lived.' *Num. 21: 9.*

'. . . in the hand of the Lord there is a cup, and the wine is red . . .' *Ps. 75: 8.*

The cup of the last supper. See *Mt. 26: 27–28.*

15TH DEGREE ARIES

First Image, Outer Symbol

A man in danger of drowning fights against the current of a stream. Deeper into the picture there are the remains of a shaky footbridge, which has just collapsed under his footsteps.

Interpretation

Janduz calls this a degree of 'treason'. People with this degree prominent may be the victims of treachery or may be traitors, themselves. This does not mean that we necessarily have here a primitive kind of symbol: it can be lived both on a low and a high level.

In daily life these people may have a difficult character and even be very disagreeable. One cannot count on them, they are two-faced and they hide their true character. They brood and mask their own unstable thought-world. On the low level of awareness they can be parasites (neg. Pi. behind Ar.) who suddenly unmask themselves at a very untimely moment. They have to own up to their deception and this can give them a temporary material loss.

They can literally do what is depicted in this image. One minute they make a human contact, and the next moment they suddenly reverse their own impulse. In reality their higher consciousness falls down and fights against drowning in the water of their own aroused feelings.

As typical Aries people they are often completely unaware of what they unleash (atomic chain reactions come under Ar.). They have no notion of the pain they cause to those who sympathise with them (Sc.–Tau. fore-axis).

In business they may be ruined, as they tend to break their promises and appointments. Their impulsiveness can drastically affect other people's destinies, although they do not foresee the effects of their actions at the time. Depending on the horoscope in general, their speculations may have no disastrous results, but there is always the tendency that these people will drag others into the stream with them.

There is a true story of a man who had the planet Venus here. He declared his love on an unstable bridge, and the girl to whom he promised a most fantastic future suddenly fell through the bridge and drowned. He never believed it had been his fault, and even accused her of not accepting his amorous advances quickly enough.

This anecdote is typical of these people. They may have a deep-rooted persecution or guilt complex. They may tell misleading tales, through which others do not easily see.

They may typically be bearers of bad news, or 'Job's comforters', who are not conscious of the fact that their negativities are sweeping others along and dragging them down. There is a great need for de-masking themselves to avoid realising this potential. They must face the fact that the 'certainties' they possess are often false ones.

On a high spiritual level these are individuals with enormous fighting power, in spite of all adversities and misfortunes. They should always be cautious of water with hidden undercurrents, threatening danger and reflecting their inner turmoil. Needless to say, they should repair or renew (Ar.) any broken human bridges in their lives.

Second Image, Inner Symbol

An American Indian is weaving a basket in the golden light of sunset.

Interpretation

These people start anew (Ar.) with the goodwill necessary to repair or weave a new work of art, something that is strong and can stand the test of time. Here we see what was needed in the first image: perseverance in building according to ancient inner traditions, even though with small outer result.

This Indian might be able to do much more, but the God-given day is approaching its end. The first image has uncontrolled activity and the man in it may have all too confidently run over a frail human construction. The Indian is embedded in the cosmos. The sunset (see also 13th Ar.) represents the end of a cycle, and here is implied the full control of one's capacity to finish a piece of tribal art before a new cycle begins.

The difficulties of the sign of Aries are given here. These people have to save energy and need to channel it wisely. They may produce less work than they had hoped, but at least what they accomplish is practical (Vi. behind Ar.), and does not suffer from the use of material that is rotten (Pi. behind Ar.). The deficiencies of such material always come to light when their work (Tau.), done with uncontrolled energy (Ar.), is brought to the test, or else it brings lies and pain (neg. Sc. before Ar.). When inspired by the golden light of creativity (Le. trine Ar.) these Aries people may weave spirit and matter together into a container (the basket) to hold the flow of cosmic energy (Ar.) used to heal and repair the broken bridges between heaven and earth, which the Indian culture can help to restore.

Biblical Parallels

'But they that will be rich fall into temptation and a snare, and into many foolish and hurtful lusts, which drown men in destruction and perdition.' *l Tim. 6: 9.*

Peter walking on the water towards Jesus, but beginning to sink, cried 'Lord save me.' See *Mt. 14: 28–32.*

Note

Anonymous poem on the weaver.

> My life is but a weaving
> Between my God and me.
> I cannot choose the colours,
> He works it steadily.
>
> The dark threads are as needful
> In the weaver's skilful hand,
> As the threads of gold and silver
> In the pattern He has planned.

See *The First American* by Ceram, for Indian basket-making.

16TH DEGREE ARIES

First Image, Outer Symbol

An upright woman bending slightly forward, keeps a balance in equilibrium, one of whose scale-pans carries a goblet of wine, while the other has diamonds, pearls and gold coins in it.

Interpretation

Janduz calls this a degree of 'chance and materialism'. People with this degree on the Ascendant, living on a low spiritual level, do indeed demonstrate what Janduz sees in this degree, namely a covetousness of beautiful and expensive objects. They weigh the pros and cons of obtaining what is within reach of their purse, and they may hanker after something long and secretly. On this level they do not strive for higher things, as they hunt only for pleasure, luxury and comfort. They do not develop great sensitivity or feeling (Cn. sq. Ar.). An egocentric pride might be their only emotion (Cap. sq. Ar.).

On the lowest level the opposition sign Libra, so remarkably shown here, might get out of balance so that they could give themselves over to drinking too much (the wine goblet, Pi. behind Ar.), or to eccentricities of behaviour. They might even exist only to collect and wear jewellery in order to make others jealous (neg. Tau.–Sc. fore-axis). On this level they are no more than arrogant boasters.

If they know a little magic (Ar.), they can summon up compassion in others and by hypnosis can get anything from those moved to help and protect them. They may be dancers, pimps, drug dealers (the scales) or prostitutes. However, they may be without ill intentions. They are caught up in materialism (Tau. fore-axis) for which they sacrifice (Pi. hind-axis) everything, although not knowing what true sacrifice is.

On a higher level these people like to study subjects in connection with fashion, precious stones, diamonds and gold. They may become such seekers as find 'gold' in the foam of the sea or among the outcasts of society.

This Aries degree has to face enormous difficulties, being so heavily opposed by Libra (the balance). Aries is a very positive male sign, but here is a female holding the balance. Therefore we have to interpret the entire Aries grail with caution, because there is something cramped here. Sacrifice and service (Pi.–Vi.), desire to work, and deep self-analysis and transformation (Tau.–Sc.) can hardly be expected; these subjects may be generous to themselves but avaricious towards others.

Do they understand that happiness consists of truly giving away oneself and one's possessions? If not, they may really have to become poor in order to learn this lesson the hard way. Fate will strike if they do not get Cancer–Capricorn under the control of their Higher Self. However, in the second image we see the solution for the highest level of Arien qualities.

Second Image, Inner Symbol

Brightly clad brownies, or nature-spirits, are dancing in the warm, dying evening light.

Interpretation

The first image seems to be cramped because of too much Libra. Here we see the same tendency. The dance comes under Libra. 'Brightly clad' is also Venus–Libra, and there is a third Libra element. At sunset the Sun is in the seventh house or in analogy with Libra. So thrice Libra in an Aries image must put us on our guard with our interpretation. The negative sides of Aries may thus get a chance here, which tend to be black-magical. Brownies are earth elementals (Tau. fore-axis), who work for sleeping humans in the night, a fact not often accepted in the left-brain materialistic Western world!

The key to this symbol lies in the presentation of the brownie or nature-spirit, and the emphasis here is on the kind of clothing worn. Usually a brownie is pictured in workaday dress, but in this image they are dressed for the dance (the cardinal cross Ar.–Cn.–Li.–Cap.) – they are not at work, not fulfilling their cosmic task.

The first image is concentrated on personal pleasure resulting from material possessions. Do these people want to work for that? They need to learn to identify with the earth and its fullness in a cosmic, right and ethical way. Taurus follows Aries. They need to learn to work with devotion. The brownies, however, are dancing and evading their duty.

The symbol of the nature-spirit indicates that these people need to direct their attention towards the still sleeping forces (of karma yoga) in earth, and to discover their will to work. Unseen help from earth elements implies interdependence, and the human obligation to co-operate. (Az.–Cn.–Li.–Cap.)

The people in the first image tend to store up so much in this short life because they lack faith (neg. Sag. trine Ar.) in a continuing life after death, and in higher things.

There is a fundamental problem in this 16th degree of Aries. When one sign is shown over-represented, all other signs begin to avenge themselves. Aries tends to be pointed in one direction thereby dulling other elements. This process can be fatal.

However let us not forget the symbol of the setting sun (or early evening light). See the 13th and 15th degrees of Aries. Here is a cycle ending, with a new one to come. Maybe the gold and the diamonds (both symbols of Le., Sun) are being weighed to serve for a new cycle of more spiritual awareness. After all, why shouldn't the nature-spirits dance at the beginning of their new day, which starts at sunset, and not be at work? Rudhyar calls this an image of 'repotentialisation' and 'becoming again like a little child': that may be the meaning of this degree.

Biblical Parallels

'Thou art weighed in the balances, and art found wanting.' *Dan. 5: 27.*

'Let me be weighed in an even balance, that God may know mine integrity.' *Job 31: 6.*

17TH DEGREE ARIES

First Image, Outer Symbol

A young student, with a book in his hand, walks through a shaded leafy lane. The rays of the sun pass through the branches and illuminate his face.

Interpretation

According to Janduz this is a degree of 'intelligent passivity', and she says that these people live a useful life, for which they prepare themselves from their earliest youth, not only by reading a lot, but also by employing an inner and outer technique to study in the right concentrated and meditative way. According to her, although a leafy, country environment is not indispensable, an outer isolation in nature will enhance their rich thought-life, and by studying in such surroundings they will develop, so that at an early age (symbol of the student), they are able to go through the world with a more or less perfect moral code.

They are sympathetic, and call forth sympathy of a discreet and solid kind from those higher than themselves, as well as those lower on the social ladder. They have a natural sense of duty (Cn.–Cap. sqs. under control), which springs up during the most complicated and, for others, stunning circumstances. They are direct and single-minded. They will be honoured for their pure and real knowledge and erudition, which can attain great heights. So far Janduz.

Their particular preoccupations will depend on the nature of their entire horoscope. On the highest level the hidden laws of nature and the universe may be disclosed to them. They can be good biologists. They are seldom eccentric, and their attitude is calm and contemplative. They love to be alone with nature for the inner experiences they receive. Nine out of ten people will not understand this, in themselves, and may try to suppress the tendency.

They seek and find their inner light (the sun through the leaves), which then radiates out from them. They have very grateful natures and use their given lifespan well.

When elderly they may increasingly wish to retreat into places where prehistoric energies still speak through matter, such as virgin woodland.

If they can acquire a good insight into the higher Plutonic level of the sign of Aries and its grail, they can live out a superior set of the twelve facets of the zodiac. They can lift up the cardinal cross (Ar.–Cn.–Li–.Cap.) to the heights of the inner planes of the invisible astral experiences, and the outer planes of emotional soundness (Cn.), as well as to the high levels of concentrated meditation (Cap.).

They can acquire a fruitful absorption (Tau.–Sc. fore-axis) of all that the Sun (Le. trine Ar.) represents. They can expand their thinking and eventually their teaching (Sag. trine Ar.). Their soul is pure, in which the mystical appreciation of nature will never be lost (Vi.–Pi. hind-axis), while at the same time they possess an independent strength to live a good outer life. However, even with the second image in the background, this first image is lacking something. The sunlight, as the symbol of the Light of the Spirit, does not quite come through. There is not yet a 'marriage' between the content of what the student takes in through his book and nature itself. Does he introject what he observes? Wouldn't he do better to listen to nature directly? Isn't it a little pretentious for this student to read a book while walking in God's creation? Shouldn't he (or she) study life at first hand, or is he reading in the actual Book of Life, which explains the universal laws of what he sees all around him? If not, then just reading a book in this sublime environment is dangerous and could make the psyche wander from the true path. This tendency is more fully explained in the second image.

Second Image, Inner Symbol

Two prim spinsters are sitting together in silence.

Interpretation

These ladies seem displaced and out of touch with the real world. Are they doing nothing (neg. Ar.)? Are they daydreaming (Cn.)? Are they observing their immediate environment? Are they drinking in nature, as the student ought to do? Are they two girls in unused 'young' bodies with very 'old' souls? The image seems very unlike Aries, which is a positive doing, forward-going masculine sign. Maybe the esoteric meaning of this silent discourse between two souls, or the two unawakened female poles within these people, is that they are detached from the constraint of outer circumstances, and of being needed by a man or a family (the entire cardinal cross Ar.–Cn.–Li.Cap.). Their way of life may be one of great dignity and even sovereignty, as indicated by 'the silence'. Or on a low level of awareness, there may be a childish attitude, incapable emotionally of facing life with its full polarity of positive and negative, male and female.

In these two images, which as Aries ones are at the beginning of the twelve 17th degrees, there is the question of what to do with the energies. There is an entire scale possible between the lower characteristics of Aries, as shown in stubbornness and primitive single-mindedness with a ridiculous and unhelpful attitude, and the higher characteristics of making most valuable to others the inner and outer purposes of the Higher Self. There will either be no contact when the spirit and soul will remain frigid, or the new energy-flow will be so abundant that these people can only sit down in awe and silence, and wait for the cosmos to burst open into a new cycle.

Biblical Parallels

The 17th degrees are the story of Israel and Judah, here the two women, waiting for their course through history.
'. . . and another book was opened, which is the Book of Life: and the dead were judged out of those things which were written in the books, according to their works.' *Rev. 20: 12.*

Conception Corrected Asc. 17TH ARIES

Queen Beatrix of Orange-Nassau   Born 31 Jan. 1938 at 09.47 hrs. in Soestdyk 52°11 N, 05°17 E. CC WAK for 282 days gives 16°17 Aries.

Before her marriage with the German Claus von Amsberg, Princess Beatrix was extremely popular as a student in Leyden, and later in her international relief work. Her nickname was 'Princess Smile, the Smiling Princess'. She is highly intelligent and prepared herself extremely well in her studies for her task of Queen and democratic Head of State, which she became in 1980. She bore three sons. See for Crown Prince-Willem Alexander's Ascendant 8th Scorpio.

18TH DEGREE ARIES

First Image, Outer Symbol

A man and a woman, standing up, give each other their right hands. They both have an air of goodness and gentleness. The man makes a gesture of protection.

Interpretation

This is a degree of 'mutual help and friendship', full of confidence. People with this degree prominent want nothing more for themselves and others than a life that unfolds itself in true openness. They give themselves out, without hurting others, although living their very own personal life-style.

It is a degree of devotion (Tau. fore-axis for Ar.) and true knighthood. These people are born with a pure and radiant character. They may be romantic and sentimental (Cn. sq. Ar.), but this also makes them pleasant. They are hospitable and respond to friendly feeling wherever they meet it, loving peace and harmony (Li. opp. .Ar.) and the gentler joys of life. They are discerning and possess good judgement. They understand much, and have something that makes other people appreciate them. They are straightforward in their dealings with others, and are never mean or domineering. They may grow into people with a high level of understanding.

The deeper symbolism of this image in the sign of Aries lies, for these people, in a perfect inner balance between their spirit (the man) or mind, (which is here the positive, masculine doing of the pioneer (Ar.)), and their intuitive, receptive, feeling side (the woman). The Higher Self, the light of the spirit, rules and protects the soul, which symbolises the entire field of their inner and outer experiences, as reflected in their astral and etheric body. Esoterically speaking, the realms of the spirit are higher than those of the soul, but we need both. We need the feelings and sensitivity of the soul for our material existence and physical incarnation on this earth. But in this image, leading towards the second image, it is not the relationship between the two which is the essence here.

The masculine side in these people is the stronger here, giving them a sense of obligation to protect and develop their awareness of beauty (the woman, leading these Aries people towards the fore-axis Tau.–Sc.), and their sensitivity for those in pain or giving birth (Sc.).

When unawakened to the concordance between the male and female side in them, they may be unbalanced and forget that their great work has to be carried out with harmony and rhythm. Otherwise they become over-protective towards others (the man). They may be carried away by their feelings, or, at the other end of the scale, may not show them at all, for fear of being accused of immorality (Ar. sq. Cap.). However, the Aries grail gives them the independent will to spiral upwards above

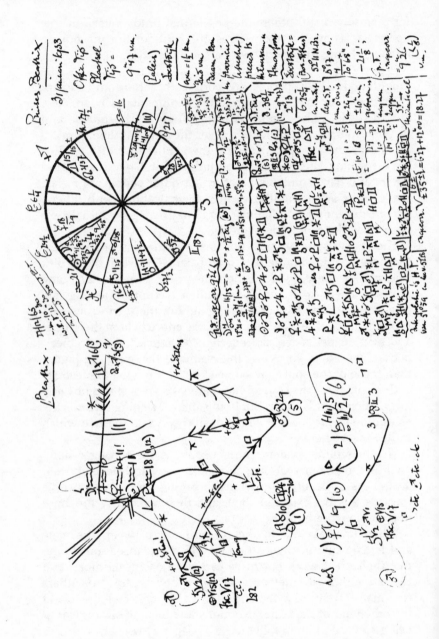

Handwritten chart of Queen Beatrix by Willem Ary Koppejan

Queen Beatrix of the Netherlands

oversentimentality and feelings of guilt (the sqs. of Cn. and Cap.), and to overcome the difficulties of the cardinal cross.

On a high level there is a great potential for creativity (trine Le.). The image is permeated with love (Le.), though these people lack the idea of passionate transformation. They may tend to be dreamers, and unsocial in the sense that they do not care to be involved in struggles for their clan or nation. This is a positive feature, coming from the inner knowledge that the spirit and the soul, as the active and the passive forces, are meant to co-operate as instruments of the higher invisible Self for the positive protection of this earth. As such they can never tolerate the polarisation leading towards war and destruction.

Second Image, Inner Symbol

An empty hammock is hanging between two lovely trees.

Interpretation

This image is a higher symbol of the first one. The two humans have become invisible. One can only assume their being together in the hammock, certainly in the past or in the future. The symbolic interpretation of this image brings us into the Chinese philosophy of detachment and the technique (Ar.) of *Wu Wei*. This speaks of such reconciliation and unification, of the spirit and the soul, that there is nothing imprinted on the physical world. The unity between the two (the trees) is sublime. Therefore the hammock seems empty.

Here is a perfect example of what a balanced cardinal cross means. In this cross there are two kinds of meditation. First there is the one that ascends through matter and climbs up by way of the five physical senses, represented by Mercury – memorising words; Venus – linking others; Mars – active movements to invoke the spirit; Jupiter – requesting and praying for goals outside oneself; and Saturn – confessions of sin and guilt.

This image, however, indicates the other form of meditation, which comes from above. The Christ-Ego radiates via the inner planes through the transpersonal planets, which means that one has to become empty of self (the hammock) and be at peace, so that the spirit can fulfil its work while one is asleep. For people of this degree, their greatest force lies in their inner being, which simply ripens without assiduous meditation and repeated prayers. Their cry 'Thy Kingdom come' is uttered without clamour. Their senses rest in nature, and they live as though in a heavenly hammock or cradle. The spirit has become equal to the soul. They have achieved inner serenity. They make the invisible visible, and what is visible invisible.

Conception Corrected Asc. 18TH ARIES

Rabindranath Tagore   Born 6 May (not 7 May) 1861 at 04.00 hrs in Calcutta 22°33 N, 88°36 E. Died Aug. 1941. CC WAK and NS for 286 days at 03.51 gives 17°20 Aries.

Indian philosopher, poet and author, writing in Bengali. He started an important educational institute, the 'House of Peace', in Calcutta and was the inspiration behind Dartington Hall in Devon, England. He lectured extensively throughout Europe, USA and Japan. His abundant writings are permeated by the beauty of the universe, and the love and consciousness of God. Translators have often oversentimentalised his original, powerful and rhythmic style, and impoverished his eloquence. He won the Nobel prize in 1913. This 18th degree of Aries fits his whole life-style and chart.

19TH DEGREE ARIES

First Image, Outer Symbol

An old man wearing a worn-out dressing-gown in a sparsely furnished room (an attic). One of the windows is cracked. There is a stool and a curtain. The door appears bolted. He is nervously pressing two sacks made of hessian against his breast. On them is written the word GOLD.

Interpretation

According to Janduz this is a degree of 'thesaurisation'. The man is a sort of treasurer, one who is collecting. On a low level people with this degree rising may be tramps, or live alone in poverty, barely subsisting. They may even be misers who beg for alms without need, or rob others. They bring their stolen wares into their little room, where they build up their collections. They gather without knowing for whom or for what purpose.

Depending on the total horoscope, they may even have a kleptomaniac tendency, the need to feel and count things in their hands, without realising why they heap up all this stuff. In this stage their mind is very primitive (Ar.), and there is no introspection, let alone any thinking about others. On this low level they are the prototype of Scrooge.

We see the cardinal cross in the negative sense of their being afraid of their emotions (Cn.–Cap.). Their attitude may be caused by a physical or mental handicap, so that they cannot just savour life. They live in a mood of repression and defence.

On a higher level all these character traits may turn into gold as they defend, for instance, their club or their country as treasurers; but in the lower type we find again all the negative elements of the cardinal cross. They are powerless (neg. Ar.) though they seem independent. They are cramped (Cap.) by unresolved experiences of the past (neg. Cn.). They do not want any sympathy or links with others (neg. Li.). They prefer to be alone, critical of mankind (neg. Vi.–Pi. hind-axis), and they gather money with greed (neg. Tau.–Sc. fore-axis), never coming to transformation through pain and death (Sc.).

However, on the higher level, their sacks may be full of the gold of heaven (pos. Tau.). Then they have the power to transmute creative energy (Ar.–Le.–Sag.) into lasting treasures of literature, arts and crafts. The old man personifies a high level of spiritual growth, and a highly developed mind full of experiences gained through time (pos. Cn.–Cap.). He is at peace (Li.) with himself and does not care that his physical garment (the body) is worn out. His genius has collected spiritual treasures. Gold comes under Leo. This is spiritual gold, the essence of all life. The attic symbolises detachment from the outer world. This individual is free within himself. The window in the attic shows that the wind (the Holy Spirit, Aq.) and the sun (Le.) can freely enter. The highly evolved types have a window towards both the inner and the outer world. The caressing way in which the old man is treasuring the sacks is symbolic too. Arms come under Gemini and so does the air through the window. Light is Leo and thinking is Sagittarius. There is a potential (Ar.) spiritual link here with ancient Hermetic wisdom (Ge.), and a general lesson in cosmology, as Aries is in an ingoing Hermetic sextile towards Gemini, and so is Gemini towards Leo, while Aries is in ingoing Plutonic trine with Leo. Much could be said about this. It leads us to the magical knowledge of the second image. Briefly it is the white (or black, according to one's level) magical power, which causes complete identification with one's spiritual nucleus (Ar.), leading to the spiritual knowledge of the True Self.

Thus this person learns the spiritual essence of life's practice, and can grow (Tau.) into a true genius, or prophet, who spares no pains (Sc.) to spread love. He will become an example of moral living (Cap.) to his entire environment (Cn.).

Second Image, Inner Symbol

A magic carpet is hovering over an ugly industrial suburb.

Interpretation

According to Rudhyar here is the 'capacity to transform everyday life by the power of creative significance, or escape in idle fancy'. This describes more or less what the first image amounts to. Magic and levitation come under Aries and so we are here in the very heart of this sign. This person needs to levitate the lower personality. The magical potentials for penetrating into the highest realms of the air (Ge.) are here. One leaves the ugly vibrations of a city that is kept going by the love of making money. This person comes out of the Babylonian confusion in search of new worlds. He (or she) may have to get out to safeguard the essence (gold sacks) that he has collected. The highly evolved can live above unbearable circumstances (Cn. neg.), in the awareness that their example makes other souls whole (Cn. pos.). The man in the street will see their example as hovering above him like the magic carpet of fairy-tales. It is the task of those who represent this Aries degree to be an example, living above the ugliness of the rat-race for the gold dust of the earth (Tau.). Their superior magical power must be used to help humanity and not hinder. The highest type will experience being caught up in the air in order to be with the Lord.

Biblical Parallels

'For the love of money is the root of all evil.' *1 Tim. 6: 10.*

The ascension of Jesus. See *Acts 1: 10–12.*

'Then we which are alive and remain shall be caught up together with them in the clouds, to meet the Lord in the air: and so shall we ever be with the Lord.' *1 Thess. 4: 17.*

Note

For magic carpet and fairy-tales see *The Arabian Nights* and Hans Christian Andersen's *Flying Suitcase.*

Conception Corrected Asc. 19TH ARIES

Wolfgang Borchert Born 20 May, 1921 at 03.00 hrs. in Hamburg, 53°33 N, 09°59 E. Died 20 Nov. 1947. CC WAK and NS for 261 days at 02.58 hrs. gives 18°29 Aries. German soldier, Nazi-prisoner, poet, writer and playwright. His classic play is *Draussen vor der Tür* (Outside the Door), which had its première in Hamburg the day after he died of starvation at the age of 26. He became the victim-hero of European youth at the time. His short life and work are a striking example of the 19th Aries.

See *W. Borchert* by Peter Ruhimkorf (Ro-Ro-Ro, 1961).

Johannes Brahms Born 7 May 1833 at 03.30 hrs. in Hamburg, Germany, 53°33 N, 09°59 E. Died 3 Apr. 1897. CC WAK and NS for 278 days at 03.30 hrs. gives 18°06 Aries.

Known as the last great classical composer of Germany. His symphonic music, vocal works and chambermusic proved him a master of the effect of sound, but it took a long time before he was generally appreciated. He had a real sense of the variety and emptiness of human life, but a strong confidence in divine consolation (*Encycl. Britt.*).

Marcel Proust Born 10 July 1871 at 23.30 hrs. in Paris, 48°52 N, 02°20 E. Died 18 Nov. 1922. CC WAK and NS for 274 days at 23.22 hrs. gives 18°05 Aries.

The famous French writer was notorious for having the character of a spoilt child. He would brood for days by himself. The title of his famous work *In Search of Lost Time* is in itself an example of the 19th Aries.

See his biographies (*Encycl. Britt.*).

Handwritten chart of Johannes Brahms by Willem Ary Koppejan

20TH DEGREE ARIES

First Image, Outer Symbol

A man equips himself for a long and hard journey. Around him there are various accessories such as a map, a blanket, a helmet and a gun. On his belt he is fixing a dagger and a purse.

Interpretation

It is rather superficial of Janduz to describe this degree as one of 'voyages and discoveries'. According to her these are adventurous, sly and sharp people, but also prudent and intelligent. They prepare themselves thoroughly for their task. She sees them destined to be colonisers, penetrating into unknown regions, prospecting oil and minerals. They are not afraid of man or beast and this is no bluff: they are armed for all eventualities! They also possess prudence and can cope with the most difficult circumstances. They are often said to be aggressive and authoritarian, but that is the judgement of their more easygoing brethren. They are to be pardoned, because they are a thousand times more dynamic than their accusers. They are courageous and have endurance. So far we have followed Janduz' interpretation.

There is more to see on the psychological level. One can see the mental conquest of the cardinal cross here. As Aries, they only grow into their true potential strength when the resistance of their environment (Cap.–Cn. sqs.) becomes so intolerable that they have to do something to avoid sinking into chaos (neg. Vi.–Pi. hind-axis). They are fighters for peace and beauty (Li. opp. Ar.). They are such forceful pioneers that it is not easy to co-operate with them. They could suffer (neg. Pi.) from the disloyalty (neg. Vi.) of adversely influenced (neg. Li.) co-workers.

When others make a failure of their projects, these people find the strength to till the ground (Tau.) and start afresh, even if it means using armed force (the dagger) to get rid of those who made the mess (Tau.–Sc. fore-axis).

On the high level their spiritual awareness is strong (the armed man), as the man is armed with the spiritual goods of the New Age. He can be a pioneer in many fields of mind and spirit. He is far ahead of the average common man. His talents are numerous (the purse) and his transmutable power is great (Tau.–Sc. fore-axis). This degree gives a strong impulse towards spiritual growth.

Second Image, Inner Symbol

A young girl is feeding swans in a park on a wintry day.

Interpretation

The first image lacks the female gentleness. The man shows too much dynamic, Plutonic, potential action. In terms of the Aries grail, the general principle is that Pisces–Aries–Taurus is the solar, spiritual side of the Aries grail. The light of this Sun-side overflows into the opposite side, which is Virgo–Libra–Scorpio, supposed to be the lunar, receiving side of the Aries grail. We can see this principle demonstrated in the 20th degree of Aries as the very male Aries of the first image overflowing into this female Libra image.

The young girl is a symbol of Cancer (Moon) and of virginal purity (Vi.). Swans come symbolically under Libra for their power and beauty (Ar.–Li.). The girl is bending towards the swans. The wintry day in our northern hemisphere is an indication of Scorpio (Nov.), with painful and cold circumstances. The park is the outcome of well-balanced planning (Ar.–Le.–Sag.) and the fruit of the pioneering mind of the first image (Tau.–Sc.). Thus it is a classic example of what Aries is to be.

The man is merely himself. He has to learn to link up with the softer female emotions in his nature and to become a receptive partner in his complementary world.

The Aries person with his high-handedness needs to exercise care for the peaceful (Li.) feeding of his emotions (Cn.), symbolised by the simple beauty of a park. Apt to be too eager for action, he must wait upon the cosmic 'right time' for his inner and outer manifestation in form (Cap.).

21ST DEGREE ARIES

First Image, Outer Symbol

A man all by himself on a raft amidst a wide, wild ocean. He is in rags, emaciated, starved and pitiable, but he is energetic and is doing his best to attract attention by signalling with a piece of cloth.

Interpretation

Janduz calls this a degree of 'isolation'. This is a word that belongs more to Pisces (hind-axis for Ar.) than to Aries, and on first sight indeed it seems to contain more elements of Pisces (isolation, shipwreck, wild ocean, rags) than of Aries, but looking deeper, the consciousness of the man is very clearly that of Aries.

On a low level these people manoeuvre themselves into a miserably isolated situation by their own impulsive acts (Ar.), which are not in rational accord with everyday practical life. They may find themselves undermined (neg. Pi.) by criticism (neg. Vi.), to an extent that threatens their very existence. Their frightening circumstances (cardinal cross sqs. Cn.–Cap.), which they have invoked in their stubborn wish for the advantages of independence (Ar.), may mount to absurdity.

As Aries, they have to go through a period of utter helplessness and impotence before they come to awareness of their true magical power (Ar.).

Outwardly there may be a period when they are deserted by all and sundry. There does not need to be a physical wreck, but there may be one in a psychological sense through enforced exile. Only highly evolved individuals realise this is needed for rebirth of the Higher Self (Tau.–Sc. fore-axis), which can only be achieved by unmasking (higher Ar.).

Even the strongest personalities with this degree prominent are risking a sad death in complete isolation, but even so they persevere. Their test comes in the last battle, when amidst all disaster they must remain upright. They will keep calling for help when others (without this degree) would have lost heart, and they get help in a 'magical' way. They could be spotted on someone else's inner radar-screen, and thus saved.

The wildness of their nature needs to be tamed. They are advised to be content with a modest place in life. They (he or she) should control their fighting spirit, and not encourage emotional scenes.

One would do well to study all the 21st degrees. This one opens in the direction of help from higher spiritual regions, which gives the solution to the problem of all twelve 21st degrees of the zodiac.

Second Image, Inner Symbol

A pugilist, flushed with strength, enters the ring.

Interpretation

According to Rudhyar this is 'complete immolation of the self in things purely physical'.

It is indeed the invincibility already shown in the first image. Here all the adverse circumstances have vanished, and there is the magical power of the ring (on different levels of interpretation) surrounding and supporting those people with this degree, so that worldly adversity has completely gone. Their intense self-assertion is justified, as it is not based on physical force alone. As Aries, having purified themselves in isolation (Vi.–Pi.), they have only to 'wish it' inwardly (Tau.–Sc.) and the spring of higher energy will flow to do their bidding.

Biblical Parallel

Job, being stripped of all his earthly goods and still standing like a pugilist, is a prototype of this image. See *Job*.

22ND DEGREE ARIES

First Image, Outer Symbol

A man with an absent-minded air is moving away from a fountain from which he has taken some water, but he lets it escape from his jar without noticing it. On the right a bear is gnawing a recumbent tree-trunk.

Interpretation

Janduz calls this a degree of 'instability and folly'. Instability is a word properly belonging to the opposite sign of Libra, but it is not inappropriate here, because these people lack right action (Ar.). They let the water of life escape, and any happiness in their life evades them. Even when they have made a good start (they have found the fountain) and circumstances are promising, the end is likely to be one of disappointment and embitterment (neg. Vi.–Pi. hind-axis), because their actions are ill-judged and their opportunities have been neglected. They will arouse the pity of others; and all this is due to their innate sloth.

So, on a low level of spiritual awareness these people can be characterised by a childish carelessness. They do not see the serious things in life. When faced with responsibility (Cap. sq. Ar.), they escape or become emotional (Cn. sq. Ar.), lacking the common sense necessary to deal with practical matters. As unawakened Aries people, they have exaggerated pretensions to knowledge which in fact is beyond their grasp.

This last feature is also indicated by the symbol of the grumbling grizzly bear, which does nothing but bite at a tree (Sag.). One can only wonder what he thinks he is doing. This indicates that these people have a streak in them which is unpredictable and foolish. They may keep silent for a long time, then suddenly flare up, show their teeth and make a scene. They can burst out like a thunderstorm (Aq., the bear also comes under Aq.). They seldom understand that their unsatisfactory situation is the result of their own want of self-discipline, conspicuously evident to others in the conduct of their lives: they cannot be guided into better courses, and they create vexation around them.

However, there is a deeper esoteric meaning in this image, which consists of two rather different parts. There is a man in this Aries degree, who is the symbol of the new and youthful potential of the spirit and the higher consciousness. The fountain is a symbol of the highest and deepest contact with the sources of life. It is a place where the essence of the earth wells up for the taking. These people have access to 'living waters', and are themselves fountains from which others may freely drink.

The key to the image is that the Aries grail is held together on either side by Pisces and Taurus. These people have a deep inner essence and a notion of the mystic side of life (Pi.), and they have a side that is well-grounded in the earth with great vision for its future (Tau.), but tragically they let these gifts lie fallow within them, wasting their highest and deepest resources.

The bear, on the other hand, is a symbol of the lower side of Aquarius. Here the fixed cross of free creation (Aq.–Le.), of working in loving co-operation (Le.–Aq.) with others, has become mere play (Le.) and idle destruction (Sc.) of what grows on the earth (Tau.). Every call for responsible action is met with a foolish grin.

This bear is behaving instinctively, but the man, whilst doing something stupid, has at least been conscious of the fountain. Both man and beast should wake up to their true being and do that to which they are called.

There is tremendous potential in this degree. If these people used their powers positively, earth would be a paradise in no time. They can be free and original, and if only they cared for their jar full of water they could use their innate qualities to open the door to the New Age.

Second Image, Inner Symbol

Gateway opening to the Garden of Heart's Desire.

Interpretation

Rudhyar changed this to 'fulfilled desires' (1973). In fact there is nothing in life which stands in the way of our true happiness: the

the door is open. Only one thing needs to be done and that is to act in accordance with our own innate being and enter through the gate with the right attitude. The garden is the symbol of Eden or Paradise, which has to be regained (like the water from the jar).

In this 22nd degree of the first sign of the zodiac one can see the beginning of all that can happen in the twelve 22nd degrees. The first image shows how wrongly humanity can misuse its energy and waste the waters of life, overlooking the fact that the earth is our paradise if we will only let her be such. The first image looks empty, but is full of unfulfilled desires.

The second image, which illustrates the higher and innermost task for the people with this degree prominent, is the total reverse. It is the inner garden, watered by the spirit. It represents the earth and her fullness, and nothing more should be desired.

These people, and humanity as a whole, need to awaken to their own neglect, and to act in accordance with the higher laws of creation to remake the garden of Eden within themselves and on earth. Through the Christ within them they can re-enter.

Biblical Parallels

'And a river went out of Eden to water the garden.' *Gen. 2: 10.*

'And the Lord God took the man, and put him into the garden of Eden to dress it and to keep it.' *Gen. 2: 15.* (Then Adam ate from the tree of the knowledge of good and evil.) 'Therefore the Lord God sent him forth from the garden of Eden, to till the ground from whence he was taken.' *Gen. 3: 23.*

'The earth is the Lord's and the fulness thereof:' *Ps. 24: 1.*

'Lift up your heads, O ye gates; and the King of glory shall come in.' *Ps. 24: 9.*

'I am the door: by me if any man enter in, he shall be saved, and shall go in and out, and find pasture.' *Jn. 10: 9.*

23RD DEGREE ARIES

First Image, Outer Symbol

On the left a man is seated on the corner of a table in a summerhouse. With a carefree air he lets the sunlight shine through a
goblet of wine in his right hand, while not far from him sit two
sinister, bad companions, who are conversing mysteriously and
looking insolently at him. On the far right three upright serpents
are fighting three other serpents.

Interpretation

From several points of view this is a dangerous degree. Janduz
interprets it as describing a person who is easily irritated,
although keenly intelligent and with an appreciation of the
arts and beauty. He is a detached connoisseur though without
an inner nucleus of ability. When one interprets the men
(consciousness) on the right, malice and fondness for idle gossip
are seen to be prominent. Their spiteful talk is impulsive (Ar.)
and uncontrolled.

On a higher level these two men symbolise concern with
occult mysteries, and an obvious interest in the wine as a
symbol of the Holy Blood and the Holy Grail.

The black and the white magical (Ar.) side of this archetypal
symbol is the source of a constant fight within these people. As
such it is a very complicated and powerful image, not only for
those who have this degree prominent in their horoscope, but
as a cosmic lesson for humanity in general. As the first of the
twelve 23rd degrees it tells the story of occult power in high
places and how it can be used for good or bad.

The two seated men represent the lower level of Aries, when
humanity masks its face and disguises itself. People at this level
have to break through their own dishonesty with themselves and
with others. They will shirk duty (Tau.) by pretending illness
(neg. Pi.), and end by becoming misers (neg. Vi.), showing all

the negative traits of the lower Aries – childish and stubborn, importunate in pursuit of rights they do not deserve. This brings them false friends and jealous enemies, attitudes in others which they have themselves called forth by misuse of their own energy. They must cease to disguise themselves from themselves and start afresh, accepting all the consequences (Cap. sq.).

We see their better self pictured in the man who is holding the glass – yes, holding the light and absorbing it. His face is pure and open and concentrated on the true mysteries (Vi.–Pi. hind-axis), and he can foresee the transformation of the earth (Tau.–Sc. fore-axis) through the light-impulse and through loving his neighbours instead of loving to gossip about them.

It is the trinity of good overcoming the trinity of evil, as the staff of Moses, through magic (Ar.), became a serpent and swallowed the staffs of the black magic priests of Pharaoh who sought power over men. An archetypal image of great importance, whose motto is 'God helps those who help themselves'.

Second Image, Inner Symbol

A woman in a summer dress carries a precious veiled burden.

Interpretation

The man of the first image is holding the symbol of the Grail as a cup in his hand. The female is the grail-bearer, dressed in the etheric white robes of the summerland, and she is veiling the chalice of the Holy Grail, whose light may be too powerful for human eyes to behold. One would do well to study the mysteries and legends of the Arthurian period in this connection.

There is inner growth needed to achieve this level, and much working out of subjective karma into objective dharma, thus turning the ages of negative thought (the veil) into positive thought and purifying white light for the earth and the universe.

These people have to go back to the source and penetrate into the deepest mysteries, which they will carry as a precious 'burden'.

Biblical Parallel

Moses' rod becoming a serpent and swallowing the rods of Pharaoh's priests. See *Ex. 4: 3* and *7: 9–15*.

24TH DEGREE ARIES

First Image, Outer Symbol

A young man lazily stretched out on a carpet, with his right arm supporting his head, plays with glittering balls, or beads, of different colours. Standing behind him on the carpet, an almost nude woman wearing only a belt beset with precious stones, is watching him with an air of dominance and disdain.

Interpretation

Janduz calls this a degree of 'no value'. According to her, people with this degree rising, or a planet there, prove to be mediocre companions on the journey of life. They dismiss weighty matters lightly. They remain childish throughout their entire life. They lack concentration and tend to lose their heads in an emergency.

They have no ambition (Cap. sq.) for an objective aim. On the contrary, their personal ambition is completely egotistical. One cannot expect them to have any strength of character. All responsibility is left to others; parents, spouses and business partners have to bear their burdens for them while they enjoy themselves. They have much imagination (Pi.–Vi. hind-axis) but not in the direction of work, rather is this faculty used to seduce. Spiritual evolution cannot be expected here.

These people are sought after for organising parties. They are good at running casinos with roulette (the balls). They are at their best in houses of pleasure, or exquisite restaurants, but they are the type that is tired even before starting to work.

In the arts they will endlessly visit painting exhibitions without ever trying to do any such work themselves. Needless to say, they prefer sensuality in the arts and in sports. Males as well as females are very sensual and passionate in an animal way. They cannot resist temptation and the lower type is the sexual prey of any gesture from the opposite sex. They may meet strange and even perverse experiences, as the lower physical type cannot give real affection, so they receive no compassion from others. Because of their sensual possessiveness they will be left alone in the end, the just punishment for their egotistical illusions and infantile daydreams. All this seems negative and indeed of no value.

Let us look further. We see a powerful young man, the Aries consciousness, lying down in idleness, which is unlike Aries and thus a great mistake. However, the image is full of potential. This young man is playing (Le.) with coloured circles (balls). He is repeating a gesture and a movement horizontally. The female, the emotional, receptive side is standing upright. The beauty (Li. opp.) of a nude has great value in itself; potentially it is the most valuable thing in this world. However, the glance of the woman is in the wrong direction; she is acting wrongly, while the young man is wrongly inactive in the cosmic symbolic sense. The woman looks down in a (black) magically dominant way.

Should not the young man, the 'animus', the male consciousness, jump up and seduce this lady, his 'anima', his female unconsciousness, and throw off her glittering belt accentuating her base chakra? But nothing happens; there is no action of the Higher Self, although all the potential elements are obvious.

Positive and negative in this image ought to intermingle, but they remain in egotistical concentration repeating the movement of their own half. This is why this image has a cosmic invalidity. The potential creation is there, but the halves present a travesty of the whole.

On the high spiritual level there is complete control over the senses and a return to the highest purity through morality, so that past mistakes and sinful experiences will not be repeated.

The highest example of this is Jesus writing in the sand, while those who accused the woman (Mary Magdalene) of being 'caught in the act' slink off one by one.

Second Image, Inner Symbol

A window curtain blown inwards, shaped as a cornucopia.

Interpretation

We have seen the man is concentrating within himself, the woman doing nothing. Both are like two closed rooms. Now in the second image a window is suddenly opened and the wind of the spirit blows in. The one room opens up into the other, and both sides see each other's potential overflowing when the contact is made.

The man has to take the woman's sanctity with the force of a storm-wind as only Aries can do – Aries has the sexual primordial impulse in its zodiacal sign. Look what kind of form the wind makes of the curtain, almost like a phallus penetrating this inner chamber. Here is the archetypal symbol of life itself. Rigidly one repeats one's own feelings until suddenly awakened by the entering storm-wind, the passion of the gale. The window can be slammed, but that will be to the exclusion of the creative power which brings the horn of plenty to the one who will receive it.

Biblical Parallel

The woman taken in adultery, whom Jesus saved from stoning. See *Jn. 8: 3–11.*

25TH DEGREE ARIES

First Image, Outer Symbol

A rider, giving the impression of force, is mounted on a restive horse and is holding the reins tightly in his hands. He looks with an air of disdain on a deformed creature, a kind of dwarf or gnome with wild hair mounted on a ram, which is making an effort to throw him off.

Interpretation

Janduz calls this a degree of 'domination'. Certainly part of the image may be called that, but the glance of disdain from the rider indicates that there is more going on than meets the eye. Janduz' interpretation speaks of intelligence, a thoughtful, strong will and a personality which can hold on in the most difficult circumstances. All this is not wrong, but it is a one-sided interpretation. Undoubtedly the symbol of the rider indicates that part of the character of people with this degree is worthy and able to floor their most powerful opponents. They are not soft or easy to get on with, and they may be even tyrannical. They have to understand that other creatures have a right to achieve their own personal aspirations. They must learn the lesson that they cannot always impose their will on others; otherwise they cause unnecessary difficulties, injuring many who do not agree with them. According to Janduz they may be a caricature of their own selves (the dwarf), but even then they hardly ever fail to dominate.

The lower level of this image is represented by the gnome, which gives these people a perverse streak, always wanting to force things the wrong way, as if possessed by an elemental magical power (neg. Ar.).

On a deeper level of interpretation we see the Aries grail and even the square-axis Cancer–Capricorn. The idea of Aries, magical power, is central. The rider is trying to make a link (Li. opp.) with another world, that of the elementals. The ram comes under Aries. The gnome has to learn from the rider how to behave. Strangely enough we hardly see the hind-axis Virgo–Pisces, unless we assume that the dwarf is about to bring chaos into the existing order (neg. Vi.–Pi.). Where is the Taurus–Scorpio fore-axis? Are these two opposing forces on the verge of making war for domination of the earth (neg. Tau.–Sc.), or is the man planning to transform the earth peacefully (Tau.–Sc.) with the help of the elemental forces? Is the Higher Self discerning the good from the bad 'little people', realising that they are merely thought-forms created by good, or bad, human thinking?

If the Aries grail principle is not controlled by the Higher Self, then automatically the square-axis (Cn.–Cap.) comes up against it. Here it is in the form of undisciplined, spasmodic and unrhythmic, out-of-time movements. The disabled dwarf symbolises wrong programming from the astral worlds. There is not enough quiet meditative emotion (Cn.–Cap.). In its absence Cancer is strongly represented. Where is the female receptivity to each other's inner and outer reactions? These two riders have no time for each other in that respect. They are centred in their own power over their own mount. The horseman succeeds in this, he even has the extra power to disdain the dwarf, but lacks exactly that power of self-control (higher Ar.).

In this image a strong one-sided concentration comes to the fore. Any planet in this degree brings its own colour into this image. For instance with Jupiter the problem is in the sphere of thinking. The riders may be concentrating on their own spasmodic thinking or they may have the reins of their thoughts very firmly under control. The man on the horse has no understanding of the way in which the dwarf thinks. To control a ram is even harder than controlling a horse.

The task for this Aries image is to develop into working for a peaceful future and to study the realms of death and trans-formation, so difficult for Aries to envisage (Tau.–Sc. fore-axis).

Second Image, Inner Symbol

A double promise reveals its inner and outer meanings.

Interpretation

According to Rudhyar, this symbolises 'fortuitous co-operation between inner and outer elements'. This is exactly what the first image needs. The word 'promise' indicates Sagittarius, one of the three fire signs (Ar.–Le.–Sag.). A double portion means that there is a reciprocal contact between rider and dwarf. The inner and outer meaning of their being becomes revealed. When delving into the deeper sources of life, their innate sense (Cn.) of responsibility (Cap. of the Sq.–axis) comes under the control of the Higher Self. The fire signs (Ar.–Le.–Sag.), in the form of a promise, lead up to new revelations which now take over in a harmonious trinity. In order to get a ram under control one needs to have super-magical power and it could be that the dwarf has far better reserves than the rider. They have to cross over and lend each other power; only then will the 'double promise' be given. This degree is the start of an inner development, which enfolds itself throughout all the 25th degrees of the zodiac.

Conception Corrected Asc. 25TH ARIES

Oliver Cromwell   Born 25 Apr. 1599 (OS = 5 May NS) at 03.50 hrs. in Huntingdon, 52°20 N, 11°00 W. Died 3 Sept. 1658. CC NS for 270 days at 03.50 hrs. gives 24°10 Aries. (Another time with Cap. Asc. has been rejected.)

English statesman. During the 1630s his eldest son died (he had eight children), and he underwent a religious conversion, entering Puritan circles. He united the nation against Charles I and took up arms against him. Cromwell wanted a reformation and a model army, but his actions led to civil war. His main blunder was to have Charles I executed. After campaigns in Scotland, he became Lord Protector in 1654 and introduced the first written constitution in English Parliament. He believed in a new Europe under Protestant rule and in a national church with freedom of worship. He massacred the Catholic population in Drogheda in Ireland, claiming that God was on his side, as if he was a Moses or Joshua, but his legacy was bitterness and dissent. He is a controversial historical figure notorious for inconsistency, for speaking 'in great fury' and for his rudeness.

See amongst many biographies *God's Englishman* by Christopher Hill (Pelican 1970).

26TH DEGREE ARIES

First Image, Outer Symbol

A royal personality with a crown and royal mantle presents his sceptre to a kneeling clerk or page. Above the royal man a large sun projects its rays onto a smaller sun above the page.

Interpretation

Janduz calls this a degree of 'facilitated success', which at first sight seems to be too materialistic for this highly esoteric symbol, although on different levels this is the truth. People with this degree rising, who apparently are hard to find in this day and age, will have a brilliant and privileged life of a kind which only comes to those who have to fulfil a great task.

The first of the twelve 26th degrees symbolises the quest for the grail in a more specific way, and this image in particular contains a deep esoteric truth. Though Janduz calls it 'projection', the larger spiritual sun is not just shining, and the smaller one is not merely reflecting the light as if it were a moon, but their rays are emanating and interpenetrating each other, which indicates a great spiritual awareness of the deeper Christ-light within these people.

Symbolically this may mean that they have two superior parts in their consciousness, which must be seen in the context of the entire chart. Their gestures and entire life-style have something truly great about them. These people are royal at heart (Le. trine Ar.) and all their Higher Self wants is to give out their inner and outer wealth. Often they even hand over their authority and knowledge of a subject to someone on a lower level of awareness, or a pupil. It can also be that, with their sceptre, they decide between life and death (see Esther 4, 5). As this is an Aries degree they are an example indeed of how one should act when one has a royal character. We must not forget that they are the kneeling page as well, which is a symbol of their modesty (Vi.–Pi., the difficult hind-axis for Ar.).

As seekers of the grail within them, it is obvious that the Aries grail must be strongly represented in this degree. From a very mystical background (Pi.) they are aware of the exceedingly high potential energy (Ar.) they have within them, with which they can see far ahead into the future (Tau.).

Their will to bring peace and right relationships (Li. opp. Ar.) is great. Unusually for Aries, they have a strong sense of humility (the kneeling page) and an inner reverence for their Creator (Vi.). They have the power to transmute and transform a situation (Sc.), seen here in the handing over of their position. Because of the strength of Virgo and Scorpio in this image, we see the three-pointed configuration of the Y here, which is the 'Y of Samos', a Pythagorean theory. This is like a catapult shooting energy straight from Aries to Libra, which can only happen when Virgo and Scorpio are strong. This also means that they radiate Libra – peace and righteousness. The suns, above both king and page, together become the symbol of the Sun of Righteousness with healing in His wings.

In the highest instance these people are initiated (Ar.) into the inner mysteries, and they can become the perfect teachers who are themselves the pupils. The master is the pupil, the pupil the master. These people have two poles of consciousness (the two suns) which are like two nuclei within their atomic being (Ar.). They may begin to understand cosmic radiation and the functioning of the atomic energies which can resurrect the body. They may fruitfully study the mysteries of the Shroud of Turin and the stories of how the grail manifests and disappears.

Second Image, Inner Symbol

A man bursting with the wealth of what he has to give.

Interpretation

The two parts of the Higher Self have become one and the energy is so abundant that it is almost bursting, like a Divine atomic explosion (Ar.), but this is not destructive because it comes from the infinite source of being, which is the consciousness itself. The giving out of spiritual wealth reaches all levels in the emotional (Moon) and physical (body) areas, circulating around the entire zodiac. These people can be almost obsessed by their potential for giving. The two suns have become one and radiate through their entire being. This is one of the most forceful degrees of the zodiac.

Biblical Parallels

Judah's blessing is 'the sceptre [which] shall not depart from Judah . . . until Shiloh [symbol for Christ] come.' See *Gen. 49: 10*.

In Esther there is the command to all the king's servants, that all who come to the inner court without being called will be put to death, except such to whom the king shall hold out the golden sceptre, that he may live. See *Esther 4: 11* and *5: 2*.

'But unto you that fear my name shall the Sun of righteousness arise with healing in his wings.' *Mal. 4: 2.*

27TH DEGREE ARIES

First Image, Outer Symbol

A man, who has just stumbled over a stone, is in danger of falling with outstretched arms near a dragon, who seems to mesmerise him.

Interpretation

Janduz calls this a degree of 'menacing decadence', which does not seem to fit the image. She interprets the man as a character who does not fit in with the laws and customs of his environment. Such people alienate themselves from their families by offending old routines and established ideas. Without much respect for tradition, they assume a more modern life-style and develop other interests. According to Janduz these people may be ill-prepared for a business or industrial life because of their heritage. They may be stripped of everything by bad advisors or traitors. They may also be hypnotised by some idea, which could cause their downfall. Prudence is needed here.

Now we have to look deeper into this symbol. The man (the Higher Self, the consciousness) is about to fall. The dragon can be either a symbol of evil, or the guardian of a threshold. It is necessary to study the symbol of the 'guardian of the threshold' (see transpersonal psychology). This dragon symbol needs to be faced with directed attention and a strong will. Even if the situation seems hopelessly difficult, the manly consciousness has to raise itself.

As this is an Aries degree there is sufficient magical power and energy to go ahead (Ar.) in the greatest difficulties. These people may attain a high social position, but the danger of falling is great. Depending on the entire horoscope, they may become a Jack-of-all-trades, always stumbling over something.

'Fall' comes under Capricorn, the square-axis of Aries–Libra. Here it is due to a misplaced ambition or a deep-seated fear of life. Part of the character of these people is draconian, with all the nastiness that implies, but the dragon can also guard gold. There may be a deep-seated lie in their life, the pretence for instance that they never have time for the right solution. They may even have poison in themselves, which can result in hypnotic fantasies and delusive dreams (neg. Vi.–Pi. hind-axis), or in a dangerous fanaticism which arises from a kind of self-hypnosis (the staring dragon).

On a high level, however, we have here the archetype of Michael or St George fighting the dragon. Then it implies an otherworldly power and tremendous concentration to overcome evil and turn it into good. People with this degree have to transmute the negative forces in the earth (Tau.–Sc. fore-axis) and overcome the powers of death, so that the gates of heaven will open. They have to make a synthesis in their lives between heaven and earth, the spiritual and the material, and show a pure way of life.

Second Image, Inner Symbol

Through imagination a lost opportunity is regained.

Interpretation

Regaining the lost opportunity is the theme of the Bible after the fall of Adam and Lucifer. Thus we have an archetypal symbol here. There is a beginning of true growth after a loss, a bereavement or a defeat (Tau.–Sc. fore-axis). It is a slow movement back towards man's creative faculties, which are recovered through true imagination (instead of illusion) and work (Vi.–Pi. hind-axis). The man (or woman) of the first image has to retrace his steps, regain his position and win back his upright attitude. Lost opportunities can only be regained by spiritual purity, which will kill the dragon within him, or without, no matter where he is called. The task here is the discovery through self-analysis of why Paradise has been lost and how it will be regained. It is *kairos*, the perfectly timed opportunity.

Biblical Parallels

The fall of Adam. See *Gen. 3.*

'They shall bear thee up in their hands, lest thou dash thy foot against a stone.' *Ps. 91: 12.*

'When I said, My foot slippeth; thy mercy O Lord, held me up.' *Ps. 94: 18.*

In the Old Testament the dragon (in Hebrew *Behemoth*) is sometimes translated as the whale: 'And God created great whales, and every living creature that moveth . . .' *Gen. 1: 21.* See also *Job 7: 12.*

It is also translated as the serpent. See *Rev. 12: 9* and *20: 2*, when this apocalyptic monster is figuratively used for Satan. 'And the great dragon was cast out, that old serpent, called the Devil, and Satan, which deceiveth the whole world.' *Rev. 12: 9.*

Notes

For *Kairos*, 'the right time' see the New Testament Concordance.
See the legends and tales of St George and the dragon, especially *George of Lydda* by Isabel Hill Elder, (Covenant Books, London).

Conception Corrected Asc. 27TH ARIES

Billy Graham   Born 7 Nov. 1918 at 16.30 hrs. in Charlotte (USA), 35°14 N, 80°51 W. CC NS for 278 days at 16.28 hrs. gives 26°15 Aries, or for 292 days (late birth) at 16.29 hrs. gives 26°58 Aries.

American evangelist, whose world-wide crusades to win souls for Christ became immensely popular after he had converted two notorious gangsters. Like a modern St George he is a 'slayer of dragons'.

28TH DEGREE ARIES

First Image, Outer Symbol

A blond lady, richly dressed, stands by herself making a gesture of reception with both hands. In the background is the hall of a palace or stately home.

Interpretation

This is interpreted by Janduz as a degree of 'favour'. It is a very special Aries degree with the strength of a hidden potential power (Ar.) in it.

Those with this degree rising possess a rich, noble and sympathetic heart (the fire trine Ar.–Le.–Sag.). They draw attention to themselves by their courage and progressiveness (Ar.), together with their tact and female graciousness. This trait in a woman may produce sensuality, a love of luxury and a rich life, but on the whole they are honourable and move in aristocratic circles – in either a conventional or spiritual sense. A man may be protected by an influential woman who is a real benefactress. This is acceptable as his potentials and new ideas deserve to be developed.

According to Janduz these people like beautiful dresses, rich food and a free rein to their passions, but they should be aware of the saying 'Take care, you are rich, so you will have to sacrifice wealth; you are happy, so unhappiness will knock on your door.'

It is clear, however, that there is a far deeper inner meaning in this image. True, this will be difficult to realise, but one can detect the entire cardinal cross (Ar.–Cn.–Li.–Cap.) here. This Higher Self is upright and beautiful and aware of it. There is great artistry and refinement of the sense (Li.opp.Ar.). The female side (receptive) has much to give and she also knows how to receive (Cn.). The environment indicates a high social background (Cap.) founded on moral principles and embedded in age-old traditions (Cn.–Cap.).

In a female way, one is shown the Aries grail. Through service and sacrifice in the background (Vi.–Pi. hind-axis) of those gone before, renewal and resurrection of the spirit (Ar.) can take place, and can be used in the future (Tau.–Sc. fore-axis) for enriching the arts. These people can even incarnate as royalty. It is a royal image of great strength and highest refinement.

Second Image, Inner Symbol

A crowd applauds a man who has just shattered a dear illusion.

Interpretation

According to Rudhyar 'a new light is shed upon cherished ideas'. The powers of renewal of the first image have been carried through in fearless revolution, which has been constructive and accepted by the masses (Cn. sq. Ar.). Aries does not shun the pain of transformation (Tau.–Sc. fore-axis). Only slack and inactive people avoid painful situations. The lady remains herself in a state of receptivity. The man of the second image transmutes his power, takes it in both hands and gives it a new value.

The task in general for Aries is to throw off masks. Here the man (consciousness) is doing just that. He is getting approval from the masses who are a symbol of Cancer–Capricorn, the square-axis of Aries. He overcomes the problems of the cardinal cross. This is a revolutionary lesson for humanity as a whole.

29TH DEGREE ARIES

First Image, Outer Symbol

A woodman at the right is felling a tree on his left. He is a robust man of humble appearance, swinging his axe high over his left shoulder. The tree has two deep cuts, and is almost felled. In the foreground to the right is an open book, in which the man studies during his periods of rest.

Interpretation

This is a degree of courageous and manly work. On the physical level it is simply hard labour. As it is an Aries degree it may be modest pioneering work, such as the felling of trees in new territories. No great fortunes may be expected. The situation of these people is toilsome: they have to fight the uncertainties of their fate. They do well in occupations involving nature, forestry, horticulture, the breeding of new species, or woodwork in general. There is a tremendous energy in these people. They plan and stimulate projects, but prefer doing everything themselves rather than leaving the management to others. Here we come to the essence of the problem in this important degree.

As the first one in the cycle of the twelve 29th degrees of the zodiac, it opens up the potential consciousness of man to be the destroyer and polluter of nature, or to become the co-ruler with the Creator by being gardeners in the paradise of Eden, as the Adamic race is meant to be. Imagine the picture in a deeper dimension. The open book is in the right-hand corner at the front, the point of the immediate future. The man, the positive consciousness, is also on the right, but he is looking away from the book and felling a tree on the left. Is the tree dead, so that the felling is a positive deed, or is he destroying age-old beauty in his primitive, self-willed fervour to 'develop'?

Historically, here is the pioneer colonist, with the axe in one hand, with which he can destroy forests and peaceful native settlements alike, and with a Bible in the other hand to force other civilisations into new beliefs. Or that book could be about forestry. There is the danger here, on a very primitive level, of a thoughtless, fanatical and feverish labour against the plan of God and nature. This is the fire trine of Aries–Leo–Sagittarius in its negative aspect.

It is the archetype of the potentially conscious human, who sees nature as something outside of himself. He has an inner drive to attack nature, to reverse things, or to convert anything living into something else (Sc. in ingoing inconj. with Ar.), till he ends up with heaps of sand (Vi.) and a lifeless desert. In his primitive stage, this human does not ask his Creator how far one is allowed to intervene in nature.

The person with this degree prominent has to learn first that all knowledge about creation is laid down in the book of life; that there is a great cosmic harmony, which is a planned equilibrium (Li. opp. Ar.). In Christian terms, this book is the Bible, wherein Adam was appointed to be the keeper of the garden, and in other terms, it is the Akashic Record, in which everything is recorded that has ever been. This person has to know these laws of nature before attempting intervention. It were better for this labourer to sit down first and read the book of life. Only then, when the essence of life is written in his blood, may he interfere with nature.

There is a striking message for collective humanity in this degree. The image shows the man felling a tree like a savage. The axe is striking deep at the root of the tree, but no precautions have been made for the moment when this tree will fall. Will it fall on the man himself, or will the book be destroyed by incautious humanity?

Let this man (consciousness) sit down and analyse his intention. There are historical examples of tree-cutting from a sense of religious fanaticism, such as St Boniface (eighth century) destroying the Holy Oak dedicated to Thor in German Hessen, or Cromwell's soldiers hewing the Holy Thorn of Glastonbury in the seventeenth century.

Many people fell trees without realising what they are doing. Once done, the action cannot be reversed. Symbolically one is unintentionally cutting one's very life-roots, and once one has fallen, death sets in. One needs to redefine one's position here and now. On a high level this tree is the symbol of the Tree of Life in the esoteric teachings of the Kabbalah. Does this man in his religious fervour dismiss these ancient Hebrew truths as 'heathen', when in fact this same wisdom is all contained in the teachings of Christ?

Anyone who has this degree prominent, especially with the Sun, Jupiter or Uranus here, will benefit greatly not only by studying the life of physical trees, but also the symbolism of the Kabbalistic tree. Such study should be undertaken with others of like mind, and this co-operation leads naturally to the higher second image.

Second Image, Inner Symbol

A celestial choir has arisen to sing cosmic harmonies.

Interpretation

Rudhyar says of this image that there is 'at-one-ment of consciousness with cosmic powers; harmonic understanding and
faith in the order and meaning of life'.

A heavenly choir symbolises the promotion of man into a
higher order of beings. When together, as heavenly orientated
earthlings, men have learned the cosmic harmonies by heart, so
that they can even sing them together, then will Christ return to
earth to establish the Kingdom of Heaven here by His example.
Then man may cut down all trees – and institutions – that do
not bring forth good fruit, and these people will be given the
collective Pluto energy to hew down all that offends the Creator
and to burn it in the fire. The opened book will reveal all who
are to be heavenly citizens, and then peace on earth will be
restored (Li. opp. Ar.). Those with this degree are part of the
tremendous implosive energy necessary for restoring this earth
to its heavenly beauty.

Biblical Parallels

'And out of the ground made the Lord God to grow every tree that
is pleasant to the sight, and good for food; the tree of life also in the
midst of the garden, and the tree of knowledge of good and evil.'
Gen. 2: 9.

'. . . if the tree fall toward the south, or toward the north, in the place
where the tree falleth, there it shall be.' *Eccles. 11: 3.*

'. . . the axe is laid unto the root of the trees; therefore every tree which
bringeth not forth good fruit is hewn down, and cast into the fire.'
Mt. 3: 10 and *Lk. 3: 9.*

'And whosoever was not found written in the book of life was cast into
the lake of fire.' *Rev. 20: 15.*

30TH DEGREE ARIES

First Image, Outer Symbol

A woman on the left, facing us, is leading a richly harnessed horse, instead of being carried on its back. Deeper in the image to the right a warrior, equipped for battle with helm and shield, faces the heavens and seems to consult the waning moon.

Interpretation

As this is the 30th degree of the sign of Aries it contains all its symbolism, which is not easy to interpret in this case. Janduz grasps part of it when she describes it as 'sentimental weakness'. Only part of this image can be characterised as such, namely the side which consults a waning moon, symbol of Cancer – emotions (sq. Ar.), and therefore not truly part of the sign of Aries itself.

The content of Aries is shown here as pioneering and battling on all levels of lower physical and higher mental activity. There is a balance between manly activity (Ar.–Mars) independently going forward, and the more feminine action of linking into, and waiting upon, the right season (consulting the Moon) (Li.–Ar. opp.).

People with this degree rising have both parts in their character, which may result in problems when the warrior side battles with, or is menaced by, the more passive and even seductive feminine feelings. The man is the symbol of the Sun, 'I' or consciousness, and is well equipped. The woman is a symbol of the Moon, the soul, the experiences. The Moon reflects light from the Sun. The woman-soul seems to act irrelevantly here as she does not use her horse (symbol of Sag.–Jup., her thinking organ) in the proper way. So there is a discrepancy here. The man is inactive, consulting the phases of the Moon (which could be interpreted as a higher activity than the woman's). She seems unaware of this Moon and is pulling her horse away from it.

Here is the essence of the cardinal cross. The Plutonic energy of renewal and the higher magical power (Ar.) can be 'bogged down' by personal emotional feelings (Cn.), and can be blocked by old stubborn traditions (neg. Cn.–Cap.), so that law and order (Cap.) get out of balance (neg. Li.). The warrior, seeking to determine the right time (Cap.) to go to battle, seems to indicate the solution for the cardinal cross problems, but why does he consult the waning moon only (Cn.-female, moon phases) and not the moon in all its phases, nor all the planets? Or does he? A waning moon, seen from the Sun in the sign of Aries, can for instance be in Capricorn or Aquarius. Is this moon a symbol of his awareness of the declining phase of the society in which he lives (sq. Moon in Cap. seen from Ar.); or does he perceive that he, as Aries, is filled with new energy lighting up an as yet invisible but harmoniously aspected new Aquarian age (sextile Moon in Aq. seen from Ar.), an age of brotherhood and holistic living? If so it now becomes clear why the woman is trying to pull her horse away from the declining society and from the new age. She does not wish to see it. She should mount her horse, turn back, follow the warrior and dare to join in the battle for a new earth. Such people could then make a magnificent synthesis of their male – female personality, of positive and negative, of old and new. They are faithful, honest fighters, and at the same time disarmingly charming and sensitive.

Second Image, Inner Symbol

Ducklings disport themselves merrily upon a pond.

Interpretation

Young ducks are a cheerful combination of sudden naive courage and an equally sudden shrinking when frightened. One moment they are timid, but the next moment they are facing dangers again. They are a symbol of Aries. The pond is a symbol of the unconscious female reservoir which is supporting them without their knowing it.

Aries is starting a new cycle and as with the ducks, the consciousness is still very young but strong in its simplicity. These people may be a bit dualistic, but they act completely independently and are content with their position in life.

Ducks need one another (Ar.–Li.). One duck on its own is too vulnerable.

Biblical Parallels

'He [Christ] must increase, but I must decrease [the waning moon of the first image].' *Jn. 3: 30.*

'As for me, behold, my covenant is with thee [Abraham], and thou shalt be a father of many nations.' *Gen. 17: 4.*

Conception Corrected Asc. 30TH ARIES

Nicola Tesla Born just before midnight 9–10 July 1856, in Smiljan (Yugoslavia), 45°00 N, 15°00 E. Died 7 Jan. 1943. CC NS for 285 days at 23.54 hrs. gives 29°06 Aries, or for 256 days at 23.49 hrs. gives 29°14 Aries.

Scientist who emigrated to the USA and is known for his far-reaching research on weather modification, instruments for interplanetary contact and other very important discoveries on which present interstellar research is based. The USSR accepted his findings when US scientists did not recognise his genius. He died in great poverty.

See *Prodigal Genius, the Life of Nicola Tesla* by John J. O'Neill (1944), and *Tesla, Man Out of Time* by Margaret Cheney (1981, Dell – New York).

Leo Tindemans, born 16 Apr. 1922 at 6.00 hrs. (R B) in Zwijndrecht (Belgium), 51°14 N, 4°18 E. CC NS for 265 days at 6.00 hrs. gives 29°31 Aries or for 279 days at 5.55 hours gives 26°49 Aries.

Belgian politician and premier (1977). He is known for his 'report Tindemans' (1975). His concept of a European Union with integration of governments was at that time revolutionary, but now in the 1990s this is becoming reality. He was the grandson of a shepherd. With Sun, Mercury, South Node and Ascendant in Aries, this last degree seems to fit him though the 27th cannot be ruled out.

CANCER

INDEX OF CANCER ASCENDANT DEGREES

1st Degree Cancer

First Image, Outer Symbol

An entire family, of several generations, is picking the grapes which are growing on the vines against the wall of their home.

Interpretation

Janduz calls this a degree of 'attachment'. This is a first degree and therefore this image must contain the elements of the sign of Cancer. Attachment is a Cancer word, which contains a range of emotions (Cn.). One could summarise all the charming character traits of Cancer people in this degree. Of course, there is parental affection and brotherly love. Cancerians care for their children and like to build their own nest, or their home, or their castle. Their own hearth is worth its weight in gold to them. However, there is a deeper level of interpretation than this outer sympathetic and emotional level.

They are amiable, sociable and, like the Moon, a bit moody, (Cn.). They tend to go up and down with the lunar phases, as do women during their monthly periods. Their life on this level of home-making is cosy. There are not a lot of difficulties. They have enough for their needs, and live by the day. They hardly ever worry, they are happily married, they eat well (Cn.) and they can grow old without being bored by family life. Family feelings are held in common, and everyone refers to what father or grandma says. They do not like to make their own decisions (Li.) or be independent (Ar.) of home. On this level, the cardinal cross difficulties have not been faced. However, there is a much deeper level of interpretation than this.

As the first degree of Cancer summarises Cancer itself, we are seeing here the plane of endless repetition, generation after generation like the cyclical motions of the Moon. This slavish conformity to tradition is, however, precisely what

Cancer should renounce, and this is shown in the Cancer grail: every degree and every sign has a meaning and a task to be fulfilled. What are all these generations doing? They are picking grapes. The grape is a symbol of the Sun (not to be confused with wine, which comes under Pi.). The vine, as a plant, is an exceptional symbol, of which Jesus was certainly aware when making use of it in parables. The vine grows tendrils to enable it to grow vertically. This straight-to-heaven tendency is Aquarian. This Cancer image is filled with people of all ages, who are all bearers of the Light and of the vertical revelations from Heaven. They straighten their backs (Le.) and reach higher they reach for the sun above them. The ripened vine represents rejoicing for the entire family. One needs courage (Le.) to climb the ladder, and one risks falling (Cap.), when one picks the highest grapes.

You may have sensed that we have been pointing all the time to the fore-axis of the Cancer grail, Leo–Aquarius, towards which Cancer has to look for its spiritual growth. For home-made (Cn.) wine (Pi.), the grapes have to be pressed and transformed (Sc.). Thus this image gives us an insight into the three water signs as well. But there is more. We can even detect what for Cancer is the difficult hind-axis of Gemini–Sagittarius. Grape-picking is a good education (Sag.) by which the young can gain insight into the wisdom (Ge.) of nature's growth. The elderly may recite and sing passages from the Holy Books on the vine and the wine, and the entire family can grasp the wisdom and the idea (Ge.–Sag.) behind it all.

In this grape-picking, the family spirit (Cn.) branches out, with everyone doing his or her best (Ar.), and co-operating (Li.) to uphold the family's reputation (Cap.). Their house wine will go on the market (Ge.) and travel far and wide (Sag.). The neighbour will drink it, the street, the country and king – yes the whole world, glorifying the Sun through which the grape ripens. This is exactly what the Cancer character needs: to help to get out of that cosy feeling of security, and into the world, and to glow in wider and wider circles until consciousness reaches universal expansion in Light and Love. And all this 'begins at home'.

Second Image, Inner Symbol

A sailor on a ship is ready to hoist a new flag to replace an old one.

Interpretation

Rudhyar calls this a symbolic act and 'a point of no return'. At this summer solstice point, the sun stops its northward motion and reverses southwards. The ship is symbolising consciousness floating on the sea of the vast unconscious (Cn.). So far Rudhyar. This individual self has had enough of sailing under the old parental and traditional flag, and now raises one of a new order. Raising this new flag means looking straight along the flagpole up to heaven. You have to straighten your back for that. You glow within yourself with enthusiasm and love, when the wind takes up and unfolds this new symbol, which was not there a minute ago (Le.–Aq.). When all the family and all the generations of the earth hoist their individual new flags, what a sea of colours that will be! Let us toast that glorious sight with a glass of home-made wine!

Biblical Parallels

'I am the vine, ye are the branches.' *Jn. 15: 1–5.*

'The angel . . . gathered the vine of the earth and cast it into the great winepress of the wrath of God.' *Rev. 14: 19.*

'Neither do men put new wine into old bottles.' *Mt. 9: 17.* (Compare the flags.)

Conception Corrected Asc. 1st Cancer

Hector Berlioz   CC for 270 days at 16.58 hrs. gives 00°13 Cancer (see 3rd Cn.).

2ND DEGREE CANCER

First Image, Outer Symbol

A well-fed dog is defending a bone against two ravenous street dogs on the left. At the right, on the street, a pretty woman is casually walking in front of a dandy, who is undecided whether to follow her or not.

Interpretation

This is one of the least enjoyable degrees of the sign of Cancer. Janduz calls it one of 'inert possession'.

It contains the material lust for possessions, combined with a sloppy kind of femininity and a coaxing half-hearted masculinity. These are the negative sides of Cancer, when motherhood deteriorates into whoring and fatherly care into the fancy-man or bully.

On a low level of spiritual awareness these people may stubbornly fight to defend possessions unlawfully acquired (neg. Cap. opp. Cn.). They consider everyone's property their own. They do not possess true creative visualisation (Le.–Aq. fore-axis), but tend to hold an unduly good opinion of themselves.

On this low level they are hardly able to earn their money in an honest way. They cannot maintain a good position in society (neg. Cap. opp. Cn.) nor keep the peace (Li. sq. Cn.), nor are they able to take the initiative (Ar. sq. Cn.). They are likely to be parasitical on others and slothful, though often seeming to be very industrious and bustling. They have a kind of slyness, which they call 'diplomacy', with which they may exploit others. They are sharp, but this is not combined with humane qualities or loving kindness (Le. fore-axis), which they need to develop more than anything else. They are lazy, and lose much time in idle chatter.

On a very low level they make the charming gangster, blackmailer or lounge lizard, exuding the glamour of the underworld and rotten through and through. Their friendship and flattery has but one end in view – their own advantage; but when their mood changes or profit eludes them, they become aggressive and supremely arrogant. Boasters as they are, the inflated ego behind all the exaggerated pretensions is easily seen by the more perceptive among their acquaintances.

Women with this degree prominent enjoy parading on the street, and love shopping for days on end. This is also the case on the more symbolic level of the emotions and the soul. They would, metaphorically speaking, rather polish their nails and make up their faces than help to heal the earth by showing motherly love for it, for instance by working in the garden.

Men as well as women with this degree prominent, especially with Venus and Mars here, can easily arouse the lower emotions (of root and base chakras) of the opposite sex, and even those of their own sex, without taking into account the consequences of their lustful stimulation. They tend to be jealous. They badly need to get off the public street, literally and symbolically, and work on their self-knowledge and self-identity. They need to feed on faith, hope and glory (Ge.–Sag, difficult hind-axis), not just for themselves but to develop impersonal energies with which to benefit a wider circle, and eventually even a whole nation (Cn.–Cap.). In politics they can defend their party against opposing factions with the tenacity of a bulldog (the street dogs).

On the higher level they may be chosen as vessels to defend the rights, and even the lives, of the people 'in the street' against crime and all enemies of the State. They may then be idolised by these people, as in the exceptional case of Winston Churchill, sometimes depicted as the British bulldog, who led the British to victory in war although in times of the Empire's decline.

Second Image, Inner Symbol

A man on a magic carpet observes vast vistas below him.

Interpretation

There is only one thing to wish for the people of the first image, who are still fastened on their own materialism. They need to elevate themselves above the world of glamour in which they are trapped.

In the first image the deep passions, and the pain thereof, can become the means of purification and transformation leading the soul to a higher level: they need to raise the consciousness from grasping to giving.

The first image is still on the defensive (the dog and bone) in an egotistical wish to hold on to the material way of life. Here, the manly consciousness relinquishes the mundane world and rises vertically in a miraculous way. This ascent by magic carpet is the beginning of an initiation into the power and energy of the resurrection (Ar.).

In this degree we see the entire cardinal cross: the dog comes under Aries–Pluto and so does the magic. Aries is square to Cancer, and so these highly active energies cause difficulties for the soft, motherly feelings and the instinct for home-making. The man on the carpet moves away from the mother country. All this is square to Libra, the binding element of relationship and marriage. The air on which the carpet floats may be Libra. Capricorn is represented in the bone on which the dogs concentrate their attention, and in the wide vista of stone-built cities under the carpet.

What these people need is to become aware of the Cancer grail in themselves. They need to show forgiving love and human spontaneity (Le.–Aq. fore-axis) and creativity, and to contact higher dimensions within themselves. On a magic carpet, away from the hustle and bustle of the streets, one is near the realm of the angels and the Creator Himself.

The difficult hind-axis for these people, Gemini–Sagittarius, is their attachment to a superficial way of living and talking, and minding other people's business (neg. Ge.), as is happening in the first image; while in the second, the wind blowing against them may be a factor to be reckoned with. They need to acquire factual knowledge, to gain inner introspection and wisdom (Ge.), and to grow into faith and hope in the higher mediating beings and guardians around them. The man on the magic carpet needs the courage (Le.) to find himself, to trust his own inner energies for self-renewal, and to look at things from the higher viewpoint of his own inner being. He needs to overcome the gravity of egotism, which pulls him back into the density of matter, by exerting an almost self-hypnotic pull upwards, towards the heavenly realms. He still needs to be sustained by outer form (carpet, Cn.-Cap.) as he is not yet daring enough to ascend without. These people may do well to study the phenomena of levitation and the Ascension.

Biblical Parallel

'And when he had spoken these things, while they beheld, he was taken up; and a cloud received him out of their sight.' *Acts 1: 9.*

3RD DEGREE CANCER

First Image, Outer Symbol

A woman is seated on a sofa in an attitude of grief, holding in her hand a bunch of faded flowers. Two men stand watching her, one with an ironic air, the other with compassion.

Interpretation

Janduz calls this a degree of 'passionate life'. Those with this degree on the Ascendant, whether male or female, do not find it easy to deal with; nor do others find it easy to deal with them. Often, it is the side of the woman that comes to the fore. On a low level these people have rather hysterical characters, and make it their profession to play the 'broken lily' or 'the lamenting lady' (men and women!). The cause of this is often their hypersensitivity (Cn.). They can be people of a degenerate imagination, whom nothing and nobody can raise from their habitual state of anxiety. On that level they simply do not want to listen to well-meant advice. Their Higher Self (the two men) stands beside them powerless, not knowing what to think of it all. They remain absorbed in their tears.

This attitude can become a habit over the years, because of misplaced greed. On the outer plane, for instance, a woman cannot stand the fact that her husband is not at home often enough to sit with her on the sofa. Or a soldier too nervous for his profession may be the laughing-stock of the regiment (the ironic man). One could sympathise with him, were the situation not so absurd. These are foolishly selfish people, lacking in elementary courage (neg. Le.–Aq. fore-axis). They often have no one but themselves to blame for the fading of their opportunities (the faded flowers).

On the lower as well as the higher level of awareness they may have very passionate and sensual natures (Cn. trine Sc. and Pi.). They may come to reflect upon (Ge. behind Cn.) their overwhelming wish to be cuddled and protected. This must be turned inward towards the inner help and protection always available from the unseen world.

Undoubtedly people with this degree prominent may have to undergo unfriendly and hurtful gestures from the other sex. If their feelings have been hurt, their positive will and consciousness (the two men) must not allow them to sit down and be sorry for themselves (the woman), for all positivity can be absorbed by self-pity.

A woman with this degree prominent could slide down into prostitution, or get herself into damaging emotional relationships with men. Woe to her if she sets out to attract male attention when her youth begins to fade away! The ensuing degradation of character, even if her own husband be the object of her frenzy, is the result of her own cowardice.

As this is a Cancer degree, however, these people ultimately have to learn their lesson by harsh experience. They have to become more careful of their moods (Moon) and less responsive to the call of the lower senses. They are too easily misled by their lightly aroused passions, which are more often than not based on pure imagination: a simple gift of a bunch of flowers does not necessarily imply a proposal of marriage.

Female emotions and moodiness (Moon) come under Cancer in general, and therefore the grieving woman is a very strong aspect in the character of these people. There is nothing wrong with pure grief and emotion, but these people have to learn to distinguish by experience the difference between the lower personal emotions that are based on egotistical (Cap. opp. Cn.) sentimentality, and those that arise from compassion. The chakras of both the solar plexus and the heart can easily be hurt by the adverse experiences of life. These people have to learn to transpose the lower energy of their flaring emotions onto the level of the heart. This can be done, because there are two standing men in the image, symbolising a double portion of will and heart-power enabling them to identify with the Higher Self. They may have a very positive wish and ability to care for sufferers. As such they make good counsellors, psychiatrists, or rebirthers (bringing these patients back to their own birth-drama) and thus they may become leaders of lost souls and rescuers of those in danger. This role is symbolised in the second image.

Second Image, Inner Symbol

An arctic explorer leads a reindeer through icy canyons.

Interpretation

The solution for the first image lies in this evolutionary development. The three elements in these people (the woman and the two men) need to come together as one in this daring and pioneering explorer, who risks his life in adverse circumstances. He cannot afford to sit down and grieve, because that would mean death for himself and the animal (symbol for the physical body) he cares for.

Following the animal's instinct and the man's higher intuition (Aq. fore-axis), their path leads them along unknown trails, which were always there on the inner astral planes. Together they can go through the hardest times (Cap., the canyon). This means that people with this Cancer degree are contacting their complementary sign Capricorn, so that they come into their own form. The woman has to spring up from her cosy couch and get on her boots and her warm clothes. The overprotected sensitivity of these people needs to be channelled into working energetically with nature towards a faraway goal, for which they are willing to face all weathers and hardships.

Biblical Parallel

This degree seems to have a parallel with the choice of land between

Lot and Abraham. While Lot thinks he will go the easy way to Sodom, Abraham bravely faces the cold north. See *Gen. 13: 11–13.*

Conception Corrected Asc. 3rd Cancer

Hector Berlioz   Born 11 Dec. 1803 at 17.00 hrs. in La Cote Saint André, 45°26 N, 5°19 E. Died 1869. CC WAK and NS for 284 days at 17.10 hrs. gives 2°58 Cn. or for 270 days at 16.58 hrs. gives 0°13 Cn.

French composer. His father pressed him to study medicine, but he gave up university for the conservatory. He lived in great poverty for many years. During the time of his fiery relationship with an Irish actress, ending in a stormy separation, he produced his best dramatic symphonies, such as *The Death of Orpheus, Romeo and Juliet* and *The Damnation of Faust.* His compositions place him in the ranks of the great Romantics. He wrote textbooks which later became important for modern 'programme music'. He had the 'extravagant emotionalism of genius' (quote: *Encycl. Britt.*). Although 1st Cancer is nearer the given birth-time, his chart and outer life reflect more the images of 3rd Cancer.

George Gordon Byron   Born 22 Jan. 1788 towards 14.00 hrs. in London, 51°31 N, 00°05 W. Died 19 Apr. 1824 in Greece. CC NS for 275 days at 13.54 hrs. (conception Paris) gives 2°44 Cn.

English poet, 6th Baron. His father squandered the fortunes of two wives. He was the son of the unhappy marriage with Lady Gordon, who was vain, capricious, mentally deranged and had a violent temper. Lame from infantile paralysis, he was maltreated, in spite of which he became an ardent sportsman, though moody and inclined to dreaming.

After Cambridge he took his seat in the House of Lords. He recorded his travels to the East in 1809. The sudden death of his mother left him desolate, though he had not liked her. His first marriage ended in separation in 1816. He went to Italy, where he became 'the prophet and champion of liberty' (*Encycl. Britt.*) and wrote most of his work. He lived with Claire. His constant companion was Shelley (see 2nd Tau.) who drowned in 1822, to Byron's great grief. He went to fight in the Greek War of Independence, but a fit suffered while there left him speechless. His dramatic last months in Greece, and his stormy life full of exaltation and gloom, provide a dramatic example of this 3rd degree Cancer. There are many books about Byron's work and life.

Maurice Magre   Born 2 Mar. 1877 at 11.45 hrs. in Toulouse, 43°25 N, 01°26 E. Died 1941. CC NS for 281 days at 11.54 hrs. gives 2°55 Cancer, or for 295 days at 11.54 hrs. gives 2°58 Cancer.

French writer of occult books. Most of his works deal with the mysteries of love, esotericism and magic, death and future life. His main interests were the Cathars and he wrote 'The Treasure of the Albigeois' (1938). The archives of his publications are at Rennes les Bains (1987).

Marie Antoinette   Born 2 November 1755, 19.30 hours (source EPA 750 of 23 July 1962 and Zenith IV, 1933) in Vienna, 48.12 N., 16.23 E. Decapitated 16 Oct. 1793. CC NS for 267 days at 19.28 hrs. gives 2°15 Cancer.

Daughter of Empress Maria Theresa and Emperor Franz I of Austria. She married the French King Louis XVI. She was very emotional in her friendships in which one can see the image of 3rd Cancer. She was surrounded by intrigues and libel, which all added to the hysterical feelings of hatred by the common people against her. There are different versions of her last years, and hours, but she comes over as an innocent victim of the French Revolution, as forgiving, and during her way to the scaffold as a truly tragic figure, displaying royal calmness and dignity. Emil Ludwig's *Marie Antoinette* is well-known amongst a great mass of literature. See also *Queen of Trianon* by Iain D.B. Pilkington (Jarolds, 1955).

Ouida   (pen-name for Maria Louise Ramé) Born 1 Jan. 1839 at 15.15 hrs. in Bury St Edmunds, 52°15 N, 00°43 E. Died 1908. CC NS for 275 days at 15.11 hrs. gives 2°10 Cancer.

English novelist, whose characters are dramatically contrasted as souls of light or darkness.

See Monica Stirling, *The Fine and the Wicked, the Life and Time of Ouida* (London, 1957).

4TH DEGREE CANCER

First Image, Outer Symbol

A table covered with the remains of a rich feast, and musical instruments, abandoned by the guests, who chase each other lasciviously.

Interpretation

Janduz calls this a degree of 'sensuality'. Fundamentally these people are materialists bent on pleasure, voluptuous and self-deceiving (neg. Cn.). On the lowest level, their ostensibly artistic interests are perverted rather than aesthetic. Typically for Cancer, their gluttony is so great as to become the unconscious driving force; they are always to be found where food, substantial or supersensible, is to be had, and may even prey on the auric emanations of others, to the extreme exhaustion of their victims, and the detriment of their own moral forces.

They are sociable and flirtatious, quick to strike up an acquaintance and prematurely familiar, all this proceeding from their greed for sensation. Of true love and unselfish friendship (Le.–Aq.) they know nothing. In short, they have abandoned the instrument, their talent, by which they could have brought music to the world.

On a higher level there is camaraderie and joviality. They can be generous, but they are still vulnerable to the wrong attractions. They may do well working with perfumes, *objects d'art*, flowers, wines and *cordon bleu* cuisine.

However, they can still show a lack of sincerity and responsibility too (Cap. opp. Cn.). There is often complacency and superficiality, and the tendency to shirk duties and evade disagreeable issues. This is most apparent in their relationships, where they will readily discard old friends for new, and precipitate drama into their lives in consequence. Who is going to clear up the mess left lying on the table, and do the washing up?

On inner levels it is often others who have to deal with the emotional débris left in the wake of these fickle adventurers into the realms of sensation. They need much self-knowledge and discipline, faith and guided meditation (Cap. opp.) to conquer their excessive sensuality and attain spiritual awareness. They should develop their artistic and musical talents.

The essence of this image is that there is a lack of mental and spiritual power. These people lack the strength to cope with difficult situations, but even so there is enough potential energy to make them succeed materially.

Second Image, Inner Symbol

A hungry cat argues with a mouse before eating her.

Interpretation

Here the deeper meaning of the first image is depicted. There is something of hypnotic coercion (Ar. sq. Cn.) and self-justification (Li. sq. Cn.) in the inner make-up of those with this degree. Like cats they are interested only in devouring the weaker creature, justifying their behaviour in terms of social necessity (Ge.). How will the mouse emerge from this debate?

These people have both cat and mouse within their personality. There is the cat-like activity and the mouse-like passivity. The lesson here is to begin a dialogue between these two elements, realising the imbalance inherent in each. Their active part should not devour their passive part, but each gain value and respect from the other.

The guests need to stop chasing each other: this cat-and-mouse game must end. If they wish to attain the high level, which this degree, and Cancer in general, can reach, they need to be honest with themselves and turn their sensuality into a new sense of morality, justice and creativity.

Conception Corrected Asc. 4th Cancer

Roberto Assagioli   Born 27 Feb. 1888 at 12.00 hrs. (source – personal information to Dane Rudhyar) in Venice, 45°27 N, 12°20 E. Died 1974. CC NS for 278 days at 12.05 hrs. gives 3°45 Cancer.

Italian psychiatrist of Jewish descent. Founder and promoter of Psychosynthesis and meditation groups. His main theme was the arguments between the lower self and the transpersonal self, to be evaluated in group workshops.

See his books *A Manual of Principles and Techniques* and *Act of Will.*

Franz Schubert   Born 31 Jan. 1797 at 13.30 hrs. (from the Housekronik), in Liechtenthal, 48°14 N, 16°22 E. Died 19 Nov. 1828. CC WAK and NS for 293 days at 13.30 hrs. gives 3°44 Cancer.

Austrian composer. His genius was revealed from the age of 17 with a composition and an essay on chamber music. He wrote a lot for the amateur orchestra in which his two brothers played violin, his father violincello and he himself viola. This shows a level of the 4th Cancer image which has not been mentioned in the text, as Schubert's own family function as his 'guests' in the family (Cn.) orchestra.

Schubert made a wide circle of friends and was always the leader of the party with true Bohemian generosity. He was 'the greatest song-writer who ever lived' (quoted *Encycl. Britt.* 1961 edn). He is best remembered for his *Unfinished Symphony*. His financial situation was often difficult.

See, amongst others, *Franz Schubert, the Man and His Circle* by Newman Flower (1928).

Harold Wilson   Born 11 Mar. 1916 at 10.45 hrs. in Huddersfield, 53°39 N, 01°48 W. CC NS for 272 days at 10.43 hrs. gives 3°13 Cancer.

British Labour Prime Minister. See his book *The Labour Government 1964–1974: A Personal Record.*

5TH DEGREE CANCER

First Image, Outer Symbol

A young tree, which the wind has detached from its sustaining post, is growing sideways. Under its branches a young girl is waiting for her beloved, who is fleeing away from her without being seen. Between them is a flowering rose-bush.

Interpretation

According to Janduz this is a degree of 'betrayal'. People with this degree prominent often have to undergo a tragic fate and course of life. Both men and women are very vulnerable and sensitive (Cn.). Their female side, or their emotional body, is full of tender confidence, but time and again they are betrayed by a hard, worldly, more masculine attitude in others.

On the physical level they may be misled and cheated, whereby the original purity and innocence of their whole character is damaged. Life is often hard for them. The disillusions and very painful deceptions which they meet are the repercussion of their own naive imprudence: they seldom realise that promises are often given by people who mean well at the time, but who break their word later. Without becoming mistrustful, they ought to be more guarded.

They may be full of love and fire (Le. fore-axis), but they lack discernment (Ge. hind-axis) and so tend to be childishly egotistical (neg. Cap. opp. Cn.). To them it seems they are being cherished and appreciated, but when this is so they are apt to lose their hold on practical necessity and their spiritual growth becomes deformed in consequence (the tree). They do not easily learn from the hard knocks which life deals them, nor from the strange and even dangerous experiences which may come their way for their much-needed enlightenment. Unless they can gain some measure of maturity they will be forsaken by those they have trusted, and unless they can bring the force of the Higher Self into their lives, an incarnation may seem to have been wasted.

On a high level of awareness there lies a far deeper experience within this degree. If spiritually evolved, these people will always realise that their roots are not really in this world. Through being tossed about in life's storms, they will learn to rely more and more on their innate strength, enabling them to stand up again. They may experience the flowering of a love that is a symbol of heavenly light. If they remain faithful to their higher calling, and know how to sacrifice everything, and relinquish their wish to be loved and possessed, their spiritual identity may grow and flower enormously. The archetype of the rose (Le.) is symbolic of the mystic centre, the heart, the beloved and perfection. (See Rosicrucians, Cirlot.)

In the image the masculine consciousness flees away. These people have to become aware of their inclination to escape, they need to realise that by this they could betray the True Self and the invisible higher worlds. Their intuitive female side is the stronger one and they should foster this inner gift. By such cherishing their astral contacts may grow so strong that these people will become a force in their world, and a mirror (Cn.) deflecting all that is base and ugly in the outer environment.

One can see the Cancer grail in this image, the female receptivity (Cn.) too easily betrayed (Cap.) by the hard ego-tistical ambition to hold a position in society (Cap.). The need for self-knowledge and confidence is the difficulty here (Ge.–Sag. hind-axis), while the solution is courage, love and intuitive understanding (Le.–Aq. fore-axis) bringing contact with the invisible world of angelic helpers.

Second Image, Inner Symbol

A motorist dies racing madly with a fast train.

Interpretation

Here the betraying sweetheart has become the cold and fast rat-race of society, with which these people try to keep up, but it is clear that this whole side of them is overdoing it so much that the only way out is death.

The first image seems to be a bit too sentimental and romantic. It needs more action and daring. The second image has too much of the fatal outer projection (Ge. behind Cn.), racing towards a goal without enough self-knowledge and control. These people need to double back on their tracks, put on the brakes and ascend to a higher life. Death, whether defined as mortality or as the termination of a certain life-style, is always a gateway and never final.

In this second image we see a basic conflict between the collective energies (the train) and the individual (the car-driver). This problem of our time is brought to the fore in this degree.

Biblical Parallel

Christ betrayed by Peter. See *Mt. 26: 69–75*.

Conception Corrected Asc. 5th Cancer

James Matthew Barrie   Born 9 May 1860 in Kirriemuir ('Thrums'), Scotland, 56°40 N, 03°00 W. Died June 1937. CC WAK and NS for 287 days gives 4° 31 Cancer.

Novelist who delighted the English-speaking world with the classic *Peter Pan* and other successful books. He never truly recovered from the shock, when 6 years old, of a brother's death (see second image).

Leo N. Tolstoy   Born 28 Aug. 1828 (OS = 9 Sept. NS) at 22.39 hrs. in Yasnaya Polyana (Russia) 54°05 N, 37°30 E. Died 21 Nov. 1910. CC WAK and NS for 279 days at 22.39 hours gives 4.13 CA.

Famous Russian novelist and moral philosopher. Best-known for *Anna Karenina* and *War and Peace*. In one of his books a major role is played by a racehorse (see second image). All forms of violence he saw as wicked. The Russian Church excommunicated him. He was very much the individual artist against the collective (see second image).

See *Encycl. Britt.* (4 pages) 1960 edn.

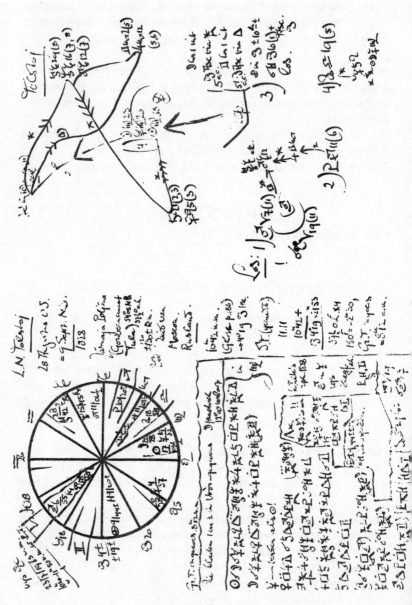

Handwritten chart of Leo N. Tolstoy by
Willem Ary Koppejan

6TH DEGREE CANCER

First Image, Outer Symbol

A man advances, dragging behind him a horse half-strangled by a line which entangles its throat. Behind them an iron gauntlet, a sabre and a riding-whip have been placed at the trunk of a tree.

Interpretation

According to Janduz this is a degree of 'brutal assurance'. This does not seem at all like a Cancer degree. It symbolises a burning energy (the man) and a brutal conquering of nature's natural resistance (the horse). Moreover, riding attributes come under Sagittarius (hind-axis) with a bit of Scorpio (iron gauntlet).

There is a great need here for moderation and control of unbalanced (neg. Li. sq. Cn.) energy. People on a low level of spiritual awareness could become hard, cruel and egotistical (neg. Cap. opp. Cn.), and work their emotions off on weaker humans and other creatures. They have the dubious advantage in this life that there are always less fortunate beings around them on whom they car. practise their slave-driving instincts.

If they have weak reasoning power (according to the position of Mer. in the horoscope), they may even lower themselves to lead a life of vengeance, on the principle of 'an eye for an eye and a tooth for a tooth'. However, as Cancer, they are very emotional and ultimately only hurt themselves.

They may be gifted with a strong intellect and the capacity to think individually (the resisting horse). Then they may resist the promptings of the spiritual will (the man). There is a discrepancy here, and they may be quite brutal to themselves. One part of them can tyrannise over their whole being, even taking a masochistic bent.

On a higher level, with positive social circumstances, they may become personalities who take on the heaviest responsibilities. They can acquire the inner power to lead both people and animals out of adverse situations, and to bring out the best in them. If only the horse would listen and obey, he would not cut his own throat! If need be, these people are able to use the whip at the right moment. They can handle a sabre to silence enemies, and symbolically, to rid themselves of bad influences. They do not shun an honest, man-to-man confrontation, common enough in medieval times. However, they often forget what weapons they possess (the gauntlet, sabre and whip are not in use). Their ideals are often rather crude (the trunk), but at least they attempt to give them form.

Even on a high level of evolution they may be heard to utter such emotionally laden phrases as *Vae Victis* – proverbially 'Woe to the vanquished!' – or 'Right, everybody out!', or 'Might is right.' In their policy to divide and conquer, there may be craftiness, but always of a morally refined sort.

The symbol is aggressive. There is a great need to go inward into one's own soul (Cn.). They often disregard the laws of the land and the rights of others (Cap. opp. Cn.). They have to learn respect, especially for the elderly and those of a higher social or spiritual rank.

On the highest level they allow others to lay the whip over them, even when completely innocent.

Second Image, Inner Symbol
Innumerable birds are busy feathering their nests.

Interpretation
Calmly preparing a home (Cn.) does not seem a characteristic of the man in the first image, unless he is trying to get the horse back to the stable where he belongs.

In the second image there is not just one individual working under his own steam, but an entire community expressing its own nature. There is no battle, no strife, no adversity, but only harmony and obedience to the laws of nature and the collective instinct to build homes for future generations with natural material (feathers come under Cn.–Cap.). Their plans may still be instinctive and not yet the formulations of conscious awareness. Their dreams may not always take the form they wish, but there is preparation for new birth.

Birds come under Gemini (hind-axis). This image shows that those with this degree need to make a sharp distinction between the inner realms of nature: between the plant kingdom and the animal kingdom, and between human and divine regions, none of which should dominate another. 'In my Father's house are many mansions,' and everyone has the right to be in his or her own appointed place.

Biblical Parallels

'Eye for eye, tooth for tooth . . .' *Ex. 21: 24.*

'And the men that held Jesus mocked him, and smote him.' *Lk. 22: 63.*

'In my Father's house are many mansions.' *Jn. 14: 2.*

'And Jesus saith unto him, "The foxes have holes, and the birds of the air have nests; but the Son of man hath not where to lay his head."' *Mt. 8: 20.*

'Yea, the sparrow hath found an house, and the swallow a nest for herself, where she may lay her young, . . . Blessed are they that dwell in thy house.' *Ps. 84: 3–4.*

Conception Corrected Asc. 6th Cancer

Thomas Ring   Born 28 Nov. 1892 at 18.00 hrs. in Nuremberg, 49°27 N, 11°05 E. Died 24 Aug. 1983. CC NS for 265 days at 18.02 hrs. gives 5°01 Cancer, which is a double Ascendant, so part of the 5th as well. Ring himself published his Ascendant as 4°23 Cancer.

German-Swiss astrologer, painter and author of many books. His work had great influence on European astrology, though none of his nine books have been translated. In 1979 the Thomas Ring Foundation came into being. A television film was made of him on his 90th birthday. An outstanding researcher – quite a few sets of data for this book have been based on his information.

See obituary in *Astrological Journal*, Winter 1983/84.

7TH DEGREE CANCER

Outer Image, Outer Symbol

A rich woman, seated under a pergola covered with flowers, accepts precious jewels from a bunch of grinning pirates (or beggars), who are showing them to one another. On the left a person in a harlequin costume, with crazy hair, forces a sheep to plunge alive into a steaming cauldron. (Note: In the Janduz version it is the woman who distributes the jewels.)

Interpretation

Janduz calls this a degree of 'mental disequilibrium'. It is a dualistic image, which indeed might contain intimations of mental imbalance. In this chaotic symbol several possibilities are not yet integrated. There is a lot of false domination and simulation of nobility. These people have to reckon with sudden very unpleasant happenings and ideas, that can spring up from their own unconscious.

The female side of this image tends to be in the foreground, as this is a feminine zodiacal sign (Cn.). On the low level of spiritual development these people often are very vain and idle, making plans that come to nothing because they are entirely self-centred (neg. Cap. opp. Cn.).

Within the 'kingdom' of the pirates, or of blind beggars, there is often a 'one-eyed' one, somewhat richer than the rest, whom they make their king or queen. Once they get hold of some money, they may spend it lavishly and behave very extravagantly.

They show much moodiness and capriciousness, combined with self-conceit. These people can switch from great goodness and generosity to a sudden cruelty which equally knows no bounds.

Janduz interprets this image with the woman distributing the jewels, but this does not seem to be in line with the lower side of Cancer, which can be very greedy and possessive (neg. Cap. opp.), while the giving out of jewels is more like Leo – the fore-axis. We give both interpretations for what they are worth.

People living this degree want to go through every emotion, from the basest cruelty to the highest ecstasy of self-giving (not of the Higher Self but of lower ego), in order to arouse deeper and deeper layers in their unconsciousness, and to bring the lower chakras into activity, especially the solar plexus, the centre of the emotions.

They may reach the stage in which they have access to so much money that they simply do not know what to do with it. They accept their riches in a rather childish, even infantile, way without true appreciation. Woe to them when they gravitate to the world, or even the underworld, drawn by their lust. The pirates may be a symbol for this underworld and may be seen as a negative streak of the collective unconsciousness, which abuses the gifts of the spirit (the jewels) and sneers at all that is precious and good. This trait may be one of the causes of 'mental disequilibrium'. The other cause is the fool (harlequin) who is forcing the destruction of his own innocent part (the sheep).

On the higher level this degree contains the true joy of a life of giving and receiving collectively (Cn.). Historically speaking piracy used not to have such a bad name as it has now. It was quite a skill and pirates received a lot of admiration – like modern members of resistance movements. Queen Elizabeth I in the sixteenth century licensed piracy on the part of her navy. When pirates had stolen a great booty, it was the custom to slaughter a sheep for a feast, and at this meal a tribute was handed ceremoniously to the pirate captain or to the queen herself. People with this degree prominent would do well to study the ethics of the Elizabethan period, and to learn from its esoteric meaning (see the Baconians, Francis Bacon Research Trust, London).

The harlequin or the fool can also have a deep meaning. This figure represents someone who does not fear to draw out the essence of truth and all the dross of the collective emotions (the cauldron) and experiences, which he may reflect as in a mirror, while playing the fool, for the advancement of learning and the self-knowledge of those who accept his teachings. The fool in fact might be the greater genius, which is the meaning of this complicated degree. There are few bystanders who can really comprehend them and give them the guidance they need. The image is full of genial but also dangerous possibilities. See note, below.

Second Image, Inner Symbol

In a moonlit fairy glade, two little elves are dancing.

Interpretation

In the first image there was the exuberant expression of the feelings (Cn.) of the woman under the pergola and the ostentatious show of male dominance over the animal world (man and sheep). All these feelings are now transformed and brought inwards on the etheric plane (the elves). Spiritual growth brings about supersensory powers, and these can only develop in man after the deeper phases of pain and grief (Cn. trine the water signs Sc. and Pi.) have been lived out. Until then one is not ready to see elves!

These people have now come to the insight that at the root of nature there are priceless energies (the jewels of the first image) activating the earth. They have arrived at co-operation with the unseen inner realms of astral riches, which look like fine-spun linen or a silk thread, becoming visible only when the lower emotions are concentrated in the solar plexus and the diaphragm becomes a mirror (the moonlight in the image), which can reflect the happenings in both the inner (the elves) and the outer world (the glade).

Such development inevitably provokes resistance in the outer world manifesting in experiences which are far from easy for these growing egos, although they now have the spiritual stamina to accept them with equanimity (unlike the predatory pirates). They learn that the dark night of the soul is, seen from the inner planes, a dance of light-energies, leading them to creativity and abundance. They will become givers, no longer foolish in their giving, but wise in the magnanimity of their inner vision. This is eternalised in the music 'The Dance of the Blessed Spirits' in Gluck's opera *Orpheus*.

Note

Harlequin   For what interest it may have, here is the Hermetic interpretation of the Pantomime. (The Chinese classic *Monkey* has similar meaning, incidentally.) Man is twofold, celestial and terrestrial. The celestial is dual, Soul and Spirit; and the terrestrial also, Body and astral Shade. These four constituent elements appear under many symbols in all sacred scriptures. In Genesis they are four rivers. In Ezekiel and the Apocalypse they are four faces of the Living Creature:

Eagle = Spirit (Jechidah); Angel or Woman = Soul (Neschamah); Lion = astral or mundane spirit (Ruach); Ox = body (Nephesch).

In the Egyptian and Greek Mysteries these four characters were the personae or masks of the sacred drama represented in cave temples where rites of initiation were performed, and this drama is the prototype of the early Christian morality play. Whether pagan or Christian, whether depicting Mithras, Bacchus or Christ, it was performed in mime at the festival of the Sun's rebirth. Vulgarised as Christmas Pantomime, this still preserves every detail and accessory of its sacred original.

The symbolism is as follows. Spirit = Harlequin; Columbine = the Soul; Clown = mundane spirit; Pantaloon = the body.

Harlequin is always masked, i.e. invisible and nameless. He wears a glittering dress of many hues, symbolising the Heavenly Bow or the Seven Divine Spirits, before the Throne of God. His rod is the symbol of Divine will and power.

Columbine is his inseparable companion. She is beautiful, obedient to his direction, but unable to work wonders except with the rod of her spouse. She is Divine only in being his.

The Clown is adroit and cunning, worldly-wise and humourous (c.f. *Monkey*). He has no power of transmutation, all his machinations are directed to gross objectives; he is the faithful presentation of the earthly mind. His colour is red. He controls his inseparable Pantaloon or body, who is feeble, supported by a stick, despicable, the fool of the play.

The ordeals of Harlequin and Columbine are none other than the Trials of the Mysteries. Their final union and eternal happiness are consummated in the 'transformation scene', which really depicts the end of all religious discipline and doctrine: the Marriage of the Spirit and the Bride.

The action of the pantomime is astronomical, depicting the

course of the Sun through the twelve zodiacal houses. Hence it is presented only at Christmas, when the solar year begins.

See *The Credo of Christendom* by Anna Kingsford. Edited by Samuel Hopgood Hart (John Watkins, 1916).

Biblical Parallels

The woman (whore) of the end-time who sits on many waters and behaves as the Queen of Heaven, trading with the businessmen of the world. See *Ezek. 16: 28; Rev. 17: 4–5; Rev. 17: 16–18;* and *Rev. 18: 3* According to some interpretations this woman is the established church, especially Rome.

Jewish tradition has it that the Queen of Sheba came to Solomon disguised as a beggar. Another tradition tells that the Saviour of the world sits at the gate dressed as a beggar. No one recognises Him.

Conception Corrected Asc. 7th Cancer

Diana Vandenberg (Blomjous)   Born 1 Apr. 1923 at 09.35 hrs. in The Hague 52°05 N, 04°18 E. CC WAK for 294 days gives 6°07 Cancer.

Dutch painter, of so-called 'magic-realistic' subjects. She is well-known for her moonlit glades with fantastic creatures, like a herd of unicorns, or paintings of the creation and cosmos. She started as a Rosicrucian and became the idol of the New Age Movement in Holland in the 1970s and 1980s.

8TH DEGREE CANCER

Outer Image, Outer Symbol

A young woman hides herself behind a column in a 'temple of Love'. She is watching a serpent in a tree preparing to drop onto a bird (a dove) on the ground.

Interpretation

This is a degree of 'abandoning of self'. Consciously or unconsciously, these people re-enact the archetypal story of Eve in her
earthy Paradise. The female side, or the soul, of those having this
degree prominent in their chart, listens to the inner serpent. In
spite of its cunning and the heavy karmic consequences to the
soul which heeds it, the Higher Self of these people does not
seem to fear the serpent, or else they are not yet awakened
to the dangers. They are convinced of the unassailability of
their feelings, so that they do not even resist inner or outer
temptations.

Women with this degree prominent may show the female
instinct to mislead men. They do not realise that they could be
gambling with their home, the happiness of the family (Cn.),
and their own personal honour. Their tournaments of love and
sex are likely to end with small profit to them.

They have a subtle power of fascination over others, with
their eagerness to make secret bonds of shared emotion, from
which the other party would do well to flee. As this is a Cancer
degree these bonds often have an emotional family background,
as between two widows, or a parent–child relationship too long
sustained. They are fond of secret ritual and the trappings of
esotericism, but they are motivated by jealous possessiveness
and the desire to dominate the emotions of others, and by this
attitude they may be fated to split communities, families and
true love relationships. Their overbearing jealousy, which may
be fed by feelings of revenge, makes them completely isolated,
inwardly as well as outwardly.

However, on a higher level these people want peace, not
strife or vengeance. This is a feminine degree, and the soul
may be only young and inexperienced (the girl). There is no
male aggression here. They are only capable of intrigue (the
serpent) and interference. What they need is not to play hide
and seek with others, which is the reflection of their own inner
structure, but to abandon their lower self completely.

Their character is a peculiar mixture of baseness and nobility.
Despite their failings, they sense that their body is God's temple,
and they can radiate love and naive innocence. Part of them is
like a white dove.

Whether they have moral resistance (the temple) against evil, depends on the entire horoscope. A man with this degree rising could more easily become a victim of a modern Eve than could a woman. On the whole the helping forces of nature are strong here (the tree), so that the real danger only comes when they are surrounded by low-centered Scorpionic people, or if they have a strong emphasis on Scorpio in their own chart (the serpent comes under Sc.).

Second Image, Inner Symbol

Rabbits in faultless human attire parade with dignity.

Interpretation

In the last image there was a lack of inner backbone (Le. fore-axis), allowing the more sensual emotions to take over. Therefore there is the need now to develop a greater inner discipline in order to become 'faultless'. The means to attain this is characterised here by the word 'imitation' (Ge.), which these rabbits demonstrate. It is a comic image, and indeed humour can bring relief from the overly intense emotions which these people sometimes engender (Cn.–Sc.–Pi., water triangle).

This group–parade is an image of intense will, and nature's willingness to evolve into something more valuable and more human.

This image is so different from the first one, and yet both have a fairy-tale atmosphere. In the first there is a reflection of the Moon in a mirror of passive absorbing energy; in the second the astral sphere of inner mysteries is hidden in this comic scene, which is transmitted by the human nervous system (Ge.), and can be controlled and disciplined by Hermetic self-knowledge. The faultless co-operation of our sympathetic and parasympathetic nervous systems is an example of how Adam and Eve, male and female, will again be faultless together in Paradise.

Biblical Parallel

'Now the serpent was more subtil than any beast of the field which the Lord God had made. And he said unto the woman, Yea, hath God said, Ye shall not eat of every tree of the garden?' See *Gen. 3: 1–24.*

Conception Corrected Asc. 8th Cancer

Paul Delvaux Born 23 Sept. 1897 at 22.00 hrs. in Antheit, Belgium, 50°32 N, 05°15 E. CC NS for 263 days at 21.52 hrs. gives 7°08 Cancer, or for 277 days at 21.54 hrs. gives 7°31 Cancer.

Belgian painter of abstract surrealism. Female figures in abstract temples and the melancholic loneliness of women are his strongest subjects. His best work, *Venus Asleep* (1944), shows Venus lying in a temple, watched by a skeleton. Monographs have been written about him in Dutch and French. Paul Elnard made a film about him in 1945.

Louis II of Bavaria (Ludwig II) Born 25 Aug. 1845 at 00.30 hrs. in Nymphenburg (Munich), 48°08 N, 11°34 E. Drowned 13 June 1886. CC NS for 284 days at 00.25 hrs. gives 7°14 Cn. (NB his grandfather Ludwig I, born on the same day, had CC 6°58 Cn. which gives them the same rising sign.)

This king was a romantic from his youth, more interested in music and theatre than in military campaigns and government. He formed an intimate friendship with Richard Wagner (see 3rd Ge.) and paid off Wagner's debts, funded the festival theatre in Munich, and then conceived the idea of building Bayreuth according to Wagner's principles. He had a dream-palace built (Swannstein), which is still a tourist attraction. He thought himself to be a reincarnation of Lohengrin. When public opinion turned against Wagner, the King was attacked for his extravagance. From 1881 the king showed severe signs of mental imbalance and violence. He was declared insane on 8 June 1886 and five days later drowned himself and his psychiatrist Dr Gudden after a fight.

This 8th Cancer certainly throws more light on this tragic king, about whom so much has been written. An outstanding illustrated biography in English is *The Dreamking* by W. Blunt (Penguin 1973).

9TH DEGREE CANCER

First Image, Outer Symbol

A young woman in the national dress of her country is walking along a path in the hills, which surround a sweet green valley where her native village lies. She is spinning with a spindle in her hands. The sun shines, and there is an atmosphere of peace.

Interpretation

Janduz calls this a degree of 'intimate satisfaction'. This image is obviously one of the most typical archetypes of Cancer. The symbols are all very Cancerian. The woman comes under Cancer as the symbol of the soul acquiring experience. National dress, as well as one's native home and homecrafts like spinning, are also symbols of Cancer. The soul is spinning the threads of life (lives). There is peace here between heaven and earth. The sun is shining over it all as the symbol of the spirit.

We find an atmosphere of inner glory here, that which every human, deep down inside, longs for. The world (Cap.) is the valley, the village. There is no great social turmoil. The environment is accepted and embedded in the good heart of nature. The mutual relationships are natural, one is known and one knows (Ge.–Cn.–Le., as the Sun side of the Cancer grail). There is happiness and health. The spirit and the soul are quiet, under control and contemplative. There is the inner conversation between the mind and the peaceful, wide-open inward side of the soul. The inner chamber is in working order (the spindle). This person can place all experiences in his (or her) astral inner home. Her industrious hands work with great patience and humility for mankind, though the result may not be spectacular. These people are turned inward, but not in negative self-defence as is often the case with Cancer.

The image lacks vigour and any hint of 'high life'. The attitude might be a bit provincial, and on the lower level there could be a non-acceptance of other life-styles, and a narrow kind of religious outlook (Sag.–Cap.–Aq.). However, in the highest instance there is spiritual self-realisation. Deep in this degree is the mother-aspect of all wisdom. Those with a planet here have to reflect on this and embody it.

Second Image, Inner Symbol

A naked little girl leans over a pond to catch a goldfish.

Interpretation

Here the valley has become a pond. In the valley are rocks, geological deposits from times immemorial. The pond contains the water of life and it reflects the heavens. Thus the down-to-earth image has evolved into a higher one.

The spinning woman may be a bit too much enwrapped within herself. Here the soul has grown into a new and young creation, a spontaneous spiritual being: a child that reaches out for the golden essences in life. Fish come under Pisces, gold is of Leo. The mystical side of nature has caught her attention and she does not see any danger in daring to reach for it. It is just a playful game, as the child will never catch the goldfish; but this childlike attitude is precious, and it completes the first image. One day she may be called to become a fisher of gold in the soul of mankind.

Biblical Parallels

'She [the virtuous woman] layeth her hands to the spindle and her hands hold the distaff.' *Prov. 31: 19.*

'Except ye be converted, and become as little children, ye shall not enter into the kingdom of heaven.' *Mt. 18: 3.*

10TH DEGREE CANCER

First Image, Outer Symbol

A majestic oak covers a large space at the edge of a stubble field in which there are still numerous sheaves. A mythical figure smilingly touches one of the sheaves full of ripe grains. It is high summer with birds on the oak tree.

Interpretation

Janduz calls this a degree of 'generous force'. It is certainly one of the most beautiful Cancer degrees. Here we have the symbol of Demeter, fruitfulness in time of abundance. Those with this degree rising, or a planet there, may be fortunate not only on the material plane, but also on the unseen (esoteric) planes indicated by the symbolic helper and protector of their harvest. The oak comes under Leo and is a symbol of the Sun. As such it was venerated by the Druids. The hand touching the grain is of Gemini, as are the birds. Thus the two sides of the Cancer grail (Ge.–Cn.–Le.) are combined in the image. This means esoterically that the opposite side (Sag.–Cap.–Aq.) can also be lived on a high level, as the entire Cancer grail is here in its purity. The true Cancer subject may evolve into a wonderful, deep, emotionally pure and imaginative person. There is no rudeness, but an extremely sympathetic, utterly feminine way of behaviour, which gives them protection. Thus we see a nature image here, that is of the highest thinkable form, reaching into heaven (Sag.–Cap.–Aq.). On a physical level, these people may be ordinary farmers who do very well, or just quiet lovers of their gardens.

Such people will find the inner wisdom of just being. Their spiritual development has no limits: they are one with God's handiwork and never hurt or damage any creature. They have something majestic in their appearance (the tree), and they may be called to manage large estates, as they are reliable and will quietly go on working, just like the farmers who went on harvesting during the air-raids of World War II, because they knew the survivors would still have to eat.

There may be loneliness in this image as some people with this degree see the unseen (the mythical figure) and may be misunderstood by more pragmatic folk. Then it is possible that they may become a little egotistical in protecting what is dear to them. On the whole they are happy and will be so even in old age.

On the highest level they may be guardians of ancient mysteries and may intuitively work on the studies of ley lines and power centres of the earth (chakras).

Second Image, Inner Symbol

A wonderful diamond is being cut into a perfect shape.

Interpretation

Rudhyar says of this image, 'Spiritual fulfilment or the acme of civilised being. Actualisation of potentialities.'

The opening of nature's chakras is shaping the light of the earth. Here in the diamond, which is of Leo, we see the Sun in a perfect form (Cap.). Hands (Ge.) have shaped nature's crystal with faith (Sag.) and discipline (Cap.) into a form which can be worn by a human being (Aq.) or used to decorate the crown (Le.) which symbolises authority over subjects (Aq.–Sat.).

Here the soul is becoming a radiant diamond. That is more than a symbol of practical value, it is the highest possible self-expression.

Biblical Parallels

Joseph's dream of the sheaves. See *Gen. 37: 7–11.*

'But they know not the thoughts of the Lord, neither understand they his counsel: for he shall gather them as the sheaves into the floor.' *Mic. 4: 12.*

A diamond is in the breastplate of judgement. See *Ex. 28: 18.*

'The sin of Judah is written with a pen of iron, and with the point of a diamond . . . Whilst their children remember their altars and their groves by the green trees upon the high hills. *Jer. 17: 1.*

Conception Corrected Asc. 10th Cancer

Isabelle Pagan   CC for 286 days at 16.41 hrs. gives 9°50 Cancer (see 14th Cn.).

11TH DEGREE CANCER

First Image, Outer Symbol

During a tempest at sea, when torrential rain beats down from dark storm clouds, a wrecked ship can be seen run ashore on the left. Beyond it to the right another ship appears to be lost.

Interpretation

Janduz calls this a degree of 'difficulties'. This is true, but only on a very low outer level. It is easy to fall into the trap of the outer image and to conclude that this person's life is a shipwreck. However, one needs to realise that this is a Cancer degree and not a Scorpio or Pisces one, although the elements of these two other water signs are present in it. Cancer is basically caring for, mothering, trying to protect. Therefore we should not overlook the unseen aspect of this image, which assumes that people with this degree on the Ascendant, or a planet prominent there, are born with the instinct to come to the rescue of others in danger, material or moral.

On the low physical level of awareness one must certainly take into account that these people may get entangled in perilous undertakings on the physical plane, or in sinister business on the psychological plane. They can only escape their fate when their plans are cancelled for them. However, for their own inner growth it is better for them to experience bankruptcy, or the wreck of their schemes, than to be spared the lessons of adversity.

People with this degree prominent are of an adventurous disposition. They love long and dangerous journeys. They feel in their element when things become risky. This may apply in all kinds of situations. On a high level they may be those characters who remain calm amid general panic, as for instance in extreme war situations or during floods and natural catastrophes.

This is a typical Cancer image, with the sea and primitive emotions coming under it. On the lower plane these people may react very primitively. Their whole life-style may be chaotic. Their outer upheavals may be the reflection of their inner inconsistency. They are at the mercy of their own moods (the waves), because they do not yet understand their emotional energies (sited in the solar plexus). On this level they will either give in to fear, or on the other hand rashly attempt deeds of bravado for which they are not qualified and which end in disaster for both themselves and others.

They need to be well-balanced (Li. sq. Cn.) and in control of themselves (Ar. sq. Cn.) before risking difficulties in their outer lives.

We can detect the entire Cancer grail in this not-so-easy degree. In its negative aspect there is lack of responsibility (neg. Cap. opp. Cn.) and formative power, no will to give out and be creative, and an absence of community spirit (Le.-Aq. fore-axis). These people are too easily depressed emotionally; they live for their own personal affections; they tend to be nervous, and they certainly need to find their true identity (Ge. behind Cn.). They may talk a lot in order to hide their lack of feeling for the real significance and direction of their life (neg. Sag. hind-axis). They need a long period of learning (Ge. behind Cn.) to attune themselves (Li. sq. Cn.), so that they can be shaped into the form (Cap.) that is meant to be theirs. A ship wrecked on a beach suggests an ending, the fulfilment of a destiny. On a high esoteric level this may mean their having come to the end of their cycle of lives.

Those with this degree who are obstinately unteachable will learn the hard way, by fatal circumstances which mirror their own irresponsibility.

On a high level they may use all these emotional upheavals to come to an artistic form, which reflects the human emotions. This brings us to the second image.

Second Image, Inner Symbol

A clown merrily caricatures all kinds of human traits.

Interpretation

Everybody knows that the greatest clowns and mimics are proverbially no strangers to sorrow, and that their humour is the badge of their triumph over suffering. They are masters in self-control. As such they represent those initiates who have won the freedom to make others see and laugh at their own stupidities.

Here also we see the Cancer grail. These people are artists in human values (Sag.) expressed in their gift of communication (Ge.). They make a sharp and subtle distinction between good and bad, right and wrong (Ge.). They understand human hearts (Le.–Aq. fore-axis). They may be inclined to get depressed (as in the first image), especially when they are too vulnerable to the inconstancy of public and critics.

People with this degree are in touch with the deepest levels of human experience (Cn.), which moreover they are able to act out. Their style is light and lively. They may wear the mask (Ar.) of an artist (Li.), to cover up their deeper inner emotions. The self-control which the first image lacks is in perfect possession here. On the negative side they can play the fool and laugh in situations where one ought to be serious and sensitive. They have to guard against becoming vulgar (neg. Cn.) by playing on the lower sensational and sexual instincts of their audiences. Their strength ought to lie in bringing out feelings of loving kindness towards others. They are born to be fund-raisers for charities and action groups.

Biblical Parallels

'. . . thrice I [Paul] suffered shipwreck, a night and a day I have been in the deep.' 2 Cor. 11: 25.

'Holding faith, and a good conscience; which some having put away concerning faith have made shipwreck.' 1 Tim. 1: 19.

12TH DEGREE CANCER

First Image, Outer Symbol

As though projected onto a night sky, we see a caduceus (the staff of Hermes encircled by two serpents) between two moons. The crescent moon at the left shows only a feeble light while the one on the right, which is almost full, shines with a magnificent brightness.

Interpretation

This is one of the most beautiful degrees in the sign of Cancer and indeed of the entire zodiac. Janduz calls this degree one of 'High Wisdom', and one could add that it is also one of esoteric knowledge, reflecting the inner light of the cosmos.

People with this degree on the Ascendant are almost always highly developed and aware of the ethereal and astral levels of their experience. They are blessed with an inner ripeness and richness accumulated throughout several lives. Outwardly they may show exceptional faculties from an early age onwards. They do not waste their talents. They may have a photographic mind (the projection), or excel in audio-visual techniques, as well as in physics and astronomy. They know how to correct the collective mistakes of the past by correcting the mistakes of their own past, and may create new things from the unseen. The moon is the symbol of Cancer. Here it is double, symbolising the old and the new phase, or the coming and going generation. The moon is also the passive, reactive side as it merely reflects the light from the sun, thus it is the symbol for the public or the masses.

On the lower level, people with this degree prominent come and go as the phases of the moon, leaving a trail of pseudo-scientific know-how behind them, that has to be reformulated by later generations. The moons are not yet full; their light is still growing. On the higher level, we can see the Cancer grail, inasmuch as there is the important interplay between light and dark, waxing and waning.

The ascending and descending (Ge.) 'snake-fire' (kundalini shakti) through the spine (Le.) when active enables one to sense the past and the inner worlds (Cn.). This is a way of experience towards holiness (Cn.) and wholeness (Ge.–Cn.–Le.). If these people achieve this state, their inner and outer mirrors (the moons) may become crystal clear (Cap.), and the caduceus then becomes the symbol of faith and healing (Sag.) and of spiritual revelation (Aq.). Thus the other side of the Cancer grail (Sag.–Cap.–Aq.) is lit up. These people have to learn, and to teach, the way to spiritual consciousness and introjection (Hermes staff), with the unification of left and right, the Ida-Pingala, and the Central River, the Shoeshoemna. Some people with this degree prominent may be great wisdom teachers, or they may excel in the fields of medicine, healing and esoteric research. They may produce ideas with the touch of genius, simply reading the astral 'mirrors' from within.

Second Image, Inner Symbol

A Chinese woman nursing a baby haloed by divine light.

Interpretation

In the first image there was only moonlight. Here it is transformed into the source of all light around the new creation. Rudhyar defines this as 'the promise to all men that God may take birth within their souls. Personality integration, illumination.' Here indeed is the Divine Imagery of the mother and child. The Christian culture knows it as the Divinity born of Mary. This is the higher side of Cancer. The inner birth of the highest in our soul is to be taken very seriously by these people (the water triangle Cn.–Sc.–Pi.).

China comes under Cancer. The loving female Chinese divinity Kwan-Yin represents the epitome of female cosmic forces, through which the light of the creation gently shines. People with this degree prominent should study the cosmological culture of ancient China, its arts and philosophy. The two images of this degree merged into one are the best example of Cancer and Divine Imagery. This astral 'imaging' and expression in form is the very essence of Cancer.

Biblical Parallels

'Moreover the light of the moon shall be as the light of the sun.' *Is. 30: 26*.

'Thy sun shall no more go down; neither shall thy moon withdraw itself: for the Lord shall be thine everlasting light.' *Is. 60: 20*. See also *Rev. 21: 23*.

Conception Corrected Asc. 7th Cancer

Albert Einstein   Born 14 Mar. 1879 at 11.30 hrs. in Ulm, 48°23 N, 10°00 E. Died Apr. 1955. CC WAK and NS for 257 days (8 month child) at 11.30 hrs. gives 11°24 Cancer.

This highly gifted genius, inventor of the theory of relativity and contributor to the quantum theory, amongst others, has opened up the possibility of explanations for many as yet mysterious phenomena in the cosmos. His Ascendant is a striking example of this 12th degree image.

See *The Universe and Dr Einstein* by Lincoln Barnett, 1950 and *Einstein, his Life and Times* by Philipp Frank, London, 1948, and other books.

13TH DEGREE CANCER

First Image, Outer Symbol

A robust man is approaching through some bushes on the left. He looks both savage and sad. Over his shoulders he has draped a recently slaughtered sheep, whose blood is still dripping. On his left (right in the picture) a big stone marks the spot where a severed human head is placed next to a dagger.

Interpretation

This is a degree of 'tragedy'. In the very sensitive sign of Cancer this is a sinister and lugubrious image. Cancer is the sign of the

instincts and emotions, and on the lowest level of awareness
these manifest in bloodshed and feuds. Absolutely everybody
has experienced and helped to create tragic examples of this
image, through their very thoughts. This is exactly what Cancer
people do not dare to bring home to their inner selves. They
often do not understand or relate to the truth 'I am guilty' or,
as a collective, 'We are all guilty of what humanity has done to
mother earth through the ages.'

For people with this degree prominent, it is very difficult to
take on personal guilt (Cap. opp.) and to have the courage to
bear a fair share in the release of the collective karma of the
human race. They tend to off-load onto other people's shoulders.
In the deep esoteric sense, they have to allow themselves to be
sacrificed like the Lamb of God 'slain for the sins of the world'.

However, they often live this degree on the physical level of
butchers, terrorists, or even hangmen; but on a more refined
level they can be excellent surgeons, or sensitive counsellors
dealing with the emotions and instincts of their clients. The
study of the psychology of instincts (hormonology) and chakras
could help them greatly, although it may be difficult for them
to bring this knowledge into harmony (Li. sq) with their own
personal feelings, and to take the full consequences (Cap. opp.)
of their insight.

The danger in this degree is the irrational way in which
these people can suddenly react with stupid and even cruel
vehemence. The next minute they may be in tears, and embracing those they have hurt by their violence; but this change
of direction is not the result of sincere reflection, and by such
uncontrolled behaviour they sever all bonds of affection. What
can make these people so dangerous is the fact that not only
are they aggressive, but they are able to exert a great and
fatal influence over others, especially those in close relation
to them. For instance, their children or partners in marriage
may go in fear of them for years, never daring to be themselves
lest they call down a new and terrible outburst on their heads.
Nothing irritates these people more than to see others going
their own way, superior to their coercion: they will struggle for
years to maintain an ascendancy. In the domestic setting they
may be very gloomy and taciturn, sulking for days (hiding in
the bushes, as it were) and nursing resentment until the next

explosion. Thus they spoil other lives around them. If given political power they may even go so far as to chop off heads (the head comes under Ar.). This they justify by reference to their position of responsibility (Cap., the stone), and they will certainly turn a deaf ear (Cap.) to any objections raised.

On a more spiritual level they may find themselves victims of terrorist action or the frenzy of an angry mob. An example is shown in the fate of Ferdinand Maximilian, Emperor of Mexico in the mid-nineteenth century.

On the highest level, as mentioned, these people may offer themselves in service to others, benefactors rather than predators on human happiness.

Second Image, Inner Symbol

A hand with a prominent thumb is held out receptively.

Interpretation

The thumb is a symbol of the Higher Self, overseeing, judging and controlling the lower passions and emotions.

Here these people, as true humans, will become witnesses of the great individual strength of the spirit they can channel. This can only happen when they have overcome the dangers of the first image, and are aware of the deepest and meanest instincts in the collective soul of humanity.

In reverse, the thumb might be turned down and this is the ancient symbol of tyrants great and small, who force through their own cruel decrees. However, as the receptive hand it is the symbol of higher receptivity and contact with the more sensitive layers in themselves and others. The thumb shows that there can be freedom (Le.–Aq. hind-axis) from sentimental illusions, and that they can truly control their lower senses. While they are developing their inner growth they may be impossible to live with, but they need to transcend their own family circle. They should guard against slander at their own table, and do nothing to further marauding of any kind.

Biblical Parallels

'Yea, for thy sake are we killed all the day long; we are counted as sheep for the slaughter.' *Ps. 44: 22.* Quoted in *Rom. 8: 36.*

'Nay, in all these things we are more than conquerors through him that loved us.' *Rom. 8: 37.*

Conception Corrected Asc. 13th Cancer

Feike Asma   Born 21 Apr. 1912 at 08.30 hrs. in Den Helder, Netherlands, 52°58 N, 04°45 E. CC NS for 286 days at 08.41 hrs. gives 12°25 Cancer.

Dutch musician, mainly known as an organist, who was popular in Canada, USA and France. There is a Feike Asma Record Library with recordings of his concerts given on the best-known church organs in the Netherlands and France.

14TH DEGREE CANCER

First Image, Outer Symbol

A magnificent star glows in a serene sky above a landscape with a bed of flowers. Nearby lies a lamb, wearing a crown also ornamented with a star.

Interpretation

This is a degree of 'renown'. It speaks in a rich symbolic language. First of all these people can be born into a famous family, and then have the chance to add fame to their already well-known name. If they are of humble birth, or born into an environment that is not spiritually inclined, they will be able to ascend above their milieu and do exceptional individual work. This is the symbol of the star. Needless to say, people with this degree prominent do well to study astronomy and what happens in the stratosphere beyond meteorological processes. They may also study plants and flower remedies, and may even discover new biological laws.

They may not be interested in the material and financial side of life. As this material side is often well cared for by the family heritage (the lamb), they can indeed leave all this behind them and become universal, knowing and teaching ancient wisdom while guided by the blazing star of intuition. They can make all things they touch radiant with starlight. They are born to dig up spiritual gold.

This degree is a highly evolved example of the Cancer grail. It has an intimate image, mild, caring and cherishing (Cn.). It also symbolises the building of a career in society (Cap. opp. Cn.), based on family tradition (Cn.). The plant kingdom, and aromas from it, come under Sagittarius, and the ancient universal knowledge hidden in this image is an indication of a strong control over the Gemini–Sagittarius hind-axis.

The light of the stars and the vastness of space in this image represent the Leo–Aquarius axis into which Cancer people need to expand. Good name and fame (Le.) are essential for these people within the wider scope of the community. The star on the forehead of the lamb is in the position of the third eye (Uranus–Aq.), which indicates clairvoyance and contact with the higher worlds. They can study the symbolism of the 'blazing star', which by some is equated with 'Shambhala' of the East. As this is a Cancer image, these people can become a mirror of the universal knowledge in the cosmos, which has been stored within the unseen layers of the earth (astral and ether, Cn.) through the centuries.

Second Image, Inner Symbol

An old man, alone, faces the darkness in the north-east.

Interpretation

Rudhyar sees in this the Wise Old Man, the archetypal figure found in all systems of symbolism. The North East to him is the occult terminology for the direction from whence the spiritual-cosmic forces enter the earth-sphere. The darkness is the intense Light invisible to our senses. So far Rudhyar.

In this image there is the immense space in which one human, as if he were Lord of Creation himself, is living, working and giving form within the universal egg (Cn.). Here is no fear, no excitement or over-enthusiasm, no unbalancing emotion. The memory storage (ether/Moon) and the brain, containing the collective memories (astral/Demeter) of this fully conscious being (Wise Old Man) are a perfect mirror (Cn.) of the cosmic space. These people are fed and filled with their own thoughtfulness, faith (Sag.) and ability to listen (Ge.). The old man knows that he receives his nobility (Le.) and inner strength by grace (Aq.). In his old age (Cap.) he also has a tremendous notion of all-round responsibility (Cap.). This is another level of the Cancer grail.

There is another esoteric reason for the symbol of the north-east. In the geographical position of 45° N, where the most ancient cultures have their origin, such as around the Aral Sea and in the Gobi desert, only the north-east is almost starless. In this direction, the emptiness of space is vast, and therefore personal and astral expansion, both ingoing and outgoing, can pulse through unhindered. At this middle latitude there is a balance between the exuberant riches, in colour and form, of vegetable life on the Equator, and the cold and icy whiteness of the polar landscape. Those with this degree prominent are facing towards the mid-point between the two extremes. They would do well to study the legendary Shambhala of Tibet, in which the human being is centred in his face. His eyes can see the Creator here on earth already, if he can sense the stars 'folded in' within all earthly things in the light of eternity. The division between light and darkness vanishes. The light does not blind, and the darkness generates phantoms no longer.

The twelve 14th degrees deal with the power of Jesus Christ to save individuals. This particular 14th image symbolises the crowned sheep as the Lamb of God, crowned in eternity and indicating that no human being shall dare to look through the north-east into the vastness of the universe, until crowned with the Christ-light. This may well be the essence of the new Aquarius–Leo Age, for which the aged man in this image is looking.

Biblical Parallels

The three wise men follow the star. See *Mt. 2: 1–10*.

'And the city had no need of the sun, neither of the moon, to shine in it: for the glory of God did lighten it, and the Lamb is the light thereof.' *Rev. 21: 23*.

The mark on the forehead. See *Rev. 20: 4*.

Conception Corrected Asc. 7th Cancer

Madame Blavatsky   CC for 293 days at 01.43 hrs. gives 13°05 Cancer. (See 30th Cn.).

Benjamino Gigli   Born 20 Mar. 1890 'a bit before midday' in Recanati, Italy, 43°24 N, 13°33 E. Died 1957. CC NS for 278 days at 11.30 hrs. gives 13°42 Cancer, or for 264 days at 11.29 hrs. gives 13°28 Cancer.

Gigli was one of Italy's greatest tenors and opera singers after Caruso (see 24th Tau.). He became the uncrowned king of the Metropolitan in New York for more than twelve years. He earned triumph in Europe where royalty gave him the highest distinctions. During World War II his magic voice enchanted German troops. When he temporarily lost his voice in 1944, German mass media faked his assassination by the Americans, to demoralise the Italians as he was that nation's darling. His triumphant career continued after the war. He played main roles in fourteen films.

Thomas Henry Huxley   Born 4 May 1825 at 09.30 hrs. (according to family bible – not 08.00 hrs. or 08.45 hrs. as given by Alan Leo in NN) in Ealing, 51°30 N, 00°05 W. Died 1895. CC NS for 270 days at 09.30 hrs. gives 13°13 Cancer, or for 284 days at 09.33 hrs. gives 13°58 Cancer.

British scientist. One of the most effective champions of Darwin's Theory of Evolution. Very concerned with education, he was occupied in campaigns against orthodox beliefs. He himself was a kind of 'scientific Calvinist', putting forward the principles of agnosticism. His grandson was the author Aldous Huxley. Amongst his work are collected essays and scientific memoirs. The 14th Cancer, second image, is appropriate for Huxley, as he spent his life in searching for the source of the creation of Man.

Isabelle Pagan Born 12 Dec. 1867 at 17.00 hrs. in Edinburgh, 55°57 N, 03°11 W. Died 10 July 1960. CC NS for 286 days at 16.59 hrs. gives 13°12 Cancer, or for 286 days at 16.41 hrs. gives 9°50 Cancer (see there). She herself favoured 10th Cancer, but that is far out of the given birth time. The 14th Cancer seems to characterise this lovely lady better.

Scottish author and astrologer. She wrote a classic on the twelve signs of the zodiac, *From Pioneer to Poet*, also *An Astrological Key to Character*, *Synthesis of Powers* and *Palace of the King*. She introduced Ibsen's plays to Edinburgh. With her interest in theosophy, she was a courageous pioneer for astrology in her day, which even *The Scotsman* in their obituary acknowledged. The symbols of the 14th Cancer fit her better than her self-chosen 10th Cancer, although the choice in this case is a difficult one.

Franz Werfel Born 10 Sept. 1890 at 23.45 hrs. in Prague, 50°05 N, 14°25 E. Died 26 Aug. 1945 in USA. CC WAK and NS for 261 days at 23.40 hrs. gives 13°51 Cancer, or for 275 days at 23.40 hrs. gives 13°56 Cancer.

Austrian author of Jewish descent. He published in Germany. He was a passionate pacifist, who, with Martin Buber, initiated the first group of active anti-militarists in World War I (1915). He married the widow of Mahler after he had moved to Vienna in 1917. A lonely 'one-world' prophet, he was far ahead of his time. He fled from the Nazis to the USA, where he died at the dawn of world peace. His writings on Paul and the Jews, and on the visionary Bernadette, together with works such as *Death*, and *The Dream City of an Emigrant*, reflect his own utter loneliness as 'world friend'. The sentiment of his poems sounds modern. This 14th Cancer image characterises him very well. The best-known films of his books are *Juarez and Maximilian* and *The Song of Bernadette*.

15TH DEGREE CANCER

First Image, Outer Symbol

Two thrones under two canopies. On the left one lies a mongrel dog asleep, and on the right one a big rat with a crown on its head lies in wait.

Interpretation

Janduz calls this a degree of 'usurpation'. It is a difficult and complicated image. There is a part that is very good here, the thrones, the canopies and the crown. However, it is corrupted and degraded by the symbols of the animals.

On what level this image is lived out depends entirely on the individual's level of spiritual development. People with this degree prominent are often either involved in, or become victims of, the basest conspiracies undermining their authority and power. The methods which they themselves use, or have to face, are abominable.

On a low level of spiritual awareness these people identify with the rats and mongrels of society, and may either overthrow their betters by guile or forcibly usurp power with the aid of the mob.

On the psychic level they are likely to possess magical power and yet deny that this is so. It could be of a base order (the mongrel dog comes under Ar.).

People with this degree on the Ascendant may suddenly get the chance to take on a leading role in a group or society (Cap. opp. Cn.), for which they are spiritually unprepared. However, they may make big mistakes and, through some twist of fate, fall suddenly from their undeserved eminence, toppled by subversion (the rats) and revolution (the dogs). This is because they themselves have neglected some of their basic duties and responsibilities (Cap. opp. Cn.) and have behaved unjustly (Li. sq. Cn.).

If they are to retain their position on the physical and inner planes, they need to seek inner wisdom, and to demonstrate its transforming effects in a change of intentions (Ge.–Sag. hind-axis). They must realise that their dominant position is held only by the grace of God (Le.–Aq. fore-axis). Otherwise they may be destroyed by opposition in the form of subversion which they are powerless to withstand, even though they are sometimes sufficiently aware of their faults to fear exposure. On the lowest level of awareness these people may be fraudulent rogues, or may themselves suffer from the machinations of impostors. More hopefully, encounters with their own conniving image in others may present them with opportunities for enlightenment.

There is the prospect of a better future in this degree. The throne is the symbol of the spiritual will to 'rule with God' (this is the meaning of *Israel* in Hebrew), to radiate goodness and to execute justice. The canopies indicate protection. As there are two thrones, they symbolise the perfect harmony between the male and female side, the yang and the yin. This can only be attained when the beasts are deposed and put in their rightful order.

Second Image, Inner Symbol

Cheerfully indolent people resting after a huge feast.

Interpretation

Marc E. Jones describes this image as 'a group of people who have overeaten and enjoyed it'. In this image the threat of a possible lapse into mob rule is turned into the simple memory of former feasts. It illustrates the alternative of withdrawal from an orgy or triumph. The dog and the rat are now just cheery idle folk enjoying themselves. This is a paradox in which all negativity turns into its opposite. The energies are transformed into positive enjoyment, and maybe even contemplation (Sag.). Here is a renewal of strength by resting and introspection (Cn.). There is the chance of new beginnings from this pause and the taking of a breather, before the duties and responsibilities of a more positive group-consciousness bring awareness of the spiritual priorities that rule over the lower instincts.

Biblical Parallels

Israel = Ruling with God. '. . . Thy name shall be called no more Jacob, but Israel: for as a prince hast thou power with God and with men, and hast prevailed.' *Gen. 32: 28.*

The Herodians had usurped the Throne of David. This is why Herod wanted to kill Jesus. See Mt. *2: 3–19.*

Conception Corrected Ascendant 15th Cancer

Alfred Adler   Born 8 Feb. 1870 at 14.00 hrs. in Vienna, 48°13 N, 16°25 E. Died 1936. CC WAK and NS for 268 days at 13.58 hrs gives 14°23 Cancer, though there is another chart which gives him 8th Scorpio for 0.15 hrs.

Austrian psychiatrist of Jewish descent, pupil of Freud and later professor in New York. He founded the school of 'Individual psychology' based on his assumption that the newly born child develops minority complexes before its first year. To compensate for this one develops a will to overpower and dominate others. This idea has been further developed in the principles of Rebirthing in the USA in the 1980s. Symbolically one could see Adler's therapeutic method evolve from this 15th degree Cancer.

Benjamin Britten   Born 22 Nov. 1913 at 19.00 hrs. in Lowestoft, 52°27 N, 01°46 E. Died 4 Dec. 1976. CC NS for 264 days at 18.55 hrs given 14°32 Cancer.

One of Britain's best-known modern composers. *Peter Grimes, Billy Budd, The Turn of the Screw* and *Death in Venice* are amongst his sixteen operas. His *War Requiem* (1962) commemorates Coventry's bombed cathedral. His motif was 'A poet can only warn'. He had great concern for the underdog. Although it is not obvious at first glance, he is an interesting example of a highly evolved 15th Cancer. He lived and worked together with his friend the singer Peter Pears.

16th Degree Cancer

First Image, Outer Symbol

A modern Samson is trying to overthrow the columns of a temple. At his feet, on the steps, lies a dead lion and lower down still a hedgehog is putting its little paw on a dead serpent.

Interpretation

Janduz calls this a degree of 'sudden triumph'. People with this degree prominent must travel a long road of inner and outer struggle. The triumph comes as the result of the last efforts. Without knowing it, and often against their will, these people, while they are involved in the process of fighting, hold out delusions to others.

They may be amiable and subtle, even too clever for those who do not understand them or their activities, on any plane. They can mislead their adversaries. Conscious of their calling, they like to wear a mask. Those around them, however, will learn one day that it is unwise to antagonise or injure these people, for they will return the hurt, and do not care how deeply they wound. Their motto is: 'Those who play at bowls must mind the rules.'

Those with this degree rising are physically strong (the Samson), even invincible, and can be good at many sports. When they are spiritually aware they are distinguished by a superiority and authority that springs from profound inner wisdom. They know the two pillars of good and evil (Ge. hind-axis, compare Ida and Pingala or Boaz and Jakin).

Bent on high endeavour, they can destroy their foes with ease. They know when to attack and when to defend, and they have perfect confidence in the justice of their cause.

They should save their tremendous energy for the right moment, and they must be above all forms of deception. They may meet many difficulties, but these should not discourage them. They have to cut out all jealousy and envy (Sc., the dead serpent), and conquer any obstacle in the way of their inner and outer victory.

They may possess a kind of bullying optimism which stops at nothing: this is the secret of their strength. They are not content with momentary results, but want to go even further, with eyes fixed on their goal (Ge.–Sag. hind-axis), because they know they are destined to succeed. By this ascent they conquer their own failings (the dead animals on the steps): every meanness (the serpent), and all arrogance (the dead lion). The soft side of their character needs to come out (the hedgehog's paw). They may remain a bit prickly and caustic (the hedgehog), but that is their normal self-protection after having been shown the highest way it is humanly possible to go. Under this shield of protection they are sensitive and full of compassion (Cn. trine Pi.) towards those around them, who have not as yet attained their own victories over the lower animal instincts (Neg. Cn.).

These people need to ascend step by step in inner growth. On the highest spiritual level they are able to forget their personal self in the struggle for a common ideal, a group or a country. In the battle of life they win the right to become masters of their destiny.

Second Image, Inner Symbol

A man holds a scroll. Before him a square is outlined.

Interpretation

Rudhyar changed this image in his 1973 edition to 'a man studying a mandala in front of him with the help of an ancient book'. He mentions that 'the square as the foundation of the mandala potentially encloses diverse contents' and 'symbolises the integration of opposing trends and multiple bipolar energies'.

The man of the first image no longer needs a temple to crush with his abundance of energy: he is now filled with wisdom. His struggle being over, he can show the world that he has returned to the root – the root pattern of his being.

These people are both the man and the mandala (square). They can attain full control over their inner and outer life. The square contains the number 4 and thus can be a symbol of completion in the world of matter. The square could also mean that there is still a struggle (in astrology the square symbolises obstacles to be overcome with pain and struggle), but these people are now so far advanced that the struggle can be that of others, whom they are now qualified to help by their advice and example. They let the Great Warrior work through them absolutely harmoniously and freely.

Biblical Parallel

Samson destroys the pillars of the house of the Philistines. See *Judg. 16: 21–30*.

Conception Corrected Ascendant 16th Cancer

Vincent van Gogh   Born 30 Mar. 1853 at 11.00 hrs. in Zundert, Netherlands, 51°52 N, 04°28 E. Died (suicide) 29 July 1890. CC WAK and NS for 271 days at 10.32 hrs. gives 15°56 Cancer. Willem Koppejan made a special study of Vincent van Gogh and came to the conclusion that 16th Cancer was his rising sign, although the register of births gives 11.00 hrs. This is one of the disputed Ascendants. For 299 days at 11.06 hrs. there is a CC of 22°18 Cancer, which seems unlikely.

Dutch painter of world fame. His method of painting had a revolutionary effect on generations of painters. His life was dramatic. He chose poverty. He lived with prostitutes and had to undergo psychiatric treatment in several institutes in France. He is remembered for cutting off one of his ears and putting it in the post. He shot himself in the south of France. His life is well documented through numerous letters written to his brother Theo. His paintings are now worth millions. There is a Van Gogh Museum in Amsterdam. His dramatic self-sacrificing power seems to be reflected in 16th Cancer.

Jan Hendrik Oort   Born 28 Apr. 1900 at 08.30 hrs. in Franeker, 53°11 N, 05°32 E. CC NS for 281 days at 08.26 hrs. gives 15°10 Cancer.

Dutch astronomer and researcher with an international reputation. He was Director of Leyden's Observatory. A planetoid has been named after him. His main research was in the Milky Way. He crusaded against astrology, which he regarded as 'unscientific nonsense', as forcefully as one might expect from someone with this degree rising.

17TH DEGREE CANCER

First Image, Outer Symbol

Under a night sky, streaked by lighting, a man is walking fearlessly from left to right, his eyes fixed on a piece of azure sky on the far right. He does not notice, on his right, a woman seated at the foot of a tree who is anxiously wrapping her clothes around her.

Interpretation

This is a typical Cancer degree, as it embodies an archetypal symbol of the spirit (man) and the soul (woman) on their way through the higher astral and lower ethereal worlds. The spirit (the man) is bravely taking the lead, overcoming the storms and the inner and outer difficulties, while the lower emotional self (the woman) is enveloping herself and protecting her inner mirror against the outer happenings and emotional disturbances.

According to Janduz, this is a degree of 'illumination'. Flashes of ideas and revelations are raining down on the spirit of this person. He (or she) is a spiritual leader, full of new plans and true ideas, not in one field only but in many (several flashes of lightning).

This person may serve as a chalice for great and new things which the angels wish to bring to humans, and may found a new life-style and control forces which have been called forth through a new age (the azure sky). Therefore he not only revolutionises old concepts, but also finds in them significant new ideas to reveal to humanity.

On a high level, this person goes through life like a raging storm. His creations leave a blazing trail behind him like a flaming whip. He may even create a new form of art. He has a charming nature, but never confuses or misleads people, always remaining aware of heaven (the azure sky) in others. Those with this Ascendant or a planet prominent, will always 'be someone', as others cannot fail to notice them. Success and honour, from above and below, are guaranteed in the end.

The weak side of this character is personified in the anxious sitting woman, who is showing the common negative reaction to fear. This is shown in the Cancer grail – the passive reaction of the Moon, the cerebral arguing about one's own difficulties (Ge.) and the preoccupation with one's own children and created forms (Le.). Yielding to the woman within, this Higher self loses sight of its great goal and highest destination (the azure sky above her), bends back towards a life-style of lesser quality, and is even inclined to sacrifice its high angelic intuitions.

This person's inclination to sink into comfortable complacency should be renounced completely, or the result will be a neurotic urge (Ge.) to do good (Le.) without discrimination. Then he may sell himself to some bogus charity, only to discover too late that he has betrayed his highest task as a human being. For all his good faith, he has put himself into the hands of dishonest persons and so allowed the dissipation of his own capacities. Rebel he may, but escape he cannot: he has forfeited all power to direct his own course.

Second Image, Inner Symbol

The archetypal soul becomes filled with life-contents.

Interpretation

Here all values and experiences are given form within a perfect inner soundboard. The soul has integrated all spiritual (Le.) knowledge.

This person has overcome the storms and has now ascended towards the Creator and is in living contact with the source. He is filled with life-contents and may draw on this for the good of mankind. The soul's archetype is to give in overflowing abundance from the source which is God for the salvation of mankind.

Biblical Parallel

The woman at the wayside, as the princess in disguise, could be seen as Tamar about to seduce Judah, the descendant of the royal line, whereby the future royal line was secured (Cn.–Cap.). See *Gen. 38: 14–30*.

Nature Parallel

The old straight track or hidden ley lines (the woman), through which nature is energised, accompanied by unusual weather phenomena, is food for the archetypal soul. See Paul Screeton *Quicksilver Heritage* (Thorsons).

18TH DEGREE CANCER

First Image, Outer Symbol

Furniture, *objets d'art* and exotic flowers (to the right) surround a man and two women playing dice. In the background is a chalice with fumes rising from it, probably of incense.

Interpretation

Janduz calls this a degree of 'ineptitude'. She says that these people are imprudent, full of plans which are exotic (the flowers), imaginative and extravagant. They might easily lose their money through gambling, and be ruined by women or unfortunate speculations.

This is indeed a degree of danger, as there is a hunger (Cn.) for exotic luxury and peculiar sensations. On a low level these people may be fascinated by the occult, and become drugged or intoxicated (incense) by their own primitive sensitivity, mistaking glamour for reality: this is so often a danger for Cancer. They still have to learn (fore-axis for Cn.) true awareness (Le.) and angelic interaction (Aq.). Their intuition is often impure, and their beliefs are too open to negative influences. Their sitting together often has some sort of 'brooding' quality, sometimes bizarre and original, but producing little Wisdom. The risk is that they may put themselves under a lower kind of fate (the dice), which is Saturn of Capricorn, the opposite sign to Cancer.

On a higher level they will learn to accept in full consciousness their own position in the development of their incarnation. They will stop playing with fate and endangering their health by misuse of exotic herbs, and will suddenly realise that they too are bound by the higher laws of the Hierarchies. Then exceptional revelations (Aq.) may come which they can no longer hide from themselves. They will see through the madness of their time – the time that surrounds them. They may begin to flower and open themselves to contacts with the higher inner astral-ethereal worlds (Cn.). The casting of the dice becomes a religious happening. Then there comes the alignment of the spirit (the man), the astral inner body and the emotional outer body (the two women), so that creativity for mankind (Le.–Aq.) can enter. Through the control of their nervousness (neg. Ge.) and apathy (neg. Sag.) it becomes possible for them to learn true wisdom and the proper use of herbs for healing (Ge.–Sag.).

Second Image, Inner Symbol

In a crowded barnyard a hen clucks among her chickens.

Interpretation

Here is the simple closed cycle of Cancer that appeals to every child, with the hen brooding on her eggs, the eggs becoming chickens and their mother making those noises of satisfaction. It typifies the eternal repetition of the cycles of creation. The chicken is never abandoned by its Creator (Le.). Listening attentively (Ge.) one can hear (Cap.) the chicken growing in its egg (Cn.). The laws of this development, under the constant supervision of the Creator, are veiled by the people of the first image, who in their gambling with life are interfering with the right course of nature. Even their games of seeming chance are bound by these rigid laws (Le.–Aq.).

People with this degree prominent will suddenly be en-lightened in this way and become as simple and humble as the creatures in this image. The meaning is that spirit, soul and body have to become one in a closed circuit.

The drug-intoxicated Higher Self of the first image has to learn the lesson of simply caring for and respecting nature as it is. A chicken is a chicken, and feeding them mash will not make them anything else. One can hardly imagine a pot-smoking hen who would dare to veil, much less change, the laws of evolution.

Chickens and hens come under Aries; they represent a new impulse of life, simple joy uninduced by artificial or hypnotic means (Ar.–Pl.). The second image corrects the misconceptions and misbehaviour of the first, enjoining adult responsibility and humble dedication to the laws of continuing generation.

Conception Corrected Ascendant 18th Cancer

Henry Rider Haggard   Born 22 June 1856 at 05.10 hrs. in Bradenham Hall, 52°38 N, 00°51 E. Died 14 May 1925. CC WAK and NS for 261 days at 05.06 hrs. gives 17°50 Cancer.

English novelist. He was in South Africa at the time when the Transvaal was returned to the Dutch (1877). His books on the English defeat there became popular. In *King Solomon's Mines* he suggested that these were at the Zimbabwe Ruins (1886). Another fantastic African story was *She* (1887). Back in England he wrote about rural and agricultural questions. He remained an eccentric with an interest in Zulu rites and other exotic customs.

See his autobiography *The Days of My Life* (1926) and *H. Rider Haggard, a Voice from the Infinite*, by P. B. Ellis (1978).

Charles A. Jayne   Born 9 Oct. 1911 at 22.39 hrs in Jenkintown, USA, 39°54 N, 75°08 W. Died 31 Dec. 1985. CC NS for 282 days at 22.44 hrs. gives 17°01 Cancer.

American astrologer mainly known for his own magazine *In Search* and his books on *epochs* and directions.

Heinrich Pestalozzi   Born 12 Jan. 1746 at 16.00 hrs. in Zurich, 47°22 N, 08°32 E. Died 1826. CC NS for 278 days at 16.00 hrs. gives 17°10 Cancer.

Swiss philosopher, writer and teacher, unknown during his life, but famous after his death for his educational theories and schools, and for the Pestalozzi village in Switzerland. He and his friends stood out against corruption, even going on hunger strike. He dressed against the fashion of his time. Helping others financially, he went bankrupt himself. He took criminal children in and taught them respect. Again he lost everything through war. He was seen as an eccentric, but at last the government gave him a castle, in which he started an international community. At the age of 81 he lost a court case owing to false accusations. He lost everything, including the castle, but started again on a farm, taking in neglected children.

N. Rimsky–Korsakov   Born 18 Mar. 1844 (NS) at 10.30 hrs. in Tichwin Nowgorod, Russia, 59°36 N, 33°35 E. Died 1908. CC NS for 292 days at 10.36 hrs. gives 17°16 Cancer.

Russian naval officer and composer of operas and symphonic poems of the Romantic period. He often based his themes on Russian folk-songs and dances. His music has great sentiment and colour. His works include *The Maid of Pskov, Sheherezade* and *Prince Igor*.

Dylan Thomas   Born 27 Oct. 1914 at 09.00 hrs. in Swansea, 51°38 N, 03°57 W. Died 1953. CC WAK and NS for 262 days at 09.09 hrs. gives 17°09 Cancer.

Welsh poet and lecturer. Bohemian, addicted to women and alcohol, he became a legend, especially in the USA where he tragically died during a lecture tour. One can find much of the 18th degree Cancer in his work.

See *The Life of Dylan Thomas* by Constantine Fitzgibbon (1965).

19TH DEGREE CANCER

First Image, Outer Symbol

On a small stage, surrounded by columns on which are fixed alternately weapons of war and musical instruments, a man in full dress uniform is standing with a lance in his right hand and a flute in his left. At his right side on the stage are a fencing gauntlet and a violin.

Interpretation

This is a degree of 'excellent performance'. It depends entirely upon the underlying horoscope whether the execution will be military or musical, or both together. On a low level this could be a person whose arrogance (Le.) is camouflaged (Cn.) by much talk. Naive persons may be attracted by the commanding physical appearance and the false brilliance (lance), only to fall victim to his or her unscrupulousness. Such people may preach a libertarian (Aq.) gospel which leads both them and others to their moral undoing. They then become ridiculous in their swift transitions from one role to another, between moods of aggressive self-confidence and timorous misgivings.

On a higher level, of course, this could represent an excellent talent for a professional actor, and people with this degree prominent are often very gifted as performers, animators or leaders of orchestras. Their intelligence can be subtle, but it has to be brought onto a higher plane. They can have an hypnotic influence on their audience (the flute of Pan). Their musical talents have to be transformed into the highest mystical knowledge of the musical laws of the universe (water triangle Cn.–Sc.–Pi.). Then they may become militant as a fighter for peace and healing.

It is a degree full of distinction and aristocracy, though rather decadent. It is important to realise that this is a Cancer degree in which public opinion about those living it can change overnight, causing them to fall into disgrace. Their outward career is always at risk from stratagem. Although they may easily become famous, they have always to be aware of the danger of becoming insincere and pandering to the fickleness of the masses.

The columns indicate that they build their life on strong foundations (Cap., other side of the Cn. grail), but even these may only be the outer props on their stage of life.

Second Image, Inner Symbol

A frail and aristocratic girl weds a proletarian youth.

Interpretation

Rudhyar writes here 'Blending of the cultural fruition of the past with the impetuousness of new blood.' Here the somewhat decadent tendency of the first image is elevated into a new unity of love above social differences, which is the Leo–Aquarius fore-axis into which Cancer has to develop, leaving show and outer man-made divisions between male and female behind them. Here is the positive creative male aspect married to the receiving female aspect, so that this Higher Self may truly become lamp and mirror in one, and demonstrate this unity in life. The underdeveloped young consciousness (the youth) has made an inner bridge to the age-old heritage of the collective unconscious folk-soul.

Conception Corrected Ascendant 19th Cancer

Richard Strauss   Born 11 June 1864 at 06.00 hrs. in Munich, 48°08 N, 11°33 E. Died 8 Sept. 1949. CC NS for 291 days at 06.11 hrs. gives 18°25 Cancer.

German composer since the age of 6 and pianist when only 4. Conductor in Munich and Berlin. Composer of *Don Juan*, *Tod und Verklärung* (1891), *Der Rosenkavalier* (1911) and many other operas, orchestral works and songs. He became a controversial figure in World War II as he was friendly with the Nazi leaders, but was proved innocent by a 'de-nazification court' a year before he died. He was married to a very prominent singer. The 19th degree Cancer fits this showman like a glove.

20TH DEGREE CANCER

First Image, Outer Symbol

A man, wearing livery and mounted on a thoroughbred, is about to ride out by the open gate of a great house surrounded by a fence. Near that gate a watchdog, seated on a cart, looks with friendly eyes at the horse.

Interpretation

This is a degree of 'service'. It is in the sign of Cancer, not in Virgo which is noted for service. The symbol of a manor-house, fenced in, comes under Cancer. This symbol indicates that people with this degree rising have access to great inner wealth. They need to be inwardly very well organised (Cap. opp. Cn.): a disorganised manor cannot survive social pressures.

These people have spiritual knowledge and radiance (Le. fore-axis). They possess a sensitive mirror within, which reflects only beauty and truth. It can reflect all the highest qualities of the planets, which correspond to human 'organs' in the astral and ethereal plane, as well as in the physical body.

The horse is a thoroughbred. As a symbol it comes under Sagittarius (hind-axis). Here it means that the ability to think is strong. These people can expand their inner space by a magnificent development of positive thinking. The conscious awareness (the man) is dressed as a servant, thus conforming with the truth 'Whosoever will be chiefest among you, shall be the servant of all'. In other words, he who does the real work and the serving in a manor-house is the true owner, and the first man in it on the inner plane. Often nowadays the actual landowner does do all the hard work himself, and so we may assume here that the man on horseback, in livery, is the landlord himself. This means that the consciousness of these people is working on the inner and outer levels simultaneously, which is the essence of Cancer. The spirit (the man) moves out of his house (Cn.) in order to make contact with the people in the world (Aq.). He wants to give (Le.) and show his aristocratic spirit and radiate his positive thinking into the hearts of others. The gate is open. There are no mental blockages.

The dog on the cart symbolises another side of these people. Such is their royalty of spirit, they could even adopt the disguise of a watchdog on a humble cart. The dog is the symbol of Aries–Pluto. It indicates the need for demasking (Ar. sq. Cn.), for the relinquishing of outer glamour, allowing these people to become what they really are, simple guardians at the gate (the watchdog). This may be their true destiny.

One might interpret this degree symbol on a lower level and see the man moving away from the manor as a thief, disguising himself as a servant, who has stolen the horse and is going to make a big display with it. In other words, this psyche is not genuine: these inflated egos imitate the talents of others. This can happen especially when Pluto in their chart takes up a difficult position.

However, this level is not often met with in this degree. Such people tend to have a very strong and beautiful horoscope with many hidden capacities and riches. They can be like kings in servants' clothes, who have to pass Cerberus, the guardian dog of the underworld, before they can proceed through the gate to a full initiation into spiritual life.

On the mundane level they can be simple people who love a rather obscure life, in which, however, they are useful. They study, and develop themselves with an absolute devotion. One may find them as civil servants, wardens, guards, nannies and grooms. Their main task is to overcome the excessive shyness which causes them to disguise themselves as servants, and to face the world openly, showing who they really are.

Second Image, Inner Symbol

A group of serenaders make merry in a Venetian gondola.

Interpretation

These people are gathered together for mutual enjoyment. The celebration is seemly and not overdone. They are representative of ancient culture, and they have chosen romantic surroundings for their game of life. Having found the group-soul through love and service they can now combine (the serenade) in joyful thanks to the Creator. This can only be when these people become completely free from any delusive ideas of status (master and man), and have attained happiness and harmony throughout their being.

Biblical Parallels

'And whosoever of you will be the chiefest, shall be servant of all.' *Mk. 10: 44*. See also *Mk. 10: 43; Mt. 20: 27* and *23: 11*.

Conception Corrected Ascendant 20th Cancer

Alexander Fleming   Born 6 Aug. 1881 at 02.00 hrs. in Lochfield, Scotland, 55°37 N, 04°18 W. Died Mar. 1955. CC NS for 256 days at 02.00 hrs. gives 19°16 Cancer.

Scientist, famous as the discoverer of penicillin. He started as a business man, but studied medicine later. As a military physician in World War I he was shocked by the high mortality from infection among the wounded, and decided to devote his life to research into prevention. 'By chance' he discovered penicillin in 1928, but had to wait till 1944 to see it in widespread use as a last resort. He never accepted any money for his discovery, sending all funds to charities.

Jean Giraudoux   Born 29 Oct. 1882 at 21.00 hrs. in Bellac, France, 46°10 N, 01°02 E. Died 1944. CC WAK and NS for 271 days at 21.14 hrs. gives 19°34 Cancer.

French author and playwright. While in diplomatic service he travelled in many different countries. These experiences are reflected in his work. The main themes are taken from Greek mythology, or from the countryside in the province where he was born and to which he always returned. One can easily see the 20th degree Cancer reflected in him.

Benjamin Peret Born 4 July 1899 at 05.00 hrs. in Reze, France, 47°13 N, 01°33 W. CC NS for 283 days at 05.05 hrs. gives 19°21 Cancer, or for 297 days at 05.07 hrs. gives 19°56 Cancer.

French *poète maudit*, specialising in evil and one of the main representatives of surrealism.

21ST DEGREE CANCER

First Image, Outer Symbol

A waning moon amidst clouds gives a feeble glow on the sea, where a dismasted ship is floating. On the left is an abandoned cart, which is about to sink into the sand.

Interpretation

Janduz calls this a degree of 'instability'. She speaks about double fatality, with the menace of unhappy voyages and the loss of one's home and haven. Indeed as this is a Cancer degree, this person is often in a state of chaos – either on the inner, emotional level or within the immediate environment, which is on the decline (the waning moon).

He does not think of the consequences (Cap. opp.) of his ways. Often he doesn't think enough about the results, which he ought to plan for (Le.) intelligently (Ge.), and there is the danger of being dragged into projects without having consulted his own inner voice. Creation should not be gambled with high-handedly.

On the physical level, the person with this Ascendant has to stabilise himself first, build his own faith, and make worthwhile plans to benefit other people (the opp. part of the Cancer grail Sag.–Cap.–Aq.). He moves too easily with the tides (Cn.) and then becomes a victim of them.

In this degree we can easily detect the two other water signs, Scorpio and Pisces. There is the death and decay of Scorpio, and the victimisation and sacrifice of Pisces. Compare this image to the image of 21st Pisces, where the sea is calm and the boat without oars. In this Cancer phase there is no symbol of a human being, thus Higher Self here is not yet aware, or in control, but can be taken over by lower elements. These people may choose the wrong partner for outward show, and then be left with the shipwreck of family life; or be emotionally tied to an unstable or mentally disturbed person. (The moon and the tides come under Cancer.) There is a lot of hysteria (Cn.) in and around this image, and on the outward plane also, their own vehicle (the cart) is full of it. They can circle emotionally round and around a happening in the past, or they can become the plaything of circumstance, for instance in show business, in a war situation, or in a healing relationship.

Depending on the entire horoscope, and whether the Sun, Moon or another planet is in this degree, this person may develop a motherly concern for social misfits and failures. Thus they may be heads of caring institutions, or healers, whom everybody adores, but this level is reached only when they bring inner and outer order into their lives. If they do not do this they are caught between Scylla and Charybdis, which Greek myth they would do well to know by heart. Their wishes are difficult to realise, and they may have to learn the moral implicit in this degree, that their life is one of emptiness (the cart) until empty of self, and until they acquire the wisdom not to rely on outer show. This is the cosmic lesson for every Cancerian.

Second Image, Inner Symbol

A prima donna sings to a glittering audience.

Interpretation

This seems to be the reverse of the first image, but it is in fact the 'inside-out' of the same symbol. This image is the elevation of the other. This 'first lady' is the centre of the emotions of the entire cast and audience, but unlike the situation when the boat was tossed around, the angry sea has become a sea

The failure inherent in the first image, with its sad solitude, is turned into success, and the power to command great popularity. The singer is giving of her talent to the delight and inspiration of her hearers, an interchange of values that was entirely absent from the first image. In the most threatening situations, or amongst the mentally disturbed, the voice of a singer can work wonders to restore the radiance of hope: there is great educational and spiritual power in this second image, with the supreme opportunity for those who have thus triumphed over adversity, to serve the public good.

Their star at last may rise and be recognised. Their influence on crowd psychology may prove greatly beneficent.

Biblical Parallel

Jesus calming the storm and the raging of the water. See *Mk. 4· 37–41; Lk. 8: 23–25.*

Conception Corrected Ascendant 21st Cancer

Salvador Dali Born 11 May 1904 at 08.45 hrs. in Figueres, Spain, 72°16 N, 02°57 E. Died 23 Jan. 1989. CC WAK and NS for 264 days gives 20°57 Cancer.

This extravagant genius painted many magic surrealistic scenes of abandoned boats and deserted beaches. He himself functioned as a 'prima donna' within his style of painting and in his extraordinary life.

See *Dali by Dali*, H.N. Abrams (New York, 1970), and *The Trutine of Hermes* by Niek Scheps (Element books, 1990).

22ND DEGREE CANCER

First Image, Outer Symbol

At the right a man is standing on the top of a hill, with a 'staff of authority' in his hand. His face is lit up by the setting sun on his left. He does not notice the torrent of turbulent water raging below him.

Interpretation

Janduz calls this a degree of 'vicissitudes'. This word does indeed apply to one of the aspects of Cancer, that of experiencing and undergoing diverse circumstances. This phase is symbolised here by the wild current rushing down the valley, with which this character may identify himself (or herself). Higher up in this human being there is, however, a strong consciousness (the man). He is an initiate of the sun, an old soul at the end of a life-cycle (the setting sun) with an excellent capacity for leadership (the staff), and strong with hope and confidence in the future. He is enlightened and radiates health and sunshine. He is also an initiate into the wisdom (Ge.) and leadership (Le.) of the grail (Cn. grail).

One is inclined to identify in this image with the magical priestly figure, who is at one with the sun. He (or she) could have a Christlike consciousness indeed, but the rushing torrent in the valley is part of his emotional make-up as well. The lower elements rebel inside this person, and the glorious strong start of their life may sink into a sea of depression. They may mature early, but in later circumstances they cannot cope. They may abandon all responsibility – domestic and professional – at the height of their career, and symbolically or even physically take to the life of a hermit. They may become great searchers of nature, perhaps as geographers, physicists or meteorologists. They are loners and seek the most dangerous places. They may disappear so completely from the social scene that one cannot even trace their steps, but this is their birthright. They know (the Sun) where their true happiness lies. They have an intense will to return to the spirit – the father – and to follow the call of their inner voice.

Physically and emotionally they have to be aware of the dangers of the swamps and moors. They are often preoccupied with thoughts of doom and apocalyptic catastrophes. They may research into morbid subjects, on which they have a good grip and can speak with authority.

On a very high level they are the prophets of the coming Armageddon, or of the restitution of the 'valley of dry bones'. Identified with the man, they are seers; identified with the torrent, they rebel against God's judgements. Their life is embedded in the vicissitudes of their national or provincial circumstances (or karma), in the light of the infallible prophecies of the Almighty judgements.

Note

This image has been 'seen' as Joseph of Arimathea landing on what is now Wearyall Hill in Glastonbury, UK, and planting his staff as a symbol of Christ's authority and His return to the Isles.

Second Image, Inner Symbol

A young woman dreamily awaits a sailing-boat approaching her.

Interpretation

Is the soul awaiting a message of hope from the promised land, or waiting to be liberated and taken from her vale of tears into a higher state of being?

The man of the first image had to experience (Cn.) the moving away from the lower planes of disturbance, and learn to stand above them. Here in the second symbol there is a clear longing for the yet greater adventure with unknown destiny, which is represented by the sailing-boat and its contents. The soul (the woman) is called by the unseen skipper who is approaching, and she dreams of a new existence after the end of this (her) world. The consciousness of the former image bravely takes the consequences (Cap.), and here the soul is also taking what comes, patiently waiting, and made young by her happy dreams of the future surprises of life (Le.–Aq.).

It is an archetypal degree of noble and courageous being, typical of all great men and women. These people are certainly not 'commoners'.

Biblical Parallels

Moses' song of God's glory, casting Pharaoh's hosts into the Red Sea. See *Ex. 15:.*

The Vale of Megiddo (Armageddon). See *Rev 16: 16–21.*

The valley of dry bones. See *Ezek. 37.*

'. . . for with my staff I passed over this Jordan.' *Gen. 32: 10.*

'Yea though I walk through the valley of the shadow of death, I will fear no evil: for thou art with me; thy rod and thy staff they comfort me.' *Ps. 23: 4.* See also *Ps. 46: 1–2.*

23RD DEGREE CANCER

First Image, Outer Symbol

On the left a man is yawning and stretching himself and about to fall beside his comrade, who is already lying down at full length asleep in the sunshine. Their tools and building instruments lie neglected on the ground and are about to be stolen by two thieves on the right.

Interpretation

Janduz rightly calls this a degree of 'negligence'. It is indeed a negative image in the sign of Cancer. On a low level these are lazy people and completely irresponsible. This is the negative, opposite side of Cancer's great sense of duty (Cap. opp.). In their past, shown on the left, they have neglected the tools and talents with which their Creator entrusted them. Now they let opportunities slip, and procrastination takes their fortune from them.

If these people identify with the thieves, they do not hesitate to steal the credit for other people's efforts, and even the material rewards. In this low expression of the image, they may go through life with a constantly spiteful attitude, even despising what they steal.

On a higher level, however, a strong Higher Self can work out some good with this symbol. Sleep is a very mysterious happening. During sleep the developed soul goes through inner experiences in which he (or she) is insulated from the lower 'waking' world of maya or illusion. The sleeping man, warmed by the sun, can sleep with full confidence in the vigilance of his comrade or guardian angel, while his higher work is carried on, so that talents pertaining to the lower self can be safely abandoned and the business of the outward world left to others. They are not the idle fellows they may seem. However, this high level of expression is a great rarity.

Second Image, Inner Symbol

A group of intellectual individuals meet for discussion.

Interpretation

The word 'discussion' means 'to break to pieces'. Intellectuals come under Gemini. They may be full of wisdom, or be hypercritical (Vi.) and abusers of the living Word. Discussion is the nucleus of science (Vi.), and can be fruitful or completely stagnant. At face value these two images do not fit each other, but they do in higher astrological symbolism.

On the lower level this second image is certainly an elevation of the first. In discussions and intellectual exchanges of ideas (the hind-axis of Ge.–Sag. of Cn.), these individuals often steal each other's ideas, or disrupt and even falsify them. Innocent and dreamy personalities are especially likely to be the victims of such plunder.

However, on the high level, through mental training (the tools), there may develop a relationship of master and disciple between the sleeping men under the sun. They mirror in their inner bank of memories (astral-ethereal body is Cn.) the spiritual knowledge of the Sun, the essence of their being, which they may be able to express in words. This is the image of 'let us reason together'. One cannot discuss anything, with the men of the first image, as they are too filled with their own petty personal experiences, and too primitive to be capable of reason. Stealing comes under Gemini, but in this second image the personal bias and selfish lust for possessions can turn into a loving (Le.) will to know and understand one another (Aq.).

For this they need to develop spiritual awareness and redeem all their past neglect of the needs and talents of their neighbour (Ge.).

This degree is a lesson in the danger of judging according to face value. What seems negative on the outside may become positive on the inside. This is an important esoteric principle in the sign of Cancer, and the interpretation of zodiacal imagery in general. There are no bad or good images as such. It always depends upon the Higher Self in what way or with what kind of energy the symbol is played out.

Biblical Parallels

'Let no man deceive you by any means: for that day shall not come, except there come a falling away first, and that man of sin be revealed, the son of perdition;' *2 Thess 2: 3*. Negligence is the 'falling away' in the end times.

'But foolish and unlearned questions avoid, knowing that they do gender strifes.' *2 Tim. 2: 23*.

We cannot discuss the Most High, supreme in His justice and might, whose goodness will never do wrong. Then therefore should we reverence Him; He regards not the learned.' (Ferrar Fenton) See *Job 37: 23–24*.

Conception Corrected Ascendant 23rd Cancer

A.J. Cronin   CC for 268 days at 03.44 hrs. gives 22°45 Cancer; see 24th Cancer.

A. C. Swinburne   CC for 266 days at 10.44 hrs. gives 22°31 Cancer; see 24th Cancer.

Peter Ustinov   Born 16 Apr. 1921 at 11.00 hrs. in London, 51°32 N, 00°00 W. CC NS for 274 days at 11.03 hrs. gives 22°43 Cancer. (Conception in mid-Europe while his parents migrated from Russia.)

British–American author, playwright, producer. Did various

other work. Cosmopolitan.

See his autobiography, *Dear Me* (Heinemann).

Jaap Wagemaker   Born 6 Jan. 1906 at 16.30 hrs. in Haarlem, Netherlands, 52°22 N, 04°30 E. Died 1972. CC WAK and NS for 269 days at 16.32 hrs. gives 22°33 Cancer.

Dutch painter, worked in Paris and Amsterdam. He made collages from materials such as shells, metals and sand. Influenced by Paul Klee (see 13th Sc.) and Van Dongen (see 21st Le.). He received several international honours and prizes.

24TH DEGREE CANCER

First Image, Outer Symbol

A flag with a royal crown is flying from the ramparts of a fortified castle on the left. Beneath it, to the right, unbridled horses snort playfully around, jumping over each other.

Interpretation

This is a degree of 'victory'. People with this degree rising can attain whatever they wish. They will have high and noble ambitions. Their character is strong, their mind active. They are full of hidden sources of energy, and do not lack opportunities in life. As this is a Cancer degree, they may well be born of ancient and even royal lineage. Their tradition points the way, and they will outdo even the illustrious forefathers in whose footsteps they follow. The future smiles and they are full of courage. Their possessions prosper in their hands. They may become good leaders and governors, and those working under them may do well also. This is all on the outer plane.

On the inner plane this degree is one of the best examples of the Cancer grail. The image is full of movement. The wind flies the flag (Ge.). The stone castle symbolises the strength of the opposition sign Capricorn. It embodies the centuries (Cap.) of glory, victory and freedom (Le.–Aq. fore-axis) of the family, the clan and the nation.

The courage (Le.) of many generations of strong men and women is embedded in the soul of these people. The playing horses are the symbols of creative thought-power (Sag.) and they are the bearers of high values (Sag.).

There may be some collective guilt (Cap.) and karma to clear (Pi. trine Cn.), as former feuds, wars and jealousies (Sc. trine Cn.) may still linger within the walls of the castle, and within the souls of the people with this degree prominent. They may reap the late fruits of their predecessors' renown. Their barns may be filled to the roof with their harvest.

These people, as Cancerians, like to make a show, although they may be very humble. They are meant to be examples of how life could really be. Others can learn a lot from them. They are honest, and tower above most of their fellows. They fill those around them with both inner and outer hope and joy.

Second Image, Inner Symbol

A woman and two male castaways on a South Seas island.

Interpretation

The first image lacked human beings. Here are two poles of consciousness (the two men), and the soul as the sensitive mirror of all experiences (the woman), wanting to leave the outer world and turn inwards. They leave home and family (Cn.) and sacrifice a good life for a more modest one. Here is a higher kind of courage (Le.), and the promise of a potentially higher fulfilment.

In the first image there was still show. Now these people have to prove that they have invincible faith enabling them to reach their inner goal. This second image indicates that inner or outer crises may occur before they can reach the high level of relinquishing everything that tied them to their past. Few achieve this great inner victory.

Conception Corrected Ascendant 24th Cancer

Hilbrandt Boschma   Born 5 Aug. 1869 at 03.00 hrs. in Kubaard, 53°07 N, 05°33 E. CC WAK for 286 days at 02.44 hrs. gives 23°26 Cancer.

Frisian writer with evangelical and pacifistic tendencies in which pure love was central. Popular writer for youth about Israel's history and its victorious battles for God, King and the land. Good at describing nature.

A. J. Cronin   Born 19 July 1896 at 03.45 hrs. in Cardross, Scotland, 55°53 N, 04°.00 W. CC NS for 296 days (late birth) at 03.45 hrs. gives 23°09 Cancer, or for 268 days at 03.44 hrs. gives 22°45 Cancer; see 23rd Cancer.

Scottish physician and author. For many years a doctor for the miners and the working class in Glasgow, his books give deep insight into the social circumstances of those days. His most famous novels are *The Citadel* (filmed in 1938) and *The Keys of the Kingdom* (filmed in 1944). His work is often autobiographical and it seems that 24th Cancer is more characteristic for him than 23rd Cancer.

Algernon Charles Swinburne   Born 5 Apr. 1837 at 10.47 hrs. in London, 51°31 N, 00°05 W. (According to Barbault, M. Jones gives the time as 05.00 hrs. with 25°57 Pisces; see 26th Pisces). Died 1909. CC WAK and NS for 280 days at 10.47 hrs. gives 23°03 Cancer, or for 266 days at 10.44 hrs. gives 22°31 Cancer.

English poet, influenced by Shelley (see 2nd Tau.) and Rossetti (see 8th Ge.). He developed his own unique style of writing and was amazingly productive. He was republican and atheist, though deeply influenced by the language of the Bible and the Classics. His fame dates from 1865 with *Atalanta in Calydon* and *Chastelard* and *Poems* (1866). His father was an admiral, his mother a devout Anglican. He broke away from his Victorian family. He had a passion for the sea. Though difficult to discern in his case, we favour this 24th Cancer degree of 'victory'.

Alexandra Pieternella Tinne   Born 17 Oct. 1835 at 22.00 hrs. in The Hague, 52°05 N, 04°18 E. Murdered 1 Aug. 1869. CC WAK and NS for 262 days at 21.58 hrs. gives 23°16 Cancer, or for 276 days at 21.57 hrs. gives 22°59 Cancer, or for 290 days at 22.02 hrs. gives 23°51 Cancer (thus thrice the same CC degree).

One of the first female explorers of Africa, and also a photographer. She twice refused the crown of the Sudan. Her expeditions were recorded in the British and Dutch press, and her own writings and unique photographs are of historical value. Her extraordinary life ended in her murder by Tuaregs in Tripoli.

See *Travels of Alexine* by Penelope Gladstone (John Murray, London, 1970) and the Tinne family papers.

25TH DEGREE CANCER

First Image, Outer Symbol

A well-armed horseman, crossing the desert sand peacefully, approaches an oasis. On the right an unbridled horse (or wild pony) runs with its mane flying in the wind, without knowing where it is going.

Interpretation

This is a peculiar image for the sign of Cancer. Janduz calls it one of 'confidence in oneself', and in general this is right. Those with this degree prominent are not easy people to get on with. They have an adventurous imagination, which shows itself especially in risky enterprises. In such circumstances they prove to have persistent strength. Their character may be restless and unbiddable. They may suddenly leave their family (Cn.), prompted by their instinct for freedom and independence (Ar.). In this they have to deal with the conflict in the cardinal cross between Aries, Cancer, Libra and Capricorn. Their sudden disappearance may give rise to scandal or trouble with the law (Cap.), and cause unbalance and loss of harmony (Li.).

The side of their character symbolised by the pony may give

them wild plans which suddenly enter their heads, and for which others in their surroundings have to pay the cost.

On a low level of awareness they may be aggressive, and they may tyrannise over others with their moodiness. They can be so hurtful that these others will give in for the sake of peace.

On a higher level, however, they are people who are not dependent upon their own family and culture. If they see the need for worthwhile work, they will go ahead with foresight. They have an eye for new things and new discoveries, and they do not mind being alone in this, or being considered peculiar, even mad.

The problem with this image is that its symbols are not typically Cancerian. These people therefore have a tremendous inner job to do in order to bring this somewhat outward-going military image onto the inner level of the second image, which is one of great inner development. Few people with this degree prominent can reach the highest levels of spiritual awareness; therefore they often fall, and so have to be aware of the pitfalls of the negative Cancer grail. For instance, if anything beckons on their horizon, they will go wild and run towards it (the pony), forgetting their previous commitments; and yet with the next mood (Moon) they race on to something else, again forgetful of intentions and not finishing their projects (neg. Ge.–Sag. hind-axis). This pattern repeats itself over and over again.

The positive side is that they are optimistic in all circumstances (Sag.). However, there is a side in them that tries to humiliate those around them who are more dutiful and conscientious (Cap.). They may be charming outside their home, but at home they can be unmannerly and militant, or unruly and lawless. They need to be aware that the negative Cancer grail tends to split the personality (Ge.), through the playing (Le.) of a different role on the outside in society (Cap.), and inside in the home, and within themselves (Ca.). This can lead them into chasing goals with fanatical (neg. Sag.) zeal. They can overpower other people (Le.–Aq.), They are themselves undisciplined, but exercise a strong will for discipline on those outside themselves.

When on this level of the Cancer grail, the square signs Aries and Libra give them a role of extreme independence (Ar.), or they may take to dabbling in magic (Ar.), by which peace and harmony (Li.) vanish and the situation becomes unbalanced.

However, people who are living this degree on a high level of spiritual awareness may overcome the dangers of the Cancer grail, and develop towards the highly evolved inner symbol.

Second Image, Inner Symbol

Leader of men, wrapped in an invisible mantle of power.

Interpretation

The man of the first image possesses this inner power in potential, but he tends to be anything but 'invisible', as he likes to show his outer superiority. Even on that level he can be a good leader of an undisciplined group. In this second image the rider has become inwardly quiet and strong. He has become a positive, strong-willed and spiritually guided Higher Self, not reacting emotionally to the materialistic impressions coming from the world of appearances.

This symbol is constantly supplied with invisible energy from within and from unconscious sources of strength (Cn.).

People with this degree need to be very highly orientated to the discovery of the inner self, where Divine Imagery has to play a role. Thus they become powerful leaders from within. They must become so advanced that they do not mind not being seen and recognised as such. Any wish for an outer show of power has to be overcome.

From playing the outward disciplinarian, their task is to become enlightened, disciplined and radiating from within.

Conception Corrected Asc. 25th Cancer

Bernard Buffet Born 10 July 1928 at 06.00 hrs. in Paris, 48°52 N, 02°20 W. CC WAK and NS for 264 days at 05.48 hrs. gives 24°19 Cancer (with a second, less likely possibility of 25°08 Cn. for 278 days at 05.54 hrs.).

French painter who became famous in the 1960s. He is known for exploiting human suffering and misery in the choice of subjects for his war paintings. The fear on the faces is almost grotesque. He is the exponent of absurdity in French art, while in French literature this is represented by his contemporaries Camus and Sartre. The prospect for his leadership of a new movement of configuration in the arts has not yet materialised. He remains rather invisible (2nd image).

26TH DEGREE CANCER

First Image, Outer Symbol

Star formations and phenomena in the dark night sky, such as meteorites and shooting stars, all seen from a plateau where cascades of water stream down from a rock.

Interpretation

Janduz calls this a degree of 'brilliancy and instability'. Her first word is obvious, but the second one, though right, needs some explanation.

These people can have a very peculiar existence and are likely to steer an irregular course through life. It often happens that their abundant energy, which they derive direct from the stellar universe, finds insufficient outlet in their work on earth, with the possible consequent splitting of the personality.

These people may achieve little for long periods of time. They ramble, they change direction time and again, so that the situation could become dangerous for their own soul-development. However, one can compare their energy with the light of the sun, breaking into thousands of facets in a tiny little drop of water, making that drop a jewel of colour. Here a whole cascade of water is lit up in this way by the stellar light.

This means that the people with this degree prominent possess enormous intuitive possibilities, and if well-disciplined (discipline is their weak point), a tremendous stream of reve-lations can be prismatically directed in and through their personality. This often gives their social and home situation a kind of fluidity, which is difficult for others to understand. They can be like a meteorite, or a brilliant falling star in the firmament of humanity: they have a great task to perform for a brief moment in time.

There may be sudden, even fatal, circumstances which force them to manifest their tremendously powerful talents in a very painful way, like the artists who have to sell their works of genius for a pittance. Or they may give themselves so fully to a project, that they are burnt up in it very quickly. It is almost impossible for them to fit themselves into the dull routine of daily life. They are hardly able to do prosaic work. They run away from the smallness and pettiness which lock them in. They cannot bear laws, rules and regulations (Cap. opp. Cn.). However, they are not just dreamers. They have the power to create forms, or express ideas which might excite or even frighten humanity. They are examples of a higher kind of human being, but they have to embody the paradoxical contradiction of this superiority with their bare existence and rough life on earth. They may be hindered and even prevented from following their high and multi-dimensional calling, especially in youth, by small-minded people who try to fence them in. However, they always break out and vanish – with pain for themselves and those they have to hurt; but that is part of their mission. On the inner level they may be driven by extra-planetary forces and bring down knowledge of stellar energy. This may make them unbalanced in the eyes of others. It could even affect their nerves and brain, so that one could indeed speak of 'mental instability' but, knowing the reasons for this, they should be forgiven, understood and helped to channel their power in their sometimes not-so-strong physical vehicle. They need to be helped to their important goal of productivity.

They can become artists or scientists, by the grace of God, able to penetrate the meaning of the as yet invisible and unattainable energies. To be good channels of their mission, they need to give themselves up completely to the higher task, without clinging to a private life of their own. They have to be careful not to ruin their physical body and bone structure (the rock), because through their bodily functions the surplus of their spiritual and mental power has to flow back and forth, between their Creator and the place of destiny for these forces. They need to fix on the stars, which are their anchor. They only need to remain open to the above, so that their being can be formed (the rock plateau) and become a bedding for the stream of feelings and emotions (Cn.) which will flow down, full of starlight, until it can be grounded and rest within the vales and dales of Mother Earth (Cn.).

Second Image, Inner Symbol

Guests are reading in the library of a luxurious home.

Interpretation

Rudhyar writes of this image (1936 version) 'Emergence of consciousness upon higher levels of being, once life has been fulfilled at normal levels. Conscious fruition.'

Having become a channel for the higher worlds in the first image, here the soul begins to realise that we are only guests on this earth, who are not meant to change, pollute and ruin the planet, as if it were our personal possession; but that those souls who are conscious of their stellar origin should enjoy themselves as guests, bathing in the cascade of the universal ancient wisdom flowing down by the written word through the ages. In the highest instance these people are able to read the Akashic records, in which all that has ever happened in the universe is stored and kept available.

Biblical Parallel

'The heavens declare the glory of God; and the firmament sheweth his handywork. Day unto day uttereth speech, and night unto night sheweth knowledge.' *Ps. 19: 1–2.*

Conception Corrected Asc. 26th Cancer

William Blake   Born 28 Nov. 1757 at 19.30 hrs. in London, 51°31 N,

00°05 W. Died 12 Aug. 1827. CC WAK and NS for 286 days at 19.26 hrs. gives 25°31 Cancer.

English mystic, poet and artist. He published his own books 'in illuminated printing'. He had an over-abundance of inspiration and the amount of work he produced is unbelievable. This brought him periods of physical and mental exhaustion. He could hardly earn a living as an engraver. In his symbolic writing he was far ahead of his time. Impoverished and unknown at his death, he is now held to be one of the greatest figures in art and literature. Rediscovered as a mystic by the New Consciousness Movement. He referred to the Glastonbury tradition by an allusion to its legend that Christ was there, in his poem *Jerusalem*. This image of the 26th Cancer is a magnificent example of his prodigious talents and character.

See British Museum, Tate Gallery, biographies and bibliographies.

Ernst Junger   Born 29 Mar. 1895 at 12.00 hrs. in Heidelberg, 49°25 N, 08°42 E. CC NS for 281 days at 11.56 hrs. gives 25°00 Cancer, or for 253 days at 12.01 hrs. gives 25°47 Cancer.

German novelist. He enlisted in the Foreign Legion while still a schoolboy, volunteered in World War I and II but then denounced war and became a pacifist. His books, such as *Heroic Heart*, were criticised as glorifying Nazi Germany, but he was persecuted by the Nazi regime himself. His theme was often the need of the conscript to rise above the world of war into the inner realms with one's 'blue pilot'. He had great influence on the younger generation.

Erich Von Daniken   Born 14 Apr. 1935 at 11.30 hrs. in Zofingen, Switzerland, 47°16 N, 07°56 E. CC NS for 276 days at 11.15 hrs. gives 25°55 Cancer, or for 262 days at 11.32 hrs. gives 29°28 Cancer (see there).

Swiss author of popular science fiction books on astronautical and extraterrestrial subjects. He rose to immense fame in the early 1970s until he was judged in a court case to be a 'pathological liar'. His bestsellers are still in demand and the last word has not been said about his work. He might prove to be prophetic. This 26th degree of Cancer fits this fantastic character amazingly well. What Daniken channels through may also give deeper insight into this 26th degree as a cosmic pore for the entry of unidentified objects and extraterrestials.

See *Ancient Astronaut Society* (USA, 1974). His *Chariot of the Gods* had half a million copies printed in 1972. Other titles *Back to the Stars* and the autobiographical *Meine Welt in Bildern*, 'My World in Pictures' (1973).

27TH DECREE CANCER

First Image, Outer Symbol

A man puts a bridle on his horse. A heifer bends its head gently towards a woman who leads it.

Interpretation

This is a degree of 'docility'.

According to Janduz, these people, have the capacity to profit by the instruction they receive, and to make their fortune by it; but they have not got the necessary will-power, and so they let opportunity slip voluntarily, through indolence of mind and body. So far Janduz.

On a low level these people can submit their capacity to think (the horse) so completely to a master (the man), that they do not profit, either materially or in their personal development, from any chance to become independent (Cn. sq. Ar.).

However, on a higher level, when being led in the right way they can learn to serve any good master, and co-operate in many ways with others, as they possess an open and adaptable attitude, ready to learn from their experiences in this world. They are in no way moody (Cn.) and are in harmony with nature (the heifer and woman). Inwardly they may give themselves completely to the task they take on their shoulders. They can be a very great silent force, enduring and persevering, especially when there seems to be no chance of success. They may live by the motto of William the Silent (Prince William of Orange, sixteenth century): 'When hope of success fails me, I remain willing.'

These people can be very good companions and marriage partners. They are capable of strong devotion. They are emotional (Cn.) but they are able to turn this into patient and persistent work. They do not bow the head slavishly, but they have the moral greatness to perform a perfect service, which will be appreciated by all who stand above them on the social ladder (Cap. opp. Cn.), or those who may serve under them or be trained and led by them. They make good teachers, concerned only with the well-being of their pupils, both spiritual and material.

Ordinary day-to-day situations may raise them to a higher level, where events will begin to show forth a higher inner meaning.

This degree bestows great potential for the development of the essential function of any planet it contains, as the image embodies the most important elements of the Cancer grail. The man is a symbol of the Cancer consciousness. He knows how to dress himself to be in tune with the spiritual level of awareness which he has reached. He owns his land. He is in harmony with his means. We can assume that his horse is a thoroughbred, which he has only to mount when he wishes to ride. The horse is a symbol of his thinking, which is noble here. The man could be a king. The horse carries him, but he needs to give it rein to be itself: he must give his thinking capacity the confidence and freedom to gallop and enjoy itself. The woman is a symbol of the receptive, mirroring side of the soul, while the docile heifer could be that part in the soul that is connected with the earth (Tau.) and its future growth.

The total image breathes space. It is not vague. It is grounded within the soil, the community and the country. It is an image of acceptance. These people need to accept their own personality. They may be too docile and require more initiative. In fact they need a fresh wind or a storm through their lives – which brings us to the second image.

Second Image, Inner Symbol

A furious storm rages through a canyon, filled with expensive homes.

Interpretation

Marc Jones speaks of this image as a symbol of 'violence and terror as divine in their capacity for lifting man out of his aplomb and demanding some manifestation of his inner ideals and enduring values'. Indeed, the tumult of the elements in a residential area, symbolic for Cancer, causes values to be played against each other out of a cosmic necessity. The docility of the first image has had a rude awakening. The cosiness of a secure home and family life is broken through by divine violence, so that these people have to rise up to the higher level of awareness of the three water signs. Their Cancerian security has to be destroyed by violence and death (Sc.). They have to learn to sacrifice and suffer (Pi.) the loss of what they built up in the past (Cn.–Cap.), so that an inner (Cn.) transformation (Sc.) and a deeper religious sense (Pi.) can be born in them. Their innate docility must rise to a greater abandonment of self. Let them welcome Divine Providence in the storms of life, when wind and rain clash with stone and soil – dynamic force with static. It is their own dynamism which must triumph.

Biblical Parallel

Gog–Magog will come like a storm and go to them that are at rest and dwell safely. See *Ezek. 38: 1–12* and the comment of Bullinger's *Companion Bible*.

28TH DEGREE CANCER

First Image, Outer Symbol

Two friends sit in contemplation on a gently sloping hill before a vast landscape. Their backs are against a tree at the left. On a branch right above their heads sits a raven as if in meditation.

Interpretation

This is one of the most balanced degrees of the zodiac. Janduz calls it 'harmony'. However, it is better to reserve that word for the sign of Libra. Here we are in Cancer, so we do well to interpret the men as being engaged in sympathetic, possibly even emotional (Cn.), colloquy, which denotes their inner state of being.

The image also gives a striking glimpse of the opposite sign Capricorn, the sign of meditation and contemplation. In fact it shows the entire Cancer grail, as the hind-axis Gemini–Sagittarius behind Cancer. We see a bird (Ge.) and a wide landscape (Sag.). The two men are in inner dialogue (Ge.) each reading the other's thoughts (Sag.). The tree against which they are leaning indicates a fully developed philosophy and power of thought. The fore-axis (Aq.-Le.) is there in the two men, in open contact (Aq.) with each other and nature. Their backs (Le.) are in line with the uprightness of their faith and being (Le.). Thus it is clear that this is a highly evolved Cancer degree. In fact for people with this Ascendant, or a planet in this degree, there seem to be no difficulties. They are contemplative, gentle, benevolent folk at one with nature. Their sympathies are deep-rooted. They like solitude, but have a natural inclination towards family life, without being limited to domesticity. Their career should be in connection with nature, in forestry, agriculture or landscaping, and they should not live and work in cities.

The lower level may degenerate into fatalism and superstition, depending on the raven's being black or white. They need to beware of the sort of meditation that is egotistical, parasitic on the astral-ethereal world (neg. Cn.-Cap.). When this occurs they may become the slaves of a meditative system which condemns them to superficiality. They may become mere dreamers and social misfits.

On the highest level, however, these people are able to scan the inner side of nature with 'second sight'. Unfortunately they do not scan themselves so easily. They need a friend, a stimulating teacher to free their innate capacities and let them grow. Then they may reach a great height as practitioners of 'occult' nature medicine, with the ability to read nature's Akashic chronicles. The bird kingdom comes under Gemini, but individual species come under different signs, so that ravens come under Capricorn. This indicates great possibilities for mediation in these people.

Second Image, Inner Symbol

An Indian girl introduces a college boyfriend to her tribe.

Interpretation

Rudhyar sees here the human soul as intercessor between primordial natural forces and the intellectual order. Indeed this soul (the girl), embedded in her own heritage (Cn.), has grown above differences and has the courage (Le.) to bring people of other backgrounds together (Aq.). She is a mediator in actuality, while the men in the former image were still only contemplating mediation, and still had to make contact with the world outside their own valley. Here is self-transcendence, and the linking-in with a higher enlightened spirit, to fertilise the collective past experiences of the soul.

Biblical Parallel

Ravens fed Elijah with bread and flesh when he was hiding by the river Jordan. See *1 Kings 17: 4–6*.

Conception Corrected Ascendant 28th Cancer

Claude Lhuer   Born 28 Feb. 1908 at 14.00 hrs. in Paris, 48°50 N, 02°20 E. CC NS for 287 days at 13.39 hrs. gives 27°29 Cancer, or for 259 days at 13.39 hrs. gives 27°33 Cancer, or for 273 days at 14.05 hrs. gives 0°29 Leo, or for 301 days (late birth) at 14.07 hrs. gives 0°52 Leo (see 1st Le.).

French painter and illustrator. She drew the 360 degrees of the zodiac for Janduz' book on which we base the first images in this present work. Although it is difficult to distinguish between a Cancer or Leo Ascendant, it feels more likely from the intimate way she drew and from her chart in general, that she has Cancer rising. See her drawings in *Beeldgids von de Dierenriem* by Helene and Willem Koppejan (Ankh Hermes, 1990).

Pir Vilayat Khan   Born 19 June 1916 at 07.30 hrs. in London, 51°30 N, 00°05 W. CC NS for 288 days at 07.17 hrs. gives 27°36 Cancer, or for 274 days at 07.38 hrs. give 01°10 Leo (see there).

Spiritual teacher, lecturer, head of the Sufi Order in the West. Son of Inyat Khan (see 29th Pi.). He adapted methods of meditation from esoteric schools to contemporary life in Western society.

King William III (King 'Billy')   Born premature 14 Nov. 1650 NS (4 Nov. OS) between 20.30 and 21.00 hrs., in The Hague, 52°05 N, 04°18 E. Die 1702. CC NS for 259 days gives 27°23 Cancer, or for 245 days (eight-month child) at 20.33 hrs. gives 27°56 Cancer, or for 231 days at 20.34 hrs. gives 27°44 Cancer – this time would confirm the historical fact that the bells began to ring for the newborn at 20.30 hours according to the historian Robb. Though 28th Cancer is highly significant, there is another CC for 259 days at 20.56 hrs. which gives 2°07 Leo (see there). Astrological literature often ascribes 1st Leo rising, which is impossible according to the CC method.

Dutch stadtholder of the Netherlands and King of Great Britain and Ireland. He landed in 1688 at Brixham, from where he led the 'Glorious Revolution'. Crowned with his wife Mary in 1689. Won the battle of the Boyne in Ireland, and went down in history as the defender of the Protestant Faith. He created the Bank of England (1694), through which he borrowed vast sums covered by private people against interest. Thus the present system was born. He was homosexual, of ill health and bad-tempered. He died from a fall off his horse at Hampton Court in 1702. Adored and hated by both British and Dutch in his lifetime, this controversial figure is worth a deeper astrological study.

Amongst many books about him *William of Orange* by Nesca A. Robb (Heinemann) is outstanding.

29TH DEGREE CANCER

First Image, Outer Symbol

In a jungle on the left a horse is tethered to a tree. It is being stalked by a tiger. On the right a man is suspended from a tree with a hangman's noose loosely around his neck, so that his toes are touching the ground.

Interpretation

This is one of the most difficult images in Cancer. According to Janduz it is a degree of 'coercion'. There is a helplessness against danger in people with this degree prominent. There is want of strength (the fastened horse and the hanging man) in their consciousness and thinking capacity. Their entire personality is inclined to make things difficult for themselves. Could it be that the man has put the rope around his neck himself and, not having done the job thoroughly, is now the prisoner of his own indeterminate deeds? Their fiery nature often misleads them (neg. Le. fore-axis) into taking steps in their lives, which can have very disagreeable consequences both for themselves and their home situation (Cn.).

On a low level of emotional control they try to shirk the consequences of their own childish and unreasoned mistakes. They may even plan revenge against those to whom they have caused pain in the first place, but this vengeance in the end hurts no one but themselves.

On another level, they may be innocent victims of intrigue and the law of the human jungle. People around them may have an interest in their downfall. It can be that others imprison them in emotional ties. The weakness of these people is that they lack the will to disentangle themselves, but remain hanging in a state of impotence unable to act on their own initiative. They are not unintelligent, though they often tie their way of thinking (the horse) to an established church or conventional system (Cap. opp. Cn.).

Their tendency to dependence upon others is far too great and they even like to surrender their personal freedom, often in emotional liaisons which are unprofitable at best and dangerous at worst. These people have to discover that they are not creatures of circumstances (Cn.) but the victims of their own passivity. They may indeed be under attack (the tiger), but this is at their own invitation, although sometimes the strength of the hostility evoked does not seem to match their naive diffidence.

Whatever befalls them is good for their own inner development. They have to learn that they must take their life into their own hands. They need to take off that cord themselves, not wait for others to do it for them. Then they should use their own hands to heal their throat area, wherein lies the chakra that enables foresight and the planning of their own future (Tau.).

Next they need to free their thinking (Sag. the horse) from the entanglements of the human jungle. They need to be alert to the fact that they could be easy prey, especially in psychically unclean places like big cities, or when in bad company.

According to Janduz 'The end of their life may be miserable and tragic, terminating in a violent death.' However, when fully aware of the pitfalls inherent in this image, these people can disengage themselves and create a magnificent rebirth of their inner, Higher Self, of which the second image speaks.

Second Image, Inner Symbol

A Greek Muse weighs a pair of new born twins in a pair of golden scales.

Interpretation

Rudhyar's keynote for this image is the 'intuitive weighing of alternatives' and he speaks of the 'power of creative imagination and the spirit penetrating into the world of manifestation' (1973 and 1936 edns).

The Greek Muse is a symbol of inspiration. Weighing comes under Libra (sq. Cn.) and indicates that these people have now gained control over the entire cardinal cross and can balance their inner and outer scales (astral and aetheric bodies, Cn.). Although these two are still split into two (twins), they are in golden balance, and by inspiration can both be lifted up to the level of creative inner vision. The tendency in the first image to

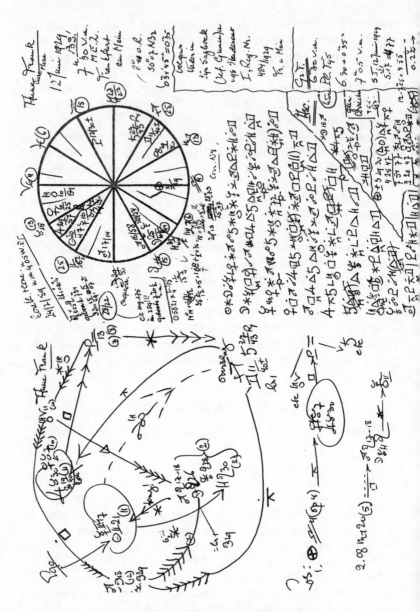

Handwritten chart of Anne Frank by
Willem Ary Koppejan

Anne Frank

be taken by surprise and by fate, and the fear of being devoured by lower passions and instincts (the tiger), is now lifted up to the level of inspired and imaginative thinking. The strangled consciousness (the man) may have died, but has been reborn in a double-sided being (the twins). The fear of the past (the jungle) has turned into joy; now the soul may rest in love (Le., gold).

Biblical Parallel

'Jesus answered . . . Except a man be born of water and of the Spirit, he cannot enter into the kingdom of God.' *Jn. 3: 5.*

Conception Corrected Asc. 29th Cancer

H. P. Blavatsky   Born 31 July 1831. CC for 264 days at 03.05 hrs. gives 28°54 Cancer, see 30th Cancer.

Anne Frank   Born 12 June 1929 at 07.30 hrs. in Frankfurt–Main, 50°07 N, 08°41 E. Died in Bergen–Belsen concentration camp March 1945. CC and WAK NS for 275 days at 07.24 hrs. gives 28°22 Cancer.

Anne Frank's diary as book and film became a bestseller in the years after World War II. She was the epitome of all the Jewish children imprisoned and murdered under the Nazi ideology of the German master race. The harrowing tale of this Amsterdam girl's hiding and capture, and her life in the concentration camp, is one of the most striking and moving examples of someone born with 29th Cancer rising. She sometimes literally describes details of this degree. If there is any truth in Divine Imagery, then it is to be found in the life and chart of Anne Frank.

30TH DEGREE CANCER

First Image, Outer Symbol

A young horse, tethered on a hill to the right, pulls at its halter in the direction of the open sea on the left. It is keeping its head so high that it does not notice a barrier which would prevent it falling over the cliff into the sea, where one perceives a barque moving away into the distance.

Interpretation

This is a degree of 'utter independence', but within certain limits. As this is the last degree of the sign Cancer, it comprises the entire sign in symbols and shows the fore- and hind-axis, or Cancer grail, as well.

Cancer is symbolised by the sea, and by the protecting fence. The horse is the hind-axis Gemini–Sagittarius. The courageous and fiery spirit pulling towards freedom is the fore-axis Leo–Aquarius. Of the two sides of Cancer, we see the outer shell more in the right side of this image, while the inner sensitivity is more clearly seen on the left side (the vessel moving towards the horizon). Thus the essence of Cancer is in the character of this degree. People with this degree rising are adventurous, and are likely to leave their place of birth in search of independence, to break away from the restrictions of family ties and small-minded associates. There is no taming their spirit, and this may give them a bad name. When they meet too much opposition they may become split personalities or fanatics (neg. Ge.–Sag.). They may not give themselves time (Cap. opp. Cn.) to learn from life. Their passion for freedom does not let them accept hardship or constraint.

They may use their strength in the wrong way. The resistance they induce in others should be seen as protective. It warns them against the danger of the fatal fall into the void which may occur if they do not control their urge to liberty.

The true Cancer will be educated by wisdom and will move in faith (Ge.–Sag.), and use all this inner power to build homes in heaven for the soul, and the souls of their friends and children (Aq.–Le.). The barque is a vessel containing many souls of their (his or her) group. The message of this image is that the individual must not set sail for the new world in a disorganised manner, but only when all the lower (animal) forces are perfectly trained into positive qualities. These people will always make their mark in the world.

Second Image, Inner Symbol

A lady of aristocratic descent proudly addresses a club.

Interpretation

A society with an aristocracy based on lineal descent and ancient tradition is the very essence of Cancer. Cancer is a feminine sign, thus this image depicts the further ennobling of the first one. The uncontrolled force of the horse is now under the aristocratic rule of self-control and proud self-respect; the coltish desire to show off is now placed in a socially profitable direction. Self-education has become transferable through speech (Ge.- Sag.) and to a wider circle (the club).

The seclusion of the ungovernable horse has now been elevated into a free contact with a wider spiritual community (Aq.–Le.), although the soul may still feel somewhat bridled by its past. However, the community is able and ready to listen. The person with this degree is now able to be in dialogue with a selected inner circle of companions, maybe even her own soul group. On the basis of this she then gives of her best to her own self-created surroundings.

Conception Corrected Ascendant 30th Cancer

Helena Petrowna Blavatsky (neé Hahn) Born 31 July 1831 (calculated as 13 Aug.) at 03.00 hrs. (sometimes given as 01.47 hrs.) in Jekaterinoshaw (Russia), 48°24 N, 35°00 E. Died 1891. CC WAK and NS for 264 days at 03.05 hrs. gives 28°54 Cancer (see there), or for 265 days at 03.08 hrs. gives 29°30 Cancer. In theosophical literature her chart has been circulated as 01.47 hrs. 'although born later'. That can only be right if she had a late birth. CC for 293 days at 01.43 hrs. gives 13°05 Cancer (see there).

Daughter of a German Commander, she married General Blavatsky at the age of 17, but soon left him. She travelled for many years in Tibet. Founded the Theosophical Society with Colonel Olcott in 1875. Her books, particularly *The Secret Doctrine*, have had great influence on modern thinking in the West.

Erich Von Daniken CC for 262 days at 11.32 hrs. gives 29°28 Cancer (see 26th Cancer).

Eric Satie Born 17 May 1866 at 09.00 hrs. in Honfleur (France), 49°26 N, 00°12 E. Died 1925. CC NS for 271 days at 08.45 hrs. gives 29°25 Cancer, or for 256 days at 08.49 hrs. gives 0°26 Leo.

French composer and text-writer. Friend of Debussy (see 23rd Le.). Nicknamed 'the velvet gentleman', he was a great eccentric, which is also evident from his own memoirs. His work made a comeback in the 1970s and is often used for background music in television.

Frederic Lionel CC for 276 days at 04.43 hrs. gives 29°29 Cancer (see 2nd Leo).

LIBRA

INDEX OF LIBRA ASCENDANT DEGREES

1st Degree Libra

First Image, Outer Symbol

On a country road in an arid landscape, a man is walking to the right with a pistol in each hand, not seeing that he is being followed by another man with a drawn sword.

Interpretation

This is a 1st degree and therefore comprises all the pitfalls that the entire sign of Libra may encounter. If one fails to realise this, one may not understand why this unharmonious symbol opens the peaceful sign of Libra. Janduz' interpretation is very superficial. She speaks of an 'unconsidered attack or wounding'. Indeed the heedlessness can be seen in the first man, and those with this degree rising may be blind to danger. Yet part of them is always on the attack. Here we come to the duality which is a characteristic of Libra. There are always two parts in the scales, and most of the time one side of their Higher Self is out of balance with the other. They always think that their goodwill is being assaulted, and often they attack before anyone has even questioned it. They battle for peace (Sc.–Tau. fore-axis) and more often than not their doubts (Li.) arise because of their hypersensitivity to criticism (Vi.–Pi. hind-axis). They have to overcome this and in their Libra grail learn to incorporate their opposite sign Aries, which stands for independent action and pioneering.

However, in this first degree, the tendency is to degenerate to a sort of super-independence and become a law unto oneself. These people may become obsessed with the idea that their family, home and reputation are under threat, and their measures of defence may even lead them into black magic (the squares of Cn.–Cap.).

The essence of Libra is to defend rights and duties. On a higher level they see a sharp distinction (Vi. behind Li.)

between good and bad, left and right. They make good judges and solicitors, whose task it is to keep society (Cap.) in moral (Cap.) balance. They have to learn to control, within themselves, the entire cardinal cross (Ar.–Cn.–Li.–Cap.).

A judge often sets new forces in motion (Ar.) without recognising the spiritual implications of what he is doing. Moreover, one has to realise that this first degree of Libra is in exact opposition to the very first degree of the zodiac, 1st Aries. This means that we are now 180 degrees further on than the first Aries impulse. Thus the man with the two pistols should turn back 180 degrees and look the primeval life-force (Ar.) straight in the face. With radiant white-magical power he could look into the eyes of the man with the sword – his own *alter ego*, thus causing him to fall on his knees (Cap.) and plead for his life. The man with the pistols could then raise up the man with the sword and give him grace (Aq.), and they would embrace (Li.). The first man would lay his hand on the head of the other in blessing, and together they would follow their path, the way of the Lord. Peace is the essence and message of Libra.

Second Image, Inner Symbol

Pierced by a dart of light, a butterfly is 'made perfect'.

Interpretation

Here the light 'kills' all that is old (Sc.) and 'fertilises' (Tau.) and marries (Li.) the butterfly as the symbol of fragile matter, so that light and form are joined in a new and perfect bond. The butterfly is the archetypal symbol of initiation by transition from death to eternal life. From the dark night of murder (man in the first image), mankind suddenly awakes and, like the butterfly, instinctively turns towards the light. These two images show the cosmological principle of how to overcome the squares of the cardinal cross by elevation from the denser planets Venus and Mars (rulers of Li.–Ar.), to the higher rulers Pluto (not of Sc. but of Ar.) and Demeter (the inner astral side of Cn.). It is little known how physical light (the sun) receives nourishment from the so-called maya (moon), in the form of our emotions and experiences in our world of matter. Only when that process is working perfectly, the true light of the Higher Self gets its 'food' from our experiences in dreams and visions which 'mirror' the immaterial forces of the unseen world. A pure ray of light is the point of no-thing in time; that moment of the eternal now in between the seconds of our world where newer forms and greater beauty (Li.) are lit up in perfection.

The paradox of it is that this process is happening all the time and everywhere in ordinary daily life. It is the way of life which St Francis showed us. The butterfly, symbol of the soul, cannot be murdered but only transformed to higher existence. The men of the first image, like the robber on the cross at Golgotha, are suddenly touched by the light and told by the King of Peace 'Today you will be with me in paradise.' Their souls are suddenly made perfect in a heavenly state of being.

Biblical Parallel

'Today shalt thou be with me in paradise.' *Lk. 23: 43.*

Conception Corrected Asc. 1st Libra

F. W. Zeylmans van Emmichoven   CC Wak and NS for 277 days at 01.55 hrs. gives 00°44 Libra. See 30th Virgo.

Joshua Reynolds   Born 16 July 1723 at 10.30 hrs. in Plympton Earl, 50°22 N, 04°07 W. Died 1792. CC NS for 294 days at 10.26 hrs. gives 00°01 Libra, which gives him part of 30th Virgo as well, or for 280 days at 10.16 hrs. gives 28°19 Virgo.

English painter, the most fashionable portrait painter of his day. He met with much jealousy from his fellow artists and was sometimes wanting in generosity himself. He was known for the richness of his deep colouring. His most famous works are in museums in the USA. His literary work comprises *Discourses* and essays on the art of painting. It is difficult to distinguish between Virgo and Libra for his rising sign, but this 1st Libra seems more likely; the second image is particularly appropriate to his style of painting, and his life, in turn, gives more depth to the interpretation of this degree.

Shirley Maclaine CC NS for 271 days at 4.05 hours gives 0.43 Libra, see 29th Virgo.

2ND DEGREE LIBRA

First Image, Outer Symbol

A sort of magician, helped by his assistant, is burning incense on the altar of his ancestors.

Interpretation

This is a degree of search for the secrets of life, which do not play a part in the concerns of ordinary people. The contact which this person has with the ordinary is minimal. He (or she) does not live in this time (Li. sq. Cap.), but in the past and future, and he tries to join the two (Li.). There is often a sad remembrance of what was, or what could have been, but this strikes a chord within him along with the future, which for him is the sustaining point of the present. He has a mighty spirit, which can circumscribe life in its entirety of past, present and future.

Ceremonial, to which these people are drawn, offers little in the way of livelihood, so more practical means have to be adopted (Vi.–Pi. hind-axis), whilst their real interest lies in their knowledge of the ancient Wisdom and their living contact with their forefathers (Ge.–Li.–Aq. trines). Following the ancient pathways they know that in fact there is 'nothing new under the sun'. They are aware of what the Sun is in reality, and the consciousness it will convey to us. For them this life is only one step in the pursuit of an eternal goal. This invisible goal needs to be reached with clean hands and the greatest devotion. Their efforts to reach it are equally unseen, but they do not lack help.

So far we have identified with the magician, but the consciousness needs to be aware of the helper as well. This is a Libra degree in which there is often a duality to be overcome. These people can do this by a study of the ancient laws and the lost religions. They need to detach themselves: by study, by meditation, and always with modesty (Vi. behind Li.), they will become truly universal and in this way bring integration out of separation.

Their capacity is great, but they remain humble and prefer to work in solitude, knowing the need to regulate energy for its proper uses. They are hermits with an open door.

As in most Libra degrees, this image is neutral. It depends completely on the higher will whether this magician and his helper are channels for positive or negative forces, whether they are black or white magicians, and whether they are calling up their ancestors for their own egotistical needs or for the good of a greater whole. The need to overcome the difficulties of the cardinal cross are obvious in this image. Magicians come under Aries, ancestors in the unseen world come under Cancer, rites and ceremonies are Capricorn and two men officiating in partnership is Libra.

In the old days, tarot readers were called 'imagicians'. The present work is a handbook for imagicians.

Second Image, Inner Symbol

A symphony is played dramatising man's heroic ascent.

Interpretation

Not only did the magicians study the images, they identified with them. In the second image this expression of universal equivalence is transposed to audible melody, a symphony in sound and form. These people manifest triumphantly the Harmony of the Spheres.

The musical expansion of this image is endless. The power of the symbol lies in the constant renewal of humble courage. These people know that every human ability derives its power, not from self, but entirely from 'God's will'. They can become willingly, and knowingly, co-operators (Li.) with the highest laws of the universe, and with them become in balance.

Biblical Parallels

The high priest and his assistant *Lev. 10*.

An example of the cosmic symphony is given in *Ps. 19: 1–5*.

'I am the door.' *Jn. 10: 7–9*.

3RD DEGREE LIBRA

First Image, Outer Symbol

A man, wearing a shirt and seated on a tree trunk, seems to be
dreaming, but his hands and feet are chained. In a house nearby
a large barred window shows a woman looking out with longing
eyes.

Interpretation

The 3rd degrees are of special importance for they deal, on an
impersonal level, with the problems of Babylon and Armageddon, which are intensifying at the end of the twentieth
century.

According to Janduz, people with this degree on the Ascendant will undergo suffering, but will be enabled to rise
above it by their faith in spiritual freedom. This may be true.
They may have to undergo physical captivity. On a low level of
awakening, their daydreaming may be an escape from reality,
which compensates for the low physical circumstances. On the
other hand they may become so depressed that they suffer
without thinking at all, and with no faith that a better life will
ever be theirs.

It is typical of a spiritually undeveloped Libra to cling to a
semblance of happiness rather than work for overall change that
will bring real fulfilment to others and themselves. They often
adopt an attitude of concentration (Cap. sq. Li.) on self, which
can easily become a wilful refusal to notice any sort of offence
from without: even physical cruelties may be tolerated in this
way, with dulled perception.

People with this degree prominent may have to experience
detention themselves, or they may work with prisoners: physically or mentally they may be enclosed, or (the woman at the
window) it may be their fate to watch over others in that state.

As a typical Libra degree this image has two components, the male and the female. The deeper meaning of this image can be better understood by taking the second one into account at an early stage of interpretation.

Second Image, Inner Symbol

A new day dawns, revealing a world utterly transformed.

Interpretation

The first image emphasises the mental side. The man is dreaming, the woman is looking eagerly, along a horizontal plane. Both the masculine and feminine are captives in the present world of matter.

What is the higher task of Libra? To answer this requires insight into the Libra grail and the cardinal cross.

The ideal of peace and happiness (Li.) needs to be realised by the individual. Nobody can give someone else peace of mind. Basically everybody makes their own peace with the inner worlds, regardless of outer circumstances. The low-level Libra lets himself be tossed around from left to right, and top to bottom, for a substitute peace based on lies (Cap. sq. Li.).

The danger in the Libra grail lies in an encapsulation of one's feelings, in which inner dreams have no connection with outer reality. Possible activities, which ought to be vigorous and independent (Ar. opp. Li.), are out of touch with the inner plane of experience. This is the ingoing square between Cancer and Libra, which means on the outer plane (aetherical – Moon) a lethargic endurance, but on the inner plane (astral – Demeter) an active task to bring thoughts for peace into harmony. That which is seen in an inner vision to be conducive to such peace needs to be brought into the outer world of matter.

This is the impersonal suffering of the planet at the end of this age, of which we all are a part. Only the quantum leap towards the opposite sign Aries can bring release. Male and female are chained in themselves, and the only way out is by exercise of the independent, fiery evolutionary force, the energy (Pluto–Mars) for transmutation. It is a power analogous with the explosion of an atomic bomb. This power has to ripen slowly (Tau.–Sc.

fore-exis) or it may be turned, prematurely, to destruction. The inner vision has to wait till it can function on the outer plane.

The essence of this second image is the preparation for the actual realisation of the Kingdom of God on earth. This will manifest through men and women who are totally dedicated and prepared for the utmost sacrifice. Only then can our planet be lit up by the higher worlds for a new dawn. It is the main mistake of humanity in general, and bearers of the Libra grail in particular, to shut their eyes to truth from above and content themselves with existence, however restricted, below.

The transforming powers of Pluto, in times and periods of absolute silence and absolute darkness, will force these people (and us all) to take seriously the idea that the inner planes softly glide into the outer planes and each is at peace with the other (Li.).

These people have to become aware that nothing in the outer world happens that is not prepared by the higher worlds, in which dwell the Angelic Hierarchies, called by God to work with man, and that every event on this planet is a mirror and message from on high.

In this degree the female side should not look out but seek to discover the processes of transformation hidden within. These people need to give the macrocosm a fair chance of reflection in the inner mirror. Their gaze needs to be reorientated towards the higher planes. Let the stars become their guides. The zodiacal astrology will receive its rightful place in the new Dawn of the Aquarian Age, for which these people should be preparing themselves and others.

Biblical Parallels

Paul's speech to the Jews '. . . for the hope of Israel I am bound with this chain.' *Acts 28: 20.*

Babylon and Armageddon. See *Rev. 16: 15–21.*

'We have also a more sure word of prophecy; . . . a light that shineth in a dark place, until the day dawn, and the day star arise in your hearts:' *2 Pet. 1: 19.*

Conception Corrected Asc. 3rd Libra

Bo Yin Ra (Joseph Schneider Franken)   Born 25 Nov. 1876 at 02.00 hrs. at Aschaffenburg, 49°59 N, 09°09 E. Died 1943. CC WAK and NS for 285 days at 01.54 hrs. gives 2°19 Libra, or for 271 days at 01.59 hrs. gives 2°21 Libra.

Great Swiss philosopher, painter and writer of many books on the world of Light. Seeing humanity 'enchained' and 'asleep' he wrote prophetically for a new age seeing 'male and female united in a bipolar creature'.

François Mitterand   CC NS for 275 days at 03.55 hrs. gives 2°15 Libra. Nearest to the given birthtime. Though this degree may fit his wartime experiences, 7th Libra seems to fit his character and statesmanship far better. See 7th Libra.

P. D. Ouspensky   Born 2 Sept. 1877 at 07.35 hrs. (N.S., Gregorian 14 Sept.) in Moscow, 55°30 N, 35°30 E. Died 2 Oct. 1947. CC NS for 279 days at 07.26 hrs. gives 2°06 Libra, or for 265 days at 07.27 hrs. gives 2°17 Libra.

Russian philosopher, writer and lecturer, well-known in psychological circles and in association (and opposition) with Gurdjieff (see 26th Li.), whose idea he promoted and with whom he later broke. He lived in London from 1924.

His most outstanding book is *A New Model of the Universe*, which is a strong indication for the second image of 3rd Libra. Other well-known books are *Tertium Organum*, and *The Fourth Way* (Routledge & Kegan Paul) and his biography by J. H. Reyner (Allen & Unwin, 1981).

Suzanne Valedon   Born 23 Sept. 1865 at 06.00 hrs. in Bessines-sur-Gartempe, France, 46°10 N, 01°28 E. Died 7 Apr. 1938. CC WAK and NS for 290 days (late birth) at 06.04 hrs. gives 2°28 Libra.

French painter, mother of Utrillo (see 11th Tau.), worked in the circus until she had an accident on the trapeze, after which she painted scenes of the circus, in her own eccentric style. She wanted to express the freedom in the air which she had experienced on the trapeze. She was a friend of Van Gogh (see

16th Cn.) and Degas (see 10th Aq.). She is an interesting example of a double Libra (Sun, Mars, Saturn, Ascendant Li.).

4TH DEGREE LIBRA

First Image, Outer Symbol

At the entrance of a field, where only half a furrow has been turned, a discouraged man looks at his broken plough, while behind him, from the right, a rider is approaching. He is rather dashing, but his horse is lame.

Interpretation

Janduz calls this a degree of 'difficulties'. However, that word is too superficial for this image. The difficulties are caused by the squares of Cancer and Capricorn with Libra. People with this degree rising or prominent in their chart have certain qualities, which for some inexplicable reason they cannot use. It is not that they have no opportunities, because that would be an outer projection, but it is something within themselves, which is the cause for a lack of chances, and for their not being able to succeed time and again. The very minute they start to work, their instruments fail, or their engine stops. They blame the outer thing, such as their vehicle or the limping horse, instead of finding the shortcoming in themselves.

As this is a Libra degree, the troubles often start within the marriage or other partnership. For instance, there is no money for repairs or buying anew: so they give up instead of putting their energy to work in a review of circumstances. It seems that they are always handicapped by circumstances, but the handicap is actually in themselves. They should never have started on a journey with a lame horse or a rusted machine – they should have been wiser. It shows that these people often overestimate their own power, and underestimate the possible resistance and inertia of matter. They ask for extra obstacles by undertaking too great a task, not realising that their planning is inadequate (neg. Li.). They have to see that their difficulties are their lessons in the school of life.

As Libra, they do not balance the pros and cons enough, because they overestimate their physical energy, while they need the Plutonic impulse of radical transformation and renewal. They need to go through hard and humble work first (Vi.-Pi. hind-axis), see through their illusions and learn to exercise foresight, otherwise they fall back into a habitual mood of 'I am always the loser' and may become social outcasts (Cn.-Cap. sq. Li.). What is badly needed becomes clear in the symbol of the second image.

Second Image, Inner Symbol

Pilgrims gather round a campfire in silent communion.

Interpretation

The men of the first image are too materialistic and worldly. They look down instead of up. The rider may be dashing and optimistic, but his thinking (the horse) is unbalanced (limping). The consciousness of both men is too inward-looking and enclosed. They need, just as pilgrims do, to gather around the symbolic fire of the inner life, and learn to do things together (Li.). They must realise that the higher forces do not stem from matter, but from that joint centre, the fire burning within the collective (the pilgrims). It is a shared aspiration for the future which draws them together.

The opposite side of the Libra grail is marked by Pisces, Aries and Taurus, which embody inspiration, resurrection and prophetic vision. If these people work on those energies, they will not be so vulnerable on the material plane, where they experience their 'difficulties'. They need to persevere (Cap.) in estimating, from within themselves, what can be accomplished individually and collectively.

Pilgrims draw energy for the rest of their lives from that silent period, and from the places of their pilgrimage, and their dedication is blessed of God, so that even when they disperse afterwards they are bound together by one high ideal.

There will be no more broken instruments nor lame steeds

when these people have brought the Highest into daily experience.

Biblical Parallels

'. . . he that ploweth should plow in hope.' *1 Cor. 9: 10.*

'An high look, and a proud heart, and the plowing of the wicked, is sin.' *Prov. 21: 4.*

Conception Corrected Asc. 4th Libra

Isaac Israels   CC NS for 263 days (regular) at 21.29 hrs. gives 3°56 Libra. In the absence of knowledge that Israels' birth was overdue, this degree should be given preference. See 5th Libra.

5TH DEGREE LIBRA

First Image, Outer Symbol

A walker, stretching out his hand to a woman whom he tries to help climb a cliff path, falls into a lake below. Several rings, or links of a chain, fall at the same time.

Interpretation

According to Janduz, this degree is one of 'threat and fall'. On a low level of awareness, this image shows the typical mistake of Libra, namely a weakness of character, especially in connection with the other sex, but without deeply passionate or sexual implications. They still have to grow and develop (Tau.–Sc. fore-axis). It is their native doubt (neg. Li.) that makes them imprudent. They do not really see the danger of indecision. People with this degree may easily form a sentimental relationship, without due discrimination (neg. Ge.–Li.–Aq.). They stretch out their hand towards those who do not deserve it, and by this may bring disaster upon themselves.

In their naïveté they believe they are able to help, only to wake up when it is too late. They may fall socially, or into moral degeneration. They may plunge into all sorts of emotional complications (Cn. and Cap. sq. Li.), so much so that others wonder where their common sense has gone, going from partner to partner and leaving one for the next as if on the principle *carpe diem* – seize the day.

On an even lower physical plane, they may get involved in clandestine or unlawful love relationships, bribery, bigamy or polygamy. They make and break partnerships in their fall (the chain and falling links).

On the more emotional level, they may be mere romanticists and only inconsequent in their feelings. The intuitive female side in them tries to climb to higher spiritual consciousness, but it is exactly that move which draws the Higher Self down into experiences of a very low collective unconscious kind (the lake). In other words, their Higher Self may fall back into repetitious tendencies induced in past lives, propensities that should have been noted as dangerous, and overcome.

The rock path (Cap.) on the cliff means that there are great possibilities for social climbing, but also the adjoining temptations and ambitions of their partners. When high on the social ladder, they may lose their position through a love affair, or a swindle, in which they have been exposed (neg. Ta.–Sc. fore-axis).

These people must learn to be more guarded and distant, so that others do not dare to approach them with their vile intentions. Symbolically it is the story of Samson and Delilah, in which Samson, the strong man, functions as the invincible Sun-aspect, the light, while Delilah, which means night, represents the temptation to give in to the dark, unawakened Moon-side. Samson cannot withstand the temptation and loses his strength and eventually his life.

People with this degree prominent have to be wary of any unlucky chance in life. Physically they have to be careful when climbing mountains and cliffs.

As this is a typical Libra degree, one cannot really diagnose, from the outside, what is wrong. It depends entirely on the complete horoscope and the place of the Sun, the Moon and Venus.

The falling of rings, or chains, symbolises the loss of loyalty towards life, and the loss of the continuity of their past, present and future lives. They need to work on their own inner peace and make it their daily bread. The way to attain this peace is symbolised in the second image. These people may have to descend into the lower regions of the earth first, following the example of the Master.

Second Image, Inner Symbol

Inspired disciples listen to the words of their teacher.

Interpretation

Knowledge, experience and insight, together with the ability to live according to one's own teachings, are all being tested here. Inner greatness calls for the highest conceivable destination. The seekers are searching along safe and orderly pathways, guided by a wise Teacher. All outer appearances are being studied, not taken at face value. The Self is now learning to listen to the inner selves. The teacher is their own inner guide. Their inner attention has now found a high and wide vantage point, the danger from below has passed, and spirit and soul are filled with true inspiration. The perils of the first image can be completely overcome by ascension to a higher plane (Li. air sign).

Biblical Parallels

The story of Samson. See *Judg. 14, 15, 16*.
Ascension. See *Acts 1: 9–11* and *Eph. 4: 8–10*.
'When he ascended upon high, He led captivity captive, and gave gifts unto men.' *Eph. 4: 8*.
'He also descended first into the lower parts of the earth.' *Eph. 4: 9*.
'Peace I leave you, my peace I give you.' *Jn. 14: 27*.

Conception Corrected Asc. 5th Libra

Comtesse Marie d'Agoult, if born premature. See 6th Libra.

Pearl Buck CC for 282 days at 12.24 hrs. gives 4°45 Libra, see 6th Libra.

Isaac Israels Born 3 Feb. 1865 at 21.30 hrs. in Amsterdam, 51°30 N, 04.99 E. Killed by a passing car 7 Oct. 1934. CC WAK for 291 days at 21.33 hrs. (late birth) gives 4°49 Libra, or CC NS for 263 days at 21.29 hrs. gives 3°56 Libra.

Dutch impressionistic painter. Son of the well-known Dutch painter Joseph Israels (see 8th Sag.). He was immensely interested in people and well-known for his street-life paintings. A close study of his life gave Willem Koppejan a strong impression of the 'Samson-Delilah' struggle in Israels' nature, and consequently the battle between light and darkness in his paintings, which made WAK choose this degree. See also 4th Libra.

Daphne du Maurier If birth overdue, CC NS for 292 days at 15.07 hrs. gives 4°47 Libra. See 6th Libra.

Frans Masereel Born 30 July 1889 at 10.00 hrs. in Blankenberge, 51°19 N, 03°08 E. Died 1972. CC NS for 271 days at 10.06 hrs. gives 5°59 Libra (see 6th Li.), or for 285 days at 09.58 hrs. gives 4°43 Libra.

Flemish painter, woodcarver and teacher. His biography by Frans Buyers is entitled *I Love Black and White*. His wood engraving technique is known as the 'Black and Whites'. He always had an intense interest in his pupils and the younger generation in general, and youngsters still listened to his inspired words when he was in his eighties, which may be an indication for the 5th Libra.

Elizabeth Taylor Born 27 Feb. 1932 in London, 52°30 N, 00.00, at 20.00 hrs. (according to the mother at 19.56 hrs. in *Astrol. Jour.* 67/68, not at 01.30 hrs. as given by Ebertin). CC NS for 263 days at 20.02 hrs. gives 4°12 Libra.

American film-actress, famous for starring in *Cleopatra*, *The Taming of the Shrew* and *Who's Afraid of Virginia Woolf?* She has been married seven times, Twice to Richard Burton. He was notorious for buying her the most expensive diamond rings. In 1987 she bought the feather diamond broach from the Duchess of Windsor's legacy in aid of Aids research. She is its American Chairman (1988). Her character is one of inner greatness, though often misunderstood. All her experiences with rings and broken marriages are indications for her 5th Libra Ascendant.

6TH DEGREE LIBRA

First Image, Outer Symbol

A farmer is ploughing his field. At the end of the field one can see beautiful haystacks, which encourage him in his work.

Interpretation

According to Janduz this is simply a degree of 'labour'. However, this is a Libra degree with Virgo in the hind-axis and Taurus in the fore-axis, therefore it is a more complicated image than one assumes at first sight.

On the ordinary physical level these people may be interested in farming and make it their occupation. Their farm, or business, may flourish. They deserve to become rich: they work hard throughout their entire life. They demand a lot of themselves and their staff. Their commercial instinct (Vi.) is great: they buy and sell at the right time (Ge.).

However, this image may be lived out on different levels. Their ideal choice of work depends on the entire horoscope. In any case they will probably be concerned with Mother Earth, and with the survival of this planet and its natural products.

Looking deeper into the symbol, we see the grail-cup of Libra clearly represented, with its squares also (Cn.–Cap.). In the first place the man is tilling the earth, which is Taurus, and is representing the primeval force of work (Vi.). In the same fore-axis we find Scorpio. Without its depth and hidden transformation, the seeds would not grow and bear fruit. Quiet growth, and deepening of their character, is very much needed for the people with this degree.

The difficult hind-axis Virgo–Pisces is almost too prominent here. It shows that these people can lapse into being too much on their own (neg. Pi.), concerning themselves excessively with economic details, thus tending to become slaves to their work (neg. Vi.). On the positive side they are very practical and decent, and have an exceptional bond with nature (Pi.).

Aries, as the opposite sign to Libra, comes to the fore in the independence of the man (consciousness) and the phase of the ploughing, which initiates a new cycle. We should not forget, however, that this is a Libra degree. These people are basically born to co-operate (Li.). They will do well when working in partnership with their boss, their partner, or their children. Their doubts about their emotional attachments, their feelings for home and family (Cn.), and their fears for their moral status (Cap.) and integrity, need to be overcome. They can do this by the use of their good intellect (Vi.) and foresight (Tau.), and by their true love for the planet and their concern that it should return to peace and balance.

Their life may not be easy. They need to do a lot of hard work in preparation for the fulfilment of their ideals (see second image). As artists (Li.), they may plough for years before they can give an inner concept (Cn. sq.) outer form (Cap. sq.). Their doubts are many, but they are loyal to their ideals. They are peaceful people and will seldom start a quarrel.

Second Image, Inner Symbol

In a trance, a pilgrim beholds his ideals made concrete.

Interpretation

This is not the way of an outer pilgrimage. The people of the first image may work so hard on the material plane that they forget the contact with the higher worlds (Aq. trine) and neglect the study of the ancient wisdom (Ge. trine). Here in this image, these people have to rise to a higher inner level (the 'trance'), and to think and see their way through, in order to reach their inner sanctuary; otherwise they remain doubters and get only disappointment out of life (neg. Li.).

The lesson from this image is that these people have to be

confronted with their own objectives. In a kind of inner dream state, they need to learn whether or not their ideal is too low, too earthbound and materialistic, and whether it is true or false. They may be slow to see this, as they are often very attached to their own ideas.

The pilgrim is an archetypal symbol of man's celestial origin, and of life as a path of return to the Centre. It shows that these people are open to faith. They need to awaken more to themselves, and to the set-up of their present life. They must not be bound by the emotional ties with their fathers and mothers, or by misunderstood relationships (sq. Cn.–Cap.).

Even though they still seem to be in a trance, at the end of their lives they will harvest respect, as it will become clear how much good they have achieved. They should wake up to the fact that they are not alone in their work or ideals, but are part of a larger, world-wide movement to make inner peace, and planetary peace, a concrete reality.

Biblical Parallels

'No man, having put his hand to the plough, and looking back, is fit for the kingdom of God.' *Lk. 9: 62*.

'. . . he that ploweth should plow in hope.' See *1 Cor. 9–12*.

Conception Corrected Asc. 6th Libra

Comtesse Marie d'Agoult   Born 30 Dec. 1805 at 23.55 hrs. in Frankfurt, 50°07 N, 08°40E. Died 1876. CC WAK and NS for 289 days at 23.56 hrs. gives 05°53 Libra. If eight-month child CC NS for 233 days at 23.47 hrs. gives 4°05 Libra.

French author whose *nom de plume* was Daniel Stern. She became the mistress of the musician Franz Liszt (See 26th Le.), to whom she bore three children. One of them, Cosima, became the wife of Richard Wagner. She wrote novels and political and historical essays. She is remembered for her interesting correspondence (See *Encyc. Britt.* – which wrongly gives her birth as 31 Dec.).

Douglas M. Baker   See 7th Libra.

Pearl Buck Born 26 June 1892 at 12.30 hrs. in Hillsboro (Va., USA), 39°40 N, 79°00 W (conceived in China). CC NS for 296 days (late birth) at 12.28 hrs. gives 5°33 Libra, or for 268 days at 12.34 hrs. gives 6°49 Libra (see 7th Li.), or for 282 days (late birth) at 12.24 hrs. gives 4°45 Libra (see 5th Li.).

American writer, famous for her book *The Good Earth* (a trilogy) for which she received the Nobel Prize (1938), written about China, where she lived as a daughter of American missionaries. This 6th Libra seems to be symbolic of her life's circumstances. In the first image one can see the Chinese agriculture of her days and in the second one the ideals of the mission where she grew up.

As well as writing novels on China, and biographies, she also wrote her autobiography *My Several Worlds* (1954). See *The Trutine of Hermes* by Niek Scheps (Element Books, 1990).

Daphne du Maurier Born 13 May 1907, at 15.00 hrs. (personal information) in London 51°30 N, 00.00. Died 19 April 1989. CC WAK and NS for 278 days at 15.14 hrs. gives 5°52 Libra, or for 264 days at 15.08 hrs. gives 5°01 Libra. See 5th Libra for 292 days.

One of the most famous British novelists. Her books are mainly set in Cornwall – *Jamaica Inn, Frenchman's Creek, Rebecca* and others. Most of these have been filmed. Dame Daphne married General F. A. M. Browning, who was one of the commanders at 'Operation Market Garden' at the Battle of Arnhem, Holland in Sept. 1944. Through personal correspondence we know how Daphne du Maurier ploughed steadily through the historical background of her subject, followed by three months almost in a trance, working in an empty room with bare walls and only a table to give form to her vision, and interrupted only by hard manual work in the garden of her Cornish estate. Her life and work is much more the personification of 6th Libra than of 5th Libra; She herself agreed to the images of the 6th.

7th DEGREE LIBRA

First Image, Outer Symbol

A large black bird (probably an eagle), with claws dripping blood, is flying low over a vast landscape. Higher up in the sky in front of it and to the right, a white triangle, with its point uppermost, is as it were suspended between heaven and earth. Its sides are surrounded by flames of light, which burn without consuming it.

Interpretation

Janduz calls this a degree of 'devouring ardour'. What she means by this is unclear. In any case, as one of the 7th degrees of the zodiac, this image is the bearer of enormous potential forces, which are not yet disciplined and integrated within the personality. It is a dualistic image, as are many of the air sign images. There is the danger of a split within the personality. These people tend to prefer the beautiful right part and to suppress the side of the dark bird.

At first sight, people with this degree rising show both sides. Within the peaceful Libra, the black bird is very unlike them. The eagle, if such it is, comes under Scorpio, the fore-axis towards which they have to grow. Their placidity then changes to sharp and analytical intelligence. They are seekers and searchers for the heights, but they often do not reach further than personal ambition and egotism will take them: for instance, they may tyrannise over an entire family to satisfy their need for ascendancy. They want everyone to dance to their tune and they can be very resentful of anyone who resists. They will even stoop to blackmail. Meantime they are blind to their own faults of character and they may be open to bribes, masking the good qualities they do in fact possess. They can be very sharp and ingenious masters of their trade. Such extremists cannot be put back on the right track with any argument.

The dark side in them (the bird) is as strongly black as the light side is white, and the weightless triangle represents the white magical forces or Plutonic energy fields (Ar. opp. Li.). These burn in the pure Libra air and move upwards towards regions of the pure white spirit. (Both symbols are venerated by the Americans/Indians.) On the credit side these people have exceptional resources. They are able to work creatively and to accomplish things whose visionary conception will only be appreciated in the far-off future. It sometimes seems as if they create things out of nothing. The secret of any true creativity lies in the fact that the 'higher up' in matter one starts bringing things into form, the more exalted the end results will be. People with this degree prominent know this primordial process. They do not spare themselves in their passion to reveal what they know to be the best. They go to the limit.

However, if at the same time their other part remains aggressive, posterity may judge them scoundrels and it may be a long time before the whole truth about them is known.

They are people who do not easily find their master in this life. If they dabble in occultism, they may follow sinister figures with enthusiasm, only to wring their neck the next, quite unconscious of any inconsistency in their behaviour (look them in their eyes, which can be burning). At the end of their lives they may become more balanced, but is this because they have not worked out their absolutely white–black attitude? They need to combine, not offset, these two parts of the image.

In their Libra grail they may live the opposite sign Aries on the worldly level of the passionate and aggressive Mars, or on the spiritually evolving level of the uplifting Pluto energies. The black bird needs to become the phoenix, the flames of the triangle have to leap over to the claws of the bird. The triangle should borrow the wings of the black bird, stop floating, and come down to earth and be grounded.

The difficult hind-axis is Virgo–Pisces. There is lack of self-criticism and true religious sensitivity. There seems to be too much of Scorpio–Taurus in this image.

The binding element between the two parts is the earth, without which they are adrift in thin air. The problem of this degree is worked out further in the second image.

Second Image, Inner Symbol

A witch feeds chickens frightened by a hawk she has tamed.

Interpretation

Witches are familiar figures in occultism and magic. On the black side they can suck and pester animals. On a higher level the 'white witches' are the herb-seekers and the healers of animals and plants. Here is a witch (white or black) who feeds (Cn.) young magical forces (chickens come under Aries). There is still the fear, characteristic of Capricorn, which sign is not yet under control (sq. Li.). The witch, who is the female side, or the soul on a certain level, has not yet fully disciplined and integrated that which she has tamed herself. The black bird with drops of blood has now become the hawk, or falcon, a symbol of the incarnating human being. People with this degree prominent need to gain control of the fears accumulated from past incarnations. Too often their intuitive understanding is not keen enough for the control of their instincts. They have to tame themselves before they can teach others: their power of transmutation is enormous, they are exceptional people with many faces behind their aims in life. Who will work this out with them? They ask to be led, but this is no mean task for the small egos which get crushed in their neighbourhood. Only the highly evolved can lift this degree up to its heights.

Biblical Parallels

On a high level the symbol of this degree bears the secret of a parable about the house of Israel: 'A great eagle with great wings, long-winged, full of feathers, which had divers colours, came unto Lebanon, and took the highest branch of the cedar: He cropped off the top of his young twigs, and carried it into a land of traffick.' *Ezek. 17: 3–5.*

This is supposed to be a parable of the king's daughters known as Tamar, Tephi and Scota, being carried away to Ireland at the captivity of Israel (eighth century BC), from whom, according to tradition, the British Royal House stems. The triangle is a symbol of the Pyramid of Giza and its secrets.

Note

The bird can also be a pelican picking its own breast so that drops of blood fall down over its feet as a symbol of self-sacrifice.

Conception Corrected Asc. 7th Libra

Douglas M. Baker.   Born 31 Dec. 1922 at 23.55 hrs. in London, 51°30 N, 00°00 W. CC NS for 282 days at 23°56 hrs. gives 6°00 Libra, which is a 'double' Ascendant. See 6th Libra as well.

English lecturer, author, mystic and astrologer. Author of many books, such as *Esoteric Astrology* based on Alice Bailey. This degree seems to fit his personality, when interpreted on a high esoteric level.

François Mitterand   Born 26 Oct. 1916 at 04.00 hrs. in Jarnac, 45°40 N, 00°25 W. CC NS for 261 days (regular) at 04.16 hrs. gives 6°09 Libra or for 289 days at 04.18 hrs. gives 6°21 Libra, or, for 275 days at 03.55 hrs. gives 2°15 Libra.

French politician and socialist prime minister till 1986. Elected president in 1988. He was a prominent fighter in the French resistance movement during World War II. See 3rd Libra.

Simon Wiesenthal   Born 31 Dec. 1908 at 23.30 hrs. (according to his mother in his book *Murderers Amongst Us*) in Biczacz, 48°50 N, 24°00 E. CC NS for 261 days at 23.26 hrs. gives 6°31 Libra, or for 289 days at 23.24 hrs. gives 6°07 Libra.

Jewish author and main prosecutor of World War II war criminals, still finding one as late as 1988. This 7th Libra fits the man and his books like a glove. He reminds us of the heraldic symbol of Germany, the eagle, having the blood of war crimes. He is like an eagle picking his victims, while fighting for peace and in defence of his vulnerable Jewish clients. He made his name with Eichmann (see 4th Ge.).

8TH DEGREE LIBRA

First Image, Outer Symbol

Two gladiators in an arena. One of them is carrying a poignard and a shield, the other fights with a net and a trident.

Interpretation

This is a peculiar image in a Libra degree. It is all fighting, action and power. Janduz calls this a degree of 'tragedy'. It is indeed one of pain and trouble, and of inner as well as outer conflicts. However, this kind of fighting has something artistic (Li.) about it. Tens of thousands once watched this art of fighting. Nowadays it can be compared with the martial arts of Japanese warriors and with yoga.

People with this symbol prominent in their character have a kind of vitality which can work out as hot temper or touchiness. They always want to argue and dispute. They like to debate. They may be deaf to sound reasoning or to practicalities.

On the highest level this is an exceptional degree, because the Libra tendency to too much peace and harmony is offset here by the urgent need for activity to find and sustain a balance. The gladiators seem to be evenly matched, but the battle could go either way.

People with this degree on the Ascendant cannot tolerate opposition. They will fight till the other bites the dust. They often have both hidden and open enemies (Sc. fore-axis), or they think they have, because their nature is inclined to suspicion. They do not always fight fair. They favour the surprise attack (Aq. trine), and are very ready to take advantage of a weaker adversary. They are not only forceful, but they can also be quite cunning and sly.

On the high level of the Libra grail they can be exemplary fighters who have the classical rules (Cap.) of fighting by heart, and their emotions (Cn.) well under control. In other words they have overcome the squares of the cardinal cross.

On the social level, these people feel happiest when they can make some form of fighting their profession. They have to defend something of public importance. They make good lawyers, advocates, or surgeons (who fight with death). They can do well in the police force, in military service, or as martial arts instructors.

As this is a Libra degree, the two sides in their character may get completely out of balance, leading to suicide, because one part in them hates the other part, or this problem may be modified so that they want only to risk a tragic death. They can avoid this state of affairs by cultivating self-discipline and mental strength. They are capable of achieving mental suppleness, elasticity and sportsmanship.

There is a good deal of outer show in this symbol. These people often need a public (the arena) to rouse their mettle. As artists they tackle their material with a fervour which almost makes them seem possessed, and as though they were engaged in a matter of life and death.

Second Image, Inner Symbol

A fireplace blazes mysteriously in a deserted farmhouse.

Interpretation

The inner fire or zeal needs to come out into the open and become the centre of their being. All the tension of the fighting and the show are over, and have turned into a most peaceful attitude of spirit, mind and body. In this symbol is the constant unseen presence of sustaining energies. There is depth in this image. One can sense hard work in the background on the farm. Why else would the farmhouse be deserted? The visitor (Ge.) is obviously welcome and trusted (Aq.). Having conquered the squares of the cardinal cross in the first image, here it is the trines of the three air signs that have come into balance. When these people have made peace with themselves, all earthly good will be provided, and they will be protected from negative forces.

Conception Corrected Asc. 8th Libra

Thys Mauve   Born 26 Nov. 1915 at 14.30 hrs. in The Hague, 52°06 N, 04°00 E. CC WAK for 281 days at 14.25 hrs. gives 7°24 Libra.

Grandson of Anton Mauve. Dutch painter, wood engraver and art teacher. He migrated to a 600-year-old cottage in a remote valley of south Devon, England, where he covers enormous canvases with lonely landscapes and deserted tin mines. He has painted murals on the old walls around his wood fire. Always in dialogue with himself, the life-style of this third generation Dutch painter is a typical example of an artist with this 8th Libra as a symbol of his personality.

Anton Webern   Born 3 Dec. 1883 at 02.00 hrs. in Vienna, 48°13 N, 16°25 E. Shot 13 Sept. 1945. CC NS for 267 days at 01.55 hrs. gives 7°40 Libra.

Austrian composer and conductor. In 1933 he wrote against Nazi influence in music. Ironically he was killed by a Canadian guard when he approached too close to the fence of a prisoner of war camp while 'in a dreaming mood'. He was one of the first disciples of Schönberg (see 18th Vi.).

9TH DEGREE LIBRA

First Image, Outer Symbol

At the left is a sick-room, where a sick person is in bed, a woman is busy and a little boy is crying. At the right a young girl in tears is seated on the ledge of a mausoleum.

Interpretation

This is quite a complicated image. The general impression is one of grief. This degree shows an archetypal problem of Libra in general. People with this degree rising may be separated from their loved ones by fate or death, but their dearest wish is to unite all that is alive, and to be completely at one with the partner, or with those they work with. However, for them life is not like this.

Following Libra is Scorpio, which holds the secrets of death and transformation. If Libra people do not make peace with these forces, they may become petrified (the girl on the stone) and shut themselves up in their negative emotions (Li. sq. Cn.–Cap.). They may have to learn to be less dependent on others, if they are not to get out of balance (neg. Li.). This may be taught by rather dramatic circumstances in which sickness, or the death of their nearest ones, may bring tragedy (Pi.), which is difficult to work through (Sc.). These people may be deprived of tenderness and love, especially in childhood. For instance, the father-figure may be chronically ill (Cap. sq. Li.), or the mother too busy nursing others (Vi. behind Li.).

There may be the danger of seeking escape from the situation by a too hasty marriage, or other untimely partnership, in which the same tendencies repeat themselves. Again they are the ones who comfort and give solace, getting very little in return. However, the need, for people with this degree prominent, is to stand up, straighten their back and turn to daily practical work (Vi.–Pi. hind-axis). They may do well nursing the sick and dying, though they will have to guard against too close an identification with their patients. Negatively, they may have a depressing influence on others, which may lead people to avoid them.

Depending on their entire horoscope, those who have this degree rising may have to work out problems and afflictions with their sixth and twelfth house, which give indications of a weak constitution and chronic diseases. Note that Libra rising always has Pisces on the cusp of the sixth house and Virgo on the cusp of the twelfth, which is another indication of professional involvement in health and healing, or in nutrition.

For their spiritual development Libras have to fill their grail-cup with the energies of Scorpio–Taurus. This causes them to be at peace with death and the decay of the earth, and their own cycle within it. Instead of reacting to death with hysterical grief, they need to accept it heroically. Death may indeed become their best friend. These are not superficial people. They can foresee tragedies, maybe even with so-called 'second sight', and they have to make themselves spiritually strong in advance, to be able to take what comes. Their young consciousness (the boy) is growing through this process. They need to learn, as Libra, that inwardly they are never alone. They are helped by the unseen angelic forces (Aq. trine). They need to learn that mourning is not always the way to remember the dead, because it holds those they love back from ascending to other realms, and it makes their own feelings cold. On a high level they begin to unite their spirit, soul and body into one harmonious whole. Spirit and mind are still weaker (the sick man and the boy) than the soul (the two women), but they can all become inspired, as the second image shows.

Second Image, Inner Symbol

Three 'old masters' (paintings) hang alone in an art gallery.

Interpretation

Libra is the sign of art. The trinity, which is the human spirit, soul and body, is symbolised here in unity. The mind has still to grow (the boy). The soul has still to go through experiences and serve (the nurse and the crying girl). The body (the mausoleum and the room) needs to go through the difficulties of physical incarnation.

The old consciousness (man in bed) needs to die in peace. Integrated wisdom and artistic energies are the harmonious result (the paintings). The horizontal mausoleum has become a vertical wall. Through high-powered initiation (Ar. opp. Li.) by way of sorrow, which makes these people creative, their sublime contentment comes out. It is the same heroic greatness which may be hidden within the first image.

They may be alone, but not lonely. They are pure (Vi.) and potentially strong (Ar.). What they form in matter by their receptiveness (Tau.), grows constantly in value in time, until it becomes perfect both in the eyes of the creator and the beholder.

Biblical Parallels

'Heal the sick, cleanse the lepers.' *Mt. 10: 8.*

Many references for the laying on of hands. See for instance *Mk. 6: 5* and *16: 18.*

'And he sent them to preach the kingdom of God and to heal the sick.' *Lk. 9: 2.*

10TH DEGREE LIBRA

First Image, Outer Symbol

A fortress in a rather ruinous state, but rooms are still in existence. The closed front gate is still remarkably well pre-served, with nails and sharp iron spikes. At a small distance to the right is the remains of a gibbet, underneath which two or three ravens pick at the ground in search of the last remnants of some flesh.

Interpretation

According to Janduz this is a degree of 'reclusion'. This image, at first sight, looks quite lugubrious, and this is indeed a sinister symbol in the deeper astral plane. Janduz says that people with this degree rising, or with an important planet here, may be 'marked by a hereditary transmission of mean and base instincts'. Apparently this is according to tradition.

Indeed there may be old karma and guilt from former lives, which have to be resolved (the ravens, Cap., searching for flesh, Sc.). Pain and violent death from previous incarnations as the legacy of karma, have to be faced. It seems to be a very un-Venusian image in the peaceful sign of Libra, but looking deeper we see the Libra grail in its almost perfect negativity.

On the outer level these people may have been spoilt children, whose security in this life has fallen away, so that they go to pieces. They may be left to fend for themselves completely and in consequence end up on the gallows, or they may have a harsh parent or guardian, who leaves them for the rest of their life with fear-complexes, or fantasies of being hanged for minor offences (Cn.–Cap. sq. Li.).

The negative side of the Libra grail comes to the fore when they cannot cope with the difficulties of the hind-axis Virgo–Pisces. Their way of life then becomes murky and confused. The opposite sign Aries, which asks Libra to be strong in its independence, becomes over-compensated in rebellion. When inner support is lacking, the fore-axis Taurus–Scorpio comes up in its negative way with greed (Sc.) for material possessions (Tau.), and they become pugnacious.

It is a statistical fact that many high-ranking military servicemen have the Sun or Ascendant in Libra, the sign of peace. This is the problem. They cannot reach that level and the end is a drama of imprisonment, exile, the gallows, or becoming enmeshed in crime or bribery. The life of people with this degree can become a ruin, as persons on the lowest level have a complete lack of conscience (neg. Cap.). Sarcastic in manner, given to theft and libel (neg. Pi.–Sc.), they are misanthropists who metaphorically speaking hang all who will not conform. Sadistic fantasies (the iron spikes on the gate) colour their existence.

However, on a higher level there are those who make an end of all this negativity by becoming social workers, detectives, criminal investigators or psychiatrists, those in other words who deal with the worst of society. They then meet on the outside that which is deep inside themselves, either left over from past lives or from a traumatic youth which they have successfully overcome. They still have to cope with the ruinous state of their inner fortress, though showing a good front door.

In the highest instance this image is exemplary of Christ's vicarious suffering and His taking upon Himself the sins of the world, on Golgotha – a world in ruins.

It is the one degree in the zodiac where everything has to be done to eliminate the last remnants of the past (karma, reincarnation), so that the power of the resurrection (Ar.) may come into play, even to the point of sacrificing one's life. This means the transformation of the body by Plutonic energy into a totally new creation, a body of light.

People with this degree prominent in their chart can work

in a Christlike manner with utter self-criticism (Vi.) and in repentance for the past, giving themselves over to God to be made better beings. The collective heritage of Adam's fall from Paradise can only be redeemed, day by day, by letting the old Adam and Eve in self be crucified. This is the deepest spiritual meaning of this awesome degree.

After this experience in physical reality, or in the inner astral realms, the soul may breathe again and come into calmer times.

Second Image, Inner Symbol

A canoe leaving narrow rapids reaches calm waters.

Interpretation

After what has gone before, time (the water) is now moving faster. It is flowing like a cataract. The canoe, symbol for the boat of life, is now speeding over the water of the inner emotions (overcoming the sq.-axis Cn.-Cap.), into calmness and peace of mind (Li.). There is the confidence that the waters of life will carry one through, if one adapts, and surrenders to anything that may happen around the corner. Manual skills (Ge. trine) and intuition (Aq. trine) are needed, and must come under the guidance of the higher messengers (Ge.) and angels (Aq.).

It is typical for Libra that in any difficult position the right balance must be kept, to manoeuvre through trouble without panic. Victory will come through courage (Le.) and a sense of destination (Sag.). As crucifixion can be a symbol of supernatural courage, so can this canoe trip symbolise great bravery with supernatural forces helping to keep the balance.

As this Libra degree reaches from the deepest to the highest planes, the great lesson here is to find and keep the Divine balance.

Biblical Parallels

Golgotha. See *Mt. 27: 33; Mk. 15: 22; Lk. 23: 33;* and *Jn. 19: 17.*

Conception Corrected Asc. 10th Libra

André Gide   CC WAK and NS for 279 days at 02.46 hrs. gives 9°29 Libra, but WAK gave preference to 11th Libra: see there.

John Lennon   (p.s. for John Winston)   Born 9 Oct. 1940 at 07.00 hrs. (= 06.00 GMT) in Liverpool, 53°25 N, 03°00 W. Assassinated in New York, 1980, CC NS for 267 days at 06.57 hrs. gives 9°42 Libra.

English pop-singer. He became world-famous as leader of the Beatles (1960), which brought a totally new era of 'Rock and Roll' into music. His and Paul McCartney's songs were genial, worthy of a double Libra, but he was also involved in introducing mass festivals, in which drug-taking was widespread. He was himself imprisoned for drug offences. His break with the Beatles and former friends seems to be a reflection of 10th Libra. He became notorious for his publicity stunts when a top world pop-star, such as displaying a photograph of himself with his wife Yoko naked in bed, on the cover of their record. He was a multimillionaire. His death was mourned by fans the world over. The medium Rosemary Brown claims to be in communication with him and to have 'brought through' his songs, which speak of loneliness, sorrow and alienation. See *Look Beyond Today* by Rosemary Brown (Bantam 1986).

Constant Permeke   Born 31 July 1886 at 10.15 hrs. in Antwerp, 51°12 N, 04°24 E. Died 1952. CCWAK an NS for 240 days (8 months) at 10.17 hrs. gives 9°33 Libra, or for 296 days at 10.05 hrs. gives 10.48 hrs.

Belgian painter and one of the most important Flemish expressionists. Shot in World War I, he lost both legs, but in a superhuman effort he even became a sculptor. In retrospect his art gives an expression of his time between the two world wars; the essence of it is the beastliness of man without heart or gentleness, but also the magnificence of his staunch invincibility.

11TH DEGREE LIBRA

First Image, Outer Symbol

A half-dressed man with a black head and body, but white hands and feet, is running and trying to jump onto the hindquarters of a centaur, who brandishes his bow in the right hand, without shooting the arrow in his left.

Interpretation

This is a degree of 'duality'. It is very important in general, but especially here, to see the entire horoscope, in order to interpret whether people with this degree rising or with a planet prominent here, could attain a high level of spiritual awareness, or whether they tend to live this image on a low level with almost bestial instincts.

The centaur is a positive symbol representing the sign of Sagittarius itself. As half-horse, half-man, these people have to sublimate their lower instincts, controlling those passions which are seated in the intestines and sexual organs (Vi.–Sc.), and the other organs of the alimentary canal below the diaphragm. In other words they have to learn to get their base and root chakras under control. At the same time their spiritual side and the upper chakras are constantly aiming at higher goals.

We can see the Libra grail here, although it is hidden. The hind part of the centaur accentuates the Taurus–Scorpio fore-axis, into which Libra needs to grow. Note: J. E. Cirlot defines the centaur as 'the antithesis of the knight, that is, it represents the complete domination of a being by the baser forces. In other words, it denotes cosmic force, the instincts, or the unconscious, uncontrolled by the spirit.'

The half-dark figure is not so easy to interpret. Is he invited to join the centaur, or is he trying to be a hindrance? There is something odd about the skin. Pigmentation comes under Capricorn (sq. Li.), as it is a question of the skin (Cap.). As the head (Ar.) is black, one might interpret this as black-magical powers (neg. Ar.). Aries is the sign opposite Libra, and represents its completion.

There is much inner tension in this image. Therefore there is 'duality' (Ge.) indeed. There is an ambiguity in the character of these people. Libra, as the sign of balance, needs to bring this ambivalence into harmony.

Having white hands and feet indicates that purity is already coming through these extremities. Hands are symbols of Gemini – higher wisdom and knowledge – and the white feet are symbolic of Pisces – purification and sacrifice – difficult for Libra, as it is the hind-axis Virgo–Pisces. They need to prevent all the black magical forces from going through their head. Wanting to jump on the centaur shows that they are sincere in their thinking, and wish for inner purification and transformation (Vi. and Sc. around Li.).

This black–white figure will still sit only on the hind parts of the horse, which means he will mingle with the centaur's digestive (Vi.) and sexual (Sc.) organs only. This may symbolise that on a high level these people need to harmonise and bring together all that which comes under Virgo–Scorpio. Esoterically speaking this has to do with the ten-sign zodiac versus the twelve-sign zodiac, which is too vast a subject to deal with here.

It is very important on what level of awareness this image is lived. A strong Mars in this degree brings out the activity and sexual energy. Jupiter strengthens right thinking (Sag.). Uranus brings it onto a more humane plane.

Because of its ambiguity, Janduz connects this degree with several dangerous personality types: hypocrites; people who can easily change their ideals; and merchants and diplomats whose ideals are for sale, and who change with the wind or the ruler of a political party.

If we interpret this on a higher level we can see these people as being idealistic, with plans which are original but very short-lived. They can easily fall back into dark and passionate schemes. However, they are open and active, and show that they want to be first in the race. They have courage and could be reckless. They may be rather idle and pedantic, but on the whole they move towards a sympathetic destiny (Sag.).

Parents, or educators of people with this Ascendant could be horse-breeders or fanatical horse-lovers. As the sexual drive is not always under control, there might be a tendency towards sexual excesses, or unwanted pregnancies.

Their goals may not always be as precise as one would wish. The centaur has got the tools in its hand, but does not use them. Their thinking is not yet fully grown. However, on the high level, they have happy, joyful natures, and when they can integrate themselves, a happy marriage or companionship (Li.) may be the result.

Second Image, Inner Symbol

A kindly old professor is teaching a class of youngsters.

Interpretation

The two rather uncanny figures of the first image have grown into a normal, kind, old teacher (Sag.), giving his wisdom to those of younger consciousness. The youngsters may be a mixture of black and white races, but at least they are whole in themselves and not a hotchpotch, such as we saw in the first image.

Here the spirit (the professor) becomes an example, worthy of being listened to and followed. Unlike the first image, here there is co-operation and goodwill. As this is a Libra degree, these people are now growing into a wise unity with the spirit and the still-learning parts of their mind. The symbol of a kind old professor is an evolution of spiritual awareness and the desire to pass on a long life's experience. His sexual activity has been sublimated into kindness (Sc.–Tau. fore-axis). His wish to help a younger generation is born out of purified and transformed (Vi.–Sc.) thinking. The youngsters are not wasting their energy in running after a mythological beast: they control their wild activity, and discipline themselves to sit still (Ar. opp. Li.), for the reception of higher knowledge. Having overcome their lower passions these people are now advanced far enough to be amiable, wise and balanced.

Conception Corrected Asc. 11th Libra

André Gide   Born 22 Nov. 1869 at 03.00 hrs. in Paris, 48°50 N, 02°20 E. Died 19 Feb. 1951. CC WAK and NS for 294 days (late birth) at 02.50 hrs. gives 10°09 Libra, which CC has preference over CC for 279 days at 02.46 hrs., which gives 09°29 Libra.

One of the most influential French authors of the twentieth century. He was known as a man who had a bad influence on youth. A homosexual, he called himself 'the man who cannot lie', which meant that he spoke the truth in a shocking way. He preached literally 'to give all passion a free rein'. In 1932 he became a Communist, but a journey to Moscow opened his eyes. Winner of the Nobel Prize in 1947, several of his plays were filmed. The best-known is *La Symphonie Pastorale*. He was a personal friend of Oscar Wilde, about whom he published an autobiographical study. See *Encycl. Britt.* and others.

In a very different way from the Austrian Emperor, Gide is a striking example of 11th Libra.

Emperor Franz Joseph Hapsburg of Austria–Hungary   Born 18 Aug. 1830 at 09.15 hrs. in Vienna, 48°13 N, 16°15 E. Died 21 Nov. 1916. CC WAK and NS for 283 days at 09.13 hrs. gives 10°38 Libra, or for 255 days at 09.14 hrs. gives 10°55 Libra.

One needs to study the dramatic life of Franz Joseph, the last emperor of the Hapsburgs, and his striking horoscope in its entirety in order to appreciate fully how fitting this 11th degree of Libra is. He pursued the false ideal of absolute monarchy, a concept which was already out of date in his own time. All his family either died young of illness, were assassinated or went mad. 'Nothing was spared him,' as he said himself in old age, when his only son was found dead in mysterious circumstances. An astro-biography based on his birth chart could be very revealing.

See biographies and *Encycl. Britt.* under 'Hapsburg'.

Constant Permeke   CC for 296 days (late birth) at 10.05 hrs. gives 10°48 Libra. See 10th Libra.

12TH DEGREE LIBRA

First Image, Outer Symbol

At the left, a woman looking obstinately behind her does not see that her steps carry her towards the brink of a ravine, into which she is about to fall. At the right, another woman, looking at herself coquettishly in a hand-mirror, arrives at the other side of the ravine, where she too is going to tumble. A small dog tries to alert her by pulling at the hem of her long dress.

Interpretation

Janduz calls this degree one of 'happy folly'. She says that people with this degree rising, on a low level of awareness, do not repent in the least about lost times in their life. Even if they look back on their path, they do not gather insight, but go on as if there were no danger.

This is quite right, but what is the reason for it? Why do they like to dance (Li.) on the edge of the abyss? Both ladies, the two sides of the soul, have climbed to the highest level of their ability, but now they feel they have arrived safely and refuse to see their possible downfall.

The sign of Libra can teach us that there are always two sides to be kept in balance, and that there is no lasting safety while on this earth, because the whole of creation is always in a borderline situation (Aq. and Ge. complete with Li., the three air signs). Ours is a fragile equilibrium which can easily be disturbed by emotions (Cn. sq. Li.), or ambition and egotism (Cap. sq. Li.).

If we interpret the gesture of the woman on the left as pausing and looking back on her life, or even lives so far, there is hope for the future, in that she is sensible enough not to follow the same direction as before, and will let the soul listen to the inner warnings of her higher intuition, and will stop and take time to meditate and pray (Sat. of Cap., also rock is Cap. sq. Li.).

The other side of the femininity of these people, the lady at the right, is in far greater danger, as this part in them, having climbed up so high, is now enraptured by its own image in the looking-glass. Having gone so far, she is so fascinated by herself, that she has fallen in love with her own beauty (Li.), so that what she is doing becomes unreal and out of place. Narcissistic love of one's own lower self and the body is psychologically far more dangerous than is realised nowadays. If the Higher Self does not elude this trap, the downfall of the soul will be catastrophic.

Weighing in the balance (Li.) which of these two females has the greater chance of tumbling down, then it is the first one, because she does not get any outer warning (the dog). Although she looks back, there is no one outside herself to hold her back from taking that one fatal step.

However, when we look deeper, it is seen that the greater chance of fatality lies with the woman on the right. She gets a repeated warning right at her feet (Pi., the essence of life through sacrifice), and at the hem of her dress (Cn., the etheric and astral body), from Martial and Plutonic energies (the dog comes under Ar. opp. Li.), telling her to wake up. The dog calls for reversal in these people, so that they may become independent of their own image. If that woman would raise her head (Ar.) and leave the mirror alone, she would immediately realise where she stood.

If she does not heed the warnings of her own inner watchdog, her fall will cause even greater damage, because she has discounted the higher impulses (Ar.) trying to hold her up on the level of existence where she deserves (Vi. hind-axis) to be. The present, which is that moment in time in which the past becomes the future, evades these people. This is the nucleus of this image.

The Libra grail is seen here in detail. One can see it in the lack of certain elements. For instance Virgo, the difficult sign for Libra, seems to be absent. What are these women doing high up there? Should they not be humble, hard-working (Vi.) servants, instead of idlers strolling along a dangerous cliff? Would they not do better to nurse the sick or do a cleaning job (Pi. Vi behind Li.)? Although they do not seem to notice them, pain and death (Sc. fore-axis) are around the corner waiting for them, and there is a deep crisis (Sc.) imminent in their existence. It is as if their astral and etheric bodies have a rift in the middle. There seems a lack of love for mother earth and the soil (Tau. fore-axis), otherwise they would sense the dangerous ravine.

The main problem lies in the cardinal cross (Ar.–Cn.–Li.–Cap.), the magical potential to turn the head (Ar.) away from the vanity in the mirror (Cn.) and to open the ear in time (Cap.) to hear the warning barks of the dog, which ask for action (Ar.). Looking back on personal experiences along the line of time, on the astral and etheric planes, and realising one's guilt, is the square-axis Cancer–Capricorn. Fate (Cap.) can be inexorable. One is confronted with it when misusing time by being absorbed in a false image of one's lower Saturnal ego. The sign of Libra, especially, can fall between two stools.

This 12th degree symbolises this general problem of the cardinal cross. The way out is indicated by the second image.

Second Image, Inner Symbol

Miners are emerging from a deep well into the sunlight.

Interpretation

We do not need to compose a hymn on the mine-workers, but they are no doubt a special species. They are a symbol of hard work and even sometimes human slavery (Vi.) in the depths of the earth (Sc.–Tau). They use their muscles (Ma.–Ar.) to transmute matter. Coal is concentrated solar energy stored millions of years ago and released once more by combustion as fuel (Sc. sq. Le.). Miners need initiative to survive in difficult situations. They are strongly individual, both as persons and as a group. The role of the miner has often been romanticised, for they constantly face death and calamity, but they are indeed a symbol of sacrifice (Pi.).

So here the two ladies have grown into awareness and spiritual readiness. The two sides of the soul have now the courage to descend to the deepest levels of existence, where they meet death (Sc.) in order to resurrect and emerge again higher up towards the sunlight (Le.), which is the heart of the Creator.

The uselessness of the first image has now turned into spiritual progress.

Conception Corrected Asc. 12th Libra

Edith Cavell   Born 4 Dec. 1865 at 02.30 hrs. in Swardeston, Norfolk, 52°33 N, 01°20 W. Executed 12 Oct. 1915 at Schierbeek (Belgium). CC WAK and NS for 264 days at 02.16 hrs. gives 11°38 Libra, which WAK gave preference over the regular CC for 279 days at 02.18 hrs. giving 12°22 Libra.

A nurse in World War I, who spied for the British in Belgium and came to a dramatic end being shot by the Germans. Her bravery became legendary, and her assassination caused a great stir in Britain and the world at the time. There is an apocryphal story that the fatal moment of her discovery as a spy came when she put the milk in her teacup first, before the tea, and not the reverse. This habit showed she was British and not Belgian. See her biography by Ambroise Got (1920), and others. Her fascinating story is given greater depth by her birth chart, and especially with this 12th degree Libra, as a background, which fits her better than the hesitating 13th Libra.

13TH DEGREE LIBRA

First Image, Outer Symbol

A marble pillar, placed at the junction of many roads, is broken at its top. On the column are the words 'Good Luck?' and 'Bad Luck?' inscribed with question marks. A man and a woman are withdrawing from the column, each taking a different road.

Interpretation

Janduz calls this a degree of 'solitude'. As this is a Libra image, there are more higher and lower levels of interpretation to be found than in the other signs, as the symbol of the weighing-scale (Li.) is both material and spiritual in nature.

Here is a classic archetype of Libra. There is a choice of many roads. People with this degree prominent can choose between good and bad. The man and woman can go together or separately. The essence of Libra is to stand in the centre (column) and to hold everything in balance and keep calm.

On a low level of spiritual awareness these people are always in doubt as to which way to go, and they become petrified (the pillar), which gives them a taciturn and even misanthropic streak in their character. They fail to pull themselves together, and they cut off the higher possibilities of spiritual growth in themselves. They close themselves to the world around them, so that they miss their chance of companionship and help that might come their way in a partner. Their own egotism and fear attracts their so-called bad luck. It depends on the position of Saturn in the chart as to which form this will take (marble comes under Cap.sq.Li.).

These people may be torn to pieces, inwardly and outwardly, by opposing ideas or conflicting advice 'Have I to remain?' 'Have I to go?' 'In which direction lies my destination?' They can have a multitude of different and equally valid choices at the same time.

It depends on the position of their Venus (Li.) and Mars (Ar.opp.Li.) whether they just wait sweetly, in which case nothing will happen, or overreact with impulsive activity, and try all the roads at once. They may create confusion (neg. hind-axis Vi.–Pi.), especially in their work. By sentimentality (Cn.sq.Li.), they bring themselves deeper and deeper into chaos. Exhausted, such a person may become a recluse, or enter a place of retreat, in order to escape the awkward contingency of taking any road at all, even literally. They linger, lonely and without understanding why, yearning for their far-away former soul.

It is a general principle that on a low level of awareness the difficulties of the square-axis hit harder and the trines work in a negative way. Here this principle works out in, for instance, trying law cases (Cap.sq.Li.), and in an emotional attachment where it is not understood that past lovers and partners have gone their own way in totally different directions. Old love affairs are cherished so much in the memory that these people may even contemplate suicide (the broken pillar) in their loss.

The three air signs can be seen in their negative aspects. There is dualism and splitting apart (Ge.). There is loss of contact with other people, through a lack of intuition and not seeking the help of higher beings. The third air sign, Libra, shows its uneasy balance and the doubting-Thomas mentality.

On a higher level of consciousness these people begin to realise that they need to consolidate the energy that is given to them, and not waste it. Instead of roads moving away from a centre, one could see these as energy lines, almost like ley lines, feeding in energy from all sides with the speed of light, so that the central being, the Higher Self of these people, becomes like a radiating star. Just as the market cross in an English village can be the centre of the town, where everybody meets, so can these people sublimate their egotistical separateness and become the centre of command in any kind of situation. They could also become a popular social 'pivot' of information, from where everybody goes their own way, happily replenished with new energy, which these people radiate from their Higher Self. They can become a stable rock of marble in the face of opposition. They grow within themselves to transcend the polarities of male and female. Their spiritual centre (the Sun in the chart) is like a round Din-stone, the place where the Vikings of old sat in judgement. They are like the seat where Macrocosm and Microcosm meet. As though in a cosmic traffic centre, they can press the button of any of the twelve signs of the zodiac, give directions and see where it leads. No wonder that this degree confers the capacity to become an all-round artist or astrological consultant. A more mundane profession would be that of a policeman on traffic duty, or working at an information centre, but such work can only be a success when these people have learned the art of spiritual concentration and keeping calm under any emotional stress (pos.Cn.–Cap.axis).

In the highest instance, these people can hear again the cosmic harmony of the spheres, and know the secret of the golden mean in philosophy, and the golden section in architecture and within themselves. They can begin to see life as a crystalline sphere or a ball of manifold colours, which leads on to the second image.

The Libra grail is seen here in the gathering of energy (Ar.opp.Li.), and in the need to search for the validity of the different roads (Vi.) and to find the essence of it all (Pi.).

By accepting 'bad luck' in the form of pain, separation and bereavement, these people will give up their longing for 'good luck' in earthly fortune and financial matters (Sc.–Tau. fore-axis). They need to spiritualise themselves in a balanced way (Li.). They should not let their feelings and memories (Cn.) become a stony burden (Cap.), but breathe out into the cosmos and give back to Mother Earth, the source of their material existence. What on earth will she think of all these different roads carved upon her skin? These people could help the earth to become beautiful again, with only as many crossroads and roundabouts as humanity needs for its survival.

Second Image, Inner Symbol

Children are blowing soap bubbles at a youngsters' party.

Interpretation

This is a symbol of the transitoriness of life in the eyes of eternity. This present incarnation, which seems solid and timeless, like a marble pillar, and which seems to have as many possibilities as there are roads into this eternity, is in fact only a tiny little moment. It is just a blob in the cosmos, and fragile as a soap bubble.

Libra is an air sign and this image is somehow the essence of this zodiac sign. Just as in the first image, concentration is needed, and one must be centred within oneself, which a child still is, in order to blow one's breath through the pipe into the soap. With this breath (Ge., first air sign) comes the intuitive (Aq.) wisdom (Ge.) to combine the three elements – air (Li.), water (Pi.) and earth (soap as a purificator has an element of Vi.–earth in it).

Becoming as children indicates the simplicity and creativity to play with all these elements together, and to bind them (Li.) into a momentous art form (Li.) of a multicoloured breathtaking wonder. Look at the children's eyes. They follow their coloured spheres in all directions (the roads in the first image). When the soap bubbles burst, they learn of the transience and vanity of earthly matter (Tau.–Sc.fore-axis). The symbol of the soap bubble is an archetype of the soul centred in its multicoloured astral body, floating through time and space.

For the people with this degree prominent, life tends to be too heavy and solitary. The great lesson for them is to see life just as a happy party-game, light-hearted and relaxing. Their art is to recreate the cosmos as one whole fantastic soap bubble.

Conception Corrected Asc. 13th Libra

Karl Georg Buchner CC WAK and NS for 267 or 295 days; see 17th Libra.

Edith Cavell CC WAK and NS for 279 days at 02.18 hrs. gives 12°22 Libra; see 12th Libra.

Pierre Loti (pen-name Julian Viaud) Born 14 Jan. 1850 at 23.30 hrs. in Rochefort, 45°57 N, 00°58 W. Died 10 June 1923. CC NS for 296 days at 23.29 hrs. gives 12°09 Libra.

French author. He entered the navy at 17 and as a sea captain he made many voyages all over the world. After being suspended from the service during the Ton-King War (1883) he became a prolific writer basing his works on his experiences in Japan, Senegal, Tahiti, China and the Middle East. An impressionist, evoking more than he describes, his novels are now outdated, but still appreciated for his description of exotic nature and his historic comments on the loss of culture in the victims of colonialism. Nine of his books have been filmed. (See *Larousse*, *MEW* and *Encycl. Britt.*)

Martin Niemöller Born 14 Jan. 1892 at 23.45 hrs. in Lippstadt, 51°40 N, 08°20 E. Died 7 Mar. 1984. CC NS for 281 days at 23.35 hrs. gives 12°34 Libra.

German clergyman, evangelist and writer. Famous for his resistance to the Nazis. He was imprisoned several times (first time 1938), for his political sermons. One of his well-known book titles is *Lord, Where Shall We Go?*. He often spoke about crossroads, such as those of State and Church, which is an indication for 13th Libra.

14TH DEGREE LIBRA

First Image, Outer Symbol

In the middle of a dressing-room is a mirror above a table on which face- and eye-masks, make-up and other properties to disguise the personality have been thrown. At both ends of the room, half hidden behind two door-curtains, a man at the left and a woman at the right peep at each other.

Interpretation

Janduz calls this a degree of 'imitation', but that is a word for Gemini, the other air sign in the trine (Ge.–Li.–Aq.). Janduz' interpretation is not very positive, but is true on a low level. They are illusionists, comedians, or personalities in multiple roles, who renew themselves in reincarnation, though not for the better. They will be applauded for their theatrical talents, as they are born for this glib profession.

It is in the theatre of ordinary life, however, that they simulate and pretend to be what they are not, as yet. Their fantasies may be amusing or dangerous. They are only imitators. Their male side (left) is flattery and leads friends astray into responsibilities they cannot carry, while they themselves are changing their personality. The female side is still more subtle and coquettish, but lacks an interesting personality. In their variety and coldness of feeling they manoeuvre their victims in a way which is not noticed by their onlookers. So far Janduz. Here we come to the deeper interpretation.

On a high level, these people have the power to 'levitate the time' (control over the cardinal cross Ar.–Cn.–Li.–Cap.). The many masks (Ar.) show the opposition sign of Libra. Dresses and paint, the veils and the mirror, are of Cancer showing the 'maya', the illusion and pretence, while the fourth sign of the cardinal cross, Capricorn, is Time.

So here the need is to de-mask the different roles and personalities in the theatre of life, cease the repetitious imitation of the past and of the show, and see the irrelevance of time compared with the true reality of the spirit.

The female and the male part seem not to know each other. They play hide and seek. There is therefore a great need to make an honest and true synthesis between the left part and the right part – the logic and the intuition, the spirit and the soul, the mental and the emotional. Then, when the integration is there, which is so needed for Libra, these people may look at themselves in the mirror and play a new role of lifting others, their audience, above time into eternity. Then they may make their comeback as comedians, acting out the lightness and amusement of heavenly things, so that life on earth takes on a new sense.

Second Image, Inner Symbol

A rich landowner takes a siesta in his tropical gardens.

Interpretation

This image seems the reverse of the first one. The other was outgoing, this one is concentrated within itself. The people of the first image should work hard and humbly for a long time, so that their riches become real. Their creative potentialities (Ar.) have to be brought out, so that everything is truly deserved.

Here the creative source (the sleeping man) is completely concentrated within his Higher Self. He is surrounded by paradise and the real fruits of his hands.

However, there is a shortcoming even in the second image. The rhythm of life has been broken. It is not in accordance with natural rhythm to sleep in the daytime in northern countries. Only elderly people may have developed the habit. The female side in these people cannot bear the hard work of half a day's creative and organising consciousness. They either shy away from their responsibilities, or they work too ambitiously. Their Higher Self therefore retires after midday to breathe again. On a high level, however, this siesta is meant to be a while spent within one's own inner self, the world of prayer and imagination. All pretence and make-believe are now over and they are merged in the rhythm of the world of reality. Their inner work, during their sleep, thus becomes of a high quality.

In the first image this Higher Self tries to play the roles of others to strengthen his own being. In the second image the Higher Self is completely enclosed in the reality of nature, and the beyond, in sleep (the tropical garden).

Biblical Parallel

'For so he giveth his beloved sleep.' Ps 127: 2.

Conception Corrected Asc. 14th Libra

Dr Albert Schweitzer   See 15th Libra for 'double' Ascendant.

15TH DEGREE LIBRA

First Image, Outer Symbol

In a polar landscape, an iceberg is silhouetted against the sea of ice, while the setting sun is disappearing in glory, creating an aurora borealis. On the ice a team of reindeer is vigorously pulling a sleigh loaded with furs.

Interpretation

This degree right in the middle of the Libra sign is one of its most significant as it shows the control over the entire cardinal cross (Ar.–Cn.–Li.–Cap.), as well as the trines (Ge.–Li.–Aq.). There is tremendous activity (Ar.), which is not hampered by the adverse and cold circumstances (Cap.–Cn.); achieving purposeful deeds and results, even when one has to travel far for them. People with this degree prominent have the capacity to see life on a grand scale, and to give form to what is seen inwardly.

This is one of the few Libra degrees in which the Libra grail is obvious. Therefore people born with this degree rising must have a superior horoscope.

Activity is of the opposition sign Aries and is the needed addition to the balancing scales (Li.). There is the full surrender (Pi.) of nature (animals have been sacrificed for their fur) and the use of technical knowledge as a service (Vi.). It is not easy, one has to fight (Sc.) to accumulate material substance (Tau.). Thus we see the hind-axis (Vi.–Pi.) and the fore-axis (Tau.–Sc.) working. What has been gathered is for food and clothing (Cn. sq. Li.). The energy for moving on the ice (Cap.) comes through the muscles (Ar.) of the reindeer, and the iron runners (Mars) on the sleigh. The iceberg (Cap.) in the sea (Pi.–Nep.) is part of their personality as a creative force, when they sacrifice (Pi.) their own ambition (Cap.–Sat.). The symbol of the sun (Le.) and aurora borealis is their radiation and purity which reaches far and wide outside themselves.

According to Janduz, based on the classic (Manilius), this symbol gives these people success in astronomical sciences, polar explorations or fur tanneries. Their entire life-style is concerned with bringing things from the cold to the warmth. All their undertakings show their original spirit (the sun), their magnificent teamwork (the reindeer) and their rhythmic (Li.) activity (Ar.), though sometimes it is all a bit feverish. The trine of the air signs is prominent in the intellectual capacity for unusual transport (Ge.) and for teamwork (Aq.).

It is an image with a wide horizon and the dynamic power to bring others in its train. There is the pleasure of conquering difficulties. The end of their life may be blessed with honours well-deserved. Their spirit is high-hearted and brilliant, though they have to be wary of personal ambition, symbolised in the iceberg which might undermine them.

Second Image, Inner Symbol

A stack of machinery parts; all are new and circular.

Interpretation

Rudhyar's words are 'Perfect and effortless participation in the universal order. Smooth approach to self-expression; inert self-satisfaction.' This means a mystic participation in the wheel of life. The Higher Self is still comprised of different personality parts which have to be arranged around the centre, the spirit of the Higher Self. As machine parts come under Virgo, we see that the hind-axis Virgo–Pisces is not completely under control. Therefore the inertia has to be overcome, especially in the beginning of one's life. This is the deeper undercurrent of the first image, where the cold polar regions suggest physical inertia, which has been overcome by the reindeer. Note that there is no human in this symbol. The Higher Self is hidden in the circular movement. This is a deep mystery. One has to study the concept of *Gilgal* in Hebrew philosophy or atomic science and the function of the circular gear-wheel as the symbol of the Eternal operating in Time.

These people always find new ways of making the world roll on more smoothly. They renew themselves, and in the end find the right work to fit their personality.

Biblical Parallel

'I shall multiply my days as the sand.' *Job 29: 18*.

Note

In Hebrew the words 'sand' and 'whirling particles' are both translated by the Hebrew word *chol*.

Conception Corrected Asc. 15th Libra

J. B. Priestley Born 13 Sept. 1894 at 08.00 hrs. (personal information to Barbault) in Bradford, 53°47 N, 01°45 W. Died 1984. CC WAK and NS for 269 days at 08.00 hrs. gives 14°02 Libra (see also 14th).

English novelist, playwright and critic. Well-known for his books about the Victorian heyday. According to his memoirs, he had a passion for exploration and he travelled extensively (see first image). He is known for his dramatic expression of theories concerned with time capsules and the walking in and out of time.

Dr. Albert Schweitzer   Born 14 Jan. 1875 between 23.00 and 24.00 hrs. in Kaysersberg, 48°50 N, 07°01 E. Died 4 Sept. 1965. CC WAK and NS for 274 days at 23.45 hrs. gives 14°01 Libra, which gives him a 'double' Ascendant image, the 14th Libra as well.

This degree is very significant for the entire horoscope of Dr Schweitzer. He was the Elzasser medical doctor and musician who sacrificed a brilliant career for the inmates of his hospital at Lambarene in Central Africa, where he became a legend in his own lifetime. He wrote many books which give him a name in medicine, philosophy and musicology. See his autobiography.

16TH DEGREE LIBRA

First Image, Outer Symbol

Near a country pub a man is strolling and gesticulating with his hands, arm in arm with two 'ladies of easy virtue'. Under a summerhouse overgrown with creepers, one sees two winged hearts pressed together.

Interpretation

According to Janduz, this person needs a strong lead and direction in his (or her) life. There is an inner superficiality and a great need for people with this degree prominent to make the mental effort necessary to get to know their true nature. From their youth onwards they may give the impression, and even the illusion, of depth and seriousness, because of their observant manner, their apparent quickness of understanding and their joyous facade, but their character traits undoubtedly tip the balance (Li.) towards the side of duplicity and a great lack of insight into their own emotional motives. The innate shortcomings may be masked (Ar. opp. Li.) by great servility. They are full of small attentions to other people, but with the sole aim of detecting their intimate secrets. Any wish to please others vanishes as soon as no more can be taken from them, in which the shrewishness of this character shows up. They may then turn to libel and slander of a superficial kind and not dangerous. After such a period, still according to Janduz, they may become completely miserable and wretched. Having conquered their negative side, they may be inclined to withdraw into an ecclesiastical order or sect, where again they may show a false spirit through flattery, deforming a sincere spiritual ideal and neglecting their true duties. Then again, they may seek to amuse their brethren and sisters with idle gossip, flirtations and flattery of their superiors.

If they stay in the secular world, they may, on the lowest level of this symbol, play the harlot, male or female, without affection but just for amusement. Marriage will eventually bore them. So far Janduz. This makes sense mainly for those with the Ascendant here.

The emotional inner female side will bring out the higher meaning of this image. On this higher level it is the spirit (the man) who has to become aware of all sorts of underhand strife (Tau.–Sc. fore-axis) and false accusations, which have to be corrected by purification (Vi.–Pi. hind-axis) before the new Kingdom of Peace (Li.) will descend on this individual. Purification will be that of the ethereal and astral bodies (the two courtesans), which will bring them to awareness of the two winged hearts. This is the aim of a noble and pure love, which in the deepest sense is love of the twin soul, not to be sought in their outer world any longer. In the end they may reach a state of inner equilibrium (Li.), in which they have conquered both their sexuality (Sc.) as an inhibition to their spiritual growth, and their chastity (Vi.) and excessive self-criticism (Vi.). Thus they may at last discover their true nature and destiny, which is to dwell with love in the 'Garden of Eden' (the summerhouse). Then this image takes the high meaning of the Kabbalistic tree of life, with one central column and two at each side.

Second Image, Inner Symbol

A happy crew is restoring beach piers wrecked by storms.

Interpretation

Here are the constructive results of transmuting the destructive forces of the first image. This person has to realise that all negative and destroying tendencies in his (or her) life arise in order to make energy (Ar.) for the true 'building stones' to build the piers, to which boats will be moored in the future.

This degree, with the others in the middle of Libra, is deeply symbolic for the restitution of the Kingdom of Peace on earth. What seems negative and sorrowful in the old dispensation will serve as means for reparation after the catastrophes. These people have to live above the storms of their emotional experiences and simply work. The two hearts-in-one will be as a pair of angels, working with heavenly will to restore our damaged planet in readiness for the descent of the New Jerusalem.

Biblical Parallel

Judah and Israel playing the harlot for Jahweh. *Hos. 1: 5–7* and *4: 15.*

The Book of Hosea, with Lo-ruhamah and Lo-ammi, is an example in symbols of the 16th degree of Libra.

Conception Corrected Asc. 16th Libra

Ralph Waldo Emerson Born 25 May 1803 at 15.15 hrs. in Boston, USA, 42°25 N, 71°08 W. Died 27 Apr. 1882. CC NS for 281 days at 15.12 hrs. gives 15°41 Libra. (There is a hypothetical chart for 17th Vi. (see there) but the birthtime of 13.00 hrs. is doubtful.)

American philosopher and famous writer. He believed in the possibility of a harmonious world, ruled by man's goodwill. His lifelong aim was to open people's eyes to the wealth and beauty to be found in the earth and in themselves. He fought for abolition of slavery. See among other books *Basic Selections from Emerson*, ed. E. Lindeman (Mentor Books) and *Poems of R. W. Emerson* (Harrap, 1900).

17TH DEGREE LIBRA

First Image, Outer Symbol

A hovel is demolished on three sides. At the fourth side an old door has remained intact. A dagger is fixed in it. On the ridge of the roof sits a mocking blackbird whistling and clapping its wings.

Interpretation

On a low level this is a degree of boastfulness and deep-seated inferiority. According to Janduz this is the malcontent type, criticising others without reason. These people always have to comment: whether it be on personal method or the law of the land, their superficiality will find fault and their mockery be carried on with a fine disregard for their own deficiency.

On this low level there is the chance that they themselves will be 'given the bird'. With this degree rising, they can be physically thrown out for their ridiculous pretentions. In spite of their shrewdness, friends and partners easily detect their hollowness and they may suffer great loss in consequence.

According to Janduz this person could become a professional whistler on the stage, or else work with birds.

On a higher level they may become ornithologists. They love the fresh air, and do not mind living in a hovel unhindered by human society.

This image shows the negative side of the two square signs Cancer (house and home), and Capricorn (law and order). As Libra, one has to balance the two, but here is the opposite sign Aries prominent, with its haughty independence. We have got the negative side of the hind-axis (Vi.–Pi.) in the dirtiness and loneliness of the image. The fore-axis (Tau.–Sc.) is shown by the overgrown hovel (Tau.) and the dagger (Sc.) in the door, which could be the silent evidence of a curse or calamity. But this is where Libra has to evolve. These people should start attending to their neglected garden (the inner as well as the outer one) and completely get rid of everything that is ruined.

On a high level the mocking bird can become a symbol of the Higher Self which has abandoned the ruins of the lower life, risen above it and closed the door to the sloppiness of the lower self. Free as a blackbird in the air, they will not be hindered by human beings who would use them as their doormat. They can spread their wings high above all the dirt and pettiness of their former surroundings.

Second Image, Inner Symbol

A retired sea captain in uniform watches ships sail away.

Interpretation

This is the perfection of the first image. The Higher Self has earned its high position of retired leader of his ships, which he can now despatch or dispense with. These ships may be the symbol of his experiences in this life, or of his past incarnations, as 'ship' means 'I' in Hebrew, or sometimes the physical vehicle of the body. The Captain has to be able to say farewell to it all without becoming diminished, inwardly or outwardly. He can now take a greater interest in life itself and receive the inner essence of all the dramatic events of the past. He will gain strength by reflection on those opportunities in the past which he may have handled inadequately, and he will realise the need for self-forgiveness with self-criticism (Vi.–Pi.). This will lead him to his resurrection (Ar. opp. Li.) in the restored Kingdom of Peace (Li.).

Note

For 'I', or in Hebrew *ani*, see F. Weinreb *Jona* (Servire, Neth.) (in Dutch and German), or his *The Roots of the Bible* (Merlin, 1986) wherein is mentioned that the story of Jonah is the journey of the Higher Self (Jonah, the dove) in the ship of the lower self.

Conception Corrected Asc. 17the Libra

Antonin Artaud   Born 4 Sept. 1896 at 08.30 hrs. in Marseilles, 43°17 N, 05°22 E. CC WAK and NS for 267 days at 08.19 hrs. gives 16°44 Libra, or an alternative CC for 281 days at 08.42 hrs. is 21°03 Libra.

His biographer Martin Esslin (Fontana, 1976) says of this French writer: 'In other epochs he might have been a prophet, an alchemist or gnostic teacher. In France of the 1930s–40s the reward for his rejection of conventional values was incarceration in a mental hospital for eight years.' From there he wrote on 'Being an authentic madman'. He relived being the crucified Christ under the name of Artaud's mother, as he claimed to be Jesus Christ, whom in the end he rejected as well as his own cancerous body. The 1968 student revolution in Paris made him their 'lodestar' as they admired Artaud's unparalleled aggressiveness, probably caused by meningitis at the age of 5 and resulting in severe headaches. He is generally diagnosed as a paranoid schizophrenic.

Karl Georg Buchner   Born 17 Oct. 1813 'about 05.30, just before morning matins at 6' in Goddelan 49°50 N, 08°30 E. Died 19 Feb. 1837 of typhus, aged 23. CC WAK and NS for 281 days at 05.44 hrs. gives 15°57 Libra (17th Li.) or for 295 days at 05.51 hrs. gives 16°53 Libra. CC for 267 days at 05.23 hrs. gives 11°58 Libra or for 295 days at 05.27 hrs. gives 12°39 Libra. See 13th Libra.

Medical student, poet and revolutionary politician, Doctor of Philosophy. Born into a family of generations of surgeons and barbers, he was a complete 'oddball' with his precocious genius at the age of 10. With his famous play *Danton's Tod* 'Danton's Death' (1835), Buchner became known as the father of social justice in Germany. Danton was an instigator of the French Revolution's Reign of Terror in 1795, and the subject of the play is his judgement after death. Buchner was almost imprisoned and had to escape to France, where he translated Victor Hugo's work (see 3rd Sc.). He moved to Switzerland, where he published the play *Woyzeck* in 1836 (about a jealous murderer and his court case). The socialist revolution of 1848 was mainly based on his ideas. His soul has been characterised as a flaming force, knowing it did not have much time here. He was strikingly modern in his nihilism and existentialism. See Sartre (12th Sag.).

See E. Johann *Georg Buchner* (Rowolt, monography 18, 1958).

Rahjiv Gandhi Born 20 Aug. 1944 at 09.50 hrs. (IWT) 04.20 hrs. (GT) in Bombay 18.55 N, 72.54 E. CC NS for 284 days at 09.54 hrs. gives 16°18 Libra. Prime Minister of India, from 1984–1989, after his mother Indira Gandhi was murdered in 1984 (see 21st Le.) when Prime Minister of India. Grandson of Brahman Pandit Nehru (see 22 Le.) Prime Minister of India between 1950 and 1964.

Henri Gheon (Henri Vangeon) Born 15 Mar. 1875 at 20.00 hrs. in Bray, 48°25 N, 03°15 E. Died 13 June 1944. CC WAK and NS for 266 days at 19.57 hrs. gives 16°15 Libra, or for 296 days (late birth) at 20.00 hrs. gives 16°52 Libra.

French physician, writer and musicologist. Making his entry as a poet with *The Solitude of the Summer* (1898) he is mainly know for his conversion to Roman Catholicism after he had to serve as a soldier in the trenches in World War I. He became the exponent of medieval Christian plays, which he revived. He left about fifteen plays in which purity and simplicity excel. As a musicologist he is remembered for his book *Promenades avec Mozart*, 'Walking with Mozart' (1932).

See *Gheon le Chretien* by Legualt (1938); *Gheon, Sa Vie, Son Oeuvre* by Raymond (1939).

Barry Goldwater Born 1 Jan. 1909 at 01.00 hrs. in Phoenix, 33°29 N, 112°01 W. CC WAK for 275 days at 01.04 hrs. gives 16°44 Libra.

American senator defeated 1964 candidate for president of USA. Known as being very radically opposed to Communist doctrines, and as an expert on North American Indian research.

Paul Kruger Born 10 Oct. 1825 at 05.30 hrs. (sunrise) in Bulhoek, South Africa, 31°47 S, 25°06 E. Died 14 July 1904. CC NS for 271 days at 05.29 hrs. gives 16°45 Libra, or for 285 days at 05.31 hrs. gives 17°15 Libra (see 18th Li.).

South African President of the Transvaal and leader of the Boer War of white South Africans against the British supremacy from 1899 to 1902. Dispute political figure, he lost the Boer War, was banished from his country and set up residence in Holland where he made friends with the young Queen Wilhelmina. Seen as a political bore or as an Old Testament prophet, he aroused the emotions of his day. He died as an exile in Switzerland. See a chapter in *The Trutine of Hermes* by Niek Scheps, (Element Books, 1990).

18TH DEGREE LIBRA

First Image, Outer Symbol

A pretty little cottage bordered with flowers, whose door and windows are wide open showing a cosy and comfortable interior.

Interpretation

Janduz calls this a degree of 'hospitality'. This image is indeed inviting. Come, let us enter here, tired after a long day's work. First we are doubting (Li.) whether we may enter. We are bemused by the scent and colours of the flowers. We assume that at the back of the cottage there are even more flowers, and inside, a cosy fireplace and a mysterious attic. Truly it seems a paradise.

Indeed it is all so peaceful (Li.) and it seems so balanced that it is too good to be true. However, there is a problem behind it, here in the middle degrees of Libra, which is essential and not interpreted by Janduz. One only understands this if one also takes into account the second image, which speaks about two men under arrest.

However, it is certainly not wrong to interpret this image on the outer (Moon) level, especially for those with the Ascendant here. They are born for outer happiness and the 'house of their dreams'. They deserve it and there it is. They are happy and serious people and they can dedicate their lives to hospitality, always keeping open house. They can share everything. Anyone can come in and use the garden. Granny may have a room for herself. The poor children of the village may play here. It is all very sympathetic, but they are not open to the essence of Libra.

This 18th degree of Libra is part of the cosmic story of the twelve 18th degrees. The basic conflict of this lies in the 18th degree Cancer and the 18th degree Capricorn. In the 18th degree Cancer there is a strange ineptitude, and in the 18th degree Capricorn are spasmodic quarrels. Therefore we must not interpret the cosiness of the 18th degree Libra in too positive a way. There is too much worldly activity (lower Mars of Ar.). It is so open that a bomb could easily be planted (Pl. of Ar.), and there is an egotistical encapsulation (Sat. of Cap.) in their striving for emotional and earthly security (Cn.).

People with this degree prominent do well to close a few windows to the world. They should open up their inside link with the upper worlds, and develop their higher inner functions (De. of Cn.) and their own inner judgement of what is, and what is not, of value according to the cosmic laws (Cn.–Li.– Cap.).

Second Image, Inner Symbol

Two men placed under arrest are being brought to court.

Interpretation

This image seems the reverse of the former one. Here everything is closed-in (Sat.). An end has been made to the cosy life. These men, the double Higher Self, will be forced inside to be morally tested. There may be a bitter aftertaste. Deep down these people may know they have made a major mistake and that they have not been truly social enough. They will have to realise that the entire world, the visible (first image) and the invisible, is their Cosmic Home and does not belong to their own little selves.

These people have to see through all this earthly cosiness and get back to the eternal values above the lunar plane. It is only by the grace of God that the door of the house is open and that nature can show its flowers. They are under arrest because they did not give honour enough to Him who gave the home. In their petty egotism (Cap.) they may have tried to steal time, or in their

over-eager misjudgements they may have brought the wrong
elements into their house. They can only rise above those failings
by accepting the consequences (Cap.) and starting anew (Ar.).

Here is an archetypal problem of humanity. Who has the
courage (Le.) to get strength from a hidden world (Sc. fore-
axis)? As a human being one will be called to account for how
one has lived in one's earthly home. Has one been hospitable
to strangers in disguise, whether devils or angels? This is the
essence of Libra's grail-cup, to strike the balance between one's
work here on earth and after death (Vi.–Li.–Sc.). What will the
sentence of the court be? What have you accumulated in this life,
to give to strangers whom you might meet here or in your new
incarnation, and what can you give in your new life, when the
sentence is grace and freedom in the beyond?

These two images together are not easy to see through, but they
are of deep inner clairvoyance, a faculty which these people on
the outer plane so often lack.

Note

Willem Koppejan's intuition led him to believe that the second images
of the 17th and 18th Libra were mixed up in Marc Jones' original version.
Please visualise for yourself whether the first image of 17th Libra goes
together with the second image of 18th Libra, and vice versa.

Biblical Parallels

'Be not forgetful to entertain strangers: for thereby some have enter-
tained angels unawares.' *Heb. 13: 2.*

Hospitality is one of the virtues of saints and widows. See *Rom. 12: 13;*
1 Tim. 3: 2; Tit. 1: 8; and *1 Pet. 4: 9.*

Conception Corrected Asc. 18th Libra

E. O. Carter Born 31 Jan. 1887 at 22.55 hrs. in Charles Parkstone,
51°00 N, 02°00 W. Died 4 Oct. 1968. CC NS for 261 days (regular)
at 22.57 hrs. gives 17°15 Libra, or for 289 days at 22.57 hrs. gives
17°16 Libra. Other CCs are too far from his given birthtime.

Architect, astrologer and writer. After his retirement from the
Forces in World War I he became president of the Astrological

Lodge in 1922. His interest in astrology dated from his 13th year. He started the quarterly *Astrology* in 1926, remaining its editor till 1959. With his pleasant character he was a guiding light to many students throughout the world. He was founder of the Faculty of Astrological Studies and its first Principal. Amongst his ten major books and numerous articles, the most reprinted ones are *An Encyclopaedia of Psychological Astrology* (1924), *Principles of Astrology* (1925), *Zodiac and the Soul* (1928) and *Astrological Aspects* (1930). See bibliography of his writings by Stephen Wells.

Paul Kruger   CC for 285 days at 05.31 hrs. gives 17°15 Libra, see 17th Libra.

19TH DEGREE LIBRA

First Image, Outer Symbol

A great block of marble on which someone has begun to carve a throne with steps, and on which a sceptre and crown lie waiting.

Interpretation

Janduz calls this a degree of 'opportunities to dominate', which in English means not so much to dominate as to govern, or have dominion over. It depends on the level of the entire horoscope whether it is domination or wise government. This person is not easy to know (the stone). They are taciturn and keep quiet about their plans, and they may get a name for being severe. On a lower level they are of a kind that does not spare others, even to harshness.

Undoubtedly there is a lot of Saturn (stone, Cap.) in this symbol, as there is a side to it of spiritual and worldly power (Cap.) which is square to Libra. We have to put the emphasis on the artistic (Li.) work that is in process. On a high level we have, therefore, to do with a perfect artist, who has made a sculpture of the highest symbol, a throne, which is nearing his inner vision

(Cn.) of the completed form (Cap.). He does not spare his energy (Ar. opp. Li.). A lot of chiselling must be done in the virginal (Vi.) matter, which has to be 'hurt' by his hammer.

Here we have an archetype of the Libra grail squaring Cancer–Capricorn and between Virgo–Scorpio. Libra needs the perfect eye for the right measures (Li.) to 'kill' matter (Sc.–Vi.) and transform it. Here this transformation is the throne for the King (symbol of the Sun).

On a high level the Higher Self is working in this way with matter in himself (or herself), and chiselling his own throne. A crown and sceptre are waiting as his reward. This work has to be done with the utmost devotion (Tau.) and with full surrender and faith (Pi.) in the Highest. Thus the other side of the Libra grail-cup, Pisces–Taurus, is filled. A new impulse (Ar.), something that has not been there before, emerges out of it.

On a high level, people with this degree rising, or a prominent planet (such as the Sun or Uranus) there, are royal and aristocratic in their behaviour, content to occupy a lonely (Pi.) position in order to work and fight for their highest ideals. Their final goal is glory and triumph for the true king, which is their own Higher Self. In the highest instance they chisel for the return of the King of Kings.

On a low level, however, these are ambitious people who do not hesitate to tyrannise over others for their own ambitious plans. When they crown themselves, the end is tragedy and ostracism. This is because they only worked for their own glory and vanity. Then the symbols of the crown and the sceptre are too high for them, and remain lying waiting while nothing is truly finished or achieved, just like this piece of marble. The fall of these people and their emptiness (no king or queen is to be seen in the image) can be great, when there is no sustaining energy (Ar.) to prevent their heart being turned to stone by their egotistical ambition. This degree reminds one of Michelangelo, whose life should be studied. In the highest instance, this throne becomes a spiritual symbol on which the supreme Ruler is enthroned amid the praises of those who love Him.

Second Image, Inner Symbol

Robbers are hiding, ready to attack a heavily armed caravan.

Interpretation

In this image we see the robbers as a symbol of protest against deserved, or undeserved, privileges and riches around authority or thrones. As long as these have to be guarded by weapons (Tau.–Sc.) there is still a fundamental lie (Tau.–Sc.). People with this degree prominent do not yet really dare to be spiritual leaders. They still use killing and murder (Sc.) to protect themselves from those who want to rob them of their crown.

As Libra is the sign of peace, the great message here is that the crown and sceptre can only be given to those who truly rule in peace, ruling their own inner self, not enclosed in stone, but fearlessly walking on the path and guarded by the Michael-forces. These people must learn everything about the enduring throne of David, and the archangels protecting its existence.

Biblical Parallels

Jahveh is *enthroned* by the praises of Israel *Ps. 22: 3.* (in Hebrew)

'. . . there shall come a Star out of Jacob, and a *Sceptre* shall rise out of Israel . . .' *Num. 24: 17.*

'. . . will I cause the Branch of righteousness to grow up unto David; and he shall execute judgment and righteousness in the land.' *Jer. 33: 15.*

The *throne of David*. See *2 Sam. 7: 12–16* and *Jer. 33: 20–22.* Also the literature.

Crown Many references e.g. 'Blessed is the man that endureth temptation: for when he is tried, he shall receive the crown of life, which the Lord hath promised to them that love him.' *Jas. 1: 12.*

Conception Corrected Asc. 19th Libra

John F. Kennedy Born 29 May 1917 at 15.00 hrs. EST in Brookline, 42°25 N, 71°20 W. Assassinated 22 Nov. 1963. CC WAK and NS for 256 days (eight months) at 14.54 hrs. gives 18°23 Libra. President of the USA from 1960. A member of the Kennedy 'dynasty' (see first image) was murdered in Dallas in his car by a shot from a window (see second image). Roman Catholic, millionaire and democrat, initiated the USA Peace Corps. Known as the strong man against Cuba and the USSR. Married to Jacqueline Bouvier (later Onassis); brother of Robert (also murdered) and Senator Edward.

20TH DEGREE LIBRA

First Image, Outer Symbol

The setting sun is shining through the arches of a cloister where a monk reading a book is approaching a small altar upon which a censer is smoking.

Interpretation

This is a very simple, archetypal image. Janduz calls it 'religious spirit'. A person born with this degree prominent is indifferent to worldly fortunes, glory, riches and fighting, or to worldly loves.

Led by serious and well-founded inner conviction (control over the sq. axis Cn.–Cap.) this person will tread a path leading further and further from the madding crowd. This is not the result of renunciation of, or rejection by, society, which is so often the case, but is because he (or she) has found the truth, once and for all, that in reality one should not be turned towards the world but direct all one's inner and outer behaviour towards the Creator. Until recently one could only retreat in religious orders, but nowadays more and more open retreat centres have been created, where it is possible to stay in peace and quiet (Li.) and live this degree openly, which is of objective world importance.

These people have beautiful (Li.) inner qualities with a real sense of sympathy and compassion. On a deeper level there is a strong (Ar.) link (Li.) with the spiritual world.

They may be laymen and saints in their own right. This cloister is open to the sun and it is not strictly ecclesiastical enclosure

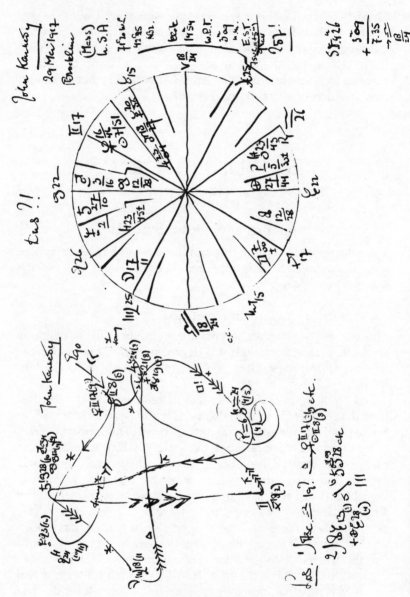

Handwritten chart of John F. Kennedy by
Willem Ary Koppejan

(Cap.). As it is a Libra degree the emphasis here is on the link between heaven and earth. The manly consciousness is a reader of the Word. He is approaching the altar with great reverence. Part of this character is the censer itself, full of eternal fire.

Sunset is the moment of prayer, and that is what is happening here. According to the Jews and early Christians the new day begins at sunset, the moment of the greatest inner thankfulness and sanctity. What then happens, hidden within, is the secret (Sc.) of the soul when penetrating into the highest and deepest essences (setting sun). At the moment of sunset in Libra, the opposite sign Aries is rising and thus one can imagine how the sun in this image is in Libra and in the seventh house. It is a trinity of peace enlightening the spirit, soul and physical body. After that glorious moment the sun dives deep down into the night side of our being and on to our own inner chamber, which is the fourth house in the chart. This leads us into the second image.

Second Image, Inner Symbol
An old Rabbi sits contentedly in a room crowded with books.

Interpretation
Originally the word *rabbi* meant no more than 'teacher'. In a way one could lay the second image over the first one. They radiate the same peace (Li.). They cherish the same values and are parallel to each other. Here is an accumulation of ancient wisdom and competent service.

All doubts and uncertainties of the lower and unbalanced Libra are overcome and this Higher Self has established the perfect balance between Gemini (books and writing) and Aquarius (being open to the higher worlds).

In connection with the other 20th degrees of the zodiac, this is the one and only degree in which the first and the second image are on the same level. As a Libra degree it functions here as a perfect example of being in balance with the outer ethereal and the inner astral world.

The most simple cosmic principle of Divine imagery is the most difficult to weigh out (Li.) unless one simply does it (Ar.).

No need to talk – just do it. That means withdrawing one's lower energies from the rat-race in order to seek inner retreat, inner silence and time for the Word. This will bring peace, harmony and a complete revival of one's own inner senses, thus blessing the world at large. To a world where people simply live these images, in the end Christ, the Prince of Peace, will return as the teacher of righteousness (Li.).

Biblical Parallels

The Hebrews had wisdom schools where teachers and prophets were found, mostly among the Ephraimites and Levites, and certainly as early as Samuel. See *1 Sam. 3: 19–21*.

Jesus is often called *Didaskalos*, which means master, teacher or Rabbi, as an official title or honour. See *Mk. 9: 5, 11: 21*, and also *14: 45*, when Judas kissed him.

The word *Rabbi* comes from the Hebrew 'to make a great man'. The inner chambers of the priest for offerings and to sanctify the people, see *Ezek. 46: 19–20*.

'Search the scriptures, for in them ye think ye have eternal life.' *Jon. 5: 39*.

'Watch and pray always.' *Lk. 21: 36*.

21ST DEGREE LIBRA

First Image, Outer Symbol

A wooden pack-horse bridge over a dried-up stream is almost demolished. On the remainder of it stands a braying donkey with a gnome mounted on its back, who is working himself up as if he wants to make a speech.

Interpretation

This is a strange and complicated image in the sign of Libra. People with this degree rising, as the outcome of the entire horoscope, often behave deplorably. On the low physical level they do nothing but 'bray', either for help or in resistance. We have expressions in our language like 'donkey work' and 'donkey's years', but here we have the typical donkey attitude of refusing to go forward.

The lower instincts of these people are rightly warning them, because their bridge from here to the other side is in such a lamentable state that disaster would indeed follow should they try to cross. The necessary linking for Libra between two opposites is not to be seen here. Moreover the rider, the Higher Self of this person, is symbolised as a dwarf or an earth elemental, while Libra is an air sign. Last but not least, the stream has dried up. The waters of life cannot get through to this Higher Self.

Janduz interprets the symbol on the outer level. She says that their position in life is desperate, while they try to sustain it with lamentations and unreasonable demands. They connive to occupy places they do not deserve, and they attract all the attention when in a group. This is of course true when concentrating on the image of the gnome. They make unwise friendships (symbol of the demolished bridge, Aq.). Their life may end in a drama resulting from their inner, and sometimes even outer, physical deformity, a distinction which they tend to cherish. So far Janduz.

This is indeed true on the outer level. Psychologically these people may suffer from the so-called 'work-shy neurosis'. They do not want to work (Vi. behind Li.). They get hysterical (Cn. sq. Li.) when society, on whose charity they live (Cap. sq. Li.), calls upon them to do their duty. They refuse to restore what they have demolished themselves, physically as well as on the inner planes.

A gnome or a dwarf in symbology is always a sinister symbol of imperfection, a form to be pitied and to be released from its earthbound state.

When the Higher Self identifies itself with such a creature, this is often a reflex or consequence of karmic guilt, which has to be overcome not by constant attention to it but by accepting a helping hand in the present, from the angelic world.

As this is a Libra degree, these people have to become at peace with themselves, pull themselves together, start working and stop braying (Vi. and Sc. around Li.). Then the other side of the Libra grail may begin to flow in, as a fruitful stream

(Tau.–Pi. around Ar.), in the form of tears and compassion for others instead of themselves, and with vision for their own and others' future (Tau.).

On a high spiritual level this image has a deeper meaning. Those with this degree prominent, especially the Sun or the higher planets, can develop clairvoyance and warn others about coming calamities and drying up of the spirit on earth.

The donkey, as a symbol of Virgo, is the pure physical vessel through which clairvoyance or clairaudience can operate. Remember the story of Balaam's ass, which halted before the Angel of the Lord. These people may develop prophetic vision (Tau.). However, on this high level there is one snag. They may become only prophets of doom, due to the evils of their own personal background, while in reality the bridges back to heaven may have been further restored than the howlers and brayers of this 21st degree realise.

Second Image, Inner Symbol

Hot Sunday crowds delight in the cool sea breeze.

Interpretation

The dried-up stream has become the wide open sea. The gnome and donkey have evolved into a group of people, though not yet individuals. Fundamental here is the delight which is so needed in the first image. This person has to link (Li.) himself anew with the freshness of nature, the cosmic laws and eternity (the tidal sea on Sunday). This will be healing for the bemoaning and lamenting person.

It is the only solution for the first image, which turns around and around in itself. The demand is to seek the sun, the spirit of light, and reach others with it so that there will be joint de-light. Their words of doom need the wind of the Holy Spirit. Let them be thankful for the group of friends who stimulate and warn them. They must embrace this crowd's delight in the new day, the Lord's Day. Unless they can share the general rejoicing in this day of peace (Li.), they will foretell their own dramatic end in the dried-up stream of an exclusive day of doom.

Biblical Parallels

Balaam, the diviner of Moab, was sent to curse the children of Israel, but the ass on which he rode saw the Angel of the Lord standing in the way three times. Then he gives his famous blessing three times: 'How shall I curse whom El has not cursed.' See *Num. 24: 10*.

Conception Corrected Asc. 21ST LIBRA

G. I. Gurdjieff   CC for 279 days at 00.13 hrs. gives 20°20 Libra; see 26th Libra.

A. David-Neel   CC for 281 days at 05.40 hrs. gives 20°10 Libra; see 22nd Libra.

G. Puccini   CC for 266 days at 01.45 hrs. gives 20°31 Libra; see 23rd Libra.

22ND DEGREE LIBRA

First Image, Outer Symbol

Two horses, one saddled and bridled, the other haltered, are waiting for their master, who takes his pleasure in sleeping on the grass. He is flanked on both sides with bags of money, which he has neglected to fasten on his pack-horse.

Interpretation

According to Janduz this is a degree of 'neglect'. There is harmony in this image, although one does not notice this at first. The Libra grail can be seen here with one's inner eye. The consciousness (the man) is asleep, so it may not be alert enough to notice that two signs of the Libra grail come to the fore. They are Taurus (bags of money), and Pisces (regenerative healing sleep). These two surround Aries, the complementary sign for Libra. There are also strong ties with Leo (see second image), and Sagittarius (the horses). Virgo and Scorpio are a bit hidden, but the man has either worked hard for his wage (Vi.) or has stolen out of greed (Sc.), and the pack-horse, whose job it is to carry other people's burdens (though he is free from it for the moment), is also a symbol of Virgo–Pisces.

As Libra is the sign of balance, it is vitally important for those with a Libra Ascendant that all the symbolic elements of the signs in the Libra grail are equally represented, apart from the opposite sign Aries. This is the case here. It shows that this is a well-developed degree, where a strong Higher Self can bring through a great deal of spiritual influence in a mild and convincing way.

Among people with this degree prominent, thinking is not very active; their minds do not dominate their actions. Often they are playing the waiting game (the horses), and their consciousness is not very much with the outside world; but they are very much at peace. We can imagine a late autumn (Li.) sun, so why shouldn't one take a chance to rest after the hard labour of harvest (Vi.)?

There is certainly no mistrust of their environment. On the contrary their confidence seems almost too great. They do not feel the need for outer protection, and do nothing about it.

On a low level of spiritual awareness, rarely found with this degree prominent, these people dream of achievement and desire to do much, but they let the best opportunities pass them by. They are not sufficiently in the 'here and now'. They are either thinking of the past or dreaming of the future. Their consciousness is not sharp, and they have no sense of right timing. In spite of their doziness, however, they are pleasant people, although their drowsy attitude may be irritating for those who are sharper. They are rich in talent, but often they are not aware of this themselves. They need to work at themselves and transmute their energy (Sc.) and look at themselves with a bit more self-criticism (Vi.).

They may literally become 'sleeping' partners in wealth, and it could be their spouse or partner who makes this happen. However, there is always a chance that they are too careless with money, and they have to be warned against the danger from theft. They will probably favour the attitude that losing one's riches does not matter, but this is exactly the danger of this degree. They ought to learn that they have to wake up to the value of consciously letting their money circulate. They need to learn about right commercial enterprise (Ge. trine Li.), working for peace, and how to use their intuition to contact the right individuals and groups (Aq.), worthy of sharing the fortune they may have gathered, on the material, as well as the spiritual, plane.

On the higher level, these people sow seeds (Tau.), and wake up their own thinking and that of others in order to find new (Ar.) and inspiring (Pi.) goals (Sag.). The richness of the symbol may lead to very high esoteric regions. These people would do well to study what happens during sleep.

Second Image, Inner Symbol

A child laughs as birds perch on an old fountain and drink.

Interpretation

According to Rudhyar, 'Here is intuitive understanding of simple souls in spiritual matters and youthful life-enjoyment.'

It is an archetypal symbol, which evokes a deep response of peace (Li.) – drinking birds at a fountain watched by a child. The fountain is a symbol of the water of life and pure joy.

We see the three air signs harmoniously represented here. Birds as a species come under Gemini. They are bearers of good tidings, singing their song in the air above our world of strife, teaching us freedom from care (Li.). The fountain symbolises the water-bearer (Aq., the third air sign), and the constant flow of inspirational intuition from higher worlds, in which the consciousness takes part while asleep (man of the first image). Children are a young and new creative love (Le.). Being a Libra degree, strong harmonising energies may flow through it, so that those with this degree prominent can do far-reaching things in the arts, or for the furthering of peace for humanity.

Biblical Parallels

'All my springs are in thee.' *Ps. 87: 7.*

'In that day there shall be a fountain opened to the house of David and to the inhabitants of Jerusalem for sin and for uncleanness.' *Zech. 13: 1.*

'But whosoever drinketh of the water that I shall give him shall never thirst; but the water that I shall give him shall be in him a well of water springing up into everlasting life.' *Jn. 4: 14.*

Conception Corrected Asc. 22nd Libra

Antonin Artaud   CC NS for 281 days at 08.42 hrs. gives 21°03 Libra. See 17th Libra.

Charles A. J. M de Gaulle   Born 22 Nov. 1890 at 04.00 hrs. in Lille, 50°39 N, 03°06 E. Died 1970. CC WAK and NS for 288 days at 03.58 hrs. gives 21°58 Libra (which gives him a 'double' Ascendant and part of the 23rd Li. as well).

French army officer and statesman, professor of philosophy and literature. He fought in World Wars I and II and became leader of the Free French and first government in 1944. See his own memoirs. In 1958 his personality united France when the country was threatened with civil war (see 22nd/23rd Li.). He has gone down in history as the president of France who wanted to reinstitute its 'glory', and who opposed Britain's entry into the Common Market. It is not commonly known that he wrote stories for children and that one of his Christmas tales became a bestseller in France (see 22nd Li., 2nd image).

Ernst Haeckel   Born 16 Feb. 1834 at 22.30 hrs. in Potsdam, Germany, 52°23 N, 13°03 E. Died 9 Aug. 1919. CC WAK and NS for 262 days at 22.19 hrs. gives 21°24 Libra, or for 276 days at 22.21 hrs. gives 21°45 Libra.

Zoologist and author. Widely read in his day, he was notorious for furthering the theory of evolution with faked diagrams and is said to have falsified a skull for scientific proof of humanity's descent from the anthropoid apes. On the other hand he was known for his tragic love poems. He 'denied the immortality of the soul, the freedom of the will and the existence of a personal God' (*Encycl. Britt.*). In his genealogical constructions of higher animals descending from simpler forms, he tried to find nature's source of life. In his way he is an example of 22nd Libra.

Yehudi Menuhin Born 22 Jan. 1917 'towards midnight' in New York, 40°45 N, 73°58 W. CC NS for 267 days at 23.41 hrs. gives 21°22 Libra.

World-famous violinist, even as a child. As a young man he had years of complete silence in which his talents were dormant (see first image), while searching for the fountain of life and finding inner peace in Eastern religion. He started the Yehudi Menuhin School in 1963 in England. He played a great part in the Bath Festivals, which breathe the atmosphere of the second image. He is known for his generosity in playing for charities. His genius made him rich, but he is just as ready to give. The 22nd Libra seems to fit his character.

See his autobiography and the literature about him.

Alexandra David-Neel Born 24 Oct. 1868 at 05.45 hrs. in St Maude, Paris, 48°50 N, 02°25 E. Died 8 Sept. 1969 (100 years old!) CC WAK and NS for 281 days at 05.45 hrs. exactly, gives 21°11 Libra.

'Madam Tibet' as she was called, became the first white explorer to enter the forbidden city of Lhasa in Tibet. She endured incredible hardship, which makes her memoirs (1956) fascinating to read. Several times she literally experienced this 22nd Libra degree. Often she had to leave luggage and horses behind and sleep on the wayside with a sack of gold under her arm. She was 56 when at last she entered Lhasa in disguise, and drank there from the 'fountain of wisdom', the purest Buddhism in the world. She wrote twelve books about religion and life in Tibet between 1925 and 1937, and twenty-seven novels about the East, but her autobiography (1956) is appropriate here as a striking example of her chart and Ascendant degree.

Isaac Newton Born 25 Dec. 1642 (OS = 4 Jan. 1643 NS) between 01.00 and 02.00 hrs. in Woolsthorpe, England, 53°54 N, 0°46 W. Died 20 Mar. 1727 (OS). He was a seven-months child. CC NS for 209 days (premature) at 01.09 hrs. gives 21°01 Libra, or for 223 days at 01.26 hrs. gives 23°56 Libra.

English natural philosopher and astronomer, one of the greatest seventeenth-century minds. He was acquainted with astrology and alchemy. He became the world-famous discoverer of the law of gravity. He is often given 20th Libra rising. However, the above very thorough calculation by Niek Scheps on the assumption of a seven-months pregnancy does not give that degree but this 21°01 Libra. This is a 'double' Ascendant containing part of the 21st Libra as well as the 22nd, which is apt for a genius. As for the 21st Libra, he said of himself 'I seem to have been only like a boy, playing on the seashore and diverting myself in now and then finding a smoother pebble or a prettier shell than ordinary, whilst the great ocean of truth lay all undiscovered before me.'

His standard biography is *Memoirs of the Life, Writings and Discoveries of Sir Isaac Newton* by Sir David Brewster (Edinburgh, 1855).

23RD DEGREE LIBRA

First Image, Outer Symbol

An elderly gentleman dressed in a long robe and wearing a square beret like the doctors and clergymen of former days, is surrounded by all sorts of instruments. He examines some liquid in the light coming through his window.

Interpretation

Janduz calls this a degree of 'aptitude for all things'. This is a beautiful symbol, and a degree of high quality in which we can see the Libra grail and also the problems of the entire cardinal cross, with the square-axis of Cancer–Capricorn showing up well. Behind Libra is the Virgo–Pisces axis. Virgo is science in general – chemistry and alchemy are the essence of it – and this is what this image symbolises.

Under Pisces comes the actual surrender to the exact studies (Vi.) of fluids (Pi.) and alchemical liquids. Here is a symbol of an old doctor, or a magician, experimenting with, and searching for, an element in liquid form. He holds it against the light (Le.) in his room (Cn. sq. Li.). He understands and lets his intuition work (Aq. trine Li.), so that spiritual revelations can flow through him. This process took place with the ancient alchemists, and now some scientists are beginning once more to admit wonder and mysticism into their work.

The axis in front of Libra is Taurus–Scorpio. There is trans-mutation (Sc.) of matter (Tau.).

The square beret on the head, which comes under Aries (opp. Li.), indicates the difficulties in the cardinal cross (Ar.–Cn.–Li.–Cap) being elevated on a metal plane and in a wise way. The esoteric meaning of the square beret was known in medieval times and was a sign of initiation by a true master in all the then-known sciences. One needs to study the cardinal cross in order to understand this. Aries, the first sign, is the beginning and the initiation of all things. In order to reach perfection as a researcher one needs to be at home, not only in the physical world, but also on the astral and ethereal planes (Cn.) as well. One needs to study the laws (Cap.) of creation and bring all these into perfect harmony (Li.). Sages like the German Jacob Boehme, Bo Yin Ra, and men of the Renaissance period are examples of individuals who had this attitude.

People with this degree prominent can become witnesses of of a very special wisdom, being at ease with all matter and their entire surroundings. They may even develop far memory, and be able to judge of their own individual merit in past lives. They can get sudden flashes of light and insight, and then their entire past becomes fluid and crystal clear. They just need to see it and write it down.

Second Image, Inner Symbol

Chanticleer salutes the rising sun with exuberant tones.

Interpretation

This is the elevation of the first image. The chanticleer or cock comes under Aries and is another symbol of initiation. Moreover the sun, symbol of the spirit, is rising. The consciousness (the master of the first image) is rising to the level of new and ultimate enlightenment.

The life of these people is a continual new dawn. They do

not need to doubt (neg. Li.) that new energy (Ar.) will be given them, day by day, promising a new age of peace (Li.) to come. With this in view they surrender all their knowledge and research to these new beginnings. They will be given the courage to persist in the face of all resistance (Cap.). They will be as sure of the coming of the world of Light as the chanticleer making his proud announcement of the coming of the dawn.

Conception Corrected Asc. 23rd Libra

Giacomo Puccini   Born 22 Dec. 1858 at 02.00 hrs. in Lucca, Italy, 43° 52 N, 10° 29 E. Died 29 Nov. 1924. CC WAK and NS for 280 days at 01.55 hrs. gives 22° 21 Libra, or for 266 days at 01.45 hrs. gives 20° 31 Libra.

Italian operatic composer, born in family of professional musicians. He made his name with *La Bohème* (1896) and *Madame Butterfly* (1904), which at first was a failure, as it was set in Japan, the land of 'The Rising Sun'. We can easily detect traces of the second image of 23rd Libra in this work. He composed this after a near-death experience with poisonous petrol fumes caused by a car accident in 1902!

See *Giacomo Puccini, The Man, His Life, His Work* (1933).

24TH DEGREE LIBRA

First Image, Outer Symbol

A beautiful solid tree is placed on a rocky height. A centaur passes under it, shooting arrow after arrow at serpents fleeing in the long grass.

Interpretation

Janduz calls this a degree of 'wisdom'. However, that is more a word to be used for a Gemini degree. Here is a symbolism which is difficult to interpret. A centaur puts us in the sphere of mythology or at least in a non-material world. A centaur is half-man, half-horse. It is a non-existent phenomenon of our natural senses. According to Cirlot the centaur is 'The antithesis of the knight, that is, it represents the complete domination of a being by the baser forces'. Perhaps this can take us a little further in our interpretation. The lower instincts, wherein man becomes beast, could point in the direction of the Scorpio–Taurus fore-axis, which in its lower unawakened form is sexual greed, the passion to kill (Sc.), and the love of money and material possessions (Tau.).

These people are half-awakened to their higher spiritual calling (the human part), but their attention is still directed towards the poisonous side of nature (the serpents). However, they are already in the process of frightening these lower passions away. They do this with an arrow (Sag.), which is symbolic of their well-directed thoughts. The centaur as a whole also comes under Sagittarius and so does the tree. Sagittarius is sextile to Libra and so we see the interesting fact that we seem to have to do with the Scorpio grail instead of the Libra one.

One of the attributes of Libra is justice and the power to judge. Seeing the tree on the height with our inner eyes, we can easily imagine this place to have been one of the ancient Celtic or Scandinavian seats of judgement, which were called *dings* and words in place names with *dan* or *don* in them may be reminders of those days. People with this degree prominent are driven by a deep, almost ancestral force which manifests itself as an intense sense of justice. Of this they are the living testimony. They can be quite harsh in their judgement and if, symbolically, the death sentence has to be given, they give it. They have keen insight and a fine nose for what is right and wrong. They do not argue, they do not doubt (neg. Li.), they go straight to the heart of matter. Their attitude towards life is a combination of mildness and sternness. They stand by word and deed for what they know as right. They may not be easy people to live with, but when they are awakened to their higher consciousness they are of an advanced inner level. They are so honest, that others can forgive their outer harshness. They are very efficient in the elimination of evils, for the building of a better world.

Second Image, Inner Symbol

A butterfly spreads its wings, showing an extra left one.

Interpretation

The centaur of the first image is not a physical reality, and here we have another image that does not exist in our physical world – a butterfly with three wings. According to Rudhyar (1973) 'The butterfly is the ancient and traditional symbol of the results of the process of spiritual rebirth. If the butterfly has three wings instead of two, a special development of an aspect of the spiritual life is shown.' In other words, there is an exceptional energy (Ar. opp. Li.) here, which can break through old forms (Cap. sq. Li) or the astral mould (Cn. sq. Li.).

The key to this image is that the extra wing is on the left. The left side is traditionally the one of the past, the 'negative' side that has to be overcome. However, in modern left- and right-brain knowledge, the left side corresponding to the right-brain is the neglected part relating to the intuition, the arts and the imagination (working with the degrees fosters this side). So in one way this extrasensory energy can be a symbol of a wild growth, and of weird contacts in the astral realms, which ought to be counterbalanced by logical and concrete computer-like brain work. On the other hand it gives an indication of a higher faculty and of a relation with an as yet unknown inner realm of new forms. It is a potential extra dimension of the Higher Self present in these people. In the sign of Libra this gives an extra possibility for higher judgement.

In the first image these people, in their zeal for justice, hunt all sorts of cruelty and injustice to the death. However, there is the danger that they may only recognise cruelty in the world outside themselves, and not as being part of their own constitution in which the passions are not yet quite under control (the beast side). Their lesson is to identify with the symbol of the butterfly, which is reminding us of life's fragility and of the manner in which we die and resurrect.

Three is the trinity of spirit, soul and body. With their superior sense of justice and balance, these people have a more than ordinary opportunity to experience the inner harmony of the oneness of their spirit, soul, and physical body, but they can as easily break into pieces and revert to their former unregenerate state in which they see evil only on the path, and not within. They need to study the laws of metamorphosis.

Biblical Parallel

The blessing for the tribe of Dan (meaning judge) is to 'be a serpent by the way, an adder in the path, that biteth the horse heels, so that his rider shall fall backward'. *Gen. 49: 16–17.*

Note

1. The Druids worshipped round an oak surrounded by stones. They celebrated the 'Yule-log' and they called the fire they kindled the 'cairn', which is related to the acorn, symbol of the oak's rebirth.

2. The best studies of transformation (metamorphosis) in nature, based on Goethe's theories, are to be found in Anthroposophical literature.

Conception Corrected Asc. 24th Libra

Camille Saint-Saëns   Born 9 Oct. 1835 at 07.00 hrs. (RB, not 6.45 hrs.) in Paris, 48° 50 N, 02° 20 E. Died 16 Dec. 1921. CC NS for 275 days at 06.58 hrs. gives 23° 06 Libra.

French composer, pianist and organist. He is remembered for his symphonic work *Carnaval des Animaux* (1886), in which he seems to express something of the 24th Libra. Liszt (see 26th Le.) whom he admired, promoted his opera *Samson et Dalila*. His best pupil was Gabriel Fauré (see 5th Tau.).

25TH DEGREE LIBRA

First Image, Outer Symbol

The midday sun throws its rays on the promontory of a cliff covered with flowers, in the middle of which a large peacock is spreading its tail in full glory. He is imitated by a turkey, and by a fantail pigeon.

Interpretation

Janduz calls this a degree of 'pretentious grace'. She characterises people with this degree as being fond of parade, and even the greatest pomp hardly satisfies them. It is not so much ostentation, as the being in love with one's self and one's own colourful beauty.

On a low level, interpreting the three symbols in one, these people are disgustingly puffed up, excessively idle and vain, and driven to the support of their pretentious life-style by all manner of swindling; and they often come out of it untouched, as they have a greater swindler behind them. This immunity is thanks to their magical power (Ar. opp. Li.). They live from excess to excess, always leaving explosive situations where they found tranquillity. Humility and composure are not to be expected of them. They harbour a deeply rooted desire to shine, to flatter and to be flattered.

However, as this is a Libra degree they often behave sympathetically, and as lovers of art they can be charming. On a higher level they live for beauty. If their underlying horoscope is harmonious, they may become happy, balanced and productive people, simple imitators of the great masters in the arts. They might do well as reproducers of original works.

The three air signs (Ge.–Li.–Aq.) are present here. Imitation comes under Gemini, the bringing together of beauty is Libra, and the group wanting to be equal on the same level is of Aquarius. The only difference is that these birds are not created equal, and therefore the two smaller one make themselves a laughing-stock.

These people are boastful. As soon as they have any success, the entire world has to know. They advertise themselves from the rooftops. In reality their behaviour is something like intoxication (neg. Ar.). They cannot remain in an environment that does not venerate them: they have to move on in the rat-race for admiration and new relationships. Some of them are the prototype of the eternal seeker for love and the 'twin-soul', the partner seldom met as they are too full of themselves and their own glory to recognise the true compassion and the kindred spirit. However, on the higher level they do indeed radiate the full sunshine on the summit of being, enlightening and warming all egotism and hardness (the cliff). They open as flowers, spreading their colours to the fullest, as in the midday of creation. Note, however, that this is not a full summer degree, but one of autumn (at least in the northern hemisphere) and thus we have to interpret all this glory as a holding on to something that is passing, or already on the decline.

We can see the square signs of the cardinal cross (Cn.–Cap.) in the image. The cliff, from which they can easily fall (Cap.) when blind to the dangers of their own eminence, is an indication of a formidable egotism (Cap.) and an unsatisfied hunger for show (Cn.), in which their personal emotions (Cn.) are fed.

Moreover the archetypal symbol of the peacock is often one of danger in myth and legend, standing for corrupted pride, as it seems to imitate, with false eyes in the tail, the solar Eye of God. Their character as such is amoral. The turkey seems good for nothing but being eaten at Christmas. The pigeon should know better, as it is a symbol of Libra itself, and should stop imitating those of a lower spiritual status and become what it is meant to be – a bringer of tidings of peace.

The core of this image is the great need for humility (Vi.), silence (Pi.) and death (Sc.) to self-pride and stubbornness (Tau.), in order to come to true Libra rest, calmness of mind and honest creative artistic power.

Second Image, Inner Symbol

A falling golden leaf teaches a lesson of life to a rebellious schoolboy.

Interpretation

Here we have a true autumnal image, a falling golden leaf. It is the deepening of the first image. When they have discovered the futility of all the lower senses in the first image, such as the racing mind, the hunger for adulation, their disharmony of proportions, their lack of faith in the goodness of creation, and their inner disruptive attitude, then the childish, rebellious, youthful Higher Self of these people may be ready to be taught some fundamental lessons. One of them is that the Bible teaches how we all fall like leaves and are no more. That is to say our sins fall away when we are reborn, here or in heaven, as part of the Tree of Life, and are no more in the lower personality. Our Higher Self is eternal as a golden leaf on the 'schoolteacher's' desk of the Creator.

People with this degree prominent do well to think of the golden autumn leaf. They should read poems on the theme. They should paint a gold leaf on the palette of their inner life, for they are no more and no less than a golden leaf themselves. Thus a golden rest may descend upon their rebellious soul.

Biblical Parallel

'We do all fade as a leaf.' *Is. 64: 6.*

Conception Corrected Asc. 25th Libra

Adolf Hitler Born 20 Apr. 1889 at 18.30 hrs. in Braunau, 48° 14 N, 13° 00 E. Suicide 30 Apr. 1945. CC WAK and NS for 265 days at 18.17 hrs. gives 24° 19 Libra.

At first sight one might have expected a more brutal image for the man who is held responsible for the assassination of millions in World War II, but this fits the Nazi leader perfectly, as the man was a megalomaniac who sacrificed everything for an ideal of self. This image, which Willem Koppejan saw as the sure outcome of his dangerous horoscope, is an extreme example of where an unbalanced Libra degree can end. The important German astrologer K. E. Krafft came to the same conclusion, calculating that Hitler was born at 18.17 hrs. with 24° 20 Libra rising. The 26th Libra (according to Janduz and Frankenbach) is a CC for 217 days (7 months child) at 18.29 hrs., of which we found no historical confirmation. The possibility of 28th Libra cannot be excluded, since this is the CC for 278 days at 18.35 hrs., which would give Hitler the same Ascendant as his British contemporary Harold Macmillan. See 28th Libra.

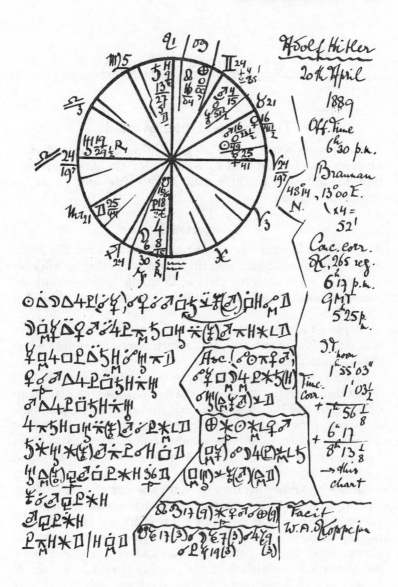

Handwritten chart of Adolf Hitler by
Willem Ary Koppejan

26TH DEGREE LIBRA

First Image, Outer Symbol

A well-proportioned man, of good physique dressed in a medieval coat of mail with a sword in his right hand, advances from the left to help a little man, armed only with a stick, to fight a roaring lion.

Interpretation

According to Janduz this is a degree of 'victory', but this is too much of an identification with the knight, assuming he will win. The image symbolises the glory of the battle (not yet won). As this is a Libra degree there are still the two sides, the undecided moment.

People with this degree rising are certainly brave and have confidence (the man on the left), which comes to the fore when danger approaches.

According to Janduz, this degree is emphasised by classical writers as being very valuable, and a degree for a great statesman or minister. This is certainly true, but we have to understand the elements of the cardinal cross in this degree. The little man is doubting (Li.) whether he will fight at all (Sc. fore-axis). Then suddenly there comes a tremendous potential (Ar. opp. Li.) in the form of the knightly figure, who is, one might say, an Aries, a Ram, who knows his own strength and even has the will to challenge the symbol of the greatest animal power, the lion.

The small man is paralysed by fear (Cap. sq. Li.) and emotionally disturbed (Cn. sq. Li.), so that he retreats (the typical Cancer way). The knight is heading forwards (Ar.), and so we see the entire cardinal cross (Ar.–Cn.–Li.–Cap.) in which, of course, are all inner characteristics of those with this degree prominent. These people are a combination of bravery and invincibility at one moment, and at the next they are indecisive and not well-equipped for life's battle awaiting them. However, there are not only the two men, as the two consciousness levels, but also the lion. They have a combative trait in their character, especially the weaker brothers, the doubting Thomases, as it were to test their own faith. The small man has to learn that his stick may contain magical power (Ar.) as did the rod wielded by Moses. He may also learn from the example of the armed knight, who is armed with superhuman force. This last point comes to the fore because there is a lion, the symbol of Leo. Leo is in Hermetic ingoing sextile with Libra.

The tension from Libra to Aries is so great here that the Uranian opposition can be imagined as a fourth, invisible figure, an angelic helper. Angels and help from above come under Aquarius, which is one of the three air signs (Ge.–Li.–Aq.). It symbolises here the New Era human being who is living above Saturnal fears. Then these three together, the men and the beast, will become one team, and as a Libra degree will make peace and disarm each other. The small man will gain some of the courage of the knight and the lion will learn to become a lamb (Ar.). Then the potential is there to do battle for the weak against worthy opponents.

As one of the twelve 26th degrees which depict knighthood and especially the seeking of the grail, this degree is an archetypal lesson for the whole of humanity, which is even more specific in the second image.

Second Image, Inner Symbol

An eagle and a white dove change swiftly into each other.

Interpretation

The eagle comes under Scorpio (fore-axis), which is the sign of transmutation. The dove is Libra itself. These birds could not interchange in the symbol if they did not have the potential energy (Ar.) of a higher identification (Ge., one of the air signs), which can only be acquired through the Hermetic knowledge that they are mediators. All birds come under one order, and all men are of another order. To reach this kind of interrelation it is necessary for both sides to understand (Aq.) each other, and to learn to balance (Li.).

It seems as if these opposing birds, as Venus of Libra and Mars of Scorpio, can never merge into each other. So it seems with the lion and the lamb, but it will happen. The white dove is the archetypal symbol of the Holy Spirit. It brings the message of the New Age when wars will be no more. The moral descent implied in the act of killing (Sc.) will become the descent of the spirit of peace upon those who have this degree prominent. They will be mediators for the Kingdom of Peace to come, when they have found the courage to beat their swords into ploughshares and plant their spears to be transformed into trees.

Biblical Parallels

'. . . your adversary the devil, as a roaring lion.' *1 Pet. 5: 8.*

'The lion shall eat straw.' See *Is. 11: 6–8.*

'. . . the Spirit of God descending like a dove.' *Mt. 3: 16* and see also *Mk. 1: 10* and *Jn. 1: 32.*

Swords into ploughshares, see *Is. 2: 4* and *Mic. 4: 3.*

Conception Corrected Asc. 26th Libra

André Breton Born 18 Feb. 1896 at 22.30 hrs. (according to Volguine) in Tinchebray, France, 48°52 N, 03°04 W. Died 28 Sept. 1966. CC NS for 259 days at 22.38 hrs. or for 273 days at 22.39 hrs. gives 25°35 Libra.

French surrealistic painter and author. He became a Communist in 1925 till Stalin took over. He was also physican and later astrologer and parapsychologist. He worked together with Apolliaire (see 29th Le.), and for a while with Dali (see 21st Cn.) whom he cursed in 1942. His main directive was to give form to the unconscious.

Jan Foudraine Born 25 Feb. 1929 at 22.00 hrs. in Amsterdam, 51°30 N, 04°55 E. CC NS for 271 days at 22.08 hrs. gives 25°57 Libra.

Dutch psychiatrist, started an alternative movement in mental health by giving attention to the consciousness of the patient. His books *Who is of Wood?* (Wie is van hout) and *Who is of Light?*

(Wie is van licht) are well known. He is obviously living this degree out as a defender of the weak in mind.

G. I. Gurdjieff   Born 13 Jan. 1877 at midnight (00.00 hrs.) in Kars (Alexandropol) in the Caucasus, 40°46 N, 43°00 E. Died 29 Oct. 1949. CC NS for 279 days at 0.38 hrs. gives 25°13 Libra, or for 279 days at 0.13 hrs. gives 20°20 Libra.

Russian philosopher, lecturer and writer. He wandered through many lands and settled in France (1922), where he founded his institute. Adored and hated as a guru, he was an early pathfinder for the consciousness movement and New Age philosophy. He was closely associated with Ouspensky (see 3rd Li.) until the latter broke with him. He had, and has, many pupils all over the world.

See *Gurdjieff: Making a New World* by J. G. Bennett (Turnstone, 1973) and *Meetings with Remarkable Men* by G. I. Gurdjieff (Dutton, 1974), which has been filmed.

Karl May   Born 25 Feb. 1842 at 22.00 hrs. in Hohenstein-Ernstthal, 50°49 N, 12°42 E. Died 30 Mar. 1912. CC WAK as NS for 298 days gives 25°23 Libra.

The life-story of this famous – or perhaps notorious – writer on battles between North American Indians and Europeans, is a fascinating and intriguing example of the first image, and his one day appearing as a fierce eagle, while the next as a messenger of peace, is characteristic of a writer who has influenced the minds of millions, both young and old, into seeing a black–white duality and loving a good fight.

Louis Pasteur   CC for 263 days at 01.59 hrs. gives 25°48 Libra (see 28th Li.)

27TH DEGREE LIBRA

First Image, Outer Symbol

A rustic and prettily enticing cottage, surrounded by a simple garden, well kept by its owner. A beautiful cedar overshadows one side of the house.

Interpretation

This is one of the most sympathetic degrees in the sign of Libra. It breathes a Venusian peace and an agreeable life-style. Janduz calls it a degree of 'good and hospitable reception'.

People with this degree prominent are not marked out for many difficulties and worries. They can be characterised as solid and quiet workers, with unruffled good humour. Though not spoiled, they will be protected. Their solidity of character and well-balanced attitude in this life is the harvest acquired in former lives. They do not just vegetate on what they have earned, but in a calm way they add to their already great spiritual capital. They devote their spare time to the beautifying of their inner and outer possessions.

They are humble and modest (Vi.–Pi. hind-axis) and their inner distinction calls forth respect from others, who instinctively see in them a protector of nature and a possible father–mother figure. They truly help the weak and poor, and any victim of injustice. They care without worrying. They combine calmness with industriousness in their occupation and business. They help friends and neighbours (balanced trines with Ge.–Aq.).

They are straightforward, and even if there is meanness around them they remain inwardly and outwardly unaffected. When they are conscious of being under Divine protection, they may be called to help bring wrongs into the open. They can do very good work for the protection of nature and the healing of the earth. They have a great and warm heart. They may have a gift for helping the sick, because of their own inner peace and contentment. They do not weary in well-doing. They are happy when all around them are well. They are people who pave the way for others.

On a high level of awareness they see all others around them as belonging to one great family. They like to raise the standards of those who are entrusted to them. This can be on a national or even on a planetary level. They have universal minds. Their life has meaning and direction. They may become more and more conscious of working with higher hierarchies, who want to use them as channels for spiritual growth (the cedar). The cedar in the Bible is a symbol of royalty with a deep esoteric meaning, and ought to be studied by these people. They may become a shining example, which is the meaning of the second image.

Second Image, Inner Symbol

A spot of light in clear skies, where an aeroplane sails calmly.

Interpretation

These words of Rudhyar imply that there is a mysterious bright light in the sky and a calmly sailing object. One could easily assume that a glider, a flying saucer or an unidentified flying object is indicated here. Whatever one visualises, the psychological meaning of this symbol is one of subtlety high above ordinary and normal levels of existence. If we take the symbol of the cedar as one of royalty, then this symbol here is a refinement of the former one.

These people are identified by a bright inner light, which is to say their superior mental status of inner peace (Li.). They sail through life calmly and as though they belonged to a superior order of creation. They deserve a superior position, because their inner strength is perfectly balanced, although this may pass unnoticed by the earthbound. They encourage others to look upwards and see that there are higher ideals in life. They are not pulled down by depressing circumstances or situations, but they ascend and live truly above them.

Biblical Parallel

The cedar. The cedar tree is a symbol of royalty in the Bible. Solomon had his temple built of cedars from the Lebanon. The highest branch of the cedar is said to be a symbol of the Royal House of David, brought over by Jeremiah to Ireland. See *Ezek. 17: 3–23*. See also the bibliography in Francis Henking's historical novel *The Tender Twig* (Cov. Publ., London, 1963).

Conception Corrected Asc. 27th Libra

Adolf Hitler If born a seven-month child, CC NS for 217 days at 18.29 hrs. gives 26°30 Libra. This degree symbol is highly unlikely. See 25th Libra and 28th Libra.

28TH DEGREE LIBRA

First Image, Outer Symbol

A windmill on a stubble field which is divided by a stream. A cord binds a small ass to the axis of the windmill. The ass is dozing.

Interpretation

Janduz calls this an image of 'servitude'. People with this degree rising often live in modest circumstances. They do everything slowly, but solidly. Their motto is 'God's mills turn slowly'. They accept their unenviable destiny in a rather donkey-like or sheepish way. It does not seem to bother them.

On the low level of this Libra degree they are indecisive. They prefer doing things which have been ordered by others, in a rather slavish manner. They are not very energetic or active. They need a more independent mentality (Ar. opp. Li.). Their consciousness is not completely roused. The dozing ass or donkey is a symbol of the hind-axis Virgo – Pisces. Sleep and dreaming come under Pisces, and an ass or donkey is a typical symbol of toil and service (Vi.).

On the lower level these people lack the imagination (Pi.) to set themselves a higher task. Their thinking is not very well-developed. They do not see the necessary details (neg. Vi.). They are badly in need of a more lively attitude to life and a really hard-working devotion to their undertakings (Tau.–Sc. fore-axis). Their initiative and impulse to action (Ar. opp. Li.) are too slight.

On the low level of awareness, where this degree tends to operate, these people remain docile and content to tread the well-worn path. They do their duty, but they do not seem to make the effort to give any meaning to their daily life. They are very willing to serve any cause and they do this correctly, but still one wonders what they get out of it. They always seem to be dozing and are tired even before they start.

There seems to be something paralysing in this degree. The ass, seen as a symbol of the human body (see the Bible and St Francis of Assisi), is roped here to a piece of machinery (the mill). These people may just manage to retain their position in life, but a big gale could sweep them away completely. They are in fact only fit for a humble job, but they need to take care not to get discouraged too easily. Most of their capacity lies dormant. They need to become more alert and they need help. However, stubborn as they are (the ass), they often dismiss good advice, so that they remain alone in their same old circle.

Second Image, Inner Symbol

A man in deep gloom. Unnoticed angels come to his help.

Interpretation

This is exactly what the people of the first image need. They lack discernment and awareness of the higher angelic realms. They tend to be gloomy, and are badly in need of spiritual sustenance, which will be freely given to all who open themselves to divine inspiration, so that revelations for the future, with the right impulses to start afresh, can channel through. Even in this second image the higher help remains unnoticed. Often these people do not even see or accept the bearers of help from the higher worlds, let alone attempt to contact them in the first place.

They need to step out of their inertia and unfruitful resignation and move towards positive acceptance of a new way, even if this is a long process. This is a Libra degree and this means the other side of the scale is always there. They only need to find the right balance. If only they wanted to be in harmony, the angels of Peace would provide inner contentment. They could suddenly realise that like Christopher they are chosen to carry the Christ on their back through deep waters into the city of Peace, the new Jerusalem of their vision.

Biblical Parallels

The ass of Balaam. See *Num. 22: 35.*

Jesus riding into Jerusalem on a white ass. See *Jn. 12: 12–15* and *Mt. 21: 5.*

Conception Corrected Asc. 28th Libra

Adolf Hitler   CC WAK and NS for 278 days at 18.35 hrs. gives 27°42 Libra. This degree is difficult to imagine as the symbol of the mad dictator responsible for World War II, though he was obsessed by his idea of Providence (second image 28th Li). In that case he had the same rising degree as Harold Macmillan. See 25th Libra.

Harold Macmillan   Born 10 Feb. 1894 at 23.20 hrs. in London, 51°31N, 00°05 W. Died 31 Dec. 1986., CC Ns for 273 days at 23.15 hrs. gives 27°56 Libra or for 259 days at 23.11 hrs. gives 27°19 Libra.

Had a Scottish father and an American mother. Severely wounded in World War I. From 1921 was part of the Macmillan Publishing House (London). In May 1940 became a Secretary of Parliament under Winston Churchill; 1942–45 Minister Allied Headquarters North Africa; close friendship with Eisenhower.

He was a pioneer of the United Europa Movement, Prime Minister of Britain 1957, initiated summit talk with the Russians (Khrushchev). In 1986 at the age of 92 he still spoke in the House of Lords. He is undoubtedly an example of a British statesman with the lifelong protection and help of higher forces (see second image).

See amongst his own works *The Past Masters* (1975), *The Winds of Change* and various biographies.

Paul L. A. van Ostayen   Born 22 Feb. 1896 at 22.30hrs. in Antwerp, 51°14 N, 04°23 E. Died 18 Mar. 1928. CC WAK and

NS for 263 or 277 days at 22.21 hrs. gives 27°57 Libra.

Flemish poet and writer. He is of historical interest, as he became an activist for the Germans in World War I. Escaping to Germany in 1918 he came under the influence of the new art movement 'dadaism' in Berlin. From his return in 1921, till his early death in 1928, he was one of the first to introduce this new art form into Belgium. (See MEW – encyclopaedia). He was a writer of 'the logical consequence of events, which become absurdities'. He is compared to his contemporary writer Kafka (see 14th Leo).

Louis Pasteur Born 27 Dec. 1822 at 02.00 hrs. in Dole (France), 47°06 N, 05°33 E. Died 1895. CC WAK and NS for 277 days at 02.08 hrs. gives 27°34 Libra, which has preference above the CC for 263 days at 01.59 which gives 25°48 Libra.

Willem Koppejan, who was an MD himself, made a study of Pasteur's life and work, and was convinced that the 28th Libra fits his chart. However, if it were known that Pasteur was born prematurely (263 days), the 'victory' image of 26th Libra could be an alternative CC Ascendant. Pasteur was the famous French founder of modern bacteriology who discovered antiseptics and a method now know as 'pasteurisation', amongst many other things. He was a convinced Christian, who knew that he was sent by his Master to help coming generations on the way back to health. Greatly respected by the medical world and his students, he taught as Professor in Chemistry at the Sorbonne (Paris) until he was a great age. Although he saved the French silk industry from collapse by preventing disease of the silkworms, he declined to profit by this: he preferred to remain poor. His genius also discovered a vaccine against rabies. His *Letters and Discourses* are still worth reading. Amongst biographies in English are *Louis Pasteur, Freelance of Science* by R. J. Dubois (1950).

29TH DEGREE LIBRA

First Image, Outer Symbol

A pond of dark water under the leaves of a forest. At its edge lies a man lazily stretched out with his hand on a book. Some weak rays of the sun penetrate through the branches, faintly overlighting the water and the man.

Interpretation

This is a degree of 'melancholic life' according to Janduz. At first sight this seems right. On the outer level people with this degree rising do not live on the sunny side of life. However, this does not make them melancholic. (Melancholy can be a feature of Capricorn, which is square to Libra.)

This is a Libra degree, which shows a facet of the Libra grail. These people readily abstain from hard, practical toil (Pi.–Vi. hind-axis) preferring to dwell in a romantic world of twin-souls and togetherness (Li.), without much activity (Ar. opp. Li.). They should prepare themselves to sow seeds for the future, which will require cultivation in depth and with passion (Tau.–Sc. fore-axis).

Their placidity can become fatal to them. In order to keep the peace they would rather retreat into nature or within themselves, than face the facts of their situation and act upon it positively. This attitude works out in them as a general trait of sadness. It is as if the sun of their spirit has difficulty penetrating the thickness of their thoughts (the leaves, trees come under Sag.).

They are too lazy to work on their own spiritual growth. They read something here and something there, but the living word does not seem to change them. However, this does not exclude a kind of useful intellectuality (Ge. trine Li.), though this is seldom creative.

On a higher level they can make their love of solitude productive by developing great erudition. They may have hidden talents and interest never noticed by the general public. On a high level they can be positive people behind the scenes, but on a low level they do nothing useful and their obscurity is well-deserved.

Too readily content with a monotonous life, in which they can be indolent, they need much help if they are to become active workers. However they can develop a wisdom with which they can genuinely appreciate the great works of art of other people. They do not want to get involved though, and therefore even in this respect they remain at a distance.

There is another peculiarity in this image. We can see the entire Libra grail here in its absence. Herein lies the esoteric meaning of this image. There is no activity (Mars–Ar. opp. Li.) crossing the inner peace (Li.). There is a new kind of higher energy here, which makes these people realise that coming pain and death are part of the process of growth towards a better future (Tau.–Sc. fore-axis). Once this is seen, they do not live on the outer level of emotions and reactions (Moon–Cn.) any more, but have retreated to the inner planes (Cn.–Demeter), where they digest the old cycle of experiences. They do not need to work now, nor do detailed study, nor do they need the noise of music to disturb the silence of nature (Vi.–Pi. hind-axis).

These people make themselves immovable in time (Cap.), in order not to stand in the way of the flow of energy into their inner self. They eliminate all the outer activity with which the horizontal world is filled. One should acknowledge the hidden courage with which they surrender to an inner process of cleansing (Vi.–Pi. axis). It is an image that is far away from all career-making and social climbing. Their heart is pure: they reverence all that is good and beautiful. They have attained to wisdom, and their intuition for what is true is far above average (Ge.–Li.–Aq. trines). Their motto could be the Druidic saying 'The truth against the world'.

Second Image, Inner Symbol

Vast masses of men push forward reaching for knowledge.

Interpretation

Rudhyar changed 'men' into 'mankind' (1973), and Marc Jones changed it to 'Humanity seeking to bridge the span of knowledge'. W. Koppejan altered 'knowledge' to 'truth' in his Dutch version.

The essence of this image in any of these versions is that the man (the consciousness will stand up at last from his prone position, and, letting the new and higher impulses come through his body, be so renewed that it is as if he can unite a whole collectivity of conscious spirits (the men) in the aspiration to a new era of knowledge and truth.

The consciousness of the first image, in a typical Libra way, is still concentrated in its own centre, which is unstable and can easily be disturbed. At the same time, this centre can be one of great stability if only this person can recognise the truth within him.

In the first image there was a dark pond, where one could imagine a life and death struggle for light between all the organisms in it. Here all these organisms have become one organic whole, of humanity or mankind, leaving their dark collective past (the pond) behind them and being attracted like a magnet to new knowledge and real truth. This will have a snowball effect. There is the deep will to build up a new economy under the highest inspiration (Vi.–Pi. hind-axis), with a community wherein war for other people's possessions (Tau.–Sc. axis) is transformed into a true vision for the future.

It is the task of these people to bring these two images into harmony. They need to withdraw first from their old habit of retreat, before they can push forward and become true pioneers (Ar. opp. Li.) enabling all mankind to find a new truth and a new knowledge. The lesson for them is to dare to be open to new impulses and views. Then they may return to the Book, in which the wisdom and truth of the ages is laid down. This book may also be the Akashic record of their own lives, which they fail to read when their consciousness remains in its horizontal position.

Biblical Parallels

'O Lord, thou hast searched me, and known me. Thou knowest my downsitting and mine uprising . . .' *Ps. 139: 1–2.*

'Thine eyes did see my substance, yet being unperfect; and in thy book all my members were written . . .' *Ps. 139: 1–16.* (See the entire psalm.)

30TH DEGREE LIBRA

First Image, Outer Symbol

A man lies on a kit-bag in a clearing in a wood. He looks frightening to a timorous hare, but he himself is terrified of the hare. However, he does not notice a sparrowhawk circling above him, or a snake ready to bite his dangling left hand, or even a wolf behind him which is about to attack him.

Interpretation

According to Janduz this is a degree of 'absence of judgement'. This is quite right for the negative side of Libra. As this is the last degree of the sign, it comprises all the dangers and also all the possibilities of Libra.

These people are not aware of the real perils that are lurking (Sc.) around them. They also do not realise how dangerous their own appearance may seem to others. They have the tendency to surround themselves with timid and fearful people Ge., the hare), not noticing that perfidious and even criminal persons are lying in wait to attack them (Sc., the wolf and hawk).

In the psychological interpretation of these symbols we need to realise that the easy identification with the man alone is wrong. All the symbols of the beasts are character traits in themselves. When studying the entire horoscope of people with this degree prominent, one can see where their weak points are, which cause these negative symbols to emerge as their Ascendant.

On the low level of consciousness these people do not have strong natures. They are like weather-vanes which turn with the smallest change in the wind. This can even bring them into physical danger. They are not as alert as they should be in the care of their own body, or about their possessions which may be stolen through their neglect.

However as this is the last Libra degree, the real danger comes if they are too sentimental (Li. sq. Cn.), or hold on too much to the letter of the law (Li. sq. Cap.). All their troubles may come through a partnership or marriage (Li.), or through relationships in which others damage (the snake, Sc.) their nerves and inhibit their better knowledge of the higher things (Ge., hand). In this experience they forget, however, that they themselves started such a relationship in the first place. They close their eyes and are deaf until the wolf of their lower passions seizes them by the throat (symbol for their vision of the future), and the sparrowhawk of their greed pecks out their eyes to blind their spiritual sight.

They have to be aware of their own attitude to life, which is one of fear on the one side (Li. sq. Cap.) and of over-concern for small unimportant things and family problems (Li. sq. Cn.) on the other.

This is the problem of Libra in the cardinal cross in general. In particular here these people will choose the way of least resistance until it is almost too late and fate is menacing them, when they may realise just in time that common sense is urgently called for to restore the balance (Li.). They should not feel secure in anybody else's hands nor trust bad advisors, who are sure to destroy their peace of mind (Tau.–Sc. fore-axis).

The wood (Sag.) indicates their mental growth. They possess a certain amount of light (we can assume the sun is shining through the open space in the wood), and an openness towards the Above. If they have the strength to stand over and above their situation spiritually, they could find new goals and build a life with their spiritual baggage (the kit-bag). They can only do this when they shake off all conscious and unconscious fears.

Second Image, Inner Symbol

A phrenologist discovers mounts of knowledge on a head.

Interpretation

Marc Jones speaks of 'Three mounts of knowledge on a philosopher's head'. This version was adopted by Rudhyar (1973) and he indicates that the number 3 signifies a state of completion and he sees this as a holistic approach to knowledge. Phrenology is more or less a lost science, but like cheiromancy (hand-reading) it will receive its rightful place again in the new (Aquarian) age, when people will be able to read each other's true being through sciences like this.

If the man (consciousness) of the first image had his inner hearing and seeing opened, these being seated in the head, he would have been warned inwardly of the approaching dangers.

In this second image the way to overcome the 'absence of judgement' is shown. These people need to learn insight by observing the structure of the heads of persons before they associate with them. They need to master this system of knowledge and develop intuition so that they can discern what in their outside world is pure and what should be avoided. They can attain real human relationships when they understand the interconnections between spirit, soul and body (the three mounts) within the dome of their own skull.

The head comes under Aries (opp. Li.). The skull itself is Capricorn and the brain, as the seat of memory and the senses, comes under Cancer (Moon). Thus there is complete control over the cardinal cross (Ar.–Cn.–Li.–Cap.). The head is also the seat of the Christ-light whence peace and balance (Li.) are directed towards the entire being.

Biblical Parallels

'But the very hairs of your head are all numbered.' *Mt. 10: 30.*

'. . . the head of every man is Christ; and the head of the woman is the man; and the head of Christ is God.' *1 Cor. 11: 3.* (Although this text is often quoted as a symbol of the relation between man and wife, in phrenology this could be taken literally.)

Conception Corrected Asc. 30th Libra

Paul Leautaud   If CC WAK and NS for 273 days at 00.52 hrs. were correct this would be his Ascendant – see 3rd Scorpio. Although his physical appearance has more of Scorpio than of Libra, the degree symbol 30th Libra fits his character better.

CAPRICORN

Index of Capricorn Ascendant Degrees

1st Degree Capricorn

First Image, Outer Symbol

In a room a boy and a girl are standing together, graciously holding hands. However, they turn their heads away from each other. The boy faces to the left, the girl to the right.

Interpretation

Every first degree of a sign gives a summary and thus we see the entire sign of Capricorn symbolised here. According to Janduz people with this degree on the Ascendant are not moody. They are friendly and pleasant to meet. They put their energies into large communal projects. They do not shirk their duty. They have strong ambitions.

They often have two jobs and are occupied with serving two masters. They are quick-witted and mentally above average. They have the faculty, to project 'an occult double', something requiring a strong brain and a disciplined nervous system. So far Janduz. This needs explanation.

Hearing comes under Capricorn–Saturn. These people are able to detect subtle differences in sound, which distinguish truth from falsehood. With this faculty they make good diplomats. They do well in the secret service of the State, or in any kind of secret organisation. Their discretion is perfect.

These two professions show the two sides of their character. Sometimes they wish to be in the eye of the world, at others they would rather be completely withdrawn. All this concerns the outer side of this image.

On a higher level, the symbol needs deeper esoteric insight in order for the entire Capricorn grail, together with the square signs in this image, to be revealed.

In order to hear well (Cap.) one needs to develop an inner faculty for listening. One needs to develop the outer and inner sensitivity to vibrations of the opposite sign Cancer. One needs an inner receiving station with radar and inner antennae. These two youngsters listen to each other with their inner being. They are a mirror (Moon of Cn.) to each other. He is responding to her male side, while she is bringing out his female side. Together they try to make a many-faceted crystal out of their fragile relationship.

The difficulty is that each wants to keep their independence (Ar. sq.) and there is doubt whether they should link in marriage (Li. sq.). This cosmic problem has not been overcome as yet in this degree, because their will to independence is still too strong, but their hands are already joined. Hands come under Gemini. Gemini–Sagittarius is the difficult hind-axis for Capricorn. The faculty of listening and counselling comes under Gemini. This is raised here already on a higher level. There is inner wisdom to bring their ideals and faith together (Sag.) so that their relationship may come to full maturity in time.

Four hands offered in mutual love and understanding (fore-axis Le.-Aq.) show that the spirit (the boy), although still young, wants to build a bridge (Aq.) towards the female, functioning as soundboard (the girl). The girl is receptive to the boy. This brings forth the masculine spirit, which she in turn feels streaming towards her. This gesture of double giving (Le.) equalises the gesture of separation made by their heads. Capricorn tends to be formal and has to learn to give and understand (fore-axis Le.-Aq.). The joined hands are a promise of growth. Their feet do not touch. Feet come under Pisces. The mystery that the bond of love brings suffering has not yet touched them. The male and female side of Capricorn are here still separate forms, not yet completely united in service to one another (Vi.-Pi.).

This symbol is very revealing of our whole society, and for those who can bear it there are tremendous possibilities for working out the entire cardinal cross (Ar.-Cn.-Li.-Cap.). There is no intervening father or mother in the image, no curious brothers and sisters to disturb the romance. One can imagine how the bond between these two will lead at last to joint responsibility for their own home, their circle, their tribe or their planet. This brings us to the second image.

Second Image, Inner Symbol

An Indian chief claims power from the assembled tribe.

Interpretation

It is easy to imagine this as an archetypal symbol of North American Indians in the Rocky Mountains (rock comes under Cap.), but it could be set anywhere and in any age. This image is the essence of Capricorn.

All the heads of the tribe are gathered around, but one is above them and speaks on behalf of all. He stands upright, and every male contributes power to the circle. All listen. Nobody can listen as well as an American Indian! They see a plan forming before their inward eye. The collective creative will is given voice and form in the chief. Their united resolution (Le.) empowers the plan, and will have effect far afield and upon neighbouring tribes.

The community is acting together, still with the personal assurance of each individual (Ar.). The masculine pole is now emphasised, which is apt for Capricorn. It is the organising sign for the welfare of the community. Listening and thinking are perfected: the spirit receives power from below and from above to bind all things together.

Biblical Parallel

Israel is based on a twelve-tribed system. Each tribe named after a son of Jacob claims its own authority direct from Jahweh. It is worthwhile to study this spiritual–political tribal system in connection with this first degree of Capricorn.

Conception Corrected Asc. 1st Capricorn

Camille Huysman Born 26 May 1871 at 22.00 hrs. in Bilzen, Belgium, 50°53 N, 05°30 E. Died in 1968. CC WAK and NS for 278 days at 21.58 hrs. gives 00°49 Capricorn or for 264 at 22.01 hrs. gives 1°34 Cap.

Belgian prime minister who played an important role in

international socialism and Belgian political life. Personal friend
of Mao Tse Tung, Red China's leader in his time. He was in
London during World War II. He published a great deal, not only
on politics but also on literature. In his long life he combined his
male and female sides.

2ND DEGREE CAPRICORN

First Image, Outer Symbol

Two men come out of a house carrying a reed (or rush) on their
shoulders, as if it were a heavy tree trunk. On the house is a
weather vane, the arrow of which is out of order and useless.

Interpretation

Janduz calls this a degree of 'impotence'. At a first glance
this seems right. Without doubt, however, people with this
degree rising are born 'tired' and have very little potential for
perseverance, or ambition. Their feverish efforts are completely
inappropriate to the work to be done. They pretend to be very
busy, and admire themselves a great deal (neg. Cn. opp. Cap.).

In the best case they make light work of difficult problems,
but there is always something childish in them (neg. Le.-Aq.
fore-axis). They do not quite understand situations and one
cannot expect them to bear the burdens of others in any real
sense. They evade any ordeal in their own lives. They are likely
to be restless and agitated, unable to be quiet, and extravagant in
various ways. Sometimes they are hampered (when this degree
is rising, not with a planet here) by a physical weakness, with
lack of muscular control and stamina.

However, this almost humorously futile image may be used by
more developed Higher Selves to mock the follies of the world.
They may make good imitators (Ge.), humorists or entertainers
for a wide public (Cap.). They may show hope and despair (Sag.),
at the mercy of the winds of chance. In the circus they may do
well as clowns, or tightrope walkers. They may also become

good thatchers or cane workers. The world may see them as odd. What they need to develop is regularity and perseverance, and an inner life of meditation based on practical experience.

However, there is a higher symbolism. We have two men, which is a doubly positive spiritual team (Aq.-Le. fore-axis). They come out of a house, which is the opposite sign, Cancer. Shoulders come under Gemini, and a tree trunk (which they take the reed to be) comes under Sagittarius. For their Capricorn grail-cup they have to make their difficult hind-axis Gemini–Sagittarius lighter. They need to raise their heavy, pessimistic Capricorn mentality, see through life's illusions (the reed) to make use of them, and acquire the faculty of optimistic thinking (Sag.). Let them get that imaginary chip off the shoulder! The reed could be made into a flute, and accompany the dance (Ar.-Li. sq.).

The symbol of the wind has a lot to do with this image. The wind (Ge.) may have broken the reed and damaged the weather vane. This may have happened through lack of knowledge and care. These people need to reorientate themselves more firmly towards craftsmanship and wisdom. They need to give out humour and fun.

This image is a complicated one. From a mercantile and social point of view, it is not a good one and may even be dangerous, but one should not forget that Capricorn is on the threshold of a new and freer age, where all may be themselves (Aq.-Le. fore-axis). For weak characters this is a dangerous degree of impotence, but for more developed Higher Selves it is freedom and courage, the chance to become a flute for the breath of God.

Second Image, Inner Symbol

Rose windows in a gothic cathedral. One has been damaged by war.

Interpretation

Here the horizontal (worldly) reed has become the vertical (spiritual) window, made by craftsmen, in love, to the glory of their Maker. Here is the creative moment given the right form.

No fancies or misconceptions here. All is perfected in the form, and by teamwork (Le.-Aq.).

In the framework of tradition, and the ethics of the group (Cn.-Cap.), people with this degree rising can provide a monument for later generations. Their spirit flowers for the future (Tau.) through persistent and detailed work (Vi.). They are in service to the religious ideals of the whole community, the group, or their own small environment.

They are not fully protected. As the weather has damaged the direction of their life, so human passions (war) can leave a mark on their soul, as the window towards heaven. When true to their religious ideals, they cannot be destroyed. Even this image teaches them the lesson of the relativity of all outer beauty and all brute force. With the symbol of the rose (window) in the centre of their heart, they can become witnesses of the Eternal.

Biblical Parallel

The rose window, of which Chartres Cathedral is the main example, has its roots in Hebrew mysticism, in the 'Rose of Sharon', a name for Jesus. The petals of the rose catch the spiritual dew from heaven, the symbolical tears of God shed of joy and sorrow for mankind.

Conception Corrected Asc. 2nd Capricorn

Camille Huysman,   If CC for 264 days at 22.01 hrs., See 1st degree Cap.

3RD DEGREE CAPRICORN

First Image, Outer Symbol

A lengthy serpent coils itself around a three-branched candlestick with all three candles burning.

Interpretation

Janduz calls this a degree of 'resplendent wisdom'. It is one of the strongest images of Capricorn. It is rather rare to have this degree rising. The Higher Self with this degree prominent needs to be exceptionally evolved. The inner power of this degree may radiate through for people with the Sun, Mercury, Venus, Jupiter, Uranus or Neptune here, but there is more difficulty with Mars, Saturn or Pluto.

As Capricorn has the tendency to crystallise things in an egotistical sense, whether on a high level of awareness or a low one, the symbolism has to be interpreted accordingly.

On a low level of spiritual awareness, these people may have a streak in their character which makes them mistrustful of others (neg. Sag.-Aq. around Cap.). They can be suspicious and sly, and even mean, in defending their own interests. This is especially the case when the energies of Mars (Sc.) come through. Then the lower side of the serpent in the symbol arouses the passions of the lower chakras such as jealousy, rivalry, a love of gossip and enmity towards others. The misuse of this symbol is seen when, in the practice of the black arts they arouse the Kundalini fire, from the base of the spine upwards, for their own ends and for power over others.

However, the same image contains all the attributes for enlightenment from above. At a higher level of awareness, the candelabra with its three branches stands for the combined activity of Spirit, Soul and Body, and indicates awareness of the threefold constitution of all Creation. With knowledge of this principle active in Nature, these people can be adepts in all branches of New Age science. They have the insight to interpret the Ancient Wisdom anew for future times, as experience rather than ritual observance: they may revive (set alight) established institutions (Cap.) when these seem to have perished.

On a still higher level they are represented by the burning candle itself, flame, wick and wax denoting the combustion or transmutation of lower into higher which the Higher Self has achieved. Flame has three colours: red (Ar.), yellow (Le.), and blue (Sag.) of the three fire signs, corresponding (again!) to three stages of combustion. Here is to be inferred the possibility of ascent through meditation to contact with the inner worlds. The intensively transforming forces of Mars (Sc.) play a great role in this process, as well as the Mars energies (Ar.) and perfect equilibrium (Li.), between spirit, soul and body (the Ar.-Li. squares under control).

We come into the most subtle esoteric regions with this image. One needs to study the Kabbalah, with its left and right column and the central middle path, and the light from Kether (the crown) descending into Malkuth (the earth). Or one can explain it in terms of the chakras, when the fully controlled Kundalini–shakti fire (the coiled serpent) ascends through the spinal column by way of the double nervous system (Ge.) from the base-chakra (Muladhara), through the intermediate five chakras, on to the Crown-chakra. Shedding light on this human process is the basis for the free flow into the second image.

Second Image, Inner Symbol

The soul as a hovering spirit is eager to gain experience.

Interpretation

Here we see an incarnating Higher Self hesitating on the threshold of an intense new life-experience. It is clearly a higher version of the first image. One of the most difficult things for Capricorn, and for all humans, is to become a total or Christed being. The highest expression of the first image fails if the form of the Higher Self, which is the spiritual counterpart of the physical body, is not motivated by the purest light. If it is, this Higher Self can work through this image as a 'pore' of the Cosmos. As such it remains above all possible limitations of the physical plane. For Capricorn there is always the danger of the plunge into the lower planes of egotistical (Saturnine) self-interest. The soul in this image is aware of this danger. Therefore it still hovers above the world, reluctant to leave the bosom of the Creator, but it has heard its call to descend on the karmic time-line (Cap.). This suspension between two planes is well-known to advanced souls. They know that every step up requires two down, into matter, with all the dangers and the pain of transmutation which incarnation signifies.

People with this degree in their chart have the task of sensing their karmic position. Esoteric (Hermetic) theory has it that the manifested universe *is* at the point of equilibrium between the centrifugal and centripetal modes of Divinity. We are sent here, but we are welcomed home. This is where we 'hover'. These people are on the borderline between etheric and astral being. If they withdraw from incarnation they do not fulfil their task. When they dive into form (Cap.) they may descend too deeply. It is a degree of yes-no, no-yes, in one. Within the framework of the twelve 3rd degrees it is the most striking example of the dual nature of these Cosmic images.

Biblical Parallel

'The spirit moved upon the face of the waters.' *Gen. 1: 2.*

Conception Corrected Asc. 3rd Capricorn

Jens Pieter Jacobsen   Born 7 Apr. 1847 at 01.58 hrs. in Thisted, Denmark, 56°58 N, 08°40 E. Died 1885. CC WAK and NS for 272 days gives 2°46 Capricorn.

Poet and novelist. His characters are usually young dreamers who through disillusion become atheists, portraits which are really of himself. He hovered between the natural science and poetry of his time. His exact descriptions of nature are sublime. This is like the soul deciding which way to incarnate. He longed for light, and wrote about the 'broken light of one's interior'. For his novels see *Encycl. Britt.*

Frederic Mistral   CC for 270 days at 18.12 hrs. gives 2°56 Capricorn (see 10th Cap.)

4TH DEGREE CAPRICORN

First Image, Outer Symbol

The entrance to a temple, the two keys of the divine world are depicted in the solar disk surrounded by a radiating corona of flames. Underneath this sign, beside the door, hangs an ancient oil lamp. In front of the entrance, a Vestal Virgin holding a lamp in her right hand, is guarding the flame of the lamp with her left.

Interpretation

This is a pure symbol of initiation. When meditating on this image, we can become aware of the cardinal cross in the form of an inner cross of light, and we can also see the Capricorn grail-cup. This image is an example of both. The temple itself is a symbol of Capricorn. It is a place for meditation and prayer, where the flickering ego (Sat.) needs to be kept under control. A temple is the house of the Father (Cap.), or the Father–Mother God (Cap.-Cn.), or of the Mother (Cn.) guarded as in this case by a virgin. Herein lies the highest idea of inner visualisation (Cn.) which is the completion for Capricorn.

The flaming sun disk above the open door is a pure symbol of the fore-axis Leo–Aquarius. The seclusion (Cap.) of the temple is broken by the open entrance, as an indication of hospitality for all (Aq.). The two keys to the divine world are doubly Aquarius and they show the borderline – or threshold – situation of Capricorn. Traditionally the disciple Peter comes under Capricorn, as the holder of the keys to heaven.

Janduz' artist drew the keys as Egyptian 'Ankhs'. One could also see them as T's (the Greek letter Tau) or the Lingua.

The square-axis (Ar.-Li.) is to be seen in the beauty and peaceful composure of the Vestal Virgin. She radiates spiritual independence (Ar.). She derives her energy for this from her Initiation (Ar.) in the magical arts (Ar.-Li.) surrounding ancient and modern fire- and light-ceremonies.

People with this degree rising (rather rare), or with a planet here, are witness to the highest aspirations in any circumstances. They have gained a height of spiritual subtlety, which can only be reached by very 'old' souls. In the eyes of the world these persons may play a humble role. This obscurity is of no concern to them. However, they will often, when elderly (Cap.), receive recognition for their inherent nobility of character. They need to be alone a great deal, and to take time for meditation (Cap.) to advance their spiritual evolution.

They respect the habits and beliefs of other people and cultures. In their own sufficiency there is room for all. They are wise in the deepest human mysteries. When in a female incarnation, they may stand for the female aspect of religion. They have to guard against division of opinions and fanaticism (neg. Ge.-Sag. hind-axis). Indeed, when they are 'old' souls, the problem of time and division into male and female no longer exists for them.

Their role in society will correspond to their position on Jacob's spiritual ladder. Whatever they do, they educate others and remind all whom they meet of their highest destination (Sag.).

Second Image, Inner Symbol

Merrymakers embark in a big canoe on a lantern-lit lake.

Interpretation

The first image radiates light, but it is a static and secluded symbol, though with a lot of potential. Here we are all together (Aq.) in the same boat. There is group consciousness of, and admiration for, the collective soul (the lake) illuminated by unseen serving hands of angels (Aq.), or by priestly Vestal Virgins.

It seems as if all the inhabitants of the planet paddle safely through the past, present and future. When old souls find their soul-group, life together is as a great feast: it is time to make merry, and give thanks to our Maker.

Biblical Parallel

'Then shall the kingdom of heaven be likened unto ten virgins, which took their lamps, and went forth to meet the bridegroom.' *Mt. 25: 1*. See also *Mt. 25: 1–13*.

Conception Corrected Asc. 4th Capricorn

Nicholas Culpeper Born 18 Oct. (OS, 28 Oct. NS) 1616 at 12.00 hours in London, 51.30 N, 0.05 W (source: his own information). Sibly and Alan Leo give him 3rd Cap., but this is impossible according to the CC. He died 10 January 1654. CC NS for 286 days at 11.59 hours gives 3.03 Capricorn, or for 272 days or 300 days at 12.05 gives 4°53 or 4°58 Capricorn.

English herbalist also well-known for his astrological and medical work. Within his short life of thirty-eight years he left nineteen books and translations. His *Herbal* with 369 remedies from English herbs, is still in print. It seems as if the 4th degree is the right Ascendant, but the 5th has also to be taken into consideration.

Michelangelo Born 6 Mar. 1475 (OS) = 15 Mar. (NS) between 01.15 hrs. and 02.30 hrs., or 'at the 8th night-hour' = 02.00 hrs., in Caprese, 43°45 N, 12°05 E. Died 18 Feb. 1564. CC NS for 292 days (late birth) at 02.27 hrs. gives 3°45 Capricorn, or for 264 or 278 days at 02.06 and 02.02 hrs. gives 28°55 or 28°11 Sagittarius (see 29th Sag.).

Italian sculptor and painter. One of the most famous artists of the Renaissance. He is mainly remembered for painting the ceiling of the Sistine Chapel in Rome, a colossal task and a miraculous technical achievement. His main sculptures are *David*, *Moses* and *The Pieta*. His incessant work, in spite of insurmountable difficulty, gives him a unique place in history. His genius reached far above his contemporaries and he was a high initiate. Although it is difficult to differentiate between Sagittarius and Capricorn as his rising sign, his physical appearance and strength as a sculptor indicate Capricorn. We favour the 4th Capricorn, which suits this highly religious initiate. The second image is reflected in the fact that he often worked through the night with a lantern or candle fixed upon his nightcap.

See *Encycl. Britt.* and numerous biographies and art books.

5TH DEGREE CAPRICORN

First Image, Outer Symbol

In a peaceful patch of countryside lies a small cottage, doors and windows invitingly open to everyone. At the left a spring is bubbling out of a stone ornament.

Interpretation

This seems to be one of the most agreeable degrees of Capricorn, which shows us straight away that this image is built on the Capricorn–Cancer axis. There is an atmosphere of assurance. The site looks harmoniously in balance (the square signs Ar.–Li. are incorporated). It seems the ideal place for retreat, or one where retired people may spend their old age (Cap.).

People with this degree rising, or prominent in their chart, are simple and without ill will. They are open towards life. They show the important trait of hospitality, and the giving of self to others (Aq.–Le. fore-axis). They have faith in human nature and no fear of burglars (Sag.–Ge. hind-axis). They are intelligent, open towards other original interpretations of life and centres of light. They have hidden sources of energy, which shows in their peaceful attitude and which attracts others who wish to link with them in bonds of sympathy (the sq. axis Ar.–Li.).

The Sun is in this degree one or two days after Christmas, 'Boxing Day' in the Western cultures, when people keep open house for their friends and neighbours. However, this degree symbol is not perfect, and we must not close our eyes to the reverse side of this open-house attitude. After all, it is a Capricorn degree and not yet an Aquarius one.

Janduz rightly calls this a degree of 'imprudent reception'. The benevolent generosity of these people can go too far. Their hospitality can be excessive. Capricorns in general need to set bounds and time-limits, but those with this particular degree too often do not dare to refuse anyone. Their goodness of heart asks no explanation or justification from those who pass through their door, and who take possession much too easily. It can even go so far that people with this degree prominent develop feelings of guilt (Cap.-Cn.) for not being hospitable enough. They become doormats. Their trust becomes too cheap, and being taken advantage of eventually empties their hearts of love (neg. Aq.-Le. fore-axis).

There is a collective cultural problem at Christmas time, when the Capricorn side of the cardinal cross (Ar.-Cn.-Li.-Cap.) brings out obligations and compulsory visits, especially between parents and growing children. Often in those days time and emotional energy are spent in direct conflict with the need for quiet meditation (Cap.), inner peace (Li.) and hibernating for gathering new strength (Ar.).

On a higher level we can also see many elements of the Capricorn grail. There are creative potentials which can be seen when these people choose to overcome their doubts and undeserved sense of guilt. They have to learn first to discern what is of value and what is worthless (difficult Ge.-Sag. hind-axis). Then they come to the perennial spring within.

On the lower level, when they are too open, and their inner resources plundered by others, they have yet to learn to guard this inner spring. This pure water of life (Aq.) comes through the rock (Cap.), a free gift (Aq.-Le.) for the fructification of the earth and its flowering in the spring.

This is a degree showing a high level of possible development, as we see the three earth signs (Tau.-Vi.-Cap.) so harmoniously worked out in the purity (Vi.) of the water, the natural rock (Cap.), and both in harmony with the earth (Tau.).

Second Image, Inner Symbol

An American Indian camp, where a fierce war dance is in progress.

Interpretation

This image seems to speak in a different language, but it gives exactly what the first image lacks. The first one was too open and too inviting. The second one mobilises all latent talent and energy for the safeguarding of one's own possessions and those of the tribe.

There is self-expression here contained in a traditional form (Cn.–Cap.), in which the entire masculine part of the community participates. It is a display of great power (Ar.), muscular and rhythmic (Li.). Whoever has seen true Indian war-dancing knows how awe-inspiring this can be and how it is better to close the doors of sensibility to it. It is a symbol of the cardinal cross on a primitive level. This image can be seen either as obsession by elemental forces, or as an awakening to the hard realities of life. An Indian war-dance comprises the evolution in time of an entire race, they dance in defence of their original well-springs and the resources of their tribal life.

The owner of the first image takes things too easily and hopes that God's water will flow for ever on his fields, but by contrast in the second image we see collective responsibility in evidence.

A solitary house is vulnerable: the duty of Capricorn is to act in concert with the community for the protection of its values against intruders.

Conception Corrected Asc. 5th Capricorn

Nicholas Culpeper   CC for 272 or 300 days at 12.05 hrs. gives 4°53 or 4°58 Capricorn. See 4th Cap.

6TH DEGREE CAPRICORN

First Image, Outer Symbol

A man enveloped in a cape advances. He stretches out his right hand, in which he holds a heart surmounted by a flame. On each of his shoulders sits a small dog.

Interpretation

Janduz calls this a degree of 'devoted affection'. This degree can be an indication of a unique love on a high level. This is not only sexual love, but devoted universal love, which cannot be broken by temptation. It may be the love of a devoted servant, or that of the creator of a work of art for his creation. As it is a Capricorn degree, we see these people in a position of authority in charitable work, social welfare and in help, wherever needed, for others. They will be faithful to their duty and true to their ideals and aims, which will grow in depth the older they become.

This image may lead people to a place of seclusion or meditation (Cap.) from where they can fulfil their high calling or mission (the cape). They may be attracted to esoteric groups who use the symbol of the flaming heart. They may bring their own burning heart towards those in need, like the mentally ill or the homeless (Cn. opp. Cap.). These people are good Samaritans, regardless of their own reputation. Their warm heart is extended but they themselves, their own higher consciousness, are enveloped in a mantle of protection which they will need against misunderstanding and gossip. The cape also protects them from disappointments on the emotional level (Cn. opp. Cap.), which might be caused by the very people whom they help most with their strength and love. When this happens their inner nature is not changed; on the contrary, their enthusiasm only becomes the greater the more the hand that has fed others is bitten.

As Capricorns of a high order, they have moral purity (Vi.) and the capacity to alleviate material need (Tau.). (So here we have the three earth signs Tau.–Vi.–Cap.)

The image shows the Capricorn grail in the heart (Le.) stretched out towards others (Aq.), symbolising spiritual growth towards an Aquarian cycle where love prevails. The difficult hind-axis (Ge.–Sag.) is under control in the outstretched hand (Ge.) and there must be an unseen ideal (Sag.). The cape can be seen as a symbol of the psychic protection of the astral and etheric bodies (Cn. opp. Cap.).

The squares of the cardinal cross are under the control of the Higher Self because the dogs, which come under Aries, create a perfect balance (Li.) by sitting on the man's shoulders. The dogs on the shoulders (Ge.) of the consciousness indicate strong energy for new initiatives (Ar.–Pluto) and the Wisdom (Ge.) to carry them through.

This is one of the most interesting images within the sign of Capricorn.

Second Image, Inner Symbol

Ten logs lie under an archway leading to dark woods.

Interpretation

In this image we see the same symbols on another level. The archway has an analogy with the mantle or cape. Wood comes under Sagittarius and is a symbol of growth and inner ascension towards heaven. Cut wood means that the thoughts of this person have been spread out and are now arranged in orderly fashion for use. The number ten has a mystical meaning. It is the One (the Creator) together with the Nought (that which is not yet created).

At the end of the dark woods we can assume there is a clearing with the sun shining through it. The movement through darkness towards light is symbolic of Capricorn when, in the Northern Hemisphere, the days begin to lengthen.

At the end of their existence on earth the power these people have received from their life's experience is immense. They move from fulfilment to fulfilment, reaching a greater fullness of sensitivity both inner and outer. Their spiritual knowledge is well organised. They may become a true example of God's image.

This image is stable. These people have their feet firmly on the ground and they work hard. They are at one with Nature. Like the flaming heart, this wood will burn and warm others.

Biblical Parallel

The symbol of the flaming heart is well-known in Christian mysticism. It parallels the experience of the disciples at Emmaus, who having met the risen Christ said 'Did not our heart burn within us, while he talked with us by the way . . .' See Lk. 24: 13–32.

Conception Corrected Asc. 6th Capricorn

Sophia Loren (Sciccolone) Born 20 Sept. 1934 at 14.10 hrs. in Naples, 40°53 N, 14°18 E. CC NS for 276 days at 14.00 hrs. gives 5°39 Capricorn (or if born late for 290 days at 14.09 hrs. gives 7°46 Cap.).

Italian actress and film-star. She went to Hollywood and made some of her best films with Cary Grant. She won several Oscars, for example for *El Cid*. Contemporary and rival of Elizabeth Taylor (see 5th Li.). She became a sex-and-love symbol for the millions. The 6th degree of Capricorn seems to fit her film-image better than the 8th Capricorn, though this has to be taken into consideration as well.

7TH DEGREE CAPRICORN

First Image, Outer Symbol

In a gloomy interior two men and a woman hold a secret meeting. It looks like a conspiracy or a seance. Miniature statues and a heart transfixed with nails are placed on a table in their midst.

Interpretation

According to the drawing in Janduz' book, one of the men is wearing a five-pointed star on his breast, and the woman has one on her tall, pointed witch's hat. She calls it a degree of 'dangerous attachment'.

This is one of the most dangerous images in the sign of Capricorn, and even of the entire zodiac. In this image there is an enormous amount of hatred gathered together, caused by personal jealousy and rivalry. This is fed by unscrupulous ambition and a lust for power (neg. Cap.). People with this degree rising or prominent in their chart, suffer from much deep-seated grief, but they are hardly ever able to transmute their genuine hurt and bitterness into anything better than mean thoughts. Often they project their feelings of hate onto the innocent, or those who simply cannot think like them.

This symbolism of the image as it is pictured shows the lower or underworld level of negative awareness. It speaks of enormous hypnotic (Ar.), black magical and binding forces, which make these people feel (Cn.) they must destroy peace and harmony (Li.) wherever they find it. Almost everybody whose adverse karma (neg. Cap.) brings them in touch with bearers of these forces falls victim to them. Their negativity often originates in an inferiority complex, which may have fed on their character from early youth. (All this is the negative side of the uncontrolled cardinal cross Ar.–Cn.–Li.–Cap.) The castle of their dreams may have fallen early to outward circumstance, or through their own karmic guilt: perhaps they had to cut short a hopeful career. Whatever the occasion of their disappointment, they project their bitter feelings and their lust for vengeance upon the outside world. They approach their victims by psychic attack, which is to say by thought. This is symbolised by the heart transfixed; nails and iron both come under Scorpio and Mars.

The twentieth century knows about the rebirth of primitive guna-guna practices, or voodooism, which are even now (1990) being used in modern parapsychological warfare. It is a proven fact that small miniatures of, for instance, a national president have been found magically pierced through heart and vital organs. It is hardly necessary to state that proficiency in the black arts argues total absence of moral development. Its roots are in a monstrous egotism and an unscrupulous greed for power.

Those who are under this degree with a higher level of egotistical consciousness often get the responsibility, or feel it as their duty, to bring lost souls back from darkness to Light. But this is a dangerous task, to be attempted only by highly schooled initiates (Ar.) whose inner peace (Li.) of heart cannot be shaken. Most of them see their criminal protégés end up in utter loneliness, their lives often terminating in total ruin.

Those on a lower level of awareness may sink into despondency and misanthropy. In reality they are much to be pitied, although it is difficult to forgive them their base practices which could end in murder or even genocide.

However, on a higher level the light bearers with this degree prominent, who may have been the victims of these sinister practices, or have helped to destroy them, need to realise that the only white magic against these attacks is the protection of the Michael light-forces, and the love and forgiveness of which Jesus Christ is the highest example. Forgiveness is most difficult here as one cannot expect awareness of guilt or any betterment in a short time. One needs lifetimes of astral soul-cleansing (Cn.), purification (Vi.) and humble work for peace (Tau.), before the spirit can become as clear as a crystal (Cap.).

Second Image, Inner Symbol

A heavily veiled hierophant leads a ritual of power.

Interpretation

The hierophant or high initiate is heavily veiled, which means that the consciousness is darkened and hidden. Therefore we cannot go along with Rudhyar's interpretation of a positive avatar, who is a highly developed soul.

This image as the follow-up of the first one may indicate a false saviour of humanity, a self-styled world-leader or a guru, who is in fact a liar and a seeker after personal power. It is easy to lead entire populations of gullible people in 'rituals of power' (Cn. opp. Cap.). Emotional crowds ask to be misled.

This is the image of the veiled consciousness of one who cannot bear the consequences of his (or her) destructive attitude towards life. The outer projection of hypnosis in the first image has become one of self-hypnosis. A ritual of verbal repetition (Ge.) is still needed at this stage to convince (Sag.) the bearers of this degree of their power. The real need is for introspection (Ge.) and a reasoned review of their thoughts and beliefs (Sag., the difficult hind-axis). Only from this level of self-consciousness may they learn to open up towards the true hearts of others (Le.–Aq. fore-axis). They need to de-mask (Ar.), to desist from their theatrical hocus-pocus (neg. Cn.), and by self-knowledge learn to think in terms of human love and understanding (Le.–Aq.). Theirs will be a long and stony path (Cap.) before they have worked out the adverse karma accumulated by their lust for domination.

Biblical Parallels

'Surely he hath borne our griefs, and carried our sorrows: yet we did esteem him stricken, smitten of God, and afflicted. But he was wounded for our transgressions, he was bruised for our iniquities: the chastisement of our peace was upon him; and with his stripes we are healed.' *Is. 53: 4–5.*

'Hide me from the secret counsel of the wicked.' *Ps. 64: 2.*

The veil of the temple was rent in twain at the moment of Jesus' death. See *Mt. 27: 51.*

Christ is the true High Priest 'By a new and living way, which he hath consecrated for us, through the veil.' *Heb. 10: 20.*

Note

Suggested reading: *Psychic Self-Defence* by Dion Fortune.

Conception Corrected Asc. 7th Capricorn

Robert A. Schumann   Born 8 June 1810 at 21.30 hrs. in Zwickau, 50°43 N, 12°28 E. Died 29 July 1856. CC WAK and NS for 263 days at 21.24 hrs. gives 6°15 Capricorn.

German composer and writer. He started his own 'New Magazine for Music' (*Neue Zeitschrift für Musik*). He is known for his songs, symphonies and chamber music. He injured his right hand deliberately so that he could not play anymore. He married the pianist Clara Wieck. He suffered from severe depression and attempted suicide. He was institutionalised and died young. His traumatic life becomes much clearer in the light of this difficult 7th Capricorn Ascendant.

8th Degree Capricorn

First Image, Outer Symbol

On the left an eagle on outspread wings is carrying up his prey from a flock of sheep and lambs. On the right side a young girl is caressing a turtle dove, which she holds in her hands.

Interpretation

This is a very dualistic image. Janduz calls it 'fierce isolation'. This is true for the left side, which gives the hard and even cruel atmosphere of the nature of Capricorn in the heart of winter with the first lambs out in the open (at least in the northern hemisphere). The right side of the image, which Janduz' artist places higher up the hill, shows us more of the opposition sign Cancer. The girl is probably a shepherdess and is caring for and protecting (Cn.) a bird (Ge.).

The combination of the two sides indicates the complexity of these people's characters. They may be either very humane and tender persons, who can be rudely hurt by the painful realities of life, or they may develop an egotistical and even bloodthirsty streak in their character, which fights fiercely for their own existence regardless of their victim's. We can easily detect the Capricorn grail in this symbolism. Birds in general come under Gemini (Ge.–Sag. hind-axis) and here we have one bird in the air and another in the girl's hands (Ge.). We do not see a Sagittarius symbol as such, but we can assume that the girl must be idealistic and have faith (Sag.) in order to do her job (Ge.–Sag. hind-axis).

These people can get far in self-knowledge and introspection (Ge.), which is difficult for Capricorn. They need to develop benevolence (Sag.) and reflect on their high ideals (the bird in the sky), whether these are egotistical or purely altruistic. They may suffer from a lack of thinking-power (Sag. hind-axis). They need to grow into the fore-axis (Le.–Aq.), which will radiate goodness and break open the humane and understanding side of their nature. One day, in the New Kingdom, the beasts of prey will not feed on lambs any more (see Is. 65). The female side in these people needs to become sensitive to what is happening in the world around them. The hardline attitude of the 'hawks and eagles' is just as much part of the mundane and political life in the world (Cap.), as is that of the peace-loving 'doves'. These people need to become both within one.

A flock as such comes under Cancer and shows the collective unconsciousness (Cn.), which may not be aware enough of the dangers in the political (Cap.) air above their heads. Lambs come under Aries. One individual lamb has been picked out. Because of their herd instinct (Cn.) the entire flock becomes a target, which means that these people do not yet have their cardinal cross (Ar.–Cn.–Li.–Cap.) entirely under control. The eagle is a symbol of Scorpio. These people need a war (Sc.), or some other upheaval (Sc.) to wake them up from their too meditative and dreamy 'isolation'. They always have to be aware of the beast in themselves, but as the eagle is one of the highest esoteric symbols of transmutation, their spirit may ascend very high, taking their rudely awakened unconsciousness in its newborn state (the lamb) with them to the top of the mountain (Cap.). There, in meditation, their spirit needs to become open to grace and the intuitive understanding (Aq.), that letting live is a more royal (Le.) attitude than bloodthirsty voracity. The eagle may learn to caress the lamb in his nest, while the girl may become more alert, like the eagle, and stand up and protect her flock against impending dangers from high places.

Second Image, Inner Symbol

In a big living-room flooded with sunlight, canaries are singing.

Interpretation

Here the integration of this personality is clearly demonstrated. The dualism of the former image has become one whole (the room) lit from above by the spirit (sun). The eagle and the dove have amalgamated in one group of happy, singing, colourful canaries, which bring joy to the listener (Ge.–Sag. hind-axis).

People with this degree let inspiration crystallise. They become like a colourful work of art, or a cosmic symphony or choir. This image does not give the impression of isolation anymore, but it is still enclosed (Cn.). The birds are caged, but unconscious of their lack of freedom (Aq.).

As Capricorn, the spirit of these people is enlightened now by light from heaven (Le.–Aq.), but they still need to transcend their lower self and enter into inner (Cn.) freedom (Aq.) beyond their self-imposed boundaries (Cap.).

Biblical Parallels

'The wolf (symbol of Sc. like the eagle) and the lamb shall feed together . . . They shall not hurt nor destroy in all my holy mountain.' *Is. 65: 25.*

'. . . my days . . . are passed away as the swift ships: as the eagle that hasteth to the prey.' *Job 9: 26.*

Note

In mythology this degree is a symbol of Icarus, who flew so near the sun that the wax of his fabricated wings melted, causing him to fall from a great height as the reward for his pride in challenging the gods (Cap.–Saturn).

Conception Corrected Asc 8th Capricorn

Carry van Bruggen Born 1 Jan. 1881 at 08.00 hrs. in Smilde 52°56 N, 06°25 E. Died 17 Nov. 1932. CC WAK for 266 days at 08.06 hrs. gives 7°22 Capricorn.

Dutch writer of Jewish Rabbinical descent. Famous in her day. She had Sun, Moon and Ascendant in Capricorn with a heavily afflicted cardinal cross. She ended her days in a mental hospital and committed suicide. Her manic-depressive life-story is a clinical example of this degree. She wrote a book, *Prometheus*, which deals with the pride of man in stealing fire from heaven. A similar subject to that of Icarus.

Sophia Loren, if born late, CC NS for 290 days at 14.09 hrs. gives 7°46 Capricorn.

9TH DEGREE CAPRICORN

First Image, Outer Symbol

A man falls near a broken key lying on the earth beneath a standing cross on the right.

Interpretation

People with this degree on the Ascendant, which is the physical manifestation of a degree symbol, tend to 'fall' on many levels. This tendency can range from being accident-prone to falling morally or politically. According to Janduz, their downfall may be due to their materialistic temperament, and they may be great spenders. It may happen that their excesses provoke their relatives, especially their father (Cap.–Sat.), if the family is affected by the loss, and the entire family (Cn. opp. Cap.) may mind their business. One way or another they will 'meet their fate' through justice, and be stopped by violent means.

The broken key may indicate that these people find it difficult to work out the right solution to their problems. The door to a better understanding remains locked to them. As this is a Capricorn degree, they may easily fall into the habit of pretending to superior wisdom, which ends in tyranny and is no more then a disguise of their impotence (neg. Ar.) to descend of their own volition to seeking co-operation (Li.). Bystanders begin to see through their childish despotism (neg. Le.), to the empty pretence, and thus they themselves bring about their own downfall. However, the cross might symbolise salvation and redemption, to be won if they will work to improve their character.

The upright cross, which we assume is of stone (Cap.), is a high symbol of the sign of Capricorn itself and has a deep esoteric meaning. On the outer level it is a symbol of organised religion, but here it represents an inner meeting with the Cross. This touches the deeper interpretation of this image seen from the Capricorn grail as a whole.

Who knows whether the fall of the man is not by the will of the Higher Self? Perhaps the broken key on the ground tells us that worldly and political preoccupations are not the right key to the meaning of existence. Or could it not symbolise that the earth itself is broken and needs to be healed?

These people may, of their own free will, step down from their high position in society, to bring healing to the wounded planet in co-operation with angels and devas (see second image). Maybe they discover one day that they need to turn everything upside-down and see all the things they took for granted from another angle. They may need the magnetic attraction of the earth and the earthly, even if only temporarily, to teach them the vanity of material values in a world where the spirit is crucified in matter. The vertical beam of the cross is rooted in the earth, but points upwards.

On a high level of consciousness (the man), these people are able to perceive and evaluate the many veils which constitute this world of illusory appearance (Cn. opp. Cap., Maya or illusion). Recognising the relativity of earthly values they can rise to the invisible planes. The sacred and profane levels of existence, and the visible and the invisible, become one in their lives. They know that the symbol of the cross in a circle (of which the Celtic crosses remind us) raises all earthly matter to a higher plane, and will protect and save them from any sort of fatal downfall or catastrophe. They may ascend to a firm faith (Sag.) in the 'Rock of Ages', through which their will (Le.) sees a wider scope (Aq.) and becomes wiser (Ge.) as time passes (Le.–Aq. fore-axis and Sag.–Ge. hind-axis). They may attain spiritual insight and leave the low level of society politics (Cap.) far behind them. This is so beautifully symbolised on the inner level.

Second Image, Inner Symbol

An angel carrying a harp comes through a heavenly lane.

Interpretation

Here is the bearer of harmony from a higher world, an angelic figure, in consciousness far above ordinary humanity yet symbolic of the human ideal.

The true Self of these people can be daily tuned to the tones of inward perfection, for the true ordering and ennoblement of life in the outer world. Thus will they be bearers of good tidings, or angels (Aq.) in the true sense of the word, as much by example as by precept. They need to sever themselves from material things and public ambition, to grasp the truth that their mundane situation is their place in a school where they are set to learn attunement with their Creator.

The symbol of the harp is significant in this connection. It is the most meaningful of all musical instruments. It has the form of the human heart, whose 'strings' must be correctly tuned if we are to make music of our lives as we are meant to do. There is much more to say about the harp, but it suffices here to note that it comprises the elements of the Leo–Aquarius grail of creativity, led by the angels (Le.–Aq. fore-axis). Only those who can see angels as reality, can learn from this important degree in the zodiac that their ministry is more real than is ever suspected today. These people will be kicked around by 'fate' and menaced by society until they realise that angels are bearing them up and watching that they do not hurt their feet on a single stone. If only they can find the courage to sever their worldly ties and turn their values upside down. Then the cross rises up in them and they become angelic examples, themselves under the protection of angels. Any egotism of lower Capricorn has been overcome. The threshold between Capricorn and Aquarius is passed, and a new humanity working in tune with the angels can be foreseen here.

Biblical Parallels

'Woe unto you lawyers! for ye have taken away the key of knowledge: ye entered not in yourselves, and them that were entering in ye hindered.' *Lk. 11: 52.*

'. . . the key of the bottomless pit' *Rev. 9: 1* and *20: 1.*

'. . . the keys of hell' *Rev. 1: 18.*

'. . . the keys of the kingdom of heaven' *Mt. 16: 19.*

'For he shall give his angels charge over thee, to keep thee in all thy ways. They shall bear thee up in their hands, lest thou dash thy foot against a stone.' *Ps. 91: 11–12.*

Many psalms speak of praising the Lord with the harp.

'. . . I heard a voice from heaven . . . and I heard the voice of harpers harping with their harps.' *Rev. 14: 2.* See also *Rev. 18: 22.*

Conception Corrected Asc. 9th Capricorn

W. E. Gladstone Born 29 Dec. 1809 at 08.30 hrs. in Liverpool, 53°25 N, 03°00 W. Died 1898. CC WAK and NS for 279 days at 08.35 hrs. gives 8°44 Capricorn or for 265 days at 08.36 hrs. gives 8°58 Capricorn.

Four times Prime Minister of Great Britain. 'Double Capricorn' (Sun and Ascendant in this sign). Gladstone's character and devotion to what he saw as his duty, made him an outstanding nineteenth-century statesman, and a first-class example of this degree. He was known to be 'more Christian than statesman.' He knew himself to be God's instrument to serve the monarchy and to be the conscience of the country. This meant to him fulfilling one's duty and obeying the laws. He was falsely accused and blackmailed when he tried to rehabilitate prostitutes. He was ahead of his time in seeing these 'fallen women' as the moral conscience of Victorian society. See, amongst others, *Gladstone, a Biography* by Philip Magnus (Murray).

Mina Kruseman Born 25 Sept. 1839 at 14.30 hrs. in Velp, 51°59 N, 05°59 E. Died 2 Aug. 1922. CE WAK and NS for 296 days at 14.34 hrs. gives 8°20 Cap.

Dutch singer, actress, writer and brilliant lecturer. She became a household name in the Holland of her days, as she was one of the first suffragettes. Some of her novels were very advanced for her time and shocked the Dutch. She certainly had a golden key in her hands, but behaving like a man, she lost her reputation and left for France, where she lived out of wedlock with a Dutchman, being against a civil marriage on principle. The Dutch feminist movement of the 1970s was called after her nickname 'Dolle Mina's'.

Her book *Myn Leven* (1877) is autobiographical.

Joseph Willem Mengelberg   CC for 272 days at 02.29 hrs. gives 8°34 Capricorn. See 11th Capricorn.

Karl Schoch   Born 5 Mar. 1873 at 04.00 hrs. in Pilgram, 52°20 N, 14°25 E. CC NS for 270 days at 04.01 hrs. gives 8°55 Cap. CC NS for 270 days at 04.01 hrs. gives 8°55 Capricorn.

Genius mathematician, who simplified astronomical calculations; known for the 'Schoch Tables'. Before the age of the computer his books were invaluable to astrologers, who thus could calculate charts as far back as 3400 BC.

Main work *Planetustafeln fur Jedermann* (Ebertin).

10th DEGREE CAPRICORN

First Image, Outer Symbol

It is night. A man standing upright holds a night-bird (an owl) in each hand. A third owl is sitting on a branch in the light of the full moon.

Interpretation

Janduz calls this a degree of 'secretiveness', but this is a rather superficial interpretation. There is a part in this degree which may be seen as 'secret' by small-minded people: the public mind quickly labels somebody 'secretive', and sinister too, if they choose to be habitually out and about after dark.

Janduz calls people with this degree on the Ascendant 'night-birds', who would do well to have a nocturnal job when everybody else is asleep, and to study occult philosophies. So far Janduz.

This degree has many more possibilities, especially on the meditative plane (Cap.). There are several elements of the Capricorn grail to be found in this image, on a level which tells us that we have to do with a highly evolved one.

People with this degree may be not very evolved spiritually, dabblers in occultism, which in their case tends to go a bit beyond its established laws. They may even practise on the fringes of black magic. In this case, however, theirs is not the dangerous guna-guna (see 7th Cap.), but they do like rituals at night involving some hidden wisdom.

On a higher level, these are people with an innate capacity for pure meditation and, of course, they are sensitive (Cn. opp. Cap.) to the phases of the moon in their meditations, especially the full moon, which mirrors the sunlight completely. This reflected light, however, represents 'second-hand' knowledge, like the astral and etheric thought-forms created by their thinking and feeling, shadows of the true light. The moon and the night-birds are symbols of these. The man is holding the owls in his hands (Ge.) and carrying on an inner conversation (Ge.) with them, although owls would normally be afraid (Cap.) of men.

The man himself is standing with a straight back as a symbol of full consciousness of spiritual being, which in contact with his Higher Self is bringing light into the darkness of this night. (One may compare this with the 12th Capricorn.)

Typically these people cannot stand the limelight, or on the physical plane, loud noises and the tumult of the world at midday. Their ideas ripen slowly inside them. They are prudent and guarded, often giving the impression of timidity. It takes a long time to discover their positive value and to penetrate their reserve. They have a talent for abstract study and occult philosophy, and they can apply endless patience to projects that take years to mature. In Capricorn nothing takes form quickly. These people know things inwardly that are hidden from others, but they go with the times and know how to wait. They never force fate: they enjoy following the course of events. Their great interest in macrocosmic processes leaves them humble, but their merits may one day be made public, and they may become important or even famous in society (pos. Cap.).

The Capricorn grail is evident (Ge.–Sag. hind-axis and Le.–Aq. fore-axis). The opposition sign Cancer, as part of this grail, is represented by the full moon. These persons need to meditate on events in the outer world. This seems simple, but is in fact very difficult. Most people are preoccupied with their personal affairs and the daily agitation of their own fretful minds. They have to expand their consciousness to embrace a much wider world.

The owl traditionally is the symbol of meditative wisdom. The owls on the hands of the man indicate a strong awareness of the hind-axis Gemini–Sagittarius (hands and birds come under Ge., and the owls in a subdivision under Sag.). During meditation these people have a great capacity for introspection and the ability to create potent thought-forms.

Trees come under Sagittarius. The presence of a third owl suggests a triangular form of thinking similar to the ancient Celtic philosophy with its triads or thinking in threes. The straight back (Le.) of the man, and the obvious contact (Aq.) with the birds, indicate growth into the fore-axis Leo–Aquarius, which also comes forth in the second image.

Second Image, Inner Symbol

On a sailing boat, seamen are feeding a tame albatross.

Interpretation

The lesson in the two images of this degree is to overcome all instinctive (Cn.) fears (Cap.), which occur during the full moon. We know the word 'lunatic'. Mental patients tend to be disturbed at this time, and we have all heard of dogs baying at the moon. It is easy to meditate on primitive and personal emotional vibrations (Moon), but it takes conscious Sun-power to meditate on objective fields of cosmic thinking. These people need to persuade (Sag.) their racing thoughts (Ge.) to slow down (Cap.), in order to get form (Cap.) in time and place (Cap.). Like the man in the first image, they should shun the limelight in order to develop their inner spiritual values and wisdom (Ge.–Sag.). These sailors have left the rat-race behind and gone 'back' to nature's energy.

During a calm, seamen have all the time in the world to meditate. They have to conquer their superstitious fear of birds of 'ill omen', but here it is a tame albatross landing on their deck.

In the first image it was Wisdom held in the hands; here it is the Mystery of the sea in the form of a tame albatross at the feet, treasures to be found only in solitude. Both images symbolise a peace and quietness which bring the bearers of this degree high up the ladder of spiritual evolution. Their Higher Self can fly high, like the albatross over the ocean in the moonlit sky.

Note

The immortal classic *The Ancient Mariner* of S.T. Coleridge (1772–1834) deals with this degree. It embodies the dream of a friend and the shooting of an albatross.

Conception Corrected Asc. 10th Capricorn

King Baudouin of Belgium Born 7 Sept. 1930 at 16.25 hrs. in Brussels, 50°51 N, 04°21 E. CC WAK and NS for 264 days at 16.26 hrs. gives 9°04 Capricorn.

Son of Leopold III (see 13th Ar.) and Astrid (see 9th Ge.); great grandson of King Leopold I (see 29th Sc.). He is married to Fabiola (see 16th Vi.). Due to his father's abdication, he became King when only 20 in the difficult post-war years. With the reserved attitude often found in those with Capricorn rising, it took his marriage to the gifted Fabiola to secure his popularity. Belgium has been blessed with a king with the wisdom of the 10th Capricorn at the helm of their ship of state.

Frederic Mistral Born 8 Sept. 1830 at 18.30 hrs. in Maillane, 42°50 N, 04°50 E. Died 1914. CC WAK and NS for 284 days or 298 days (late birth) at 18.40 or 18.38 hrs. gives 9°54 or 9°28 Capricorn. Or for 270 days at 18.12 hrs. gives 2°56 Capricorn, see there.

French poet from Provence. Famous for his poem *Mireio*. His writings are important in connection with the Cathars of that area.

11TH DEGREE CAPRICORN

First Image, Outer Symbol

At the right a king on his throne leans forward to a messenger, who has approached him from the left and with a deep obeisance presents the king with a sealed parchment held in his outstretched hands.

Interpretation

This is a degree of 'responsibility', according to Janduz. People with this degree rising may be responsible for important papers, such as are held at a bank, a post office or in any other civil or governmental service.

On a higher level they are responsible for religious or political correspondence which may be highly confidential. This is the physical side of the messenger. With this degree on the Ascendant, the other side of the symbol shows that they may have very high standing in the country and be in personal service to a royal family, or belong to the nobility. They may serve a Minister of State, or may be such themselves. They may be on the receiving end of petitions. As this is a Capricorn degree, their professional duties may be inherited from their father (Cap.) or be rooted in tradition (Cap.–Cn.).

On a lower level there is the possibility of diplomatic scheming, which can deteriorate into subservience. If this is their attitude, these people may fall into disrespect.

Their manner may be taciturn, as they are accustomed to carrying responsibility for much that is secret.

As a spiritual symbol this degree indicates that the spirit of these people can ascend (Cap.) to the highest regions of inner and outer awareness.

The hind-axis Gemini–Sagittarius is represented in the messenger, the bringer of good tidings, which come from all the twelve sides of the zodiac to the king, the symbol of the Higher Self in the middle. Nothing escapes the attention of a true spiritual king, who represents our own innermost centre. The king is in contact with all his subjects. This is the Aquarius–Leo fore-axis into which Capricorn needs to expand. The symbol of the Sun (Le., the king), right in the middle of the Capricorn grail, gives tremendous spiritual responsibilities within the tradition of the past (Cn.), thus giving their grail-cup a firm basis for ascension into physical, etheric and astral worlds of experience.

Second Image, Inner Symbol

Pheasants display their brilliant colours on a vast lawn.

Interpretation

The king of the first image is bound by ritual. He needs his messengers to keep him informed. He still has his eyes on the outside world.

The pheasant is in some respects a higher symbol of the king. Although coming under Gemini as a bird, pheasants as a species are one of the advanced birds of the Sun and come under Leo (fore-axis). Their brilliant colours are radiating from within. There is no need for messages (Ge.), because they themselves are the mediators of a multicoloured Creation. They display great inner richness and have a style of exquisite royalty. Amongst these birds on the lawn, we see no distinction of rank. This is a proud group of royal equals, completely safe and free to show their true colours. There are great possibilities for spiritual creativity.

This is a degree of *noblesse oblige*, if idleness and vain-glory do not mar it.

Biblical Parallels

The story of King Nebuchadnezzar's dream. See *Dan. 2*.

The story of King Belshazzer and the writing on the wall which nobody could explain, so that Daniel was brought into the King's presence. He rebukes the king saying 'You have not glorified the God who holds in his own power your breath of life and destiny.' *Dan. 5: 23* (Moffatt translation).

Daniel reveals the writing on the wall and is proclaimed as ranking third within the realm. See *Dan. 5: 7, 16* and *29*.

Note

In China the pheasant is the allegorical animal of light and of day (see J.E. Cirlot).

Conception Corrected Asc. 11th Capricorn

Joseph Willem Mengelberg   Born 28 Mar. 1871 at 02.30 hrs. in Utrecht, 52°05 N, 05°06 E. Died 22 Mar. 1951. CC NS for 272 days at 02.29 hrs. gives 8°34 Capricorn (see 9th Cap.) or for 286 days at 02.35 hrs. gives 10°20 Capricorn.

Dutch conductor who raised the Amsterdam Concert Gebouw Orchestra to international level. He was famous in his heyday, but lost his good name during the German occupation when he conducted for the Nazis. He was dismissed in 1945.

Niccolo Machiavelli   Born 4 May (not 3, OS, 13 May NS) 1469 at. 4.00 hours into the night in Florence, 43.48 N, 11.18 E. This means 4.00 hours after sunset and not 4.00 hours a.m. (compare Leonardo da Vinci, 8th Sag.). According to calculations by NS sunset was at 18.24 GT. The night hours were 61 minutes, so that the birthtime is 23.13 local time or 22.28 GT. CC NS for 261 days at 22.59 hrs. gives 10.10 Capricorn or for 275 days at 23.11 hrs. gives 13.14 Capricorn (see 14th degree). All known charts for 4.00 hrs. a.m. with Taurus rising (see Wemyss' *Wheel of Life* vol. III, p. 91) are wrong according to this new information.

Italian politician, diplomat and writer. He was counsellor for war affairs in Florence. As diplomat he was sent to European rulers, which gave him the concept for his notorious *Il Principe* 'The Ruler', or 'The Prince' (1513), for which Cesare Borgia was his model. In our century Mussolini (see 20th Sc.) twisted Machiavelli's ideas and used them for his Fascist dictatorship. Machiavelli was not the villain he is often held to have been, but a prophetic historian who stood at the turning-point in history between rule by a degenerate medieval Church and the rise of national states with absolute rulers. His life as a 'messenger' is an interesting example of the 11th Capricorn, which also adds weight to the calculations of NS. See *Encycl. Britt, Machiavelli and His* Times' by D. E. Muir (1936) and an Italian film about him, *La Mandragola* (1965).

12TH DEGREE CAPRICORN

First Image, Outer Symbol

In the light of the full moon a dog, incited by his master on the right, chases a fox, which, having a head start, is gaining ground.

Interpretation

Janduz calls this a degree of 'velocity'. Indeed when superficially observed it gives an impression of speed. With this degree on the Ascendant these people make a quick impression. They may excel at running, riding and of course hunting. They like risky undertakings, which indicates on the inner planes that they have an active spirit. They have the squares of Aries (action) and Libra (balance) well under control. They can make rapid decisions, especially when they have to attack.

On the whole we can distinguish three types of people in this image, although ideally speaking all its symbols should be integrated into their personality. There is the fox which is subtle, sly and cunning. We have a Dutch saying 'The fox loses it hair but not its tricks', and there are English equivalents which also fit Capricorn 'What is bred in the bone (Cap.) will not come out of the flesh' and 'The fox may grow grey but never good'. In the Middle Ages the fox was a common symbol for the devil (neg. Cap.) and an expression of base attitudes and of the wiles of the adversary.

Then there are the symbols of the man, the moon and the dog. Taking the man first (the consciousness), these people on a low level of awareness may let others do their dirty work for them, and they treat these deputies like dogs. On a higher level they have the vigilant mentality of the policeman or detective in the pursuit of terrorists and perpetrators of all sorts of crimes that shun the daylight. On the more intellectual level they are searchers in archives, researchers of genealogies, or guardians of the treasures of a museum.

The full moon symbolises a more contemplative side of their nature, but they are not as meditative and aware of the full moon and its importance as the people of the 10th Capricorn, where we see a man and owls in a meditative position at full moon. In this 12th image there is too much exaltation, nervousness and lack of time (neg. Cap.) to look up into the sky and contemplate what is going on in the heavens. These people live in a kind of dream-state because they are not aware of the waves of energy present in the elements during the full moon. Therefore they are easy victims of negative forces, which they call up themselves when they do not have their exalted emotions under control. They can be caught by 'fate', which may lead them into physical or mental imprisonment, or even exile. They may be excluded from undertakings they themselves initiated (Ar.) and from the very people they most wish to make their partners (Li.).

However, the dog (Ar.) in the middle of the image symbolises the energy which these people possess. Their will (the man) can make this energy work, and by the right guarding and directing of it they may attain control over the inner and outer situations of life (Cn. opp. Cap.). Needless to say they may be excellent at training dogs for police or rescue work.

On a higher esoteric level they may indeed develop the psychic ability to do rescue work on the inner invisible planes, preferably in their sleep-state at night. However, for this work they need to forgo pursuit of outward objectives and attain a meditative purity (Cap.) with which they can mirror the feelings (Cn.) of others. They need to discern the goodness in humanity (Le.–Aq. fore-axis). This is the apotheosis of that low consciousness with which they so energetically (Ge.–Sag. hind-axis) detected vice, sometimes by excess zeal transgressing the laws of nature.

Second Image, Inner Symbol

Natural wonders are depicted in a lecture on science.

Interpretation

The possible offence against nature's laws in the first image is transmuted here. These people have discovered the wonders of nature and can even teach about them now (Ge.–Sag. hind-axis on a higher level). This image detects the deeper layers of the microcosmos in all its minutest detail and in everything that is growing on earth (the three earth signs Tau.–Vi.–Cap. in harmony). The manifest universe proceeds, by stages, from its cause, the unseen Creator: only those made sensitive by long searching can find and declare this truth.

The lesson of this image is that the world is one great miracle for those who know that all is created in the deeps of cosmic silence. Agitation has no place here. Self-control is necessary before we can grasp, and impart to others, the complexity of our links with all Nature in this (by no means incidentally) sub-lunar world of ours.

These people need a knowledge of cosmography, and they especially need to make a study of the Moon.

Biblical Parallel

The ancient festivals of the full moon, which were pagan and, the meditations during the new moon, which were Israelite, with their culmination in Easter, are times and seasons to be remembered.

Conception Corrected Asc. 12th
Capricorn

Arthur Koestler Born 5 Sept. 1905 at 15.30 hrs. in Budapest 47°28 N, 19°03 E. Committed suicide 3 Mar. 1983. CC WAK and NS for 284 days at 15.29 hrs. gives 11°42 Capricorn.

This English-Hungarian writer and former Communist is known as a nervous, cynical, passionate intellectual, who bore the consequences of his philosophy in taking his own life and that of his wife. He is a striking example of this degree. He wrote *Darkness at Noon*, *The Sleepwalkers* and *The Thirteenth Tribe*, amongst many other books. He sponsored the Koestler Foundation, a laboratory for psychological and ESP research in

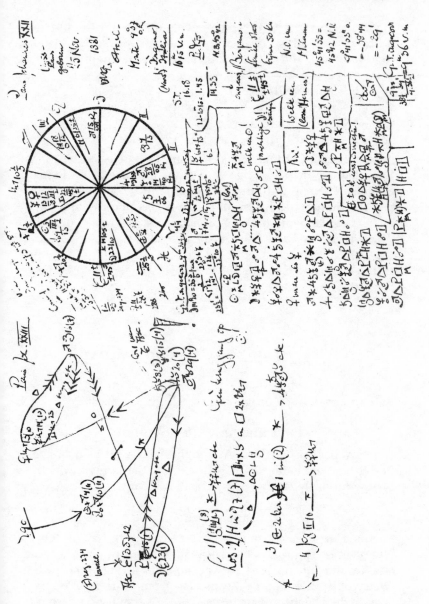

Handwritten chart of Pope John XXIII
by Willem Ary Koppejan

England. He exposed the experiments on rats for the psychological research of the 1960s as inhuman. In 1984 the Foundation concentrated on the validity of astrology in different professions.

Pope Johannes XXIII (A. G. Roncalli)   Born 25 Nov. 1881 at 10.15 hrs. in Sotto il Monte, 45°42 N, 09°37 E. Died 3 June 1963. CC WAK and NS for 288 days at 10.15 hrs. gives 11°43 Capricorn, or for 274 days at 10.16 hrs. gives 12°03 Capricorn (see there).

Italian priest, Cardinal of Venice in 1953, elected Pope in 1958. During his short five-year reign he moved the Roman Catholic Church into the twentieth-century mainstream of modern human behaviour and thus he became the first pope to be popular with the common people. See his biography *I Shall be Called John* by Lawrence Elliott (1974).

H. F. Verwoerd   If CC for 274 days at 15.57 hrs. gives 11°38 Cap. See 17th Cap.

13TH DEGREE CAPRICORN

First Image, Outer Symbol

A harrow lies in a bare field. At its right stands a man with a small upright serpent in his hand. He is exciting the serpent, which is hissing furiously.

Interpretation

This is a degree of 'critical spirit', according to Janduz. On a low level of spiritual awareness, these persons like to tease and wound others. This can be done in an aggressive way with words, or by other means. They can be really base and achieve their egotistical goals (neg. Sag.) by fraud and treachery. They may have a sharp tongue, using the sting of irony and the needle of sarcasm. Their criticism is fierce: it may drive their partners and companions to desperation (Li. sq. Cap., Ge.–Sag.

hind-axis). They sow distrust amongst families and groups (neg. Le.–Aq. fore-axis). They may even undermine other people's faith and self-confidence by ridicule, on the pretext of developing their inner growth. They do not hesitate to blacken other people's characters. They tear down the sanctuaries of others, and leave them sitting in the ruins. On this level these people are a public menace. They deliberately excite base passions and like to see others become jealous. When in positions of power, they make empty promises of promotion to subordinates whom they in fact despise and eventually disappoint (neg. Sag.).

However, as with any degree, the level on which this symbol is lived out depends on the development of the Higher Self.

At first these people may merely be acute analysts of their own passions and emotions, but later they can ascend to a great height of impartiality (Li.) and accordingly act with much dignity. As such they make good judges and psychoanalysts. With an evolved Higher Self, they may go in search of the hidden sources of power (serpent comes under Sc.), and seek out the works of humanity throughout history (Cap.), that witness the greatness of mankind. It may become their aim to revive these in a newer and nobler form (the trine Tau.–Vi.–Cap.). Still on this higher level, however, they may have no reverence for tradition or outmoded ways of thought, which it is their task anyhow to expose (Ar.). Their highest goal will be to serve a renewed society, or by breaking down the old, to bring forth the New Kingdom (Le.–Aq. fore-axis).

The harrow can become a tool for working the soil so that others may sow (Tau.) the seed and harvest the grain (Vi.). It is a typical cold winter scene, symbolising the tough and cold-blooded character of Capricorn. These people may not seem very productive, but all they need to do in order to sow positive seeds in others is to go into themselves and meditate. Their great inner need is to soften the sharp edge of their hypercriticism, and to free their own spiritual fecundity for the benefit of others. For this they are often too egocentric, and have difficulty in transcending their lower, fretful ego. On the highest level, they may be able to plant prophetic suggestions (Tau.) to purify the barren or polluted earth (Vi.) and thus exercise a great and effective force for humanity.

Second Image, Inner Symbol

Beneath snow-clad peaks, a fire-worshipper is meditating.

Interpretation

Here we see a higher concentration of the former image. The man, who provoked the serpent's power, has realised he played with fire, and that he needs a more respectful attitude towards the Kundalini-fire in him, and the element of fire in his meditations. The consciousness is elevated to the central force. In the first image there was an uncontrolled descent towards the depths of the unconsciousness. This is now replaced by subtle thinking and the crystallisation (the snow) of energy, a triumph over all the base and devious passions in the lower psyche. These people remain cool and their work is done in silence and meditation, from whence go out impulses both creative and consuming.

It is a Capricorn degree in which we can learn how great is the resistance of matter. Capricorn is symbolised by a stone, indicating what a stumbling-block our own lower nature can be.

14TH DEGREE CAPRICORN

First Image, Outer Symbol

A harp is placed on a carpet of flowers while a man with the head of a falcon tries to vibrate the strings.

Interpretation

Janduz calls this a degree of 'harmony'. It is a two-sided symbol. People with this degree rising may show a strange mixture of shortcomings and the most beautiful qualities. Often they have talent, and even a gift for music and composition. They may get far in their career, but the symbol of the man with the falcon-head shows that the easy performance of the genius has not yet developed. They still have to go through many hours of hard practice.

These people are day-dreamers, a characteristic which often masks tremendous egotism (Cap.) and unfulfilled ambition (Cap.). They may be aware of their talent, but this is not always firmly grounded.

On a low level there may be a show (neg. Cn. opp.) of sympathy, but just around the corner in their character there is excessive jealousy and calculation which can suddenly turn cynical and sarcastic. Often these people feel themselves to be undervalued (neg. Sag. hind-axis) exponents of their art. Scorning the public (Cn.), they are apt to criticise their preceptors.

On a higher level of awareness they may succeed in self-criticism and become constructive critics of the arts. (This is the earth triangle Tau.–Vi.–Cap.) Now there can be growth without rivalry. It seems as if their nature changes and begins to vibrate to a higher octave on the strings of the cosmos. They learn to sacrifice the lower self for the sake of pure art, and begin to listen to the heartbeat of the universe. The harp has the form of a heart, and it is the most sacred and healing of musical instruments. These people are rich in healing power and may understand the subtle gradations of acoustics. The laws of rhythm and harmony in the arts, crafts and architecture have their special attention. They may be craftsmen carving beautiful bird or flower symbols on instruments.

The falcon has an esoteric meaning and these people may benefit from studying ancient Egypt and medieval falconry. Psychologically, however, their character has not quite grown into full understanding. A man with a bird's head still has an animal nature and has yet to form (Cap.), the models of the astral world (Cn.) by experiencing and thinking them through, before he can play the harp in full perfection.

Second Image, Inner Symbol

In a dense jungle we see a perfectly preserved Mayan bas-relief.

Interpretation

Here is a high symbol of Capricorn. Time, as such, comes under

Capricorn and here is a form (Cap.) carved in stone (Cap.), the hardest matter, which has lain in silence (Cap.) since time immemorial (Sat. in Cap.). This relic of ancient culture makes no claims and nobody knows who made it, but one feels the divine creative inspiration in and behind it, formed 'through' man into a crystalline form.

The symbol means that these people ascend to anonymous immortality and will leave a harmonious thought-form on this earth, having conquered their lower self through profound self-awareness and release of any form of personal ambition and selfishness.

Biblical Parallels

David playing the harp for the depressed King Saul. See *l Sam. 16: 16–23*.

Prophesying with the harp. See *l Chron. 25: 7*.

'My harp also is turned to mourning' *Job 30: 31*.

'Praise the Lord with harp.' *Ps. 33: 2* (and others).

Note

In Egyptian religion the god Ra is depicted as a man with a falcon's head. Horus was the falcon-headed deity.

Conception Corrected Asc. 14th
Capricorn

Karel Jonckheere Born 9 Apr. 1906 at 01.00 hrs. in Ostende, Belgium, 51°13 N, 02°55 E. CC WAK for 266 days at 01.01 hrs. gives 13°56 Capricorn.

Flemish writer. Sometimes called the 'sphinx-like poet'. He is mainly know for his linking the cultures of Belgium and the Netherlands and for his excellent description of his travels amongst the arts of the world, which makes him a good example of the second image.

André Malraux Born 3 Nov. 1901 at 12.00 hrs. (RB) in Paris, 48°50 N, 02°20 E. (A circulating chart of 16.00 hrs. with Aries rising is not according to the Registrar of Births.) CC WAK and

NS for 275 days at 12.01 hrs. gives 13°45 Capricorn.

French writer, art-psychologist and politician with Chinese Communistic sympathies. He fought the Fascists in the Spanish Civil War, and the Nazis as an active French resistance worker in World War II. Close to de Gaulle (see 22nd Li.), he became Minister of Information in 1945 and of Cultural Affairs in 1959. He is known for his Museum 'Imaginaire', which is a photographic inventory of art forms through the ages and their metamorphoses, and he expressed this in his book *Metamorphosis of the Gods*. His life and works seem to have been a constant search for the archetypal image of the 14th Capricorn. In the 1920s he went to Laos in Asia to hunt for bas-reliefs in the jungle (see 2nd image) where, accused of being a Chinese Communist spy, he was arrested, attracting world-wide publicity.

His best book, *The Conquerors*, deals with a Communist takeover of China, some twenty years before it actually happened. He admired Lawrence of Arabia (see 17th Le.), whose work he translated into French. There are numerous studies about his work in both French and Dutch. See *André Malraux* by Jean Laconture (1973) and his own *Antimemoires* (1967).

15TH DEGREE CAPRICORN

First Image, Outer Symbol

At the left stands a tripod and brazier from which flames are leaping high. At the right a man is standing with a dead sheep on his shoulders. He is half sacrificial priest and half butcher.

Interpretation

This is a peculiar image with many esoteric elements. It hardly seems to belong to a Capricorn degree. Janduz calls it one of 'ardent life'.

On many levels of awareness there is sacrifice (Pi.) or destruction (Sc.) performed by these people as a ritual or as a profession.

They may become butchers, or have to do with defence in a military or patriotic sense.

As politics and governments come under Capricorn, these people on a low level might be revolutionary types, or ardent conspirators, always stirring things up. They may hunt down their objective with cruel persistence. They can literally sacrifice innocent people (the sheep) on the altar of their political or personal ambition.

On a higher level, for instance with the Sun here or a planet of the fire or air trine, the symbols of the tripod (the trinity) and the fire prevail. They may have high and altruistic ambitions without calculating the cost (which is rare for Sat. – Cap.). They may indeed become honest, and be very active as missionaries, priests or explorers. They are indefatigable and do not get depressed by setbacks (neg. Cap.). Their faith in their goal is enormous (Sag.– Ge. hind-axis) and they gradually evolve to be free and dynamic leaders of their group (Aq.– Le. fore-axis). Thus their influence and activity is felt at home and nationwide (opp. sign Cn.). Customs and traditions of ancient religions and peoples (Cn.) interest them. They recover hidden knowledge (Ge.) and re-present it for the New Kingdom (Aq.). Their forté may lie in archaeology, ley line research or esoteric temple-work.

The tripod indicates high and pure spiritual morals structured and based on the triads and the trinity of life. When their burning passions are transformed and made available for the service of mankind, they become guides and lead their flock of sheep on spiritual and esoteric paths. This may lead them in turn to the shambles politically, or even physically, as they may be sacrificed to the ignorance of the common herd.

Second Image, Inner Symbol

In a hospital, a children's ward filled with playthings.

Interpretation

At first sight the two images do not seem to be connected, but they are. In a world split by fanaticism (Ge.–Sag.), oppressed by human sacrifice, the heartsick children of God need to be healed with special care, not by fiery rituals but by simple gifts from heaven (Le.–Aq.).

The man of the first image can escape suffering by his ardent and constructive attitude to life, but in the second image the ego becomes humbled by its helplessness, ready to become a child again and gently healed with the simple pleasures which life itself provides. In the symbol there are no children, but their toys are waiting for them to come and be healed. No rituals, no politics, just simple healing enjoyment.

Biblical Parallels

Animal sacrifices. See Num. *15,18* and *19*.

Christ the lamb slain. See *Rev 5: 6* and *13: 8*.

16TH DEGREE CAPRICORN

First Image, Outer Symbol

An able horseman mounted on a beautiful horse is passing from left to right in the foreground. In the distance is seen another man playing the clown on his horse. He is riding bareback and the horse is bolting.

Interpretation

These symbols represent two totally different characters within these people. The best thing for them, of course, is to make a synthesis of the two symbols (Ge.–Sag. hind-axis). It is a degree of 'gallantry and proud courage'.

Identifying with the first man, their consciousness is of an aristocratic nature in full control of their thinking (the horse) and has their lower self fully in hand.

On the physical level, these people may be owners of horses, or have as their profession the training of horses, animal healing, horse-racing and so forth. The second side of their character has the same interests but in a more eccentric form.

They may be involved in risky adventures where courage and much originality of thinking is needed, but they have things far less under control.

The first man does everything according to the rules and goes down well-trodden paths. His thinking is evolving towards a perfected form (Cap.) of beauty. Here we see the cardinal cross (Ar.–Cn.–Li.–Cap.) striving towards perfection. The energies (Ar.) and unbridled actions are brought into a beautiful harmony (Li.) by binding the emotions (Cn.) with discipline (Cap.).

The clown on the wild horse is in a way evolving more towards the freedom and childlike play of the fore-axis Leo–Aquarius, which is just what the static Capricorn needs. They are eccentric, free and spontaneous (Aq.), giving their thinking (the horse) free rein (Le.). Thus they will learn more from their experiences (Cn. opp. Cap.). The first man has concentrated too much on formality, without and within. The second man may suddenly break away in a violent flight of emotion, but he may, because of his audacity, get further in life's circus and in the eyes of God's 'cloud of witnesses'.

The combination of the two symbols gives very highly evolved people, who are deep thinkers. They have productive concentration, which, when combined with original courage, takes command of the most grotesque situations. One moment they may play the fool, and the next put on the formal uniform of *haute école*. As such they may be born teachers, which brings us to the second image.

Second Image, Inner Symbol

Schoolgrounds filled with youths in gymnasium suits.

Interpretation

This is the inner and outer synthesis of the former image. The impulsiveness of the circus artist is now subdued to dependence on school rules wherein games and education are combined. The youths in the symbol are all alike in physical appearance. There is creative teamwork (Le.–Aq. fore-axis), and the energy of the one is combined with that of the other in a natural way. Life is still a game in preparation for a place in disciplined society.

There is spontaneous enthusiasm here and a love of sport, which spirit aids the learning process for intuitive and original contact with others. No marked contrasts here (Ge.) but sportive open-mindedness and love (Le.–Aq.): the horsemen have merged into one.

Biblical Parallel

'. . . exercise thyself rather unto godliness.' See *1 Tim. 4: 7–8*. NB In the original Greek, the word 'gymnasium' is used for 'exercise'.

17TH DEGREE CAPRICORN

First Image, Outer Symbol

In a landscape of the 'Isle de France' a personage of importance (or it may be Louis XIV in Versailles) looks down on a courtier at the left making a deep obeisance.

Interpretation

Janduz calls this a degree of 'elevation'. This word of course fits the upright figure but does not cover the entire image. Janduz' interpretation is not very adequate as she does not see that this symbol is split into two halves. According to her, the left side of the image with the courtier symbolises the people without backbone, who are servile in an irritating way. They are inclined to flatter but always in order to get a higher position (Cap.). They have a good nose (Sag.) to seek out those who can serve their egotistical ambition. They tyrannise over those under them, cajole those above, and may even resort to terrorism. They give favours only when it is worth their while.

Janduz goes on to say that those symbolised by the royal figure are blessed by the gods, happy, quiet and in favour with the world. From obscurity, they may even rise to hold a position in the royal court. Autocratic royalty and divine right becoming ever more rare in this world, the symbol could mean that the subject will raise himself by his own abilities. These people are far-sighted and their intelligence, hard work and fluent speaking may bring them towards a high position in regional and national government. So far Janduz.

We have to give a deeper interpretation in the light of the Capricorn grail. This is a typical Capricorn degree in the observance of duty and subordination, whilst admitting the show and pomp of the opposite sign Cancer. Around Cancer are Gemini and Leo. The Cancer-phase is illustrated by the two men (king and courtier) reflecting each the vapidness of the other.

Capricorn has to develop towards the fore-axis Leo–Aquarius and to acquire true royalty, by way of true nobility totally free from pomp and false show. The reign of Louis XIV symbolises absolute monarchy even though historically it was a period of utter decadence. One can learn from such a time-symbol (Cap.), whether placed in seventeenth-century France, the Egyptian dynasties or a dictatorship of the present day. The essence is that this person has two sides to him, and that as Capricorn he needs to rise above (Sag.) his own egotism and its mistaken ideas of elevation (Cap.–Saturn).

Second Image, Inner Symbol

A repressed woman finds psychological release in nudism.

Interpretation

Here the cork is out of the bottle of all the 'do's and don'ts'. Any nonsense of outer status has gone. The entire court has a bath! The woman, symbol of the Moon (Cn.), is as naked as Eve in paradise. It means that the conventional (Cap.) men of the first image must learn to get rid of all pretensions and social inhibitions.

All relationships will be reviewed, especially those between the spirit, mind and body. Here is the cardinal cross (Ar.–Cn.–Li.–Cap.), in the highest Self, stripping the body until the soul is bare (Cn.) and only harmony (Li.) is left and the beauty of the pure form (Cap.). Only then can the two signs around Cancer, Gemini and Leo, begin to speak the language of creation and true Being.

The danger for Capricorns is that they remain fixed in the hierarchy of the first image. It is a Capricorn tendency to stick to the outer form, which is of the satyr – Saturn. In this second image there is psychological (logic for the psyche) release (Aq.) from all the artificial conventions and traditions decreed by social caste.

The symbol of the nude woman can only be mirrored (Moon–Cn.) by the essence of the Higher Self. Within the hierarchy of the universe, spirit, soul and body are a trinity and have to be naked to one another in order to be complete.

Biblical Parallel

Humbly consider each other the better man. See *Phil. 2: 3–9.*

Note

See the apocryphal story of Suzanna in the bath.

Conception Corrected Asc. 17th Capricorn

Emperor Napoleon III   Born 20 April 1808 at 1.00 hrs. (official records) in the Tuileries near Paris, 48°50 N, 2°20 E. Died 9 Jan. 1873. CC WAK and NS for 277 and 291 days at 01.14 hrs. gives 16°23 and 16°31 Capricorn, or for 249 days (premature) at 0.58 hrs. gives 13th Capricorn. Though this is nearer the birthtime, it seems unlikely.

Son of Louis Bonaparte and Hortense. He became President of France after the Revolution of 1848 and reinstated the royal throne. He became involved in the Crimean War (1855) and lost the Franco-Prussian War of 1870–71, when he was taken prisoner in Germany. He retired in Chislehurst, England, where soon after he died. This 17th Capricorn seems to fit his life, in which at the end he was stripped of all his royalty.

Raymond Poincaré Born 20 Aug. 1860 at 17.00 hrs. in Bar-le-Duc 48°46 N, 05°11 E. Died 1934. CC WAK and NS for 266 days at 17.10 hrs. gives 16°58 Capricorn. (Other corrections improbable.) Double Ascendant: See 18th Cap.

French statesman. Minister of Fine Arts and Religion in 1893, and Minister of Finance 1894–5. Prime Minister in 1912 and during World War I till 1917. He saved the French economy in the 1920s. His appearance to the world was undoubtedly a representation of the first image of 17th Capricorn. See *Encycl. Britt.* (1964).

Johan August Strindberg Born 22 Jan. 1849 at 08.00 hrs. in Stockholm, 59°20 N, 18°00 E. Died 14 May 1912. CC WAK and NS for 272 days at 08.00 hrs. gives 16°08 Capricorn, or for 286 days at 08.01 hrs. gives 16°28 Capricorn.

Swedish author and playwright, one of the greatest of his century. Influenced by Swedenborg (see 26th Sag.) and spiritism. Most of his work is autobiographical about his parental home, his strong individualistic and pessimistic personality, his three marriages, his relationship with God and his fear of nationalism. He struggled with his own lower side of excessive pride and utter despair on the other hand. Being often suicidal, the story goes that he tried to contract pneumonia by climbing naked in a tree on an icy cold Swedish night, with the unexpected result of becoming physically healthier for a long time. Isn't this a striking example of the second image 17th Capricorn?

Most of his work is in Swedish and German. See in *Strindberg, Introduction to His Life and Works* by Mortensen and Downs (1949).

Joseph M. W. Turner Born 23 Apr. 1775 at 1.15 hrs. in London, 51.30 N, 0.05 E, died 19 Dec. 1851. CC NS for 261 days or 289 days at 1.15 or 1.13 hrs. gives 16.41 or 16.30 Capricorn. There is a CC for 174 days at 1.04 hrs. which gives 13.59 Capricorn (the 14th and 15th, which for a man of genius cannot be excluded, though we stick to the given time).

England's greatest landscape painter of the 18th century. He was famous for his new interpretation of light, expressed in his paintings of the sea and the sun. See *Sun rising through*

Vapour (1807). Much of his work is in the National and Tate Galleries in London. Though difficult to discern, he may be seen as embodying the 17th Capricorn on a high level, with the symbolism of the king being transformed into his urge to give the sun form on canvas.

Encycl. Britt. devotes three pages to him, with bibliography. A. J. Findberg's *Complete Inventory* (1909) and biography (1939) are still the standard works on Turner, though there are many others.

Dr H. F. Verwoerd   Born 8 Sept. 1901 at 16.00 hrs. in Amsterdam, 52°17 N, 4°54 E. Assassinated in South Africa 6 Sept. 1966. CC WAK and NS for 274 days at 16.17 hrs. gives 16°06 Capricorn, or at 15.57 hrs. gives 11°38 Capricorn. See 12th Cap.

Editor of the pro-German *Transvaler* in World War II. He became instrumental as Prime Minister of South Africa in the separation of South Africa from Great Britain. Being a fanatic supporter of separation between the races, with white supremacy, he was murdered by a white Greek usher during Parliament.

Though the 12th Capricorn is nearer the given time, this degree, which is an archetype for the master and slave mentality and the emotional liberation from it, seems more appropriate for the man who was the main exponent of Apartheid.

18TH DEGREE CAPRICORN

First Image, Outer Symbol

On the left, a man standing upright looks as if he has been cut in half at the waist. On the right, two men are fighting savagely.

Interpretation

This is a degree of 'quarrels'. According to Janduz there are great dangers in this image. Indeed on the lower physical level there is impotence. These people are not fit physically to bring

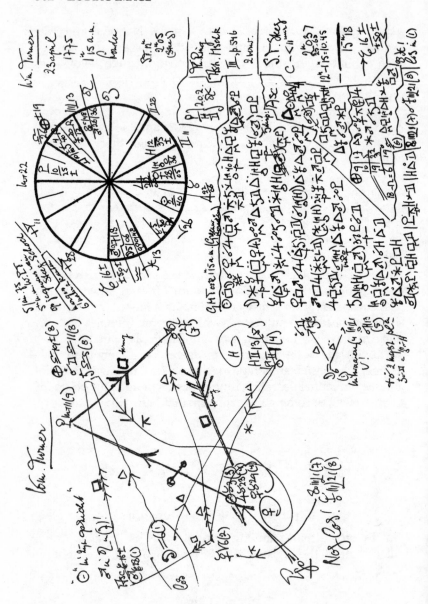

Handwritten chart of Joseph M. W. Turner
by Willem Ary Koppejan

undertakings to a good end. They do not know how to control themselves. They tend to become petrified and turned to stone by terror (neg. Cap.), which shows in their eyes. They are easily disturbed emotionally (the solar plexus) and tend to overreact (the gap in the man's middle). They may scream and complain, or raise their fists and make a lot of noise about nothing. They enjoy fights, battles, the tactics of the Mafia or displays of medieval jousting, but only as spectators.

On this unawakened level, their weakness of character and cowardly ill nature is easily detected. They pretend to a strength which they do no possess and, fearful of being found out, they keep other at arm's length. An exchange of opinions, let alone a heart-to-heart relationship (Le.–Aq. fore-axis), cannot occur. A defensive manner and brooding silences (neg. Cap.) may develop. On this level they are difficult to get on with. They are secretive, and easily hurt others by their very presence though they may not realise this. They are easily offended, intolerant, and ever ready with self-justification.

On a more psychological level these are people who are often divided in themselves. They can foster fixations (neg. Cn.) formed by misunderstandings and quarrels with their parents, or even left over from past lives (Cn.). One certainly cannot blame parents or teachers for not understanding this complicated problem of an underdeveloped or, at the other extreme, an oversensitive solar plexus, or even, as the image seems to indicate, no diaphragm at all! There are as yet no schools fully able to bring out the best in children with this degree prominent, except perhaps those based on the teachings of Rudolf Steiner.

Sometimes they need (right side of the image) to be brought out into the open for a healthy contest. On the physical plane this can be achieved in sport, or on the mental one by a combat of minds. However, they seldom dare to be challenged in a forum of opinion.

Fear (neg. Cap.) is their biggest stumbling-block, and the cause of all their doubts (neg. Li.) and lack of initiative (neg. Ar.). They swing between aggression and uncertainty. When called upon to do something positive, they have no time. One can see them making a shell (Cn.) of formality (Cap.) and assuming an air of high rank, which can only give a ridiculous impression and result in isolation. On this level they become unhappy purely by reason of their own guilt (neg. Cap.), and their suppressed and unrealised emotional attachment to some incident in the past.

On the physical level, these people need to develop their sense of co-ordination. They would do well to study Eastern types of wrestling and control of the body, such as Tai Chi, or fencing, where forms of 'crossing over' from left brain to right brain are exercised.

They need to become conscious of their weak diaphragm (man on the left). They will benefit from studying any therapeutic method, which practises a responsible way of opening the chakras (of which the solar plexus is one) as power-points of energy. This is what they lack. They need to visualise their spine as a column of light with two energy channels crossing twelve times from skull to coccyx. This brings the fatal split between their upper and lower half together.

Highly evolved individuals with this degree may become teachers (Sag.), yogis or natural health therapists, helping to heal a split world sick of dividing itself into head or heart, mind or body. They need to become aware that everything functions according to diagonal laws from left to right, and top to bottom, of which the second image is the symbol.

Second Image, Inner Symbol

The Union Jack flies from a new British destroyer.

Interpretation

The first image was a symbol of division into two halves and being in a clinch. In the second image the reverse is happening. The two halves have come together in the red cross of St George and the diagonal red cross of St Patrick, both on a white background, and the white diagonal cross of St Andrew on a blue background. Together they form Britain's national flag which is deeply symbolic, not of division, but of union. It is the symbol of a united kingdom within these people. Here is the pure challenge to overcome the inertia of the first image.

In meditating on this image, these people need to overcome their preconditioned pro-or anti-national feelings, and lift themselves onto a higher plane. Here there is magnificent self-realisation with a full and pure consciousness of authority and strength. The period of doubt and indecision (neg. Li.) has been surpassed by the command (Cap.) that all the forces should pull together (Ar.–Li.) and take a new initiative (Ar.). The result is this proud display of invincibility at sea. The lower emotions are no longer divided, they are being steered together. The proud independence, which is shown by a British warship with its flag, can be a cosmic symbol of the sign of Aries, the very sign under which England traditionally comes. The sign also of atomic fission superseded by fusion.

These people can 're-member' their cosmic origins in those twelve stations within their spine, as the twelve tribes of Israel of which Britain is the symbolic head (Ar.). The Union 'Jack', which means 'Jacob', directs these people, and all who are concerned with understanding this degree symbol, back to the 'Covenant' of the archetypal patriarch (Cap.) Jacob. It can also stand for binding together his twelve scattered sons.

The missing link in the middle of the man of the first image is found unexpectedly in this present-day symbol of the second image. The open-minded study of this Capricorn degree can be a source of food from heaven for us all. It could bring an end to all quarrelling and, what matters more, to all wars. Then this ship can sail back to harbour.

Biblical Parallels

See the literature on the Union Jack as a representation of the colours to be worn by the priests and placed on the tabernacle as prescribed by Moses. *Ex. 25: 4; 26: 1–36;* and *Num. 4: 5–9.*

Conception Corrected Asc. 18th Capricorn

E. A. D. E. Carp   Born 4 June 1895 at 22.30 hrs. in the Hague, 52°00 N, 04°30 E. Died 1963. CC WAK and NS for 268 days at 22.30 hrs. gives 17.42 Cap.

Dutch psychiatrist and professor at Leyden University 1930–63. Prolific writer on psychiatry (5 vols.), psychotherapy (10 vols.), and the problems of life and death. He started his own psychiatric clinic 'Endegeest', which became known internationally. He surrounded himself with patients and their problems, as shown in this first image. Amongst his favourite subjects were the split personality and the 'aetheric double' which 'mirror' his 18th degree Capricorn. He moulded generations of Dutch physicians and was one of Willem Koppejan's tutors. See Bibliography at Leyden University Library.

A. Rodin   CC for 285 days at 11.44 hrs. gives 17°47 Cap. See 22nd Cap.

19TH DEGREE CAPRICORN

First Image, Outer Symbol

Battered by a raging sea, a piece of rock emerges from the tempest. On its platform a half-naked man is standing, with two feet on each leg, and as if rooted in the rock.

Interpretation

This is a degree of 'stability', says Janduz. However, this is not a quiet stability, it is an act of resistance for one's own safeguard. The entire personality (the man) is firm and energetic, outwardly cold-blooded but inwardly burning.

People with this degree on the Ascendant are straightforward. Their self-confidence gives them daring (Sag.), and deep down they are very sincere and high-spirited. Outwardly they may seem hard on themselves and others, but inside they have deep feelings (Cn.) and a great heart (Le. fore-axis).

They may stand completely alone, but their isolation they know and accept. They (men or women) want to calm the storms and bring the elements back into balance (Li. sq.). When emotions are aroused in their vicinity (neg. Cn.), they are the ones to remain detached by exercising self-discipline and inner perception of the real truth (Aq.).

There is a lot of ambition in this symbol and great self-awareness. If necessary these persons may take the highest ranks by storm, where they will have to withstand cataclysms and disasters which in many cases they have unleashed themselves. They pursue their aims with whirlwind energy.

On a lower level their energies are rather veiled, but one can suspect enormous sources of power. They have to work against much resistance and win their way slowly, in spite of great difficulties. Theirs is seldom an easy and happy life, but they can throw their will and vital force into it, and push forward to their true place, which is firmly founded. Their faith can be as strong as a rock. Their beliefs are grounded in their religion and in timeless traditions.

Feet come under Pisces. Feet to each side, with ten toes coming out of each leg, seems bizarre, but the symbol stresses how strong their religious (Pi.) foundation is. They may live a life at sea, or be members of the crew of a lifeboat or, more symbolically, serve the church in a minor capacity, or act as part of a medical rescue team. They are the ones who will not panic – steady as a rock.

On an enlightened level, they may become examples to their fellow beings.

However, unless they face the elements and dare to sacrifice the ego, they become petrified and isolated. Rock is the symbol of eternal safety. A rock remains stable and safe whatever happens, as are the faithful who trust in the Rock of Ages.

Second Image, Inner Symbol
A five-year-old girl proudly does her mother's shopping.

Interpretation
The austerity of the first image has been softened. The heavy battle with the elements has come to its end. A new cycle of young human feelings has begun and these people can become glad and playful again. The raging emotions around them have been stilled, enabling the growth of powers of motherly protection, thus fitting them for an important task.

It is now their business to gather inner food (Cn. opp. Cap.) for others, and then they can begin to nourish themselves on that which others have produced and made wholesome. They may even contact the great horn of plenty, the source of life, which is God.

Rudhyar calls this image one of 'accelerated growth' and entitles it 'group-performance'.

The soul here is certainly becoming responsible (Cap.) for the well-being of a great group-soul or its spiritual family. It shows the motherly element (Cn.) newly displacing the somewhat formal and fatherly authoritarian will (the man of the first image).

Biblical Parallels

The parable of the 'wise man who built his house upon rock and the rain descended, and the floods came, and the winds blew, and beat upon that house; and it fell not: for it was founded upon a rock.' *Mt. 7: 24–27.*

Peter is compared with a rock. *Mt. 16: 18.*

Christ is the Rock. *1 Cor. 10: 4.*

Conception Corrected Asc. 19th Capricorn

Sebastian Kneipp Born 17 May 1821 at 23.30 hrs. (source *EPA* magazine nr 305) in Stephansried, Germany, 47°50 N, 10°15 E. Died 17 June 1897. CC NS for 283 and 255 days at 23.28 or 23.30 hrs. gives 18°05 or 18°38 Capricorn.

With the Kneipp health products still on the world market we are without doubt well grounded here in this 19th degree where Kneipp undoubtedly had his Ascendant. When a theological student he became undernourished and got tuberculosis. He cured himself with fresh water and became a nature healer and developed water cures and massage with essential oils from plants, unknown in his time. Nowadays aromatherapists and bodyworkers widely use these, and one can buy Kneipps shampoos in supermarkets (see second image !). As a priest in his village and later in a monastery, he was consulted by thousands of patients. Amongst them were royalty and many of European nobility. His rockfast faith was known far and wide and is still working within the many modern Kneipp societies propagating his methods as an alternative model for healthy living.

20TH DEGREE CAPRICORN

First Image, Outer Symbol

Having grabbed its mistress's jewel box, a domesticated monkey is adorning itself with the contents before a mirror. It is putting on airs and graces while its mate grimaces behind its back.

Interpretation

This is a degree of 'imitation'. There are clearly two different levels of interpretation. People with this degree rising can, on a unawakened level, be vulgar, idle, cheap or just vain. They like to imitate the latest fashion, perhaps copying a star just seen on their television screen, or they will ape a celebrity by wearing, for instance, the same hat as the Prince or Princess of Wales. On this level they may be amusing, and even show a certain intelligence, but on the whole their standards are very low.

With a more constructive use of this image, they make good models, comedians or actors. As such they may be excellent imitators. Their mime is full of life. They may have good control over the movements of their hands (Ge.). In these professions they may have to travel a lot (Sag.). Monkeys come under Gemini. Thus we see the difficult hind-axis (Sag.–Ge.) very prominent here.

The second monkey adds to the doubly imitative aspect of Gemini. The difficult axis for Gemini in its turn is Taurus – Scorpio. Their disposition tends to be jealous. They like gossip, and do not really add anything positive to any conversation. They borrow, then lend out the loan, thus manoeuvring themselves into the most ridiculous chain-situations. With great charm, they can adorn themselves with other people's ideas, works of art, jewels and what-have-you. The mirror comes under

Cancer (opp. Cap.) and reflects the empty pretensions involved. On a higher level they make splendid photographers and cameramen, mirroring human follies and portraying people's feelings to their faces.

On a high level it is an example of one of the degrees which give a higher solution to the entire Capricorn grail. These people dare (Le.) to see themselves in the mirror (Cn.) and to expose themselves openly (Aq.). Their innate honesty (Aq.) compels them to self-examination (Ge.) and recognition of their most negative Capricorn traits, such as fear of life, and selfish ambition. They bring positive adaptation (Sag.) to all their thinking. After facing their faults squarely, they dare to play again, in a creative way and with a growing warmth of heart (Le.). At this level of development they are able to laugh at themselves, not easy for Capricorn, and see the absurdity of any kind of showing-off in public.

More often than not the second monkey is externalised, in the sense that accusation and envy are characteristic of their behaviour. However, by this they confront their own conscience, because they mirror their own shortcomings in others.

From imitation they have to discover their own glowing creative self. They need more isolation in order to give form to their artistic abilities. They may not have sufficient concentration to become highly creative artists, but they could profit from classes or apprenticeship in arts and crafts.

Second Image, Inner Symbol
Through the empty church, the choir is heard rehearsing.

Interpretation
The empty hours passed in nothing but imitation, as depicted in the first image, have now been transformed into a building with a positive use, empty still, but filled with the sound of music. An invisible ray of hope streams through these people. The door to the temple is open, and anyone from outside can enter in to listen and be refreshed. This is the reverse process of the first image, where all is externalisation.

For those who have eyes and ears to understand these

symbols, the monkeys become human choirboys with all their nerves alert. The mirror becomes the walls which bounce back (Cap.) the collective emotions (Cn.) of the singing choir. The divided attention of the two monkeys becomes the united concentration of listeners and singers, who rehearse in order to be ready for the first day of a new cycle.

Biblical Parallel

'. . . a book of remembrance was written before Him for them that feared the Lord and that thought upon His name. And they shall be Mine, saith the Lord of Hosts, in that day when I make up My jewels; and I will spare them, as a man spareth his own son that serveth him.' *Mal. 3: 16–17.*

Conception Corrected Asc. 20th Capricorn

George Adamski Born 17 Apr. 1891 at 02.00 hrs. in Bromberg, Poland, 53°10 N, 18°00 E (personal information) CC WAK as NS for 289 days at 01.56 hrs. gives 19°40 Capricorn.

Author on flying saucers (UFO's). His books became bestsellers until it was found out in the 1950s that most of what he wrote was faked. For instance, he did not work as a professor in astronomy at Palomar Observatory in California, USA, but was a stallholder selling peanuts (see the monkeys) at its entrance. During his visit to the Queen of the Netherlands, much more was discovered to be merely embellishment, and when this came out into the open it caused a scandal. Whatever the truth may be about Adamski's supposed travels to Venus and his meetings with their inhabitants, this 20th Capricorn degree symbol fits him 'as a spacesuit does a spaceman'.

21ST DEGREE CAPRICORN

First Image, Outer Symbol

In a study one sees a high lectern, on which is an open

manuscript in the form of a folio, with pages covered in hieroglyphs. On a table there are scientific instruments.

Interpretation

This is a degree of 'renewal'. The trend is to renew scientific ideas. The people with this degree rising have great perseverance with high moral and ethical standing. As true Capricorns, they go their way calmly and do not fear to stand alone, either inwardly or outwardly. That they must is a command from the cosmos, in order that they may form their true selves. Their attention is focused on the search for facts and reasoned conclusions, which they have anticipated intuitively right from the start of their study.

On an outer level, they may be successful publishers, librarians, archivists, or just lovers of ancient manuscripts and beautiful bindings with which to decorate their bookshelves. The lectern may indicate that they have some religious or monastic interest. However, more often these people may play an important role in scientific research, in which new and alternative methods are being introduced. They seek new ways to rehabilitate old scientific traditions. They are not dogmatic. The hieroglyphs may mean that they seek to recover lost cultural values. They search for a better understanding, and can see through inscriptions into their source with the inner eye.

They are not 'un-modern'. Their work is one of reinterpretation. They may even do this with 'computer hieroglyphs'. On a high spiritual level they reach an understanding of alchemical secrets. They may be great parapsychologists and seekers into the occult, who can point out the direction for humanity's development. They may even leave the mundane sciences behind them, after having investigated these.

According to Janduz, the spirit of the 'Neo-Pythagoreans' is in this degree. These people indeed have great thinking power (Sag. hind-axis) and research the microcosmic and macrocosmic structure of the divine worlds, or in other words, the etheric and astral planes. They may go so far as to start a new school of thought (Sag.), which will add value to the culture on this planet.

On a high level of the Capricorn grail they are the true mediators (Ge.) of the energy from the cosmos, which is trying to manifest on this earth.

They can be peremptory and 'hard' at the right time (Cap.), which they sometimes need to be to enable them to achieve what is necessary. They may become well-known and honoured, as indeed they deserve.

Second Image, Inner Symbol

A relay race. Each runner springs eagerly into place.

Interpretation

In this image, co-operation (Li.) is at its highest, with every runner starting a new track (Ar.), exactly on time (Cap.), with the right sensitivity (Cn.) towards the others. Thus it symbolises the cardinal cross under control.

If the race is held in an arena, the movement of, for instance, the flaming torch, comes back full circle. This is a symbol of the Sun and symbolises the movements of the entire cosmos in all its layers, or planes of manifestation.

Developing from the first image, these people can, step by step, begin and develop relationship with all layers of existence, as does the scientist. They need teamwork for this process, with full commitment of the total self. These people are aware that the fire (Le.) is carried by all the members of the group in turn (Aq.) or by the group soul as a whole. Their life's plan depends on those who run before and after them. Thus they develop in line with the creativity of others (Le.–Aq. fore-axis).

Biblical Parallels

'. . . rejoiceth as a strong man to run a race.' *Ps. 19: 5.* See also verses 1–6, which compare the heavens and its circuits with this strong man.

'. . . let us lay aside every weight, and the sin which doth so easily beset us, and let us run with patience, the race that is set before us.' *Heb. 12: 1.*

Conception Corrected Asc. 21st
Capricorn

Max Reger Born 19 Mar. 1873 at 03.30 hrs. in Brand 49°40 N, 12°10 E. Died 11 May 1916 in Leipzig. CC WAK and NS for 283 days at 03.37 hrs. gives 20°41 Capricorn.

'German composer of piano, violin and orchestral works. Teacher Royal Academy Munich, and Leipzig Conservatorium. He turned out work after work and is especially remembered as a contrapuntist, and for his complicated compositions.' (*Encycl. Britt.* 1961)

22ND DEGREE CAPRICORN

First Image, Outer Symbol

On a plot of cultivated land, giving the impression of prosperity, a pair of oxen is ploughing a new furrow. In the distance a solidly constructed farmhouse is visible.

Interpretation

Janduz calls this a degree of 'labour', which is a simplified interpretation. Of course agriculture, the earth, and her products are the territory in which these people may best exercise their capacities and demonstrate their zest for work. They can be good organisers (Cap.) of their business (Vi.) when directors or owners, as they possess the right kind of authority (Cap.), especially when it has to do with cultivating the earth (Tau.) and mining (Cap.). The earth triangle (Tau.–Vi.–Cap.) is well-balanced here.

They are not exuberant, jovial leaders (Sag.–Le.), but of the duller, more materialistic kind who could degenerate into petty dictators. People with this character work best when they work exactly according to 'the clock', dead on time (Cap.). Materialistically speaking they do well. They just might inherit

(Cn.) a manor. If so, all they would have to do should be to let it go on as their forefathers (Cap.) did.

On a high level they really put their heart into their undertakings, and they recognise themselves as being a part of the organisation, and of the times and seasons of nature itself. They know they are subordinate to the higher forces and elements and to the laws of form-giving and crystallisation. Through this they ascend a little higher on the karmic ladder, when they learn to control their too-fruitful imaginations and see their task simply as labour that has to be done. So far we follow Janduz.

Interpreting the image on a deeper level there is the fact that the oxen are starting a new furrow. Oxen come under Taurus and are primitive, hard-working, but sluggish animals, not aware of their own strength. The consciousness (a man) is not mentioned here. The oxen exactly parallel what was done before. It is important to realise that this is not a Taurus degree, but a Capricorn one, and so the repetition day in and day out, and working on and on in a traditional way, could be dangerous. He thinks that he will go on for eternity filling his belly and adding to his savings.

However, this person as Capricorn ought to be aware of the times, the political trend (Cap.), the danger of sudden changes (Aq.), and learn to change direction and be open to the new ideas of younger generations and to a new age (Aq.). This is symbolised in the second image.

Second Image, Inner Symbol
Defeated general yields up his sword with noble dignity.

Interpretation
This general, or the Higher Self who has reached high rank, was once a little boy who dreamed of getting a high position in society by hard work and good military discipline. Everything may go well, as well as in the first image, but the soldiers under his command may begin to venerate him too highly. He may begin to think himself supreme and his authority unquestioned, until the day the enemy enters his country. He is then called to the highest post in the country, with orders to

fight to the bitter end. He tries to bluff his way through, but his tactics are outdated (neg. Cap.) and his traditional strategy equally old-fashioned (neg. Cap.). He ought to have studied the up-to-date methods of his opponents, superior both in arms and leadership (Aq.–Le. fore-axis). The new conquers the old, so that this high-ranking officer, here the symbol of the old order, has to surrender his sword, here the symbol of his authoritative word.

The true spiritual gain here is in his noble dignity of bearing, showing acquiescence in a new and better order, one perhaps in which we learn to love the enemy and to pray for him. This can only be done by the individual of high spiritual standing, who prays humbly at the same time to The Most High impartial Creator of all.

Oxen do not pray: they are creatures of the soil, and nothing beyond their unthinking labour is expected of them. The distinguished soldier of the second image, who has attained high rank under the discipline of life, must yield self-esteem to his yet Higher Self – no foe, but emissary of the coming new order of the world under the dominion of Christ.

Biblical Parallels

'They shall beat their swords into plowshares.' *Is. 2: 4* and *Mic. 4: 3*.

'Beat your plowshares into swords.' *Joel 3: 10*.

Conception Corrected Asc. 22nd Capricorn

Queen Elizabeth II of Great Britain Born 21 Apr. 1926 at 2.40 hrs. (1.40 GT) in London, 51.32 n, 0.05 W. Commonwealth of those days. CC NS for 261 days at 2.41 hrs. gives 21°48 Capricorn.

Eldest daughter of George VI and Elizabeth, she is married to Prince Phillip, with whom she has had four children. At the death of her father in 1953 when she was only 27, she was called to the throne and crowned according to the ancient traditions and surrounded by the pride of the nation and the glory of the Commonwealth of those days. With this 22nd degree she represents a period of British supremacy and government which has declined, whilst she plays her role and fulfils her task according to the rules in an immaculate way. With this degree symbol of the 22nd, however, she is the Queen who will be asked to hand over the ruling rod of power to a larger European Community (1992) Or is she destined, as prophecy says, as a descendant of King David, to save the British monarchy and steer Great Britain through a swordless period (see second image) into the hands of the 'returning Christ or second King David, the Prince of Peace'? James IV is quoted to have said; 400 years ago: 'The greatness of England starts with Elizabeth I and will end with Elizabeth II.'

Auguste Rodin Born 12 Nov. 1840 at 12.00 noon, in Paris, 48°50 N, 02°20 E. Died 17 Nov. 1917. CC NS for 299 days at 11.58 hrs. gives 21°43 Capricorn, or for 285 days at 11.44 hrs. gives 17°47 Capricorn.

French sculptor and painter, famous for his *Thinker*, *The Kiss*, and *The Burghers of Calais*. The last one could be seen as an expression of the second image 22nd Capricorn (the siege of his city). He was an immensely hard worker and though it is not easy in this case to differentiate, the CC 22nd Capricorn seems to be nearer the mark of this genius. Numerous replicas of his sculptures have been made, such as his later work *The Hands*. His former home in Paris houses the Rodin Museum and a second museum is in Philadelphia (USA). He was a close friend of Rilke (see 17th Vi.).

Note

This was written before Niek Scheps chose the alternative rising degree of 18th Capricorn in his *Trutine of Hermes* (Element Books, 1990). He devotes an entire chapter to substantiating his choice.

A. Toscanini CC for 297 days (late birth) at 02.58 hrs. gives 21°22 Capricorn. See 24th Capricorn.

23RD DEGREE CAPRICORN

First Image, Outer Symbol

A blindfolded woman pulls a man along by the hand. As he follows her, in his haste, he overthrows the table on which they seem to have had a romantic meal.

Interpretation

Janduz calls this a degree of 'danger'. However, this word is too general for the specific dangers of Capricorn–Saturn. According to Janduz, those with this degree prominent are indeed prone to fatality, which comes through imprudence. This person does not reckon with obstacles and is heedless of advice, which could prevent the catastrophe.

It is often the woman, or the female pole in the man, that is uncontrolled and puts events in motion.

In this image there are male and female symbols. Both sides in these personalities are a direct danger to the equilibrium of their environment. They upset family relations and break love-bonds by their sudden independence. Here we see the cardinal cross in its negativity (Ar.C-n.Li.–Cap.).

Through the existence of the animal in them, these people may find themselves suddenly at the mercy of their egotistical emotions (Cn.–Cap.) and their craze for luxury, for which they are prepared to sacrifice everything; or they may live in a luxurious environment, which they could not permit themselves to do if their conscience (Cap.) functioned along the laws of cosmic love. They are capable of all sorts of extravagances and may consume an entire fortune or inheritance to satisfy their greed, which, however, is never satisfied (the meal, Cn.). They can bluff their way through life, ignoring the voice of conscience, wasting their time, and The Time, in superficialities and in a way that can only be shown by the negative Cancer (opp. Cap.).

They are often very intelligent, and shrewd enough (Ge.–Sag.

and Aq.–Le. around Cap.) to realise that they ought to be living a more useful life. They will laughingly agree when that suggestion is put to them, but they will not change. After a while they are no longer the amusing lover, the charming companion, or the agreeable employee, as of old. Time infallibly exposes their selfishness, the bare bones (Cap.) of them, as it were. Often their bones, literally wear out and become spongy for want of blood to the bone marrow, and this deprivation is the direct result of their moral evasiveness: life lived on this level brings them serious disease. Saturn is the ruler of the bones and, as it is also the ruler of Capricorn, this image represents the symbol of the negation of what Capricorn stands for: high morality and a healthy skeleton. Meditation and visualisation of these requisites can help to heal.

The effects of negation are tragic for these people, but entirely their own fault, caused by the outward projection of their thinking (Ge.–Sag. hind-axis). They need to learn loving-kindness (Aq.–Le. fore-axis) and the will to give, otherwise they deteriorate rapidly in social status. However, there is a deeper insight in this symbol.

The woman has a blindfold around her head (Ar.) symbolising the conflicts (Ar.–Li.) in the cardinal cross. These people do not wish to unmask and show their true feelings. There is a lack of fresh and positive action, although there is a lot of movement with a goal (Ge.–Sag.) in view. The will (the man) is debased so that the good inner food (Cn.), needed to build their lives, is abandoned. Thus spiritual possibilities are being given to the dogs or the dustbin (the food knocked over).

The essence of all this is that they are too much bound to pleasure for the purpose of killing time. They need to transfer their interests to the inner level (Cn.) and acquire insight into the entire Capricorn grail.

The reason for the degeneration of their bones, and morals, lies in the disastrous working of the transpersonal planets, when these people do not open themselves up as a cup. The Higher Self needs to let through the cosmic energy. In short they need to recognise their guilt (Ge.–Hermes), burn up the dross, make a completely new start (Ar.–Pluto) and open up to the inspiration which is ever ready to come through to them (Aq.–Uranus). Thus their own intelligence (Mercury), their activity (Mars) and persistence (Saturn) can be built up and their backbone straightened, so that they receive new courage for life. Let them learn that they must not throw all the good from the invisible world under the table, and they will be rewarded.

Second Image, Inner Symbol

A soldier receives decorously two awards for bravery.

Interpretation

Salvation can only be achieved by going 'up'. These people need to stand erect again, like soldiers, and without the blindfold. They need to look life straight in the face. Then life itself will not forget them. They will be rewarded, and rightly so, because they have overcome the many problems of the first image. For this their sense of responsibility needs to be reawakened. Alertness alone is not sufficient: they should not sit down and wait till the goose with the golden eggs comes along, for she will not come if these people do not first show courage and enterprise.

Their male and female side (their Sun and Moon in the chart) need to 'soldier on', and indeed do what the Cosmos requires of them, with due recognition of its moral imperatives.

The two awards are for their two sides after they have repaired what they destroyed, and have set the table again to serve others, as the gallant soldier has done. And for this, hard work is needed.

Conception Corrected Asc. 23rd Capricorn

Doris Doane Born 4 Apr. 1913 at 01.57 hrs. in Mansfield, USA, 42°00 N, 71°15 W. CC NS for 263 days at 01.58 hrs. gives 22°24 Capricorn.

Writer and astrologer, connected with the 'Church of Light' (treasurer/seer) and author of *Thirty Years of Astrological Research*. Well-known researcher, her zone timetables are invaluable.

Jacob Moleschott   Born 9 Aug. 1822 at 18.30 hrs. in s'Hertogen-bosch, 51°41 N, 05°18 E. Died 20 May 1893. CC WAK and NS for 281 days at 18.28 hrs. gives 22°38 Capricorn.

Dutch physician and philosopher, became a professor at the University of Heidelburg in Germany. His scientific work became internationally known because of his book *Kreislauf des Lebens* (Circulation of Life), which propagated an extreme materialism, foreshadowing Russian Communism. Because of this he was dismissed from the university as 'immoral and a danger for the German State'. His pupils, however, stood up for him with a wreath 'for his bravery'. After this he was called to Turin and Rome and nominated senator. He lectured and did research there as Professor of Pathological Anatomy. He became very popular with the Italian students and remained so till his death there.

See his autobiography, also articles in *Medisch Tydschrift*, 1893, 1948 and 1953.

24TH DECREE CAPRICORN

First Image, Outer Symbol

A cooper is finishing a new barrel and fixing on the last circular iron band, thus assuring its rigidity. On another recently finished barrel stands a goblet half-filled with wine.

Interpretation

This is a degree of 'quiet and simple happiness'. The symbol speaks of an unpretentious life-style. Work is being done steadily and freely.

On the ordinary social level, these people succeed in trades concerning basic crafts such as carpentry, the making of furniture, and jobs that have to do with breweries, wine or cider-making and the like.

They are solid, well-grounded people, full of common sense. They are not insensitive, but have learnt to buffer themselves against the shocks that flesh is heir to. Their integrity is high, and they are fair with themselves as well as others. They are noted for their forthright logic (Vi. trine Cap.), though not dogmatic. They stick to their decisions (Li. sq. Cap.), and when they take a stand, it is with reason. Born peacemakers, they are a blessing to their associates.

Being intelligent, they are open to chances of promotion in their profession. They are slow to adapt to new methods, but when they see change eases their work, they go with the times.

They are homemakers (Cn. opp. Cap.), and they tend to care for their family in an altruistic way. They avoid rows. They can control themselves, and demonstrate the fact that an honest and regular working life, within the frame of their given time and space, is of far greater value than indulging in all sorts of exciting and ephemeral activities (Sag.–Ge. hind-axis). They do not exaggerate. They are examples of humility and simplicity, and with all this virtue they are not bores.

These people can radiate the depth of their thought-life (Sc.–Sag. behind Cap.) and their compassion for the suffering of their fellows (Aq.–Pi. around Cap.). Their work is a vocation. Their motivation comes from a very high level.

On whatever social plane they live, their spiritual qualities will be of such value to others that they are recognised as examples to be followed. They may become master-craftsmen, and teach others who are less evolved, being drawn always towards the humble and lowly of heart. They are the ones who fulfil their task in the knowledge that nobody else is going to do it for them.

The concept of *dharma* plays a great role in their lives, whether consciously or unconsciously. They may simply take upon their own shoulders other people's karma and work it out to the finish with them. Being of high spiritual standing, they are incarnated exactly where they wished to be; they fit harmoniously into the mosaic of their zodiacal place.

The glass on the barrel symbolises the finishing of a cycle of lives. The fruits of their labours are being pressed into their grail-cup (Sag.–Cap.–Aq. opp. Ge.–Cn.–Le.), as the essence of their being. This may show in their style of life unknown to themselves, but a good observer sees how this essence is within their hearts and is flowing into their simple zeal for work and craftsmanship.

Second Image, Inner Symbol

A woman walking towards the sure haven of a convent.

Interpretation

Here the devout tranquillity of their disposition is shown even more clearly. This image speaks of the protective kindness of life as a reward for all those who bring to it the quiet stream of true existence. Such people invoke and respond to the inner guidance which is always available. Wherever they are, they are there at the right time. Heaven is waiting for them.

The working craftsman of the first image may be concentrating (Cap.) a bit too much on himself and his craft. Here in the second image, the female side of intuition is arriving at a greater group-awareness. Personal boundaries are broken down, and a transpersonal working community is entered. However, as this is a Capricorn degree, the group is still not yet entirely free (Aq. fore-axis), but embedded in rules and dogmas (Cap.). To be truly free from personal ties (Cn.–Cap.) and to dare to be a freelance creative individual (Le.–Aq. fore-axis) is very difficult for a Capricorn, but that is the direction for his (or her) spiritual growth.

Biblical Parallel

'Blessed are the meek, for they shall inherit the earth.' *Mt. 5: 5.*

Conception Corrected Asc. 24th Capricorn

Warren Kenton   Born 8 Jan. 1933 at 08.30 hrs. in London, 51°30 N, 00.00. CC NS for 283 days at 08.32 hrs. gives 23°46 Capricorn.

Writer under his own name and his pen-name Simon Halevi. Course leader and lecturer, known as one of the best contemporary Kabbalists, which he combines with New Age teaching and astrology.

Amongst his many books *The Anatomy of Fate*, on Kabbalistic astrology, stands out as a title for someone with Sun and Ascendant in Capricorn.

Arturo Toscanini   Born 25 Mar. 1867 at 03.00 hrs. in Busseto near Parma, 45°00 N, 10°04 E. Died 16 Jan. 1957. CC WAK and NS for 283 days at 03.05 hrs. gives 23°30 Capricorn, or for 297 days (late birth) at 02.58 hrs. gives 21°22 Capricorn (see 22nd Cap.). Italian conductor, he had his own orchestra in Turin, was leader of the Scala in Turin, and the first director to conduct completely by heart. His last concert was in the Carnegie Hall in New York.

Vivekananda   Born 12 Jan. 1863 at sunrise (06.49 hrs.) in Calcutta, 22°23 N, 88°30 E. Died 1902. CC NS for 279 days at 06.51 hrs. gives 23°13 Capricorn.

Swami, disciple of Ramakrishna, he wrote *Raja Yoga*, which became a classic by which he introduced the esoteric philosophy of yoga to the Western world. He travelled to Europe and studied Christianity, but decided to remain Hindu. He was one of the first to build a spiritual bridge between East and West.

25TH DEGREE CAPRICORN

First Image, Outer Symbol

In a kind of amphitheatre occupied by a standing public, darts launched by an invisible hand traverse the space. One is close to the target, another one passes it by. A third one fastens itself in a fish-tail suspended above the target.

Interpretation

Janduz calls this a degree of 'decline or decadence'. As this is a Capricorn degree, these people are in the first place ambitious to come into the public eye. However, there is not much spiritual power in them. They are dynamic only in the outer world. Knowing that they are not very strong inside, they simulate firmness, self-discipline and self-education, but only superficially (Ge.–Sag., the difficult hind-axis for them).

They make plans, but often these are so fantastic or even idiotic that they overshoot the target. These people give the onlooker far too high expectations, which they cannot fulfil. Instead of going up they are spiritually on the decline, they even carry with them an air of imposture; but, for all their guile, like an alarm clock set to the wrong time they disturb others only momentarily. The end is that they themselves become the target of attack from unfriendly arrows of thought. They can avoid this outcome by disciplined mental training, so that the darts of their thoughts do not miss the target.

We can see the Capricorn grail here. There is the invisible hand moving the darts (Ge.–Sag. hind-axis). Darts is a game both for individuals and for teams (Le.–Aq. fore-axis). In order to hit the centre of the target deep concentration is required, almost as though meditating (Cap.) and they must have their emotions completely under control (Cn. opp. Cap.). The fact that some darts in the image miss the target, indicates that these people have not yet mastered this art. They have to overcome jealousy, irritation and all other hostile attitudes towards others, which bring only separation and sadness. They may cherish the ambition to excel, but there is still quite a way to go before they will love their enemy, or even the opposing team! They have to learn teamwork, and how to be a good loser.

In professional sports, like darts or skittles, they may have a few triumphs, but praise can soon turn their heads and unless they are coached very well, they come to nothing.

On a lower physical level, they attract nervousness. They often find helpers whom they drain of their vitality, especially those who try too hard to keep them on the straight path. They may be so easily influenced as to have no will of their own. Their tragedy is that they miss the mark time and again. (The dart player does not show himself.)

On a higher level of awareness these people know that all outer form is transient and that they must turn within to find their strength in the invisible sources of energy. From there, one dart goes in a straight line right to the heart of the matter (the target). Their salvation is to identify with that strong line from within, forgetting all about the distractions around them. The fish-tail (Pi.) which seemed so out of place may then become a symbol of initiation at a higher level into hidden mysteries (Pi.).

Second Image, Inner Symbol

Little boys frolic upon soft rugs in an oriental store.

Interpretation

Rudhyar leaves the boys out in his 1973 version, but they are just that which gives the essence to the image. Children come under Leo, and a group of them is Aquarius. This is the fore-axis which is so needed for these people to soften their ambitious hearts. Marc Jones speaks of a rug dealer. Rugs give an impression of softness and in the Middle East they are used for prayer and meditation (Cap.). A finished rug is a product of long, disciplined and humble work wrought with great patience.

These people need to refine their senses and through meditation they can learn to observe a richness of colour within themselves, which gradually begins to show patterns as they work and exercise their spiritual self. Just as dart-playing needs manual skill and concentration, so does the making and choosing of the right pattern for a rug. These people are like rugs: it takes a long time before they develop spiritually, but once they have found their true pattern through meditation and prayer, they can be like little boys playing happily in the fabulously diverse rug-store of the universe.

Conception Corrected Asc. 25th
Capricorn

Abbé Henri Breuil Born 28 Feb. 1877 at 05.00 hrs. in Mortain (France), 48°40 N, 00°50 W. Died 14 Aug. 1961. CC NS for 277 days at 04.57 hrs. gives 24°01 Capricorn (double Ascendant with part of the 24th as well).

French priest and archaeologist, discoverer of prehistoric art in caves in France and northern Spain. His reproductive drawings of 1906–8 became the famous Altamira paintings, which were immensely popular as postcards all over the world. His work has been compared that of with Picasso and Chagall. However, as an abbé he was too modest to accept this, simply attributing his talents to God's grace.

Erwin Rommel Born 15 Nov. 1891 at 12.00 hrs. in Heidenheim, 48°40 N, 10°08 E. Forced to commit suicide 14 Oct. 1944. CC NS for 281 days at 11.52 hrs. gives 24°33 Capricorn, or for 267 days at 11.50 hrs. gives 24°01 Capricorn, which would make him a double Ascendant with part of the 24th Capricorn.

German general under Hitler's Nazi Regime. Opponent of General Montgomery (see 6th Le.) in the battle of El Alamein in N. Africa in 1942. Though fighting for Nazi Germany, he was a man of great integrity. He roused Hitler's fury when he contacted the Allies in the autumn of 1944 in an attempt to obtain a peace treaty. He was forced to swallow poison. His moving end makes worthwhile reading in the well-documented biography by the British author Liddall Hart.

See also *Rommel* by Desmond Young (1950, 1969).

26TH DEGREE CAPRICORN

First Image, Outer Symbol

A regatta of sailing boats on the coastline of a wide and calm sea. To the right, along the beach, begins a pine forest to which a pathway leads.

Interpretation

This is a symbol with several aspects, and one cannot simply call it 'maritime life' as does Janduz.

On the outer physical level this person can certainly be attracted towards regattas, motorboat races or ocean cruises. Or he (or she) may be attracted to forests and beaches. However, there are deeper things hidden in this symbol. There is a good deal of the virginal nature of Virgo and Pisces in this image, but Capricorn does not seem so obvious here, unless we look closer. In order to take part in a regatta, each crew needs to be disciplined, to work exactly on time, and to be in the correct place in line. This is an exact example of the meaning of Capricorn.

The beach and the path are essential here. They are both striking symbols of Capricorn. Like Capricorn, the beach is the dividing line between two worlds, the sea and the land. The interplay between rock and water forms sand and clay. This is the perfect symbol in nature of the cosmic earth-triangle Taurus (clay), Virgo (sand) and Capricorn (rock). The people with this degree prominent can be an example of harmonious living on earth.

The pathway is an archetypal symbol for Capricorn. It is very often an object in meditation (Cap.). It may lead these people to a higher level of consciousness. A pine forest comes under Sagittarius and indicates clear and one-pointed thinking, directed straight to heaven.

The difficult hind-axis is represented in the wood (Sag.) and in the curvature of the sails under the wind (Ge.) at the left, indicating a good balance. We see an almost classical painting before us.

The fore-axis Leo–Aquarius seems lacking. But is it? There must be people (Aq.) sailing (Le.) these boats. And the boats must be in perfect formation (Aq.) with one flagship leading (Le.).

Thus we really can say that this image is a perfect example of the Capricorn grail. It indicates that people with this degree can become exceptionally well balanced and have a foretaste of the Holy Grail.

As one of the twelve 26th degrees, it points towards the seeking of the Holy Grail. These people are not just ordinary seekers on the path. They are in search of the 'third eye', the extrasensory faculty (Neptune), which brings the visible and invisible planes together (see second image).

With this search as their unshakeable (Cap.) centre in day-to-day life, they may function in many stations in society, from fishermen to admirals, from holiday-makers to foresters. It does not matter where they are, for the search is within them (Cn. opp. Cap.).

They have a strong character, with a charming manner. They are proud and able to show backbone. Their sense of justice is well-developed, sometimes showing in sudden anger, especially when they see team-spirit violated or good leadership flouted.

Any fleeting ill temper (neg. Cap.) will or should be accepted by those around them, as they are really highly developed Capricorns without the ambition, calculation, or negative fears, which this tenth sign of the zodiac so often shows. Their goals are pure (Sag.). They are resolute, and yet still able to give and take.

Second Image, Inner Symbol

A nature spirit dances in the iridescent mist of a waterfall.

Interpretation

This is Rudhyar's 1973 version, which makes more sense than the 1936 version of 'a radiant sprite', though they can mean the same. This second image clearly contains a higher version of the first. Here is the horizontal opposition of water to earth lifted up to the level of mist above the ground and the vertical waterfall. The calm temperament of these people has found elevation in daring to relinquish material security (the horizontal coastline). They come into more subtle vibrations of the atmosphere. The spirit moves out of the body, and the Higher Self gets control over the lower. They get their strength from inexhaustible reservoirs from above, which are connected with their inner receptiveness and soul (Cn.).

The horizontal action of the first image has reached exaltation. It lives, it is a force. It is full of promise. It is still fluid.

Here is a synthesis of the Capricorn grail on a higher and more inner level. We can all benefit from meditating on this beautiful and allusive image.

Conception Corrected Asc. 26th Capricorn

W. H. Auden Born 21 Feb. 1907 at 06.00 hrs. in York, 54°00 N, 01°00 W. Died 28 Sept. 1973. CC NS for 283 days at 06.00 hrs. gives 25°36 Capricorn, or for 269 days at 06.00 hrs. gives 25°44 Capricorn.

English writer and poet. Took American nationality and acted as a 'liberating force' for other poets. He tried to revive traditional poetry. His best-known work is *The Age of Anxiety* (1947) and his collected poems *The Dyer's Hand*, in which one can often find expressed the mood of this poetic 26th Capricorn, which fits Auden so well.

27TH DEGREE CAPRICORN

First Image, Outer Symbol

On the edge of a forest a man walks alone, towards a field in the middle of which stands his home, small, solid and ornamented with a vine.

Interpretation

According to Janduz this is a degree of 'solitude'. This is self-willed seclusion, a feature of Capricorn. These people want to have time at their own disposal. Their personal taste is for solitude, so that they can think their own thoughts uninterrupted by chat (Ge.–Sag. hind-axis), and live in peace from the demands of public life (overcoming the squares of Ar.–Li. for Cap.). Their bent is for study, and their need is for quiet in which to formulate their ideas, which may be expressed through their hands (Ge.).

This shows that this degree is an evolved version of the Capricorn grail. These people are concentrated thinkers (Cap.–Sag.). They may be a bit asocial (neg. Aq.) and self-centred (neg. Le.), but passing through this phase they may find the spiritual courage (Le.) to contact others by telepathy (Aq.).

On a low level of awareness they may be just dreamers and idlers, procrastinators with no persistence and averse to taking trouble for others or for themselves. However, this level is unlikely to come to the fore in these people, because the man (the consciousness) has a sense of direction and he walks at the boundary of the forest and the fields, where live the most varied natural species. Wood comes under Sagittarius and borderlines are of Aquarius, so that we have the man surrounded by the two sides of the Capricorn grail.

These people face their own spiritual house and centre. They know that popular regard is transient, and that in the end they must turn homeward and within. Few people with Capricorn prominent in their chart do not fear to enter into their own inner life, with its astral and etheric emotions and reactions (Cn. opp. Cap.). However, in this image their house is said to be solid, there is no need for fear. Moreover it is surrounded by a vine. The vine is a Leo plant, and its juice made into wine is Pisces. It is a symbol of the New Kingdom where everybody will live peacefully under their own vine.

Receiving energy from higher worlds, these people prefer to remain obscure and even poor, so long as they can be free. They should not make concessions or compromises which could coax them back into public life.

Although having this high moral attitude, they still need to be alert to the dangers of the general Capricorn traits. They can become intolerant, unable to adapt their way of thinking to that of newer generations, and tenacious of the belief that 'it was better in my time'. Thus they cease to educate themselves, their imaginary authority a mask for inadequacy. They need to guard against this arrogance, any gruffness of manner, and a feeling of melancholy when alone, because this solitude is their greatest gift from heaven.

Second Image, Inner Symbol

Men climb a sacred peak: below the world, above peace.

Interpretation

Marc Jones calls this a 'mountain pilgrimage'. If the man of the first image deteriorates, there comes a division between below and above, or up and down. The individual consciousness (the man) has now advanced into group awareness (the men). Life becomes a pilgrimage, where all together serve a Holy aim. Together they reach the top, and not in competition as in the rivalry of public life.

This second image assumes shared understanding of the aim, with no suspicion in their minds of ulterior motive or that there is any form of exploitation among their associates in this ascent or even black magic with manipulation (Li.–Ar. sq. Cap.) behind this climb. Even so there is still the ambivalence. Why strain towards some sacred peak, when sanctity can be found at home? Who knows that they will not meet the Tempter himself on that high mountain? As Capricorn they still need to understand (Aq.) that illumination is given from above, and cannot be taken by conquest.

These people do not stand apart from the rest of humanity. They should not consider themselves 'holier than thou'. Pilgrimage, yes, but not privilege, for there is no separation in a holy Creation where all life is one.

Biblical Parallel

'. . . the devil taketh him up into an exceeding high mountain, and sheweth him all the kingdoms of the world, and the glory of them; And saith unto him, All these things will I give thee, if thou wilt fall down and worship me. Then saith Jesus unto him, Get thee hence, Satan.' *Mt. 4: 8–10.*

28TH DEGREE CAPRICORN

First Image, Outer Symbol

A well-dressed man is standing upright balancing an iridescent globe on his head. In one hand he is holding a sextant and in the other a pair of compasses.

Interpretation

This is a degree of 'precision'. People with this degree on the Ascendant have a great and brilliant intelligence and a strong cosmic awareness. This image suggests an interest in astronomy and cosmology, or geology and working with crystals. These people may also have mathematical capabilities.

On the inner level, they may be gifted with a mighty imagination and power of visualisation, so that they may see forms in the inner world or on the astral plane. They may be good aura-readers (the globe), or soul-researchers, which may make them into psychologists capable of crystallising the laws (Cap.) governing the psyche in written form, and by scientific methods, such as the measurement of human intelligence, intuition and perception.

They have a gift for asking the right questions and could be destined for worthwhile research, which may advance in times to come (Cap.), spreading their light far and wide. As Capricorns, they tend to appear conventional and cool. Unless they have planets prominent in the fore-axis Leo–Aquarius, they may be so walled-in by their scientific rules (neg. Cap.), that there is no room for the understanding of others. They need to develop intuition (Aq.) and warmth of heart (Le.), to give depth to their extrasensory perception. They should then guard against the waves of emotion they may meet, and by which they could be submerged. Another danger is that they can become fanatical about their own field of knowledge (neg. Ge.–Sag. hind-axis).

They make good teachers, but tend to lack originality (Aq.) and genius (Le.) (unless their complete chart shows otherwise). They have great respect for the past and their predecessors (Cn.).

On a mundane level, people with this degree rising may excel as builders, architects, technicians and in professions or hobbies that require exactitude.

According to tradition (as far back as Manilius), the metal-smelters and burners of china clay also come under this degree. In our time we can imagine them working in porcelain factories, with smelting furnaces, and as potters or glass-blowers.

Wherever they can build themselves a scientific reputation, they have the perseverance to finish a given task. They succeed, but there is a limit (Cap.) to their exceptional capacity to make a career, because they often put their own ambition (Cap.) too much in the centre, with too little regard for their colleagues.

With Mercury in this degree, the tendency is more towards scientific ability, while Jupiter brings illumination and heightening of philosophical thinking. Saturn here may make this image more concrete, while Uranus may let these people ascend to heaven to show them flashes of true genius. Neptune enhances the imagination.

On the inner esoteric level, this image is an example, not only of the Capricorn grail, but of the human grail itself. Many are seekers for the Holy Grail, which is invisible to them though some see it as a light in the corona (halo), or as the inner crown on the top of the head, exactly as shown by the man in the image. Crystal is the purest form of matter and a crystal ball is sometimes seen as the purest representation of the Holy Grail on earth.

In occultism, the terrible power of the crystal is known and feared (Cap.). Traditionally Atlantis was submerged by the scientific misuse of crystal-power (neg. Cap.).

Modern scientists have yet to become fully aware of the power of the tiny crystal (laser beam emitters for instance). There is also the rediscovery of healing-power through crystals, which are pure catalysts for the human psyche.

Thus in this degree a tremendous cosmic law is revealed for those who are aware, and are straight upright channels (the man), for light or for darkness.

The Capricorn grail image is also underlined by the symbols of sextant and compasses, symbolising the fore-axis (Le.–Aq.) and hind-axis (Ge.–Sag.) forming the grail-cup (Cap.–Cn.).

This image is one of the most important ones of the zodiac and it gives the bearers of it great responsibility.

Second Image, Inner Symbol

The aviary of a rural mansion filled with singing birds.

Interpretation

The first image is very concentrated and silent. The second one is the reverse. It is all movement. Birds come under Gemini. The rather severe intellectuality (Ge.) has freed itself, and though still caged it has now become light-hearted and singing. Participation with others is what the consciousness of the man needs to attain. These people must get out of themselves and join in the choir of their group soul. Thus they wil become more playful, fruitful and creative. When in the right rural environment, together with others, their talents of the first image may be shared with all. Thus they become the heart of the group and true examples of a Capricorn grail-bearer.

Conception Corrected Asc. 28th Capricorn

Carl G. Jung   Born 26 July 1875 at 19.20 hrs. at Keswill 47°36 N, 09°19 E. Died 1961. CC WAK and NS for 281 days at 19.18 hrs. gives 27°03 Capricorn.

NB There are other charts with Aquarius rising claimed to be correct for him which had to be rejected after careful research, as 19.20 hrs. is personal information and 28th Cap. fits the entire horoscope. This remarkable Swiss psychiatrist and author of many books was the pupil of Freud, but broke away to become the exponent of the collective unconscious and healing with mandalas. He was the predecessor of transpersonal psychology, and many more streams dealing with the consciousness. The book you are now reading owes a great deal to his genius. Taking his whole chart into account, he is a highly evolved example of this 28th degree.

Jung was also the amateur builder of his own work-tower on Lake Constance.

Recommended biographies are: *Jung and the Story of our Time* by Laurens van der Post (1976), and a biography by Colin Wilson (Aquarian Press).

29TH DEGREE CAPRICORN

First Image, Outer Symbol

A statue, of a beautiful naked woman, lies flat in the grass at the edge of a pond in a deserted landscape.

Interpretation

Janduz calls this a degree of a 'contemplative spirit'. One might assume that contemplation in these conditions could be uncomfortable and inappropriate. However, symbolically there is an influx from the signs behind Capricorn. The pond is a pool of dark depth, which betokens Scorpio. Growth in it is somewhat hidden, which is of Sagittarius and indicates that the contemplation coming up from the depth is not quite full-grown, but expanding.

As this is a Capricorn degree, the spirit of contemplation takes the form of a woman in people with this degree prominent. She represents the soul, but here she is made into a statue, not upright, but lying hidden on the ground.

These people, and especially those with the Ascendant here, are identified by being in a sense 'unfinished'. They lack practical sense. They prefer to ignore hard realities. There is an air of melancholy incompleteness around their personality. If yielding to depression, these people gradually go into a fatal decline, and the great artistic talents, which they undoubtedly possess, may filter away through neglect.

However, on a higher level of awareness, they can be very good artists, sculptors, poets or musicians. They like to work alone. Their creations often have a dreamy atmosphere. They can be inspired by the magical beauty (Ar.–Li. sq. Cap.) of nature, but there is often more shadow than light in their work. Although they can give form to their thoughts with intense joy, they are not bearers of sparkling light. They create best from an inner solitude (Cn.–Cap.) and their work is leavened with calmness and silence. They accept fate with a silent and stoical courage.

They do not seek emotional relationships in life; they would rather live alone than adapt themselves to an inferior partner. They possess a deep source of inspiration, but outwardly they appear cool. They can have great imaginative and visionary powers, and achieve a very exceptional style in their work. They add something, which could be defined as 'aroma of the personality'. They may be influenced by those who went before them, and especially by Greek art, but they are capable

Handwritten chart of C. G. Jung by
Willem Ary Koppejan

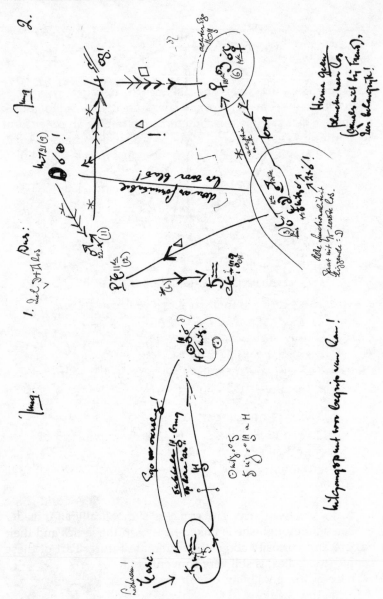

Dynamic flow in C. G. Jung's chart as seen by
Willem Ary Koppejan

of adding something in a new form, which they can call personal and their own. They may develop authority in their field, which is the result of their pure inner concentration.

They may live a public life and enjoy art in a passive way, but sometimes they miss their chance to develop their inner talents and it seems as if their latent creativity cannot break through. Their spirit is too contemplative to give an outer form to anything. They may make many plans, but there is some resistance preventing them giving these final form, unless they can break out of their inhibitions. This inner resistance may be a source of suffering for them, as they have a just appreciation of their superior potential. They may reflect a picture of Mother Earth herself, whose beauty has been so sadly neglected by the world at large.

Second Image, Inner Symbol

A gypsy reads fortunes in the teacups of society ladies.

Interpretation

According to Marc Jones this is 'A woman reading tea-leaves'. Rudhyar sees in the reading of tea-leaves a modern version of certain types of procedure used by the priests of ancient religions, and to him it is 'the ability to see the Signature of hidden meaning in every occurrence'.

In this image the essential jump into the unknown, towards becoming an exceptional human being, is being made. There is creativity here but it is still on a low level. The woman of the first image, who was a statue, has now come alive in the gypsy. The female side of these people is still on the level of a game for ladies at a tea-party. The gypsy is symbolically an outsider in society, although she is linked here with the ladies and their anxiety and curiosity about their intimate future. Part of these people (the ladies) is still very conventional.

There is the possibility of subversion here, of reducing the work of the medium to vulgarity. The original potential for contact with the higher world is being debased for use in a game of black magic, prematurely giving form to future time which is still growing from within (Cn. opp. Cap.). This is always the danger for Capricorn. This gypsy might misuse her original intuition and understanding for the pleasure of a power-trip, but the ladies will not understand this. They ought to be able to read the tea-leaves themselves! Tea, symbolising Leo (fore-axis) indicates that there is pure spiritual energy for creativity. It also symbolises the giving of warmth, which the first image lacks.

These people could do better than play the medium's game, because they can inspire others, especially women in society, with their vision of the new and better world which must replace the loveless self-seeking of the old.

This degree is an interesting phase in the twelvefold development of all the 29th degrees of the zodiac.

Biblical Parallel

'And because iniquity shall abound, the love of many shall wax cold.'
Mt. 24: 12.

30TH DEGREE CAPRICORN

First Image, Outer Symbol

A man plays the flute in the midst of an aviary where the birds are tame and, round about, brilliant balls are falling like fireworks.

Interpretation

This is a degree of 'magnetic power'. For people with this degree rising, this power can be expressed in a kind of personal charm. This charm can go in many directions. In the first place, through a magic flute or any other enchanting musical instrument. The historic archetype of this image is the Pied Piper, who first freed the town from its rats by hypnotising them with his music and later, when the magistrates did not want to pay for his 'magnetic power', charmed away all the children into a cave from which they were never to be set free. This story gives us the essence of this 30th Capricorn degree, which, as all the other 30th degrees, contains the fullness of that entire zodiac sign.

This is a highly developed Capricorn image and we see its grail very well symbolised.

Fireworks (the balls) come under Aquarius. The man stands upright and channels his power through his spine, which is Leo (Le.–Aq. fore-axis). Birds come under Gemini. Here they behave confidently, which is Sagittarius (Ge.–Sag. hind-axis). The flautist needs to have full control over his breath (Ge.) and he plays on the emotions and feelings (Cn. opp. Cap.). This whole scene is still caged in (Cap.). Even the square signs (Ar.–Li.) can be detected in the way the birds are enchanted (Ar.) by the music (Li.). This indicates that these people have overcome the difficult hind-axis. Their capacity for concentrated meditation and introjection is fully developed. They look so innocent and homely, but their power over others can be formidably magnetic.

It depends on the individual whether that power is used for good or evil. They may be exceptional healers, drawing out the imbalances and blockages, or be very good at organising conferences, or being entertainers or producers, or simply games' masters. They may be trainers of animals, or even snake-charmers.

As this degree asks for the highest moral (Cap.) perfection, one should not be surprised to see that hardly any bearer of this image is a true representative of it. To avoid the task it sets, they may compromise by superficially entertaining others and surrounding themselves with artificial glamour. They may then lack the true human force (Aq.) and courage (Le.) not to prostitute their brilliant powers for their own ends.

On the downward path they may indulge in black magic by hypnotising others for selfish reasons, or by playing a self-styled 'master' or 'guru' role. In a harmless way, they may charm people into travelling to far and romantic countries. They do well as tourist operators and film or television producers.

On a high level they are mystics, whose expansion of souls calls forth an irresistible echo in the souls of others. They may attain to profound knowledge of the inner worlds and their deepest mysteries. They may be fascinated by the nature spirits, and follow the pipes of Pan. The danger in this degree is always that of being misled or leading others astray.

Second Image, Inner Symbol

The directors of a large firm meet in a secret conference.

Interpretation

The first image spoke of the dangers inherent in superior knowledge and power. This image takes the first one out of its magical atmosphere and makes it concrete and responsible. The power of these directors may elevate them to rule in society. As such they are the essence of Capricorn.

They may be the spiritual and social leaders of their country, or of the world, and rule with justice and right action (Li.–Ar.) from their inner secret chambers, responsible to God alone. They may be unseen helpers-in-need. However, they may equally misuse their power to manipulate others.

Symbolically there is spiritual growth in this degree. In the first image there is only one single consciousness, while in the second, there is a group-consciousness. Here we see a greater whole operating unseen to produce new activities. Teamwork depends on the contribution of individuals to the joint undertaking, which is under collective control.

Biblical Parallel

'As a cage is full of birds, so are their houses full of deceit: therefore they are become great, and waxen rich.' *Jer. 5: 27.*

Conception Corrected Asc. 30th
Capricorn

Johfra (Frans van den Bergh) Born 15 Dec. 1919 at 10.30 hrs. in Rotterdam, 51°55 N, 04°29 E. CC NS for 278 days at 10.30 hrs. gives 29°35 Capricorn.

Dutch painter, who migrated to the south of France. Known as a magical-realist. Formerly married to Diana (see 7th Cn.). His second wife is also a good painter. He became internationally known through his paintings of the twelve signs of the zodiac, which were sold as posters and cards all over the world. With his esoteric and New Age philosophy his work undoubtedly shows the 'magnetic' power of this 30th Capricorn.

BIBLIOGRAPHY

See also the references in the text concerning biographies and autobiographies of sample charts.

Bible

Authorized (St James) version of 1611.

Bullinger, E. W., *The Witness of the Stars*, London, 1893, reprint Lamp Press, London, 1960.

Companion Bible, with structures and appendixes by E. Bullinger, Samuel Bagster, London, 1964.

Strong, James, *Exhaustive Concordance of the Bible*, Hodder & Stoughton, London, 1890 (22nd edn., 1955).

Weinreb, F., *Roots of the Bible*, Merlin Books, Braunton 1986.

Astrological Degrees and Symbols

d'Abanus (13th century), Astrolabium Planum, ed. de Giunta, Venice 1502 (Amsterdam, University; London, Warburg Library) see literature under Franz Boll and A. Warburg and articles by T. de Jong in Part II of the present work.

Cirlot J. E., *A Dictionary of Symbols*, Routledge & Kegan Paul, London 1962, paperback edn 1983.

Janduz, *Les 360 degrés du Zodiaque, symbolisés par l'Image et par la Cabbale*, Niclaus, Paris, 1938 and reprint 1977.

Jones, Marc E., *The Sabian Symbols in Astrology*, Sabian Publ. Soc., New York, 1953 edn. (reprinted by Shambhala Publications, Boulder USA).

——*The Sabian Manual*, Shambhala Publications, Boulder USA, 1976.

Jung, Carl G., *Man and his Symbols*, Aldus Books, London, 1964; Pan Books paperback 1978.

Koppejan, Willem A., *De 360 Gradenbeelden van de Dierenriem*, The Hague, 1956.

——*Beeldgids von de Dierenliem*, 3 Vols, Ankh Hermes, Deventer, 1990.

Manilius, *Astronomica*, Loeb Classical Library, Heinemann, London 1977. Also translation by A. Housman, 1933.

Maclaine, Shirley, *Going Within*, Bantam, New York, 1990

Rudhyar Dane, *The Astrology of Personality*, Lucis Press, USA, 1936.

——*An astrological Mandala: The Cycle of Transformation and its 360 Symbolic Phases*, Random House, New York, 1973. Paperback edn 1974.

Conception Correction Method

Scheps, N. *The Trutine of Hermes* .... Element Books 1990.

Creative Visualisation

Shone, Ronald, *Creative Visualisation*, Thorsons, Wellingborough, 1984.

Knight, Gareth, *The Treasure House of Images*, Aquarian Press, Wellingborough 1986.

Steinbrecher E., *The Inner Guide Meditation*, Aquarian Press, Wellingborough, 1982.

White, Ruth, *A Question of Guidance*, C. W. Daniels, Saffron Walden, 1988.

Encyclopaedia and Reference books

Encyclopaedia Britannica, 1961 GB edn

Grand Larousse, Paris, 1962 edn

Moderne encyclopedie der wereldliteratuur, Paul Brand/de Boer, Hilversum, 1977.

GLOSSARY

Archetype 'primordial images inherited by all' (Oxford Dictionary).

Aquarian Age or New Age Here used for the coming 2,000-year cultural period in which the Sun's precession through the equinoxes will be in Aquarius for 2,168 years after the Piscean era in which we now live. Although many people in the prematurely termed New Age movement assume that we are already in the Aquarian Age, I follow in the footsteps of WAK and astronomical calculations indicating that we are now (c. 1990) in the 180-year Piscean phase of Pisces and will not enter Aquarius before 2160. Liquidation of the old and conscious preparation for the new era is already happening now, hence the constant reference in this book to the New Age of Aquarius or the Kingdom of Heaven in Biblical terms.

Astral body Energy field on the inner level around the etheric body. It comprises the energies of the inner (higher mystery) Uranus, Neptune, Pluto, Persephone, Hermes and Demeter, functioning as an astral mirror for the Self.

Aura An energy field, comprising subtler 'bodies', which interpenetrates but also radiates out beyond the physical body (definition Ruth White '*A Question of Guidance*,' p. 174).

CC Conception correction: an astrological method for correcting the exact moment of birth by way of calculating the epoch of gestation time, thus finding back the true minute of conception. See N. Scheps, *The Trutine of Hermes*, (Element, 1990).

Cardinal cross Four signs of the zodiac comprising Aries, Cancer, Libra, Capricorn.

Chakras Energy wheels on the inner level linking the astral with the etheric body and connecting on the outer level with the glands in the physical body. There are seven main chakras in a vertical row in the centre.

Dharma Living according to the impersonal laws of the universe.

Etheric body The first invisible body immediately around the skin. It registers the emotional sensations and reactions of what is around us on the outer level. It works as a mirror and is connected with the Moon in the chart.

Fixed cross Taurus–Leo–Scorpio–Aquarius.

Fore-axis Axis of the two opposite signs in the zodiac following the Sun-sign. Such is Virgo–Pisces for Sun in Leo.

Grail The mysterious cup before the seeker, filled with light and overflowing with the water of life.

Grail astrology An interpretation of the chart, developed by WAK. See page 9 of this book.

Hind-axis Axis of two opposite signs in the zodiac, which the Sun in a sign has just passed, such as Cn.–Cap. for Sun in Leo.

Ingoing aspects After the opposition the faster planet is moving towards the slower planet. Thus Moon in Taurus is ingoing square Sun in Leo.

Inner level The invisible level of the astral plane, the inner emotions and the chakra's. Responding to the images of the inner (Sabian) symbols in this book.

Introjection A Jungian term meaning the psychological faculty of taking in and bringing onto the inner level one's experiences instead of projecting and blaming others for one's own failings.

Introspection Looking within oneself in an inspecting way.

Karma Eastern expression for the laws of cause and effect. In Old Testament terms it is 'an eye for an eye'. In Christian sense it comprises the individual and collective sins, which will be wiped out by grace, forgiveness and love. This creates good karma.

Mutable cross Gemini–Virgo–Sagittarius–Pisces.

Mystery planets Following the research of the Dutch Astrologische Werkgemeenschap we work with three undiscovered planets, which are energy points on the inner plane. These are Persephone, the higher ruler of Taurus, Hermes, the higher ruler of Gemini, and Demeter, the higher ruler of Cancer.

NS New Style calendar in contrast with OS, Old Style. Also, according to context, Niek Scheps, when a conception correction has been calculated by him.

Outer level Level of the five senses, the visible environment and physical emotions like anger, laughter. Responding to the images of the outer symbols (Janduz).

Outgoing aspects Before the opposition the faster planet is moving away from the slower planet. Thus Moon in Scorpio is an outgoing square to Sun in Leo.

Persona A Jungian term, meaning mask. Here it is used for the image on the Ascendant degree, which is the key to the entire personality.

Sevenfold Man The complete man and woman consist of seven bodies, known in Eastern philosophies and Western anthroposophy. WAK wrote about this in connection with astrology and the Bible.

Will The point where the Higher Self links with the cosmic or Christ-consciousness, which radiates through the Sun (in the chart), and with the heart of man and woman. With the (free) will one is able to say yes or no to challenges and opportunities in life.

INDEX OF CARDINAL SIGN
ASCENDANT DEGREES